The Future Ain't What It Used to Be

Also available from the Citadel Symposium on Southern Politics:

Second Verse, Same As the First:
The 2012 Presidential Election in the South

A Paler Shade of Red: The 2008 Presidential Election in the South

The Future Ain't What It Used to Be

★ ★ ★

The 2016 Presidential Election in the South

★ ★ ★

*Edited by Branwell DuBose Kapeluck
and Scott E. Buchanan*

The University of Arkansas Press
Fayetteville
2018

ISBN (paper): 978-1-68226-053-1
ISBN (cloth): 978-1-68226-054-8
e-ISBN: 978-1-61075-630-3

22 21 20 19 18   5 4 3 2 1

♾ The paper used in this publication meets the minimum requirements of the American National Standard for Permanence of Paper for Printed Library Materials Z39.48–1984.

Library of Congress Control Number: 2017954142

Contents

Preface

This edited volume is the ninth in a series of analyses of presidential elections in the southern states that began in 1984. The series was published by Praeger Publishers through the 2000 election. A state-by-state study of the 2004 presidential election was not published in edited book form but rather appeared as a special double issue of the *American Review of Politics*. In 2008 and 2012, analyses were published by the University of Arkansas Press. While the presidential election has been the focus of each volume, other important aspects of contemporary southern electoral politics have also been addressed, including congressional and state elections and the overall status of party development and competition in each of the eleven southern states of the former Confederacy. This volume adopts the general organizational plan of the previous publications, including an introductory chapter, a chapter on presidential primaries, a chapter on issues in the 2016 presidential election, chapters on each southern state, and a conclusion summarizing lessons from the 2016 election cycle.

We are appreciative of the support of those who have made this book possible or who have contributed to the atmosphere in which this work was created. The Citadel Foundation provided indispensable financial support for The Citadel Symposium on Southern Politics, a biennial conference that for over three decades has brought together a community of scholars engaged in the study of southern politics and that has, in the process, helped to develop the network of contributors involved in this study.

We also wish to thank David Scott Cunningham, editor in chief at the University of Arkansas Press, and Joseph Muller, the copyeditor, for their support, patience, and guidance during the publication process.

Introduction

The premise of this book is that the South constitutes a unique political and cultural region of the United States. Oceans of ink have been spilled covering the cultural contributions of the South. It has its own literature, cuisine, manner of speaking, and mores, to name just a few distinctive aspects of the region. It is also considerably more religious than the rest of the nation. The region is particularly important in American politics as it has tended to be considerably more monolithic in its voting behavior. The South was once a Democratic bastion. However, the civil rights efforts of nonsouthern Democrats in 1964 began to drive a wedge between the partisan affinities of white southern Democrats and their preference for the racial status quo and states' rights. Like most political realignments, change did not happen overnight. Slowly but surely, however, the region flipped its strong support from the Democratic Party to the Republican Party. This change began at the national level when Barry Goldwater won five Deep South states in 1964 and appeared complete when Richard Nixon won all eleven states in 1972. The Democratic solution was to nominate a southern candidate. This proved a successful southern strategy in Jimmy Carter's 1976 run and was repeated with limited success in Bill Clinton's 1992 and 1996 campaigns. The Republicans countered with their own southern candidate in Texan George W. Bush, retaking the South in 2000 and 2004.

The 2008 and 2012 elections represent a departure from this regional strategy. Democrat Barack Obama, having been born in Hawaii and serving as a senator from Illinois at the time, was decidedly nonsouthern. Neither did Republican contenders John McCain (2008) and Mitt Romney (2012) have any bona fide southern credentials. In 2008, Obama carried three peripheral South states: Florida, North Carolina, and Virginia. These are also states with significant in-migration, so just how distinctly southern they were by 2008 is questionable. Obama again won Florida and Virginia and only narrowly lost North Carolina by 2 percentage points in 2012. The absence of a southerner at the head of either major party ticket in 2016 continued this trend and made predicting the winner in these three states, which were crucial to Hillary Clinton, more difficult.

In contrast to its intermittent success at the national level, the Republican Party has made significant inroads in southern state governments.

States in the Deep South were uniformly one-party Democratic in 1964, but by 2016 the Republican Party held control in each of these five states. In 2008, the GOP controlled 46 percent of seats in southern state legislatures, and by 2016 it controlled 63 percent of legislative seats and the governorship in every state except Louisiana, North Carolina, and Virginia. In addition, every southern state legislature was held by the Republican Party in 2016.[1] Given this trend, it is hard to claim that the region has become more like the rest of the United States. The South continues to exhibit strong one-party tendencies.

It is this relative lack of party competition that makes the South a pivotal region for presidential candidates. It has also made the South an area of significant academic scholarship. The Citadel has been proud to host the biennial Symposium on Southern Politics since 1978. The symposium was founded by the late Tod Baker, Laurence Moreland, and Robert Steed, all professors in The Citadel's Department of Political Science. Every two years, academics from across the country meet in Charleston, South Carolina, to discuss the South's unique position in American politics. The conference has resulted in a number of books on southern politics, many of which were the product of collaborations among symposium participants. The *American Review of Politics* has also regularly published the best work presented at the conference. Since 1984, the organizers of the conference have published a book on the role of the South in each presidential election. These books were published by Praeger Publishers through the 2000 election, and the 2004 election was covered in a special edition of the *American Review of Politics*. More recently, the University of Arkansas Press picked up the reins for 2008, 2012, and now 2016. Prof. Scott Buchanan and Prof. DuBose Kapeluck continued the tradition first established by Baker, Moreland, and Steed.

The following chapters document the historic 2016 presidential election in the eleven southern states of the former Confederacy. We have followed the format of V. O. Key's *Southern Politics in State and Nation*.[2] This groundbreaking book analyzed southern politics on a state-by-state basis. Similarly, each chapter in this volume covers the presidential race in one of the southern states and includes a discussion of election outcomes for federal offices and state-level political trends. We also include a chapter on the issues driving the 2016 election, a chapter on the primary elections in the southern states, and a concluding chapter.

The 2016 presidential election was one for the history books. Vying for the nomination in the Republican primary season were seventeen candidates that included such party stalwarts as Jeb Bush, John Kasich, and Ted Cruz. By May 3, only Ohio governor John Kasich remained out of these mainstream candidates. Emerging triumphant was billionaire hotelier and celebrity Donald Trump, a candidate vilified by the GOP establishment and, arguably, not a candidate with particularly sterling conservative credentials. The Democratic primary was also a divisive affair. The presumptive candidate, Hillary Clinton, faced a strong opponent in Vermont senator Bernie Sanders. Running from the left, Sanders appealed to younger and more left-wing Democratic activists. He also possessed a refreshing honesty that many felt was missing in Hillary Clinton. Sanders finally withdrew from the race in mid-July and endorsed Clinton. The resulting two-way race between Trump and Clinton was widely thought to be Clinton's to lose. Almost daily, Trump would make some outrageous claim, tweet something inflammatory, or engage in over-the-top barbs. Hillary had her own problems, most notably the now-infamous WikiLeaks release of her emails. One has to go back to the Tilden-Hayes election of 1876, or perhaps even to the Jackson-Adams election of 1828, to find such rancor and mudslinging.

We argue there were three overarching themes expressed by Donald Trump in the 2016 presidential election: illegal immigration, the economy, and America's role as the leader of the free world. Trump ran an "America First" campaign, which he presented in detail in his inauguration speech.[3] He called for imposing substantial limits on immigration, to the point of building a wall at the US-Mexican border.[4] While the economy had steadily improved since the 2008 financial crisis, wages had largely stagnated at the lower and middle income levels. To remedy this, Trump promised to extricate the United States from trade agreements he believed worked to the disadvantage of American workers.[5] Finally, Trump advocated for reducing American military engagement in the Middle East and making other NATO countries pay their "fair share."[6] These grand themes were established by Trump, and Hillary Clinton's campaign largely reacted to them. There were also a host of other social issues—gay marriage, transgender bathrooms, and civil rights (particularly treatment of blacks by law enforcement)—that attracted significant attention.

How would voters in southern states react to these issues, and which candidate would be advantaged? A particular problem for the Trump campaign was the loss of the Latino vote, which has become increasingly important in at least two southern states, Texas and Florida. Even in Georgia, as Patrick Miller notes in his chapter on the issues in the election, by 2016 Latinos comprised 7 percent of exit poll voters. While

Democrats have always polled better with Latinos, their large numbers in Florida and Texas increasingly make them a constituency that cannot be written off by the GOP. Relatedly, Trump was perceived to be unsympathetic to African American claims of police mistreatment. Now that Obama was not on the ticket, would black turnout decline in the southern states, or would African Americans return to the polls in high numbers, energized by Trump's perceived slights?

Another wrinkle in the 2016 campaign was Trump's protectionist agenda. In GOP circles, this was an about-face for which he attracted the ire of many establishment Republicans. Southern voters have historically been in favor of free trade, beginning when the region's economy was primarily agricultural. Moreover, the region, because of its lack of unions, low taxes, and low regulation, is the recipient of substantial foreign direct investment.[7] This appeal, no doubt, was aimed at voters in the Rust Belt, but how would it play in the southern states that had benefited more from free trade?

The South is also known for its strong support of the military. Would Trump's call for American disengagement on the world stage strike a defeatist chord? On the other hand, his tough talk on terrorism would likely find a more receptive audience among southern voters. Admittedly, antiterrorism was a valence issue for which both candidates advocated strong measures. However, some of Trump's policy prescriptions were more ruthless (and were apparently submitted with less thought) than Clinton's, prompting her to refer to his rhetoric as "demagogic."[8]

Perhaps the biggest disconnect between Trump the candidate and the average southern voter was his personal life. Trump had been married three times and had children from all three marriages. He had been on record as supporting gay rights in general and same-sex marriage in particular.[9] Trump was not a regular churchgoer and did not seem to be a particularly religious person, which was at odds with the largely evangelical religious voter in the South. Nonetheless, he was endorsed by the influential Jerry Falwell Jr., president of Liberty University, a Christian university in Lynchburg, Virginia. He also received the lukewarm support of James Dobson, the influential founder of Focus on the Family and the Family Research Council.[10] Overall, evangelical leadership sided with Trump in the election, though he may have represented the lesser of the two evils to them. One notable holdout was Russell Moore, who heads the political arm of the Southern Baptist Convention. Moore was actively opposed to Trump and critical of Trump supporters.[11]

Finally, there was the issue of the rural-urban political divide. This has emerged as a persuasive theory of the support for Trump among working-class rural whites in the country. These were whites who had in the past given their support to Democratic candidates. The theory, which has come to be termed "the politics of resentment," claims that rural white Americans had been ignored for too long by both parties.[12] Their natural political home had been the Democratic Party. However, working class whites began to perceive the Democrats to be increasingly globalist and unduly concerned with correcting ethnic and racial injustice, giving short shrift to the needs of poor white Americans. This "politics of resentment" has been used to explain Trump voters' surprisingly strong showing in states like Ohio, Wisconsin, and Michigan. It is doubtful that there are many southern white rural Democratic voters. Of more interest, however, is the degree to which southern urbanites' and suburbanites' voting behaviors changed in the 2016 election.

These and other themes are explored in the following chapters. In addition to a thorough discussion of the presidential race in the respective southern states, the authors also cover important electoral outcomes in lower-level races. Our 2008 presidential election book was titled *A Paler Shade of Red* in deference to the three southern states that crossed the partisan Rubicon to support Barack Obama. The 2012 election witnessed a retreat from this premature political prognostication, hence the title *Second Verse, Same as the First*. Polling in the lead-up to the 2016 election indicated that Trump could likely lose Florida, Georgia, North Carolina, and Virginia. It seemed possible the South had truly become more like the rest of the nation, but as the results trickled in, we saw that the future ain't what it used to be.

I

The Setting and Nominating Process

1

The 2016 Southern Electorate

Demographics, Issues, and Candidate Perceptions

Patrick R. Miller

The 2016 electoral map in the South varied little from the one that southern voters produced four year earlier. Only Florida switched partisan hands in the presidential race, swinging from a narrow plurality win for Democrat Barack Obama to a narrow plurality win for Republican Donald Trump. The stability in the region's electoral map, however, obscures the critical role that the South played in 2016. Trump's victories in ten of eleven southern nominating contests proved crucial to his avoiding what many thought could have been the first contested Republican nominating convention since 1976,[1] and Hillary Clinton's sweep of every southern primary—with overwhelming support from African American voters[2]—helped preserve her frontrunner status for the Democratic nomination against Bernie Sanders.

Nor did the tumultuous general election ignore the region. Virginia, North Carolina, and Florida reprised their 2012 roles as swing states, joined by Georgia as demographic change there continued to transform its electorate. These states represented 46 percent of the South's electoral votes. And through a volatile campaign, polls showing Trump with just single-digit leads in South Carolina and Texas had media speculating about underdog Clinton wins there;[3] even the generally cautious

Cook Political Report only rated those two states as "likely Republican" rather than safe on Election Day.[4] Though most of the South ultimately and unsurprisingly went Republican despite the drama of getting there, the region nevertheless shows substantial demographic and issue cleavages within its electorate. This chapter examines those divisions as they manifested in the 2016 presidential contest, focusing especially on how the South was distinct—or more often, not distinct—from the national electorate.

Political Fundamentals in Southern States

Election forecasting models that are not based primarily on horserace polls suggest that "the fundamentals" determine presidential-level results: macropartisanship, approval of the incumbent president, and various economy-related factors.[5] Table 1.1 shows, in the left-hand columns, the vote shares for the two major-party nominees in southern states and how they compare to 2012 results. The small remainders of the vote went to third-party and independent candidates. To the right are Gallup data detailing how survey respondents in each state in 2016 responded on questions of partisanship, ideology, Obama approval, health insurance status, and employment status.

Like Obama, Clinton performed best in Virginia, also home to her running mate, Sen. Tim Kaine. Her worst performance—just 33.7 percent of the vote—came in her former home state of Arkansas. Clinton generally lagged Obama's 2012 vote in the South, perhaps because she was a nonincumbent and because several high-profile third-party or independent candidates—Gary Johnson (Libertarian Party), Jill Stein (Green Party), and Evan McMullin (independent)—reduced the typical two-party vote share. Two states deviate from this trend. Clinton bested Obama's vote share in Texas by 1.8 percent, making it one of just four states—including Arizona, California, and Utah—where she outperformed him. She actually won a greater share of the vote in traditionally red Texas than in Iowa and Ohio, two constant swing states.[6] Clinton also matched Obama's vote share in Georgia. Whether this pattern in both states reflects demographic change among voters or something peculiar to 2016 cannot be assessed.

Trump ran close to the Mitt Romney vote share across the South, slightly outperforming in some states and slightly lagging him in others. The biggest deviation came in Texas, where Trump did 4.9 percent worse in the overall vote than Romney. Nationally, Trump beat Romney's performance in twenty-three states, usually by small margins.[7] Only five of those were in the South, indicating no particular regional concentration in any pro-Trump vote swings. Like Romney, Trump performed worst in Virginia. His best state was Alabama, whereas Arkansas had slightly bested Alabama as Romney's best state.[8]

Despite great publicity around alternative candidates, they did not prove especially popular in the South. Collectively, Johnson, Stein, and McMullin did not break 5 percent of the vote in any southern state, though they performed much better in many states outside of the region.[9] Thus, southern voters were reluctant overall to deviate from major party options, and their collective preferences did not show substantial deviation from 2012.

The partisanship columns in table 1.1 show the percentages of Gallup respondents who identified explicitly either as partisans or as independents leaning toward major parties. Partisanship is the strongest predictor of individual vote choice.[10] Accordingly, the states that were in aggregate more closely divided in partisan identification were also generally the most competitive. Given the sampling error inherent in polling,[11] southern swing states—Florida, Georgia, North Carolina, and Virginia—were essentially evenly divided, with neither party enjoying more than a negligible 2-point identification advantage. Most remaining states had at least double-digit Republican advantages that matched comfortable Trump wins. Deviating somewhat, the 4-point Republican advantage in Texas lagged Trump's 9-point win there, and the 5-point Republican advantage in Louisiana did not match Trump's 20-point win there.

Partisanship strongly predicts presidential approval, and it did so especially strongly when partisan polarization in approval numbers was historically high under presidents George W. Bush and Barack Obama.[12] Logically, Obama's approval numbers in southern states generally followed the pattern of state-level partisanship. He generally fared better in 2016 in states where partisanship was more closely divided and worse in states where Republican identification was more advantaged. Obama had net positive approval ratings in Florida, Georgia, Texas, and Virginia, but he was in negative territory by as many as 19 points in Arkansas. While assessments of Obama may have affected how some less partisan southerners voted in 2016, the approval of most people likely just reflected their party loyalties.

Ideological conservatism remained dominant in southern states in 2016. Conservative self-identification enjoyed advantages over moderate self-identification, ranging from 1 point in Virginia to 16 points in

Table 1.1. State-Level Political Characteristics

	Clinton		Trump		Partisanship		Ideology			Pres. approval		Unin-sured	Unem-ployed
	Vote	v. 2012	Vote	v. 2012	Dem.	Rep.	Cons.	Mod.	Lib.	App.	Dis.		
AL	34.4	−4.0	62.1	+1.5	35	52	47	31	17	41	57	13.6	5.9
AR	33.7	−3.2	60.6	0.0	34	49	45	34	17	39	58	10.2	4.0
FL	47.4	−2.5	48.6	−0.4	43	41	36	35	23	51	45	14.6	4.9
GA	45.4	0.0	50.4	−2.8	42	43	39	36	20	49	47	15.6	5.3
LA	38.5	−2.1	58.1	+0.3	41	46	44	34	17	43	53	12.5	6.2
MS	40.1	−3.7	57.9	+2.6	38	49	46	33	15	44	52	17.2	5.7
NC	46.2	−2.2	49.8	−0.6	43	42	40	34	20	48	49	13.6	5.0
SC	40.7	−3.4	54.9	+0.3	36	48	42	36	17	44	52	13.1	4.4
TN	34.7	−4.3	60.7	+1.3	37	48	43	34	17	41	55	11.8	4.8
TX	43.2	+1.8	52.2	−4.9	39	43	40	35	20	49	46	20.5	4.6
VA	49.8	−1.4	44.4	−2.9	43	42	37	36	22	51	45	9.8	4.2
National	48.0	−3.0	45.9	−1.3	44	40	36	36	24	52	45	10.8	4.6

Sources: Vote share: David Leip, "Dave Leip's Atlas of U.S. Presidential Elections," http://uselectionatlas.org. Unemployment: US Bureau of Labor Statistics, https://www.bls.gov/lau, https://www.bls.gov/opub/ted/2016/unemployment-rate-declines-to-4-point-6-percent-in-november-2016.htm. All other data: "State of the States," Gallup, http://www.gallup.com/poll/125066/state-states.aspx. Comparisons to 2012: Patrick R. Miller, "Demographic and Issue Cleavages in the Southern Electorate," in *Second Verse, Same as the First: The 2012 Presidential Election in the South*, ed. Scott E. Buchanan and Branwell DuBose Kapeluck (Fayetteville: University of Arkansas Press, 2014), 3–20.

Note: All table entries are percentages.

Alabama. Yet in no state were conservatives a majority. As discussed later, issue questions from the exit polls suggest that this symbolic attachment to the conservative label does not necessarily translate into conservative policy preferences among voters on major campaign issues like immigration and trade. Many self-identified conservatives actually hold liberal policy preferences on balance, whereas self-identified liberals are typically policy liberals in reality.[13]

Real-world conditions under incumbent administrations often affect voter evaluations in presidential elections,[14] but two such indicators show little relation to state outcomes. First, the percentage of Americans lacking health insurance declined since the implementation of the Affordable Care Act.[15] Compared to 2012 Gallup data,[16] the uninsured share of the population declined in every southern state during Obama's second term. The smallest decline was in Alabama, where just 4.4 percent of the population went from uninsured to insured during this period. The greatest decline in the uninsured was 11.3 percent of the overall population in Arkansas—reducing that state's uninsured population by more than half.

Second, the official unemployment rate also declined between November 2012[17] and November 2016. Drops in southern states ranged from 0.4 percent in Louisiana to 4.3 percent in North Carolina. Though a swing state experienced the largest unemployment decline during this period, the region's competitive states did not consistently perform the best on this dimension. Thus, there is little evidence that southern electorates were responding to health care and employment improvements under Obama and rewarding the Democratic candidate accordingly.

Significant Subgroup Voting Patterns

The National Election Pool (NEP) no longer conducts state-specific exit polling in all fifty states during presidential elections, though the national exit poll may still include voters in every state given its sampling method. In 2016, the NEP conducted exit polls in the six southern states that *Cook Political Report* identified as competitive: Florida, Georgia, North Carolina, South Carolina, Texas, and Virginia. Though these six constitute a majority of the states of the old Confederacy, they are not necessarily representative of the five excluded states: Alabama, Arkansas, Louisiana, Mississippi, and Tennessee. Given this incomplete polling coverage, it is not possible to talk collectively about southern voters per se. But the available NEP data allow some inferences regarding how voters in most southern states differed from each other and from the national average.

Minor-party candidates were unusually strong in 2016, even if diminished in the South. When looking at the national data, it was not uncommon to see that changes in support for either Trump or Clinton among certain demographic groups, as compared to the 2012 breakdown for those groups, did not necessarily result in corresponding movements toward the other candidate. In some demographics, both nominees ran behind the Obama and Romney vote shares, with voters supporting third candidates in greater proportion than in previous elections. Table 1.2 shows the presidential vote by group at the state and national levels. For each entry, the Clinton vote is to the left and the Trump vote to the right.

Race

Race persisted as a significant cleavage among voters both nationally and regionally. Trump received just 8 percent of the African American vote nationally, barely better than the 6 percent that Romney won in 2012.

That share varied marginally in southern states, ranging from 4 percent in South Carolina to 11 percent in Texas. Conversely, Clinton won 89 percent of Africans Americans nationally, down slightly from Obama's 93 percent share in 2012. Her state-level performances among black voters ranged from 94 percent in South Carolina to 84 percent in Texas and Florida. Generally, then, the typical pattern of Democrats overwhelmingly winning black voters continued.[18]

Latino and Asian voters are a growing force in southern electorates. In Georgia, for example, together they comprised 4 percent of 2008 exit poll voters,[19] but that grew to 7 percent in 2016—certainly enough to decide close statewide elections. Whereas Latinos were captured in large enough numbers to allow for state-level estimates of their vote in every southern state surveyed except South Carolina, only in Virginia were Asian voters found in adequate numbers. Trump lost both groups to Clinton in every state where projections were possible. His state-level Latino vote share varied between 27 percent and 40 percent, though the section on Latinos later in this chapter questions the accuracy of those estimates.

Nationally, Trump ran behind Romney's share of the white vote by 2 percent. In the three states where 2012 exit polls were available, there was no clear pattern of substantial change among whites between the two elections. Trump exceeded Romney's share of white voters by 3 percent in Florida, but he did worse by 5 percent in North Carolina and 2 percent in Virginia. Nonetheless, white voters in the polled states supported Trump at rates consistently above his national share. His 59 percent in Virginia most closely reflects his nationwide performance, and he ran farthest ahead in Georgia, where he won 75 percent of whites—1 percent less than John McCain received there the last time exit polls were conducted.[20]

Gender

Clinton's status as the first woman major-party presidential nominee invites questions about how that milestone affected the gender gap. In 2012, Obama won women by 55 to 44 percent but lost men by 52 to 45 percent. Nationally, that gap widened slightly in 2016. Clinton won women by 54 to 41 percent, but Trump won men by 52 to 41 percent. In comparison to his national performance, Trump fared 2 percent worse with women in Virginia, where he received only 39 percent of their votes, but he beat his national numbers by 2 to 10 percentage points in every other surveyed state. However, only in South Carolina did Trump win more women than Clinton, beating her by 6 percent among female voters there. Conversely, Trump won men in every state polled, either matching his national vote share or exceeding it by up to 8 percent.

Minority women have been among the most stalwart supporters of Democrats in recent decades, and white women have often been more malleable in their voting preferences.[21] Trump performed poorly with black voters of both genders nationally. His state-level performances among those voters marginally danced on either side of his national share without substantial deviation. Trump also suffered landslide losses amongst Latinos of both genders nationally, but his state-level performances showed more deviation than was observed among African Americans. For example, he did 9 percent better with Latina women in Florida than he did nationally and 10 percent better among Latino men in Texas. However, the subgroup estimates of vote shares among minority voters in exit polls often came with large confidence intervals, so projecting whether these deviations among Latinos were real or a sampling-error artifact is difficult.[22]

The vote among whites by gender follows a common pattern wherein Virginia most closely resembles national vote shares while other states exhibit more substantial deviations. Trump did only 2 to 3 percent better among white men and women in Virginia than he did nationally, but he ran up to 18 percent ahead with both in Georgia. Clinton's losses among white women both across the country and across the South, along with the close resemblance between her national performances with whites of both sexes and those of Obama from 2012, suggest that white voters were not especially motivated in aggregate either to support or oppose her because of her gender. This does not preclude, however, the possibility that candidate gender has effects on voting that are indirect and not observable in simple voting preferences.

Age

Age persisted as a significant voting cleavage.[23] Trump lost voters under forty-five years of age nationally. The two exceptions to this in the South were his wins in the thirty- to forty-four-year-old age group in South Carolina and Texas, where he outperformed his national vote share in this demographic by 10 and 7 points, respectively. He won voters forty-five or older both nationally and in each southern state polled. His performance among voters sixty-five or older resembled his national vote share most closely in Virginia. Trump generally outperformed the national vote in these two age brackets in every other southern state, beating his national numbers most strongly in Georgia and especially among the oldest voters.

Education

Education was an unusually strong divide in national voter preferences in 2016, with Trump generally performing better with non-college-educated voters and Clinton besting him among voters with at least a four-year college degree. But while Trump lost college-educated voters nationally, that was not consistently replicated in the South. Trump lost voters with at least a college degree only in Virginia, where his performance matched his national numbers. Just as he did nationally, he lost southern voters with postgraduate degrees in four of six southern states, winning them only in South Carolina and Texas.

This education gap has been growing since 2000, especially among whites.[24] Media speculation about the possibility that white women would support Clinton in strong numbers focused especially on those with college degrees because of their generally stronger pro-feminist attitudes.[25] While Clinton defeated Trump by 51 to 44 percent among college-educated white women nationally, in the South this pattern was replicated only in Virginia. Otherwise, Trump performed markedly better among college-educated women across the states surveyed than he did nationally, winning them in each. Further, both nationally and in the South, an education gap emerged among whites of both sexes wherein Trump consistently outpaced Clinton among those without college degrees. Underscoring the heft of this education gap, nationally and in four southern states, Trump actually performed better among non-college-educated white women than he did among college-educated white men.

Religion

As Republicans typically do, Trump won white evangelicals overwhelmingly. He tied or outpaced his 80 percent national share of this demographic in every southern state, earning up to 92 percent of their vote in Georgia—3 percent higher than Clinton's share of the black vote there.[26] Trump earned just 37 percent of non-evangelical white voters nationally, losing that demographic in every southern state polled with vote shares within 5 percent of his national performance.

Place Type

The urban-rural divide much publicized after the election[27] was replicated in the South. Trump won just 34 percent of urban voters nationally, though his state-level shares varied between 29 percent in Georgia and 46 percent in South Carolina. Conversely, he won 61 percent of rural voters, though the exit polls showed much greater variance in that demographic in the South. Trump lost rural voters in South Carolina by 54 to 40 percent, perhaps because of the state's relatively large rural African American population. However, he won rural voters in the other five states, earning a high of 70 percent of their vote in Texas.

Trump won suburban voters nationally by just 4 percent, a relatively even split. While he won suburban voters in every southern state polled, his margin varied substantially from low single digits in Virginia and Georgia to landslides of roughly 20 percent in the Carolinas. Suburban counties, curiously, experienced some of the South's most notable electoral swings, favoring Clinton in most cases. She was the first Democrat since Jimmy Carter to carry Cobb, Gwinnett, and Henry Counties in suburban Atlanta and the first since Lyndon Johnson to carry Fort Bend County in suburban Houston. She bested Obama's margins in vote-rich suburban counties like Loudoun and Prince William in Virginia and larger counties with urban-suburban mixes like Mecklenburg and Wake in North Carolina. And though Clinton lost many large urban-suburban counties like Tarrant, Collin, and Denton in Texas, Trump often won them by smaller margins than Romney. As the South becomes more urbanized and its suburbs more racially diverse, suburbia may be the key to Democrats' future viability in the region—a possibility all the more ironic because suburban growth in the South helped effect its Republican realignment.[28]

Issues, Candidate Perceptions, and Voting Patterns

Most state exit polls included issue questions and items assessing candidate perceptions. Table 1.3 shows questions that were posed in at least three southern states, focusing primarily on major campaign issues. Parentheses indicate Trump's vote margin within each cell. Minor campaign issues such as climate change and gun regulation were sporadically included on southern exit polls, and those limited data cannot inform broader analysis. Issue and candidate attitudes in the South generally resembled national ones, with some small differences that may

Table 1.2. Presidential Vote by Demographic Group

	FL	GA	NC	SC	TX	VA	National
Race							
Black	84/8	89/9	89/8	94/4	84/11	88/9	37/57
White	32/64	21/75	32/63	24/70	26/69	35/59	89/8
Latino	62/35	67/27	57/40	—	63/34	65/30	66/28
Asian	—	—	—	—	72/26	—	65/27
Gender							
Women	50/46	54/43	52/45	45/51	49/47	56/39	54/41
Men	43/52	37/60	38/56	35/59	37/57	43/52	41/52
Race and gender							
Black women	87/6	94/5	95/3	—	88/9	91/7	94/4
Black men	81/10	83/15	82/14	—	78/14	84/13	82/13
White women	36/60	26/70	37/60	30/64	29/66	41/54	43/52
White men	28/67	16/80	27/68	18/76	23/71	29/65	31/62
Latina women	63/34	—	69/28	—	69/28	—	69/25
Latino men	60/36	—	—	—	53/41	—	63/32
Age							
18–29 years	54/36	63/33	57/35	43/43	55/36	54/36	55/36
30–44 years	54/39	51/44	49/46	44/51	45/48	53/40	51/41
45–64 years	43/56	41/57	43/55	37/62	39/59	47/50	44/52
65+ years	40/57	31/67	37/60	39/58	35/64	45/52	45/52
Education							
High school or less	51/46	39/57	44/54	38/58	48/49	44/52	46/51
Some college	45/49	46/51	42/52	36/58	41/54	44/51	43/51
College degree	42/54	49/49	47/50	43/52	41/53	51/44	49/44
Postgrad. degree	56/39	50/47	52/44	43/54	47/48	61/33	58/37
Whites: Education and gender							
Women with college degree	37/60	34/63	45/53	36/58	35/59	50/44	51/44
Women without college degree	33/62	18/78	29/67	23/72	23/74	29/66	34/61
Men with college degree	32/64	21/76	32/65	24/72	26/66	40/54	39/53
Men without college degree	25/70	11/85	20/71	14/78	19/77	19/75	23/71
Evangelical							
Yes	14/85	5/92	17/81	11/86	12/85	14/80	16/80
No	53/41	66/31	63/32	62/32	55/39	59/35	60/34
Place type							
Urban	53/41	68/29	60/35	49/46	53/42	59/34	60/34
Suburban	43/53	46/51	36/60	33/62	37/58	47/48	45/49
Rural	36/61	29/67	39/58	54/40	26/70	41/56	34/61

Source: National Election Pool, "Exit Polls," *CNN Politics*, 2016, http://edition.cnn.com/election/results/exit-polls.

Note: All table entries are percentages. Vote shares entered as Clinton/Trump vote.

stem primarily from divergent partisan and demographic balances in the region.

Top Issues

Of the four choices in the exit poll, a majority of voters nationally ranked the economy—broadly defined—as their most important issue. Voters ranked terrorism as their second priority, with foreign policy and immigration closely competing for third place. This pattern repeated in every southern state polled. Nationally and across these states, Trump substantially lost voters prioritizing foreign policy, but comfortably won those ranking immigration and terrorism as most important. Economy voters were more mixed: while Trump lost them by 11 percent nationally, they were rather evenly split in most southern states. These data deserve skepticism, though. Voters prioritizing other issues are forced to choose one of the listed options as a false priority, and the issues that voters rank as their most important often simply reflect those issues that their preferred candidates emphasize.[29] Thus, most respondents who chose terrorism likely supported Trump because as Republicans they were echoing their nominee's campaign priorities, not because his attractiveness on the issue independently wooed them.

Economics and Life Standards

On most economic matters in the exit polls, southern voters generally reflected the national electorate in their preferences and how those related to vote choice. Roughly 60 percent of voters across table 1.3 rated the economy as "not so good" or "poor," though among these voters Trump exceeded his 31 percent national margin by 7 to 20 percent in southern states. Conversely, only about one-third of voters across contexts rated the economy as "excellent" or "good," and Trump suffered losses among these voters in the 56 to 71 percent range.

Nationally, the plurality of voters felt that their "financial situation" was "about the same" as "four years ago," and these voters were closely split between Trump and Clinton. Unsurprisingly, voters rating themselves "better today" strongly favored Clinton, and those saying "worse today" overwhelmingly voted Trump. Voters in Florida, Georgia, and Virginia generally reflected this pattern; however, small pluralities in the latter two states gave "better" responses, and southern voters saying "about the same" were somewhat more likely to vote Trump than voters nationally.

Table 1.3. Issue Attitudes among Voters

	FL	GA	NC	SC	TX	VA	National
Most important issue							
Foreign policy	12 (−33)	11 (−31)	14 (−18)	9 (—)	13 (−17)	11 (−41)	12 (−27)
Immigration	10 (+39)	14 (+51)	10 (+42)	13 (—)	13 (+16)	10 (+41)	13 (+31)
Economy	48 (−3)	56 (0)	55 (−7)	54 (+3)	49 (−1)	56 (−11)	52 (−11)
Terrorism	26 (+12)	17 (+17)	18 (+30)	20 (+45)	21 (+28)	20 (+8)	18 (+17)
National economy							
Excellent/ Good	34 (−69)	41 (−71)	35 (−61)	—	38 (−56)	42 (−65)	36 (−59)
Not so good / Poor	66 (+39)	59 (+51)	65 (+38)	—	62 (+49)	57 (+43)	62 (+31)
Financial situation versus four years ago							
Better today	27 (−57)	37 (−44)	—	—	—	39 (−55)	31 (−49)
Worse today	27 (+42)	26 (+75)	—	—	—	27 (+53)	27 (+58)
About the same	44 (+8)	36 (+7)	—	—	—	34 (+3)	41 (−2)
Life for the next generation of Americans will be							
Better than today	32 (−33)	38 (−22)	34 (−29)	51 (+4)	38 (−21)	36 (−28)	38 (−21)
Worse than today	65 (+38)	69 (+42)	70 (+44)	71 (+48)	79 (+62)	70 (+45)	63 (+32)
About the same	43 (−10)	43 (−11)	37 (−19)	41 (−8)	41 (−11)	35 (−24)	38 (−16)
Effect of international trade							
Creates US jobs	39 (−21)	—	38 (−26)	—	—	41 (−35)	39 (−24)
Takes away US jobs	34 (+42)	—	39 (+45)	—	—	46 (+22)	42 (+32)
Does not affect US jobs	14 (−30)	—	14 (−38)	—	—	10 (—)	11 (−35)
Illegal immigrants should be							
Offered legal status	70 (−29)	73 (−25)	69 (−24)	—	71 (−10)	73 (−35)	70 (−28)
Deported to home country	23 (+87)	21 (+64)	25 (+65)	—	22 (+81)	24 (+73)	25 (+69)
Immigrants to the US today							
Help the country	59 (−40)	—	58 (+40)	—	55 (−35)	60 (−52)	—
Hurt the country	28 (+74)	—	29 (−71)	—	31 (+71)	35 (+62)	—

Source: National Election Pool, "Exit Polls," *CNN Politics*, 2016, http://edition.cnn.com/election/results/exit-polls.

Note: All table entries are percentages. Trump vote margin by group in parentheses.

In prospective life evaluations, the plurality of voters nationally expected "life for the next generation of Americans" to be "better than today" and supported Clinton by 21 percent. This repeated in most southern states, though Trump won these optimistic voters in South Carolina, and the plurality of North Carolina voters expected "worse" conditions. Across contexts, Trump won voters expecting deteriorating conditions but lost those expecting stability.

Trump campaigned heavily on the purported negative effects of trade. Nationally, the plurality of voters believed that trade "takes away U.S. jobs." Trump won that bloc while losing those seeing trade as net positive or neutral. This pattern generally replicated itself in the South, though most voters in Florida marginally saw trade as a job creator.

Immigration

On the major campaign issue of immigration, there again appears little difference either among southern electorates or in comparison to voters nationally. By a three-to-one margin, respondents nationally preferred offering "legal status" to illegal immigrants over deporting them, with Trump losing voters with more liberal immigration preferences but winning those with more conservative ones. Immigration preferences replicated almost perfectly across southern states, though with somewhat larger variation in Trump's vote share on either side of the issue. And though perceptions of whether immigrants helped or hurt the country were not asked for in the national exit poll, there was only small variation in beliefs across southern states on this: 55 to 60 percent of southern voters saw immigrants positively, and approximately a third in each state saw them negatively. On this item, Trump again won by large margins among southern voters who viewed immigrants negatively but lost handily among those with positive assessments.

Candidate Perceptions

As compared to past candidates, both nominees suffered from relatively high negative perceptions among voters.[30] Thus, their individual qualities—both trait perceptions and the general affect toward them—may have been voting "issues" for many Americans. Table 1.4 shows candidate evaluation questions from the national and state exit polls. Again, southern voters generally resembled the national electorate.

Nationally, roughly 80 percent of voters held favorable assessments of either Clinton or Trump, splitting about evenly in their preferred candidate. Unsurprisingly, each candidate overwhelmingly won voters who viewed only him or her positively. Only 18 percent of voters disliked both nominees, with Trump winning them by 18 percent. This pattern generally repeated across the South. Clinton enjoyed favorability advantages in four states—including three she lost—ranging from net 2 percent to 9 percent. Voters in Georgia and South Carolina reported net positive ratings of Trump, by 2 percent and 11 percent margins, respectively. The share of southern voters viewing both candidates unfavorably ranged from 13 to 19 percent, and Trump won these voters across the region by margins of 12 to 37 percent. Thus, despite some variation in state-level numbers, southern voters generally resembled the national electorate in being divided between the candidates and in their tendency to support Trump if they viewed both candidates negatively.

Southern voters also did not vary substantially from voters nationally in either their selection of the most important candidate quality or their candidate ratings on specific traits. Nationally, 39 percent of voters ranked "can bring change" as the most important candidate trait, while "right experience" and "good judgement" were closely matched for second and third place respectively, and "cares about me" lagged in fourth. Trump won only national voters who prioritized change, losing the others to Clinton. This pattern generally repeated across southern states. Voters ranked change as the most important quality in all six states—with some variation in the spread amongst voters by state—and this was again the only subgroup of southern voters that Trump won.

Nationally and in the South, voters were generally divided over which candidate was "honest and trustworthy" and "qualified," but they scored Clinton higher on "right temperament." For all three trait dimensions across contexts, each candidate again overwhelmingly won those voters who ranked only him or her positively. Trump comfortably won voters who responded that neither candidate was qualified or had the right temperament, but voters who said that neither candidate was honest or trustworthy showed greater variation and much closer division both in national and state numbers.

Each candidate had major negative storylines that dogged them and may have reinforced certain negative perceptions among voters. For Clinton, it was her use of a private email server and subsequent investigations into that use.[31] For Trump, it was his comments about women—rating their beauty, insulting them on the basis of gender, and referencing reporters' menstruation—exacerbated by audiotape in which Trump

Table 1.4. Candidate Perceptions among Voters

	FL	GA	NC	SC	TX	VA	National
Candidate favorability							
Both	2 (—)	2 (—)	1 (—)	1 (—)	2 (—)	1 (—)	2 (—)
Only Clinton	43 (–98)	41 (–98)	41 (–97)	34 (–100)	39 (–99)	45 (–97)	41 (–97)
Only Trump	39 (+98)	43 (+97)	40 (+97)	45 (+99)	37 (+97)	36 (+98)	36 (+97)
Neither	14 (+37)	13 (+37)	16 (+36)	19 (+30)	19 (+37)	17 (+12)	18 (+17)
Most important quality							
Cares about me	16 (–31)	16 (–31)	17 (–16)	17 (–3)	14 (+5)	12 (–34)	15 (–23)
Can bring change	40 (+72)	41 (+70)	38 (+80)	49 (+70)	34 (+71)	41 (+66)	39 (+68)
Right experience	21 (–80)	19 (–79)	20 (–84)	18 (–78)	24 (–71)	24 (–81)	22 (–83)
Good judgment	18 (–32)	20 (–14)	21 (–42)	13 (—)	23 (–21)	20 (–40)	20 (–40)
Honest and trustworthy							
Both	1 (—)	1 (—)	3 (—)	1 (—)	2 (—)	2 (—)	2 (—)
Only Clinton	31 (–98)	37 (–97)	35 (–100)	28 (–96)	28 (–98)	37 (–92)	34 (–96)
Only Trump	35 (+97)	39 (+97)	38 (+98)	43 (+99)	37 (+97)	33 (+95)	31 (+96)
Neither	25 (–6)	19 (–2)	31 (+12)	26 (+7)	29 (0)	24 (+1)	29 (+3)
Qualified							
Both	7 (—)	5 (—)	4 (—)	—	6 (—)	2 (—)	5 (+49)
Only Clinton	45 (–92)	45 (–95)	45 (–94)	—	42 (–90)	50 (–93)	36 (–92)
Only Trump	36 (+100)	37 (+98)	40 (+96)	—	39 (+99)	35 (+96)	42 (+97)
Neither	10 (+70)	12 (+44)	10 (+53)	—	12 (+74)	12 (—)	15 (+51)
Right temperament							
Both	6 (—)	5 (—)	5 (—)	—	7 (—)	3 (—)	5 (+57)
Only Clinton	47 (–88)	47 (–92)	47 (–93)	—	43 (–86)	51 (–81)	49 (–85)
Only Trump	35 (+96)	36 (+98)	36 (+98)	—	34 (+98)	31 (+94)	29 (+95)
Neither	9 (+53)	10 (+54)	11 (+71)	—	14 (+51)	11 (—)	14 (+55)
Clinton's private email bothersome							
Yes	63 (+47)	63 (+58)	—	—	69 (+50)	62 (+39)	63 (+45)
No	35 (–80)	36 (–88)	—	—	30 (–80)	37 (–85)	36 (–85)
Trump's treatment of women bothersome							
Yes	66 (–40)	65 (–35)	—	—	63 (–33)	72 (–42)	70 (–36)
No	32 (+84)	34 (+81)	—	·—	35 (+77)	26 (+86)	29 (+77)

Source: National Election Pool, "Exit Polls," *CNN Politics*, 2016, http://edition.cnn.com/election/results/exit-polls.

Note: All table entries are percentages. Trump vote margin by group in parentheses.

implied that he sexually assaulted women.[32] Asked whether these stories bothered them, southern voters again showed little variation from voters nationally. Roughly two-thirds of voters across polls said that both stories were "bothersome," with this proving a major division in vote choice.

Southern Latinos

The South's growing Latino population is key to Democratic hopes of making the region more electorally competitive. Quality survey data on Latinos is often difficult to produce because of sampling and language challenges unique to Latinos.[33] While exit polls include some Latinos, the representativeness of those Latino respondents is dubious, and their subsample sizes are often too small to produce highly reliable estimates of subgroup behavior.[34]

Latino Decisions (LD) specializes in polling Latinos. LD conducted national and state polls of Latinos likely to vote immediately before Election Day, including in Florida, North Carolina, Texas, and Virginia. Table 1.5 reports national and state LD polling data on questions related to vote intentions, candidate perceptions, and issues. Latinos were more liberal than the broader national and southern electorates, which is unsurprising given their stronger group identification as both Democrats and liberals.[35] Southern Latino voters generally reflected the Latino electorate nationally; however, Florida Latinos were marginally more conservative on some measures, which perhaps stems from the historical Republican roots of Cubans there. For example, Clinton's 79 to 18 percent win among Latinos nationally was roughly reproduced in all southern states except Florida, where LD projected that she would win by a somewhat smaller 67 to 31 percent margin.

LD asked respondents about the most important issue facing the Latino community that they felt politicians should address. Latinos nationally prioritized immigration somewhat over the issue of the economy and jobs, and both of these issues markedly outpaced education and health care. Immigration topped Latino voter concerns in every southern state except Florida, though the margin of its prominence above the economy was generally greater at the state level than nationally. Florida Latinos slightly prioritized the economy and jobs over immigration, though 10 percent selected terrorism—an option given only to Florida respondents, perhaps because of the massacre in June of forty-nine people at the Orlando LGBT nightclub Pulse.

LD also asked about President Obama's Deferred Action for Childhood Arrivals (DACA) executive order on immigration enforcement. Southern Latinos differed little from Latinos nationally in their DACA assessments, except that Florida Latinos again expressed slightly more conservative attitudes. Nationally, 82 percent of Latinos supported the executive order to

Table 1.5. Vote Choice, Issue Attitudes, and Candidate Perceptions among Southern Latinos

	FL	NC	TX	VA	National
Vote choice					
Clinton/Trump	67/31	82/15	80/16	81/15	79/18
Most important issue					
Economy and jobs	35	29	29	27	33
Education	10	13	12	12	15
Health care	11	10	18	11	13
Immigration	33	46	39	49	39
Terrorism	10	—	—	—	—
Obama DACA executive action					
Strongly support	53	67	56	64	61
Somewhat support	22	20	24	20	21
Somewhat oppose	4	2	5	8	4
Strongly oppose	13	4	10	5	9
Stopping Obama immigration executive action					
Strongly support	23	18	17	16	18
Somewhat support	11	7	8	8	8
Somewhat oppose	13	10	18	10	15
Strongly oppose	47	58	55	59	52
Clinton perception					
Truly cares about Latinos	58	59	65	61	57
Does not care about Latinos	33	32	29	30	33
Hostile toward Latinos	6	4	3	4	5
Trump perception					
Truly cares about Latinos	20	11	18	11	13
Does not care about Latinos	26	27	31	28	29
Hostile toward Latinos	49	59	48	57	55

Source: "2016 Election Eve Poll," Latino Decisions, http://www.latinovote2016.com.

Note: All table entries are percentages.

some degree. Support topped 80 percent in every southern state except Florida, where support reached only 75 percent, and opposition was marginally higher than elsewhere. Asked about the executive order in the negative, Latinos across contexts expressed majority opposition to stopping it. Attitudes among Florida Latinos were somewhat more conservative even though they still supported DACA.

Candidate trait perceptions also showed little difference between national and southern Latinos. Nearly 60 percent of Latinos nationally perceived Clinton as truly caring about Latinos, while only 33 percent saw her as not caring, and 5 percent, as hostile. That division was closely mirrored among southern Latinos. Conversely, 55 percent of Latinos nationally saw Trump as hostile, 29 percent as not caring, and just 13 percent as truly caring. This breakdown of Trump attitudes was generally reproduced in the South, though Florida and Texas Latinos were somewhat more positive about him than Latinos nationally.

The Southern Electorate

At its peak drama, the 2016 election teased observers of southern politics with the possibility that the region could see electoral competition at the presidential level not witnessed since Bill Clinton and Jimmy Carter were candidates. Ultimately, the South's Electoral College map reverted to the largely Republican red that has recently dominated it. But the map obscures growing political competition in the region. The South now includes three to four certifiable swing states—Virginia, which arguably now leans Democratic; North Carolina, torn from the safe Republican column in the Obama elections; the perennially competitive Florida; and Georgia, where demographic change gives Democrats a credible, though still young, hope of flipping the state. And as the region evolves, even Texas may join them.

The past several elections in the South suggest that the nature of political competition in the region may now stem from demographics more than any uniquely southern characteristics—or, for that matter, policy factors like unemployment and uninsured rates that seemed uncorrelated to electoral results. Bill Clinton brought Electoral College competition to Florida, as expected, and he also brought it to Arkansas, Georgia, Louisiana, and Tennessee,[36] states that Al Gore and, to a lesser extent, John Kerry also seriously contested.[37] Certainly, Clinton won those states with strong support from black voters, but they were also states that, compared to their regional counterparts at the time, had a greater share of whites—especially rural whites—who were still loyal to the Democratic Party.[38] With southern whites now more realigned with the Republican Party, states like Arkansas and Tennessee seem out of Democrats' reach. Rather, their hopes in the South now center on higher growth states where increasing racial diversity and an influx of relatively more liberal northern whites are changing basic electoral math.

Southern exit poll data also underscore the importance of demographics in driving regional politics. Despite the differences among the six southern states polled, on most issues and candidate perceptions, the electorates there roughly reflected the national electorate, sampling error aside. It is difficult to be sure, then, that any set of attitudes or traits separated the southern voter—if such a voter even exists beyond name only—from the American voter. Even in comparisons among southern states, no major differences were observed apart from the reflection of somewhat more conservative attitudes on some measures in more Republican states. These results may disappoint both observers hoping for evidence that "southern distinctiveness" persists and those who believe that southern states themselves show significant political variation beyond the effect of demographics on the shape of state-level partisanship. If the future of southern politics indeed hinges on demographics—the growth of Latino populations, the drifting apart of socioeconomically high-status suburbs and working-class and rural areas, the balance of white evangelical to secular voters—then these trends deserve more serious attention from casual observers and scholars alike.

2

The 2016 Presidential
Nomination Process

Seth C. McKee

After eight years of President Obama, in 2016 the White House was ready to welcome a new occupant. Typically when there is a true open-seat presidential race (i.e., no incumbent and no vice president seeking the office), a crowded field emerges. On the Republican side, after being shut out the last two cycles, seventeen legitimate contenders sought the greatest political prize.[1] By contrast, only two viable candidates competed for the Democratic nomination.[2] To no one's surprise, former Secretary of State Hillary Clinton decided to make another presidential run, but she did not completely clear the field. Clinton faced an unexpected and vigorous challenge from the politically independent and self-avowed democratic socialist senator from Vermont, Bernie Sanders.

Clinton outlasted Sanders to become the Democratic standard-bearer, but she fell short in the general election when the Republican Donald Trump pulled off a remarkable Electoral College majority by winning most of the so-called battleground states and carrying three must-win states that last voted Republican in the 1980s.[3] The story of how a real estate mogul and celebrity entertainer managed to become the next resident of 1600 Pennsylvania Avenue will be told as long as the United States endures. But Trump had to begin his journey by running the gauntlet in the same series of primary and caucus contests that have selected each major party nominee since 1972. More often than not, in this post-reform era of presidential nominations, the American South has played an outsized role in the selection process of the major party candidates, and this was the case once again in 2016.[4]

In this chapter, the 2016 presidential nomination process is examined with respect to the importance of the South in shaping the selection of the eventual Democratic and Republican nominees. The South punches above its weight in presidential nomination contests because most of its states vote early in the nomination calendar. Further, the mixture of voters who participate in southern party primaries can advantage those candidates favored in the region as the nomination process moves forward. Of course, it is common knowledge that the partisan balance in southern politics tilts heavily in favor of the GOP, but this reality creates an intriguing dynamic in primary contests, where the fight is limited to intraparty bouts. The pronounced differentiation in the coalition of voters who participate in the South's Democratic and Republican primaries directly influences the viability of those who run for a major party nomination.

The chapter proceeds as follows. First, the importance of political timing is discussed and assessed. Next, the changing nature of southern primary electorates is emphasized, and the 2016 Democratic and Republican nomination contests are analyzed. The chapter is concluded with a discussion of the South's role in selecting major-party presidential contenders.

The Importance of Timing

As the old adage goes, timing is everything, and this saying is certainly applicable to elections. First, there is a mood that prevails in any given year, and candidates who best reflect the desires of voters are clearly advantaged.[5] In 2008, the electorate was looking for a change, and eight years later a large segment of voters were again in the mood for a change. Democrat Barack Obama was the beneficiary in 2008, and Republican Donald Trump capitalized in 2016.[6] Second, when and where elections take place are fundamental factors in presidential nomination contests. The preferences of voters vary considerably with changes in location and the extent to which candidates are known by the public. Because of her long political career, Hillary Clinton was universally recognized. Likewise, billionaire Donald Trump enjoyed near universal name recognition because of his decades in the entertainment spotlight, during much of which time he portrayed himself as a cunning tycoon on the reality show *The Apprentice*.

The South has a history of going early in the post-reform presidential nomination process, so candidates who are better known by and can appeal to its voters earn a privileged position as the competition unfolds. In the late 1970s, the South Carolina GOP made a successful bid to establish their state as the first in the South in primary contests, and eventually their Democratic counterparts followed suit.[7] More generally, the South tends to hold contests earlier than the rest of the country, a trend motivated by a desire to prevent the selection of Democratic nominees who hailed from the North and were viewed as too liberal for southern tastes. Thus, in 1988, thanks to the collusion of southern Democrats who still ruled the roost in the region's politics, Super Tuesday was born.[8] Every southern state except South Carolina (which held caucuses on March 12) held its Democratic primary on March 8, 1988.[9] Since 1988, the coalition of states joining together to create Super Tuesday has changed considerably, but the South has always been generously represented on this early date in the nomination calendar.

Table 2.1 lists the dates for the Democratic and Republican nomination contests in 2016. With respect to southern states, frontloading was the name of the game in 2016. All eleven southern states held primary contests, and they were finished by March 15, when Florida and North Carolina were the last to conduct their primaries. After March 15, when the South was done with the nomination process, twenty-four states and the District of Columbia had yet to weigh in on the Democratic competition, and twenty-one states still remained for the GOP race. Following recent tradition, South Carolina went first and by itself, setting its GOP primary for February 20 and its Democratic primary for a week later on February 27. On Super Tuesday, March 1, half a dozen southern states administered their major party primaries: Alabama, Arkansas, Georgia, Tennessee, Texas, and Virginia. Louisiana was the only southern state on March 5, and Mississippi was the lone southern state on March 8.

With respect to party, the bunching of southern states early in the nomination process benefited the respective Democratic and Republican frontrunners, Hillary Clinton and Donald Trump. In the case of Clinton, her victory over Sanders is directly attributable to her performance among southern Democratic primary voters. With regard to Trump, southern frontloading served to winnow his competition down to two opponents who persisted after the ides of March: Sen. Ted Cruz of Texas and Gov. John Kasich of Ohio.

The South was key to Clinton's capture of the Democratic nomination because of its disproportionately large share of African American voters, who backed her overwhelmingly. Table 2.2 shows the percentage of the popular vote and the share of pledged delegates earned by Clinton in each contest type (primary or caucus), in each of four regions (North, South, Deep South, and peripheral South), and in each of two time periods (races occurring through March 15 and those taking place after that date, when all southern states had conducted their primaries). Regarding the popular vote, Clinton did only slightly better than Sanders in the North (52 percent), but dominated him in the South (67 percent), especially in the Deep South (76 percent) with its majority-black Democratic primary electorate. She performed markedly better in primary contests

Table 2.1. The South Goes Early in the 2016 Presidential Nomination Calendar

Date	Democratic contests	Date	Republican contests
February 1	IA[c]	February 1	IA[c]
February 9	NH	February 9	NH
February 20	NV[c]	February 20	SC
February 27	SC	February 23	NV[c]
March 1	**AL**, **AR**, CO[c], **GA**, MA, MN[c], OK, **TN**, **TX**, VT, **VA**	March 1	**AL**, AK[c], **AR**, **GA**, MA, MN[c], OK, **TN**, **TX**, VT, **VA**, WY[c]
March 5	KS[c], **LA**, NE[c]	March 5	KS[c], KY[c], **LA**, ME[c]
March 6	ME[c]	March 8	HI[c], ID, MI, **MS**
March 8	MI, **MS**	March 12	DC [convention]
March 15	**FL**, IL, MO, **NC**, OH	March 15	**FL**, IL, MO, **NC**, OH
March 22	AZ, ID[c], UT[c]	March 22	AZ, UT[c]
March 26	AK[c], HI[c], WA[c]	April 1–3	ND [convention]
April 5	WI	April 5	WI
April 9	WY[c]	April 9	CO [convention]
April 19	NY	April 19	NY
April 26	CT, DE, MD, PA, RI	April 26	CT, DE, MD, PA, RI
May 3	IN	May 3	IN
May 10	WV	May 10	NE, WV
May 17	KY, OR	May 17	OR
June 7	CA, MT, NJ, NM, ND[c], SD	May 24	WA
June 14	DC	June 7	CA, MT, NJ, NM, SD

Source: Josh Putnam, "Presidential Primaries and Caucuses by Month (2016)," *Frontloading HQ*, https://goo.gl/XVi82Y.

Note: All table entries are percentages. Southern states are shown in boldface. A bracketed "c" next to a state abbreviation indicates a caucus contest.

(57 percent) than in caucuses (only 35 percent). And mainly because of her strength in the South, Clinton performed notably better through March 15 than thereafter: 5 percentage points better in primaries and 15 percentage points better in caucuses, which is interesting since only northern states held caucuses. Because most delegates are awarded via a proportionality system, the share of delegates Clinton garnered closely reflects her popular vote.[10] Nonetheless, it is worth pointing out that in the North, Clinton and Sanders broke even with 1,460 delegates apiece.

Table 2.2. Clinton's Popular Vote and Delegate Share by Region, Contest Type, and Timing

	Total	Through March 15	After March 15
	Popular vote share		
Type			
Primary	57	59	54
Caucus	35	39	24
All	56	58	54
Region			
North	52	—	—
South	67	—	—
Deep South	76	—	—
Peripheral South	64	—	—
	Delegate share		
Type			
Primary	58	58	52
Caucus	34	40	27
All	55	60	55
Region			
North	50	—	—
South	68	—	—
Deep South	76	—	—
Peripheral South	65	—	—

Source: Popular vote data compiled by author from David Leip, "Dave Leip's Atlas of U.S. Presidential Elections," https://goo.gl/ng0Rf. Delegate data compiled by author from Wilson Andrews, Kitty Bennett, and Alicia Parlapiano, "2016 Delegate Count and Primary Results," *New York Times*, July 5, 2016, https://goo.gl/P3e6AL.

Note: All table entries are percentages. Delegate share only refers to the pledged delegate count based on a state's nomination contest. Data were computed based on the votes cast for Clinton and Sanders.

It was her landslide support in the South that propelled, sustained, and secured Clinton's bid for the 2016 Democratic presidential nomination.[11]

In contrast to southern voters' central role in Clinton's success, the South played the role of validating the Trump candidacy and helping to cull the Republican field. Trump was not significantly more successful among southern voters, but the timing of southern contests quickly whittled down his Republican opposition.[12] Trump was the plurality candidate in every region of the United States. That is, he consistently won more votes than his competitors, even if his vote share was typically less than a majority, which was to be expected in a crowded but swiftly dwindling field of Republican contenders. At the start of the Republican competition in the Iowa caucuses, there were a dozen candidates vying for the GOP nomination. After South Carolina, only four serious candidates remained: Trump, Cruz, Kasich, and Sen. Marco Rubio of Florida. And despite Cruz's surprise first-place finish in Iowa, Trump was the clear frontrunner and led the pack from New Hampshire to the end, which unofficially came on May 3 with the Indiana primary.[13] Long before Indiana, however, at the conclusion of the vote tally from Super Tuesday, it was evident from Trump's strong performance irrespective of region that he would be the GOP nominee. After Rubio's humbling loss in his home state of Florida on March 15, Trump only had to worry about Cruz and Kasich, and neither proved a credible electoral threat.

Southern Primary Electorates

Thinking back to the long era of the Democratic Solid South, it is no wonder that the contemporary ascendancy of the GOP receives so much attention. In fact, prior to 2016, the 2000 presidential nomination cycle was the only time southern Republican primary voters outnumbered their Democratic peers.[14] Table 2.3 displays the total votes cast in Democratic and Republican primaries in the southern states in 2016. Almost twenty million votes were cast, and over 60 percent were delivered in the GOP primaries. Only in Louisiana did more voters participate in the Democratic primary. At 0.2 percentage points, the Republican participation margin was the narrowest in North Carolina, but the South-wide Republican margin was over 22 percentage points. With Republican electoral dominance in southern politics has come notably greater participation in GOP nomination contests.

A major storyline in southern Republican electoral hegemony is racial sorting along partisan lines. As a growing number of white voters align

Table 2.3. Votes Cast in Southern Primaries: Republican and Democratic Contests

State	Rep. (#)	Dem. (#)	Rep. (%)	Dem. (%)	Rep. margin (%)
South Carolina	743,667	368,577	66.9	33.1	33.8
Alabama	860,652	396,851	68.4	31.6	36.8
Arkansas	410,920	221,020	65.0	35.0	30.0
Georgia	1,295,964	765,366	62.9	37.1	25.8
Tennessee	855,729	372,222	69.7	30.3	39.4
Texas	2,836,488	1,435,895	66.4	33.6	32.8
Virginia	1,025,452	785,041	56.6	43.4	13.2
Louisiana	301,241	311,776	49.1	50.9	−1.8
Mississippi	416,270	227,164	64.7	35.3	29.4
Florida	2,361,805	1,709,183	58.0	42.0	16.0
North Carolina	1,149,530	1,142,916	50.1	49.9	0.2
South	12,257,718	7,736,011	61.3	38.7	22.6

Source: Data compiled by author from David Leip, "Dave Leip's Atlas of U.S. Presidential Elections," https://goo.gl/ng0Rf.

Note: Data were aggregated based on all votes cast in Republican and Democratic primaries. States are shown from first primary contest (South Carolina) to last (Florida and North Carolina). Boldface indicates a change in the date of the primary contest; that is, Alabama, Arkansas, Georgia, Tennessee, Texas, and Virginia all held their primaries on March 1 (Super Tuesday).

with the GOP, an increasing share of the Democratic electorate is comprised of African Americans.[15] Table 2.4 documents this latter phenomenon by presenting the black share of Democratic primary voters in Deep South and peripheral South states using exit poll data from 2004, 2008, and 2016. Louisiana was the only southern state not surveyed in 2016. Over this period, the percentage of African American voters declined in just three peripheral South states: North Carolina, Texas, and Virginia. In the eight other states, black participation has grown—particularly in those states where the GOP is currently most dominant, the Deep South states of Mississippi and South Carolina and the peripheral South states of Arkansas and Tennessee. Of course, the Deep South warrants more attention because in these five states, African Americans are the majority of the Democratic primary electorate, and if this group is cohesive in their voting behavior, then their preferred candidate is greatly advantaged.[16]

Table 2.4. Percentage of Black Voters in Southern Democratic Primaries

State	2004	2008	2016	Difference
Deep South				
Alabama	—	51	54	+3
Georgia	47	51	51	+4
Louisiana	46	48	—	+2
Mississippi	56	50	71	+15
South Carolina	47	55	61	+14
Peripheral South				
Arkansas	—	17	27	+10
Florida	21	19	27	+6
North Carolina	—	34	32	−2
Tennessee	23	29	32	+9
Texas	21	19	19	−2
Virginia	33	30	26	−7

Source: All data are from the National Election Pool state exit polls for each state's Democratic primary contest and can be found online via *CNN Politics*. The 2004 primary data are available here: https://goo.gl/iEu4n1; the 2008 primary data are available here: https://goo.gl/KV4TBW; and the 2016 primary data are available here: https://goo.gl/i4qhkY.

Note: There were no exit polls of voters in Alabama, Arkansas, and North Carolina in 2004 and no exit poll of voters in Louisiana in 2016.

But the differences between southern Democratic and Republican primary electorates do not begin and end with race. As table 2.5 shows, these voters differed across a broad range of characteristics in 2016. Given the large share of African Americans who participated in Democratic primaries, Republican primary voters have become a remarkably white lot.[17] Indeed, outside of Florida and Texas, which have substantial Latino populations, only in the demographically dynamic states of Georgia and Virginia did the white share of the GOP primary electorate fall below 90 percent. The relatively small, albeit burgeoning, Latino segment of the southern primary electorate tended to participate more in Democratic contests, especially in Texas.

There was also a pronounced gender gap in southern primary electorates. In the ten southern states listed, women were always the clear majority of Democratic primary voters, ranging from a low of 57 percent in Arkansas and Virginia to an impressive high of 64 percent in Mississippi.[18] By contrast, the gender balance was much more even in

Table 2.5. Comparing the Characteristics of Voters in Democratic and Republican Primaries in Southern States

Characteristic	Primary	SC	AL	AR	GA	TN	TX	VA	MS	FL	NC
White	D	35	40	67	38	63	43	63	24	48	62
	R	96	93	96	88	94	82	86	93	78	94
Black	D	61	54	27	51	32	19	26	71	27	32
	R	1	4	2	7	2	3	9	6	3	2
Latino	D	2	1	3	7	2	32	7	1	20	3
	R	1	1	1	3	1	10	2	1	16	1
Female	D	61	60	57	62	58	58	57	64	58	58
	R	49	51	48	51	50	50	47	50	51	50
Older than 44	D	66	61	65	64	64	58	59	60	65	61
	R	73	66	74	69	75	68	68	71	74	67
College-educated	D	40	51	44	54	56	51	64	43	48	58
	R	54	44	45	53	51	53	60	44	53	51
Earning at least $50,000	D	39	45	49	57	56	62	71	36	50	57
	R	73	59	65	74	67	78	81	63	67	68
Independent	D	16	20	24	20	23	26	22	13	18	28
	R	22	27	32	25	33	27	29	20	22	30
Liberal	D	54	57	50	56	61	59	68	51	54	56
	R	1	2	2	3	2	2	3	1	3	2
Moderate	D	35	32	34	36	32	34	29	40	37	35
	R	17	20	17	18	16	17	25	15	27	19
Conservative	D	11	11	16	9	7	7	3	10	9	9
	R	81	78	82	79	82	82	72	84	70	79
Urban	D	13	58	34	16	55	58	22	31	52	42
	R	23	32	25	5	28	36	15	1	40	34
Suburban	D	27	20	24	64	24	33	53	26	42	23
	R	48	47	47	62	35	41	58	39	49	47
Rural	D	60	23	41	20	21	9	25	43	5	35
	R	29	21	28	33	37	23	27	60	11	19

Source: 2016 National Election Pool state exit polls for each state's Democratic and Republican primary, *CNN Politics*, https://goo.gl/i4qhkY.

Note: All table entries are percentages.

Republican primaries. With respect to age, as a population, Republican primary voters were older (forty-four years old or older) than their Democratic peers in every southern state.[19] There was not a distinguishable pattern regarding the percentage of Democratic and Republican primary voters with a college degree, but the income gap was prominent and showed up in every state primary. The income disparity between parties was greatest in South Carolina and Mississippi, and this should perhaps be expected because of the correlation between race and poverty and partisanship in Deep South states whose very large black electorates are almost exclusively aligned with the Democratic Party.[20] Republican primary voters are much more likely to be the haves in southern politics.

Given the short-term political conditions at the time of the 2016 election cycle, which prompted two antiestablishment candidates to run from the left (Sanders) and the right (Trump), it is notable to see the portion of political independents participating in Democratic and Republican primaries. As expected, because the South is a heavily Republican region, a higher share of independents participated in GOP primaries.[21] Next to race, ideology was the starkest dividing line for Democratic and Republican primary voters. Liberals comprised 50 percent or more of Democratic primary voters in every state, whereas conservatives simply dominated the Republican primary electorate (from a low of 70 percent in Florida to a high of 84 percent in Mississippi). Because conservatives constituted such a large share of Republican primary voters, it follows that moderates were more plentiful in Democratic primaries (ranging from a low of 29 percent in Virginia to a high of 40 percent in Mississippi).

Finally, Democratic and Republican primary voters in the South differed with respect to location. Democratic participants were more prevalent in urban areas with the exception of South Carolina, and Republican primary voters were more prevalent in suburban locales with the exception of Georgia. There was no consistent gap in the share of Democratic and Republican primary voters located in rural settings, and this can be explained by the fact that there is considerable diversity in the residential patterns of blacks and whites. In the North, African Americans are much more concentrated in urban areas, whereas in the South, because of the history of slavery, large numbers of black voters reside in rural Black Belt regions that cover vast swaths of territory in the Deep South states.[22]

The data from table 2.5 make it evident that Democratic and Republican primary voters in the South were distinguishable across a number of characteristics, and this accords with the modern narrative of partisan polarization. To the extent that the typical Democratic and Republican primary voter is distinct on several demographic features, politicians running under a major party label can emphasize positions that pit their partisan coalition against the other, as opposed to striking themes that unite voters across partisan lines.[23]

The Democratic Contest

As mentioned above, the South proved an electoral boon for Hillary Clinton because its substantial black Democratic primary electorate backed her over Bernie Sanders. But race was just the most salient factor aiding Clinton's nomination bid. As will be shown, the former first lady, senator, and secretary of state dominated her lesser-known rival. As is typically the case in nomination politics where the partisan label is held constant, voters grasp for other cues to decide which candidate to favor; and more often than not, traits that connect the voter to the candidate loom large in the voting calculus.[24]

Although it would be tough to make a case that Clinton is a southerner (she has never claimed to be), she spent decades living and working in the South as the wife of an ambitious Arkansas politician, and this familiarized her with the region's voters. By comparison, Sen. Bernie Sanders represents the New England state of Vermont, one of the smallest and least racially diverse states in the country. Sanders is also Jewish, an identity he shares with only a small minority of southerners, and he hails from Brooklyn, New York, a place truly foreign to most southern voters, Democrat and Republican alike. In this section and in the one that follows, the major party nomination contests are assessed via an examination of the popular vote amassed by the leading candidates and their performance according to various voter characteristics captured by the exit polls.

Figure 2.1 displays the percentage of the popular vote won by Clinton and Sanders in each southern state's Democratic primary and also their overall performance in the region. South-wide, the vote split 67 to 33 percent in Clinton's favor.[25] In every southern state, Clinton bested Sanders, and her vote margin was largest in the Deep South, reflecting its substantially larger black electorate. The ranking of Clinton's vote share from greatest to least was as follows: Mississippi (83 percent); Alabama (80 percent); Louisiana (75 percent); South Carolina (74 percent); Georgia (72 percent); Arkansas (69 percent); Tennessee (67 percent); Texas (66 percent); Florida (66 percent); Virginia (65 percent); North Carolina (57 percent).

Figure 2.1. Southern Democratic Primary Vote Shares

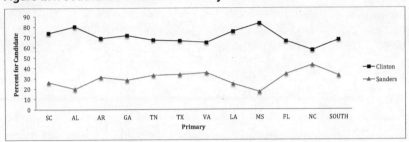

Source: Data compiled by author from David Leip, "Dave Leip's Atlas of U.S. Presidential Elections," https://goo.gl/ng0Rf.

Note: Data were computed based on the votes cast for Clinton and Sanders.

Table 2.6 shows the percentage of the vote Clinton won according to various voter characteristics documented in the 2016 Democratic primary exit polls for ten southern states. Clinton was the preferred choice among a strong majority of voters in virtually every category of voter listed in table 2.6.[26] Rather than systematically examine the results for Clinton, it is much more efficient to simply note the rare instances where Sanders was preferred. First, only in North Carolina did a majority of white Democratic primary voters favor Sanders. Second, corroborating the fact that nationwide Sanders was overwhelmingly favored among younger voters (millennials), he lost the seventeen-to-twenty-nine-year-old category to Clinton only in Alabama and Mississippi.[27] In keeping with the evidence that independent voters were more inclined to support the anti-establishment change candidate in the 2016 election cycle, Sanders only lost this group to Clinton in the Deep South states of Alabama, Georgia, and Mississippi.

There is some irony to the 2016 Democratic nomination contest in the South. In 2008, Barack Obama won the Democratic nomination because he dominated Clinton among black voters in southern states.[28] Eight years later, Clinton assumed the role of Obama and dominated Sanders in the South because of overwhelming black support. As shown in table 2.6, Clinton's share of the black vote was 80 percent or higher in every southern state, and in no other voter group did she perform so well. Essentially the same African American primary electorate that spurned Clinton in 2008 chose to elevate her to the Democratic nomination in 2016.

Table 2.6. Clinton's Dominance of Sanders in Southern Primaries: Percentage of the Clinton Vote by Voter Characteristics

Characteristic	SC	AL	AR	GA	TN	TX	VA	MS	FL	NC
White	54	59	62	58	57	57	57	68	53	[43]
Black	86	91	91	85	89	83	84	89	81	80
Latino	—	—	—	—	—	71	—	—	68	—
Male	68	73	60	66	64	61	57	79	57	49
Female	79	80	76	76	70	70	70	85	70	59
17–29 years old	[46]	52	[42]	[46]	[39]	[40]	[30]	62	[35]	[28]
30–44 years old	75	77	53	65	56	58	57	79	64	50
45–64 years old	77	82	80	80	76	75	72	90	72	62
65+ years old	88	85	81	80	82	87	85	91	70	69
High school or less	86	85	72	80	77	76	67	93	68	65
Some college	71	75	64	69	65	64	61	84	62	54
College degree	70	75	63	71	59	65	57	74	63	52
Postgrad. degree	70	78	76	70	69	66	69	84	64	53
Earning below $50,000	76	80	69	70	62	66	60	83	65	52
Earning at least $50,000	68	76	69	72	67	66	65	83	65	51
Democrat	80	85	80	77	74	75	71	87	71	65
Independent	[46]	52	[41]	51	[45]	[46]	[42]	66	[41]	[34]
Liberal	70	76	66	66	63	62	60	81	59	52
Moderate	78	82	74	79	73	73	69	86	71	59
Married	72	—	72	—	72	—	—	87	68	61
Unmarried	73	—	64	—	61	—	—	81	57	52
Urban	70	76	73	71	72	67	68	86	63	57
Suburban	70	73	58	71	62	63	62	78	68	53
Rural	77	84	72	77	61	74	67	84	51	53

Source: All data are from the 2016 National Election Pool state exit polls for each state's Democratic primary contest, CNN Politics, https://goo.gl/i4qhkY.

Note: The vote choice for Latinos was only registered in Florida and Texas. Voters in Alabama, Georgia, Texas, and Virginia were not asked about their marital status. Where the Clinton percentage of the vote is in brackets, Sanders received a higher percentage.

The Republican Contest

The battle for the Republican nomination was a more complicated affair, if only because of the greater number of contenders. To be sure, Trump was the frontrunner, but before he could wrap up the nomination, many opponents would have to drop out, and they did. Coming out of the gate in Iowa, there were a dozen Republican contenders. After the contest in South Carolina, which was the third nationally and the first in the South, former Florida governor Jeb Bush bailed, and the eccentric political amateur Dr. Ben Carson exited after the March 1 Super Tuesday contests. Through the remainder of the southern GOP primaries, it was Trump versus Texas senator Ted Cruz, Florida senator Marco Rubio, and Ohio governor John Kasich. Nonetheless, because of Bush and Carson's core supporters, the popular vote shares displayed in figure 2.2 for the four aforementioned leading candidates have been computed on the basis of votes cast for the last six candidates running (including Bush and Carson).[29]

Popular support in the GOP contest in the South can be described as giving Trump the lead, placing on a second tier the southern Latino (and Cuban American) contenders Cruz and Rubio, and dropping the midwesterner Kasich down to a third tier. As shown in figure 2.2, Trump was only beaten in Texas, by the Lone Star State's native son Ted Cruz. It might have seemed that a tough-talking New Yorker with questionable GOP

Figure 2.2. Southern Republican Primary Vote Shares

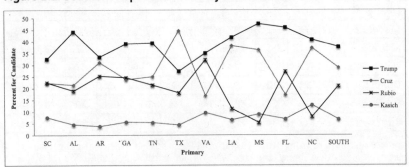

Source: Data compiled by author from David Leip, "Dave Leip's Atlas of U.S. Presidential Elections," https://goo.gl/ng0Rf.

Note: Data were computed based on the votes cast for the six leading candidates in the southern Republican primary contests: Trump, Cruz, Rubio, Kasich, Carson, and Bush.

credentials would have a difficult time relating to southern Republican primary voters, but this was not the case. Trump's outsider persona in an outsider year with a divisive message that championed the agenda of the white majority struck the right notes with southern Republican primary voters. As for Cruz and Rubio, in part because of their regional ties and conservative views (especially in the case of Cruz), they garnered a sizable share of the southern Republican vote. Meanwhile, the most moderate and foreign candidate (the Buckeye State is a long way from the South), Kasich, could not muster much traction south of the Potomac, where he managed to avoid a fourth-place finish only in Mississippi and North Carolina. In the South, Trump took 38 percent of the popular vote, and the undisputed plurality winner was trailed by Cruz with 29 percent, Rubio with 21 percent, and Kasich with 7 percent.

As in table 2.6 in the last section, table 2.7 shows a host of voter characteristics from the 2016 primary exit polls in southern states.[30] But unlike table 2.6, which displays vote shares, because of the more crowded Republican field, table 2.7 simply records the name of the Republican candidate who was the plurality vote winner for each voter category. For instance, in the Republican primary in Tennessee, Trump swept every category of voter. By contrast, in the only southern state Trump failed to carry, Texas, Cruz won every category of voter except for those making less than $50,000 per year and those who identified themselves as ideologically moderate. As evidence of identity politics and the friends-and-neighbors factor, Cruz captured the Latino vote in Texas, while Rubio was the Latino favorite in Florida.

As Trump averred on the campaign trail, he was smitten with the "poorly educated," and the feeling was mutual; he only lost those with a high school education or less in the Lone Star State.[31] By contrast, the one group with which Rubio was consistently competitive was the most educated voters (postgraduates). What is perhaps surprising but speaks to Trump's impressive primary performance and eventual general election victory is that he was preferred among Republicans and independents as well as conservatives and moderates. Trump even consistently carried the evangelical (born-again) vote, the most stalwart Republican faction within the contemporary GOP.[32] Of course, the broader takeaway from table 2.7 is that outside of Texas, Trump's name is pervasive. He was the consensus plurality candidate in a congested Republican nomination contest.

Table 2.7. Trump, the Plurality Candidate: The Candidate Winning the Most Votes by Voter Characteristics

Characteristic	SC	AL	AR	GA	TN	TX	VA	MS	FL	NC
White	Trump	Trump	Trump	Trump	Trump	Cruz	Trump	Trump	Trump	Trump
Latino	—	—	—	—	—	Cruz	—	—	Rubio	—
Male	Trump	Trump	Trump	Trump	Trump	Cruz	Trump	Trump	Trump	Trump
Female	Trump	Trump	Trump	Trump	Trump	Cruz	Rubio	Trump	Trump	Cruz
17–29 years old	Cruz	Trump	Cruz	Trump	Trump	Cruz	Rubio	Trump	Trump	Cruz
30–44 years old	T/R	Trump	Trump	Trump	Trump	Cruz	Rubio	Cruz	Trump	Cruz
45–64 years old	Trump	Trump	Trump	Trump	Trump	Cruz	Trump	Trump	Trump	Trump
65+ years old	Trump	Trump	Rubio	Trump	Trump	Cruz	Trump	Trump	Trump	Trump
High school or less	Trump	Trump	Trump	Trump	Trump	Cruz	Trump	Trump	Trump	Trump
Some college	Trump	Trump	Trump	Trump	Trump	Cruz	Trump	Trump	Trump	Trump
College degree	Trump	Trump	Trump	Trump	Trump	Cruz	Rubio	Trump	Trump	Cruz
Postgrad. degree	Rubio	T/R	Rubio	Rubio	Trump	Cruz	Rubio	Trump	Trump	Cruz
Earning below $50,000	Trump	Trump	Trump	Trump	Trump	Trump	Trump	Trump	Trump	Trump
Earning at least $50,000	Trump	Trump	Trump	Trump	Trump	Cruz	Rubio	Trump	Trump	Cruz
Republican	Trump	Trump	Trump	Trump	Trump	Cruz	Trump	Trump	Trump	Trump
Independent	Trump	Trump	Trump	Trump	Trump	Cruz	Rubio	Trump	Trump	Cruz
Moderate	Trump	Trump	Trump	Trump	Trump	Trump	Rubio	Trump	Trump	Trump
Conservative	Trump	Trump	Trump	Trump	Trump	Cruz	Trump	Trump	Trump	Cruz
Born Again (Evangelical)	Trump	Trump	T/C	Trump	Trump	Cruz	Trump	Trump	Trump	Cruz
Urban	Rubio	Trump	Rubio	—	Trump	Cruz	Rubio	—	Trump	Cruz
Suburban	Trump	Trump	Trump	Trump	Trump	Cruz	Rubio	Trump	Trump	Trump
Rural	Trump	Trump	Trump	Trump	Trump	Cruz	Trump	Trump	Trump	Trump

Source: All data are from the 2016 National Election Pool state exit polls for each state's Republican primary contest, *CNN Politics*, https://goo.gl/i4qhkY.

Note: Candidate name is the plurality vote winner. In some cases, the vote share was split between two candidates; e.g., born-again Arkansans split their votes between Trump and Cruz (shown as "T/C" in the table). The vote choice for Latinos was only registered in Florida and Texas. Only in Virginia did Trump fail to win the plurality of votes among respondents who were not born again (among this group, Rubio was the plurality winner). The vote choice was not registered for urban voters in Georgia and Mississippi.

Conclusion

In 2016 the South played its typical leading role in vetting presidential nomination contenders. The region has a disproportionate influence in the nomination process because most of its states conduct their primaries earlier than the rest of the nation, and this was once again true in 2016. Indeed, the South is often pivotal in deciding the fate of both the Democratic and Republican hopefuls, but this time around it was only a kingmaker for the Democratic Party.[33] In what is fast becoming a pattern in southern Democratic primaries, Hillary Clinton easily prevailed over Bernie Sanders because she won the lion's share of the black vote. As it had Barack Obama in 2008, a decisive advantage among the South's African American electorate gave Clinton an electoral cushion that propelled her all the way to the Democratic nomination. When southern black voters unite behind a Democratic candidate, the South becomes a formidable firewall that is hard to overcome for any candidate who performs poorly among this group, which comprises the base of the Democratic coalition.[34]

On the Republican side, the South did not exhibit a particular proclivity for New Yorker Donald Trump, the GOP frontrunner. If anything, Trump endured his greatest electoral test in the South because of competition from three legitimate rivals who called the region their home: Ted Cruz, Marco Rubio, and Jeb Bush. But Trump aced this early challenge because, as was true throughout the United States, he was the preferred choice of most voters. In other words, like their northern counterparts, southern Republican primary voters gravitated toward the "change" candidate who promised to "make America great again." Given their early placement on the nomination calendar, the southern states winnowed the field down to three contestants: Trump, Cruz, and Kasich. But just as Trump proved to be the consensus choice in the South, he easily dispatched his last two rivals after the final two southern primaries were held on March 15 because a clear plurality of voters also favored Trump in the North.

In the post-reform era of presidential nomination politics, it is always better to go earlier than later. Invariably, it seems, in any given election cycle there will be several states whose contests occur at the end of the nomination calendar when the winner is a mathematically foregone conclusion. The states of Iowa and New Hampshire have recognized this political reality for decades and now they jealously guard their first-in-the-nation status for holding their respective caucus and primary contests.

Likewise, South Carolina makes sure that it will always be the first to weigh in when the campaigns turn in a southerly direction. The South is the largest section of the United States, containing the second and third most populous electorates in Texas and Florida. Thus, because most of the South makes a habit of going earlier in the nomination process than other regions, it will continue to leave a larger imprint on who ultimately becomes the major party nominee in presidential politics.

II

*Elections in
the Deep South*

3

Alabama

Republican from Top to Bottom

Shannon L. Bridgmon

The 2016 presidential election cycle in Alabama was characteristically predictable in an otherwise unpredictable year. The Democratic and Republican primaries reflected the political environment of low political competition that also characterized congressional and state level races. Alabama's congressional delegates all won reelection with little or no competition, and no statewide races for state offices drew any Democratic candidates. Alabama remained thoroughly Republican: no Democrat holds statewide office, and the GOP extended the legislative supermajority they already had in both chambers in Montgomery.

Although Republican Donald Trump dominated the polls in the state, Alabama voters did consider and weigh the issues of personal scandal related to sexual exploits, charges of corporate and public corruption, and a newly vacated Supreme Court seat. However, each of these issues occurred within the realm of Alabama's government, not presidential politics.

The 2016 Primaries

The Democrats

Democrats in Alabama were most effective in 2016 as participants in the Democratic primary system. Both Bernie Sanders and Hillary Clinton made campaign stops in Alabama seeking to mobilize voters for the March 1 Super Tuesday primary. Bill Clinton campaigned at Alabama State University on Hillary Clinton's behalf in February.[1] She visited the state several times between October 2015 and March 1, including stops in Birmingham and Montgomery. One appearance in Birmingham was at a fundraiser for the Alabama Democratic Conference (ADC), the political caucus seeking to represent African American interests within the party.[2] Bernie Sanders held a rally on Martin Luther King Jr. Day in Birmingham to a crowd of approximately seven thousand people. His remarks highlighted his participation in the March on Washington in 1963 and the civil rights movement.

The Sanders rally and Clinton ADC appearance vividly illustrated the dynamics of the Alabama Democratic primary. The Sanders rally drew young white voters to an event that would have conventionally been suited to an African American audience, while Clinton's dinner at an exclusive suburban venue was to support the African American power caucus in the state. While the ADP's endorsement of Clinton appears to have been natural, her appearance at the event and the subsequent endorsement proved polarizing among Alabama Democrats. The Alabama Democratic Party has split into two factions in recent years, and the dominant ADC caucus has been accused of punitive behaviors against the ever-shrinking white presence in the party.[3]

Although a vigorous campaign between Bernie Sanders and Hillary Clinton played out in many areas around the nation, Alabama's Democratic voters remained solidly in support of Hillary Clinton. She carried every county in the state, receiving 78 percent of primary votes statewide (compared to the 42 percent of the primary vote in her 2008 campaign against Barack Obama). Her margin of victory was highest in the Black Belt and urban areas with large African American populations.[4]

Exit polling reveals the rise in support for her among all groups since her first run in 2008, when she lost to Barack Obama. In 2016, her support was highest among women of color of all education levels. She also carried 60 percent of white men, 58 percent of white women, and 91 percent of African American voters, reflecting her strength across all categories of Alabama Democrats. This is a significant improvement over her performance in exit polls from 2008, an election that was marked by racial voting in which only 16 percent of African American respondents voted for her. By 2016, she had earned the solid support of the African American community in the state. In that contest, her primary support came from white voters and all voters over age 60.

Sanders's largest totals were in counties in the northern section of the state.[5] Polls indicate his strongest support among young white professional men earning over $50,000 per year,[6] but Clinton still carried a majority of that demographic group. Although Clinton's primary support in Alabama dipped to 59 percent of voters during February, her success in carrying Alabama was never in doubt.[7]

The Republicans

Alabama's Republican primary voters have enjoyed growing prominence in determining the party's nominee since joining the Super Tuesday slate in 2008. Previously, Alabama's primary was held in June, long after a clear front-runner and presumptive nominee had emerged. In 2016, candidates courted Alabama GOP voters and officials seeking any advantage in breaking out of a very crowded field. Alabama's conservatives are not a monolith, yet Donald Trump established an early momentum in the state that proved difficult for other candidates to overcome.

The biggest moment of the 2016 primary campaign in Alabama came early and set the tone for what was to unfold in other states. Donald Trump's campaign rally in Mobile on August 21, 2015, drew an estimated crowd of thirty thousand enthusiastic spectators. It proved to be the largest rally during the campaign and signaled to the Trump camp that he might actually be a competitive force in the race.[8] Sen. Jeff Sessions appeared onstage with Trump, voicing support for hard-line immigration policies. This appearance served as a de facto endorsement and was followed by several staff joining the Trump campaign.[9] Sessions again appeared alongside Donald Trump at a campaign rally of fifteen thousand in Huntsville two days before the Alabama primary, becoming the first senator to endorse Trump. Sessions himself became a trusted advisor to Trump for the remainder of the campaign.[10]

Other candidates campaigned throughout the primary season, unwilling to cede the state to Trump. Both Marco Rubio and Ted Cruz campaigned across the state, each hosting rallies in December and February. Rubio's last stop was in Huntsville, where he delivered harsh words for Donald Trump and promised added investment to national defense and

America's space program.[11] Huntsville is home to both NASA and defense installations. Ben Carson made a campaign stop in Mobile in November and reappeared in Montgomery the day before the primary, although he had suspended his campaign by that appearance.

The 2016 primary election results were decisive. Donald Trump carried every county in the state with 43 percent—a clear plurality—of the vote. Ted Cruz finished second, with 21 percent, and Marco Rubio finished third, with 19 percent. Ben Carson hit the 10 percent mark statewide, and John Kasich earned 4 percent of votes. Across the state, there were clear rank-order preferences as Cruz and Rubio were interchangeable on either side of the 20 percent mark for second place.

In both 2008 and 2012, Republican support of presidential candidates followed a north-south division, with northern Alabama voters supporting the strongest evangelical candidates (Mike Huckabee or Rick Santorum) and southern Alabamians preferring hawkish candidates such as John McCain and Newt Gingrich. In 2012, urban areas supported Mitt Romney, reflecting an establishment orientation. In 2016, Trump received an outright majority in scattered counties throughout the state, performing strongest in the Hill Country in northern Alabama. His weakest support was in the east-central area of the state, and he won 37 percent of voters in the Sixth Congressional District. Both Cruz and Rubio performed their best in this district, where Trump was weaker, indicating a direct tradeoff in support. Rubio also did slightly better in Birmingham and Huntsville, both areas that Mitt Romney carried in 2012.

Given the tones of the campaign messages from candidates, Alabama GOP primary voters clearly favored hard-line messages. A CNN exit poll revealed 78 percent favored a temporary ban on Muslims entering the country and 58 percent of respondents believed the next president should be "outside the establishment."[12] This discontent was reflected by the vote totals. The only candidate to deliver what was considered an establishment message and break 1 percent of the vote was John Kasich (4.43 percent). In 2012, 19 percent of exit poll respondents indicated that experience was a top candidate quality; by 2016, "experience" was not listed as a candidate virtue in polling, but 36 percent of respondents reported that the ability to "bring about change" was the most desired candidate quality. Although one can point to the crowded field of twelve candidates on the ballot, something else was afoot. In 2012, Rick Santorum received 31 percent of primary votes, dropping to just 617 votes statewide in 2016. Santorum's message did not appreciably change over four years and could hardly be considered moderate. The political mood shifted from 2012 to 2016 among GOP primary voters. While the majority (59 percent) of 2012 respondents identified the economy as the most important issue, and 80 percent were "very worried" about the economy, by 2016 only 33 percent thought the economy was the most important issue, and those who were "very worried" about the economy dropped to 68 percent. In Alabama GOP exit polls in 2012, terrorism did not register as one of the top four issues voters identified as most important. In 2016's primary exit polls, 26 percent of respondents reported terrorism as the most important issue in the campaign.

In GOP primary voter preferences among various demographic groups, Donald Trump carried every category with respect to education, income, religious devotion, veteran status, and self-identified ideology.[13] However, that support was not uniform across all groupings. Trump's support levels were most striking in groupings by gender and educational attainment. Fifty-two percent of male respondents voted for Trump, while only 36 percent of female respondents did. While a slight gender gap had existed in 2012 (4 percent margin), this gap widened in 2016.[14] Despite differences between the genders, Trump still emerged with more female support than any other candidate (Marco Rubio was the choice for 23 percent of female respondents). As education levels increased, support for Trump decreased.[15] The inverse of this pattern emerged among those who supported Marco Rubio, John Kasich, and Ben Carson. These patterns of 2016 stood out as notable because no clear link appeared between voter educational levels and candidate preference in 2008 and 2012 Alabama primary exit polls. Although these trends reveal nuances among voter preferences, it is crucial to note that Trump still emerged as the plurality choice among all groups and carried every Alabama county in the primary.

Polling also revealed a dichotomy in the Alabama GOP electorate. First, almost half (42 percent) of respondents indicated they would not be satisfied if Donald Trump won the nomination. An overwhelming share (78 percent) of voters indicated that shared religious beliefs affected their vote, yet 39 percent of this group still voted for Trump.[16] Forty percent of respondents indicated that they had decided whom to vote for over a month before the primary, with over half of this group voting for Trump. These characteristics paint a picture of a majority of Alabama Republicans who were led by religious beliefs and a strong plurality who opposed Donald Trump's candidacy. However, hard-line messages on immigration and a dissatisfaction with establishment Republicans made Trump appealing early to voters, and they stuck with him.

General Election for President

The presidential general election campaign and outcome were largely unremarkable in terms of campaigning and outcomes in Alabama. While Secretary Clinton and Mr. Trump both visited the state several times during their primary campaigns, neither appeared in Alabama following their respective nominations. Both candidates shifted their focus and resources away from Alabama during the general election. No official Clinton campaign events were held in the state during the general election. Former president Bill Clinton appeared at a private fundraiser on her behalf in Daphne on July 13.[17] She did receive the endorsement of the *Montgomery Advertiser* and the Alabama Media Group, representing the *Birmingham News*, *Mobile Press-Register*, and *Huntsville Times*. Few official Trump campaign events were held. Donald Trump Jr., the candidate's son, appeared as his surrogate at a fundraiser in Birmingham in October.[18] In late October, Trump's "victory bus" toured the state, with several Alabama Republican officials acting as surrogates for the nominee, including incumbent candidates Rep. Robert Aderholt and supreme court justice Tom Parker.[19] The tour was largely geared toward mobilizing voters for down-ticket races and recruiting new party volunteers and activists.[20]

What should have been a comfortable and mobilizing campaign for a Republican nominee proved to be awkward and lacking in voter enthusiasm. Trump's brash style and comments about minorities proved more uncomfortable for Alabama voters during the general campaign. Nevertheless, no significant backlash at the polls was expected. However, the *Access Hollywood* audio recording from 2005 did have an indirect effect on the Alabama campaign for other candidates (if not Trump) as Republican candidates gambled on whether to distance themselves from Trump or embrace him in the fallout. Jeff Sessions offered unwavering support for Trump, and Alabama Republican Party chair Terry Lathan expressed support to minimize damage.[21] Rep. Bradley Byrne of the First Congressional District initially stated that Trump was unfit for the presidency and urged him to step aside to let Mike Pence serve as the nominee, warning of certain Clinton victory if he failed to do so.[22] However, his district's lack of outrage (and even constituent backlash) and Lathan's support prompted him to reaffirm his support for Trump.[23]

Congressional and Statewide Campaigns

Alabama mirrors other Deep South states' congressional representation patterns, with Republican senators, a Republican-dominated House delegation, and one Democrat representing a majority-minority district. Results from 2016 maintained the status quo in the Alabama delegation, returning all seven House members and Sen. Richard Shelby to Congress (see table 3.1). While the partisanship of each safe seat reflects voter preferences in the state, district lines both reinforce the partisanship of each district and protect the incumbency advantage from general election threats.

Competition may have increased in some primary elections as populist and Tea Party elements have challenged traditional establishment Republican members since 2010. First District representative Bradley Byrne, a former Democrat who is now a moderate Republican, ran unopposed in the general election but was challenged from the right by Tea Party–endorsed Dean Young in a rematch, following a narrow victory in a 2013 runoff. Second District representative Martha Roby faced a high-profile challenge from vocal critic and Tea Party opponent Becky Gerritson. Rep. Gary Palmer of Alabama's Third District handily defeated his Tea Party opponent, while Fourth District representative Robert Aderholt faced a nominal opponent from an out-of-district challenger.[24] The challenge was both legally permissible and a long shot, but it represented growing dissatisfaction with Aderholt's two decades in Washington as part of the Republican establishment. After fighting a competitive primary race in 2012, the Tea Party's Rep. Mo Brooks was the only congressional Republican not to draw a primary challenger in Alabama. He was also the only member of Alabama's congressional delegation to self-identify as a Tea Party Republican. As establishment Republicans drew increased challenges from Tea Party elements on the right, the incumbency advantage appears to have been stronger than ideological dissatisfaction among conservative primary voters in the state.[25]

The expected electoral success of Alabama's congressional incumbents was not without political upheaval. Following the release of the *Access Hollywood* recording of Donald Trump's comments about women, several Alabama Republicans condemned the remarks, including Governor Bentley and Representatives Palmer, Brooks, and Roby. Representative Palmer called on Mr. Trump to go beyond a simple apology and actively seek forgiveness for the remarks, while Representative Byrne called on Mr. Trump to step aside as nominee. However, it was Rep. Martha Roby who made the largest splash, publicly stating that she would not vote for Trump.[26] While the remaining Republican candidates walked back their criticism of Trump over several days, each vowing to vote for the GOP nominee, Roby held fast to her promise. The backlash against Roby from

Table 3.1. Alabama Federal Election Results

Candidate (party)	Vote (%)	Votes (#)	Incumbent change (%)
President			
Hillary Clinton / Tim Kaine (D)	34	725,704	
Donald Trump / Mike Pence (R)	62	1,314,431	
Gary Johnson / Bill Weld (I)	2	44,211	
Jill Stein / Ajamu Baraka (I)	0	9,341	
US Senate			
Ron Crumpton (D)	36	744,848	
Richard C. Shelby (R)	64	1,331,317	−1
US House			
First District			
Bradley Byrne (R)**	99	206,873	+31
Second District			
Nathan Mathis (D)	40	111,640	
Martha Roby (R)*	49	134,450	−18
Write-in	11	29,548	
Third District			
Jesse Smith (D)	33	93,806	
Mike Rogers (R)*	67	174,875	+1
Fourth District			
Robert Aderholt (R)**	99	235,531	0
Fifth District			
Will Boyd, Jr. (D)	33	101,577	
Mo Brooks (R)	67	204,791	−8
Sixth District			
David J. Putman (D)	25	83,396	
Gary Palmer (R)	75	244,788	−2
Seventh District			
Terri A. Sewell (D)**	98	228,948	0

Source: Alabama Secretary of State, http://goo.gl/62QhiN.

*Incumbent.

**Incumbent Representatives Byrne, Aderholt, and Sewell ran unopposed.

her constituents was immediate and sustained. Roby was blackballed from a GOP event in her district, and a write-in campaign for her primary challenger was launched to defeat her in the general election.[27] While Gerritson's write-in campaign did not cost Roby her seat, 11 percent of the votes in the district were written in, lowering Roby's margin to a mere 9 percent over Democrat Nathan Mathis. Following the election, Roby quickly sought to move past the flap. She restated that she was committed to serving her constituents—even those who voted against her—and that she looked forward to working with Trump's administration.[28]

Statewide elections in 2016 consisted of four offices, and the ballot also contained a slate of fourteen constitutional amendments. Three incumbents in the Alabama Supreme Court ran for reelection unopposed in the general election, keeping all nine seats on the courts safely in Republican hands. Justice Tom Parker faced a challenger in the Republican primary but easily warded off any threat to his third term, earning 73 percent of the votes. The remaining statewide seat was for president of the Alabama Public Service Commission. Incumbent Twinkle Andress Cavanaugh faced former commissioner Terry Dunn in the primary but kept the seat, earning 63 percent of the vote. She drew no general election opposition from the Democrats.

The labyrinth of provisions in the Alabama Constitution that hinder basic representative governance perpetually result in a list of opportunities for voters to engage in direct democracy through the amendment process. All fourteen amendments on the ballot were approved statewide by voters, including eliminating age limits on nonjudicial state officials, limiting legislative access to park system revenue and partially privatizing it, increasing local authority for limited policy actions, and clarifying the impeachment process in Article VII, a timely measure.[29]

Political and Institutional Upheaval in State Government

While the presidential election of 2016 was national political theater reflecting concerns of trustworthiness, temperament, and personality, it was par for the course in Alabama politics. Although no elections were held for executive and legislative offices, the institutions of government in the state were rocked by scandal and legal action. By the end of 2016, the leader of each branch of state government had been brought down or crippled. The governor faced impeachment charges and a criminal investigation, the Speaker of the Alabama House of Representatives was convicted of twelve felony charges and removed from office, and Chief Justice Roy Moore was judicially suspended from the court by a judicial conduct board.

Speaker of the House Mike Hubbard (R-Opelika) orchestrated the Republican takeover of Alabama's legislature in 2010 with supermajority margins in both houses. He quickly became Speaker and ushered in an ambitious legislative agenda, including a sweeping ethics reform package. In June 2016, he was convicted of twelve counts of corruption for using his public office for personal gain, violating the very laws he pushed to create.[30] He is currently seeking a new trial after being sentenced to four years in prison.[31] However, the prosecution of his case spilled over into the governor's mansion.

Gov. Robert Bentley was reelected for his second term in 2014, facing negligible challenges for the party's nomination and handily beating the Democratic opponent with 64 percent of the vote. As a constitutionally weak governor, Bentley dealt with revenue crises and a stubborn legislature as well as could be expected during his first term. As the investigation into Speaker Hubbard was unfolding, Governor Bentley interfered in the investigation by obstructing the participation of the head of the Alabama Law Enforcement Agency. As the drama unfolded, Alabamians learned of an extramarital relationship between the Governor and his political advisor, Rebekah Caldwell Mason. Further investigation revealed the governor misused state resources in covering up both the relationship and his involvement in influencing the Hubbard investigation.[32] The House Judiciary Committee convened an impeachment committee, but the process has been suspended for several institutional reasons. First, the Alabama Constitution never specified the votes necessary for conviction in the state senate, hence the appearance of an amendment on the general election ballot. Secondly, Atty. Gen. Luther Strange opened a grand jury investigation into Bentley's activities and has subsequently requested a suspension in the proceedings while the criminal investigation proceeds.[33]

Further complicating matters was the governor's power to appoint the replacement to fill the seat of former senator and current attorney general Jeff Sessions. What should be a straightforward process became the ultimate political game as Governor Bentley drew out the deliberations for the selections and pitted hopefuls against each other.[34] Ultimately, he selected Luther Strange to fill the seat—the very man whose office was investigating him but who also slowed the impeachment process. He then appointed former Marshall County district attorney Steve Marshall as state attorney general to replace Strange for the remainder of the term.

Marshall has officially recused himself from any future investigation and appointed a supernumerary district attorney to take over the case.[35] Ultimately, Bentley resigned the governorship and pled guilty to two misdemeanors, agreeing never to serve in public office again. Considering his limited compliance with the proceedings and continued political dealings with his paramour, the deal was the most favorable outcome available to Bentley.[36]

For the second time, Alabama Supreme Court chief justice Roy Moore was removed from office by the Alabama Court of the Judiciary.[37] As the administrative head of the unified court system in the state, in 2015 Moore had ordered county probate judges to halt the issuance of same-sex marriage licenses in defiance of a federal court order. The court of the judiciary suspended Moore without pay for the remainder of his term; however, as of this writing, Moore is mounting an appeal in unchartered territory. The Alabama Supreme Court has recused itself from hearing the matter, leaving the appeal up to a hastily constructed panel of retired justices.[38] Moore opposed the process, dramatically walking out of the courtroom as the judicial lottery process began.[39] He has also refused to clear out his office and entered into a public feud with former colleague and acting chief justice Lyn Stuart.[40]

Analysis

The results of the 2016 elections in Alabama reflect well-established trends in southern political development and a continuation of patterns since 2000. Alabama continued to support Republicans in the presidential election, with the difference in support for each party's nominee slightly widening from previous elections. Donald Trump received 62 percent of the vote, carrying all of the same counties as Mitt Romney with the addition of Conecuh and Barbour Counties, which President Obama had narrowly won in 2012.[41] Evidence of the decline in Democratic voting each cycle continued. Hillary Clinton received just 34 percent of the vote, 4 points fewer than President Obama's 38 percent in 2012 (see table 3.2). Turnout was slightly lower than 2008 and 2012 rates, as expected.[42] Sixty-two percent of registered Alabama voters turned out to vote.

Hillary Clinton received her largest vote shares in the Black Belt counties, all of which were in the lowest income group. Historical voting patterns based on geographic trends persisted. However, the trend since 2000 has been clear—rural areas comprised of lower-income whites have been voting more Republican at all levels. Most Alabamians outside of urban areas and the Black Belt also have remained solidly Republican.[43] Donald Trump's widest vote margins were found in more affluent suburban counties and in the northern Alabama Hill counties.[44] Hill counties offered the weakest support for Clinton, with outcomes much lower in comparison to those since 2000. Democratic support in all the northern counties in the state has also dropped since 2000. The largest Republican gains have occurred in these northern counties and also in the southeastern area of the state known as the Wiregrass. Support for Clinton in the Black Belt mirrored that for President Obama, and Democratic support actually increased in urban and coastal counties.

With regard to racial voting, the 2016 election further highlighted the enduring questions of race and politics in Alabama. Some questioned the possibility of increased Republican strength as a backlash against an African American president. Coupled with the overall partisan developments in the state, it appears there existed a lack of support for Democratic candidates in general. Clinton's performance dropped markedly in comparison to President Obama's; however, partisan voting in Alabama was certainly correlated with race. Larger proportions of whites lead to higher levels of Republican presidential voting. Clinton's weakest electoral performance occurred in counties with populations that were less than 15 percent African American. Counties with larger African American populations voted at higher levels for Hillary Clinton than whiter areas. This may also have occurred in urban areas; population estimates listed in table 3.2 reflect updated census data through 2014. Ten out of the eleven counties that were majority African American in 2014 had experienced drops in African American population since 2010, extending demographic patterns that began in 2000. During the same period, metropolitan and especially suburban counties saw a rise in African American populations.

Income distribution may shed light on voting patterns, indicating a Republican surge within the middle groups of county-group characteristics. The greatest amounts of Republican support did not occur in counties with the highest income groups but in those counties whose median incomes were between $34,000 and $43,000. While solidly urban areas such as Birmingham and Montgomery continued to favor Democrats, Republican performance remained steady in rural areas and outlying areas beyond urban centers.

The election results also reinforced the importance of party labels in Alabama. Partisanship was a strong influence on down-ticket races as well, with most contested state and federal races favoring Republicans by similar margins. Whether congressional success was a reflection of partisanship or an incumbency advantage, Alabama's incumbent congressional delegation enjoyed safe (or unopposed) races. Partisan advantage may have been so strong that it warded off even the threat of a Democratic challenger in a statewide judicial or administrative race. No identifiable race that occurred in Alabama during 2016 could be characterized as competitive. This also held true in the general election, and one could argue it was reflected in the presidential primaries, as well.

Alabama's lack of political competition within the state may cost it media and party resources for mobilization, for Democratic campaigns,

Table 3.2. Alabama Democratic Vote by County Characteristics

Characteristics	2016	2012	2008	2004	2000
	Clinton	Obama	Obama	Kerry	Gore
Total	34	38	39	37	42
Median family income					
Less than $34,000	60.3	50.0	50.9	48.3	53.7
$34,000–$43,000	24.5	28.5	31.4	33.7	42.2
More than $43,000	29.1	37.3	40.3	36.7	40.8
African American pop.					
Less than 15%	16.0	22.4	24.3	27.5	35.5
15%–40%	29.8	41.9	42.1	38.5	43.0
More than 40%	59.0	48.0	59.0	53.2	55.9
Urban pop.					
Less than 20%	33.5	33.7	32.2	34.2	42.4
20%–49%	32.4	31.4	30.1	31.2	38.7
50% or more	35.0	39.4	43.8	39.9	44.0
Region of state*					
Tennessee Valley	22	29.3	31.8	36.9	44.1
Hill Country	21	26.7	26.8	27.7	35.6
Black Belt	62	62.8	60.9	56.7	60.5
Wiregrass	26	29.1	28.6	26.7	34.2
Coastal	33	27.5	29.1	27.5	31.4
Metropolitan	46	44.5	47.8	42.9	46.1

Source: Compiled by the author from data supplied by the Alabama Secretary of State and US Bureau of the Census. Regions of the state determined by the author and listed in text endnotes.

Note: All table entries are percentages.

and for public opinion and exit polling. Nevertheless, Alabama may continue to influence national politics beyond its electoral preferences. Jeff Sessions's early and ardent support of Donald Trump earned him the nomination and subsequent confirmation for US attorney general. Many are now looking to see how this selection will shape the future of the Department of Justice and its priorities in the Trump administration. It also sent ripple effects through Alabama state politics, as the appointment of Luther Strange to fill the seat Sessions vacated upon confirmation has breathed new life into further investigations into corruption in the state.[45] As Bentley's successor—Lt. Gov. Kay Ivey—took office, pressure was mounting for an investigation into any quid pro quo between the former governor and Luther Strange regarding the Senate appointment, and there were calls to move up the special election for the seat that Bentley slated to occur along with the midterm elections of 2018.[46]

Conclusions

Alabama's political participation and governance continues to be a Republican stronghold. The Republican trend in presidential voting that began in the 1950s continues to erode Democratic influence down to the local level. The dominance of the GOP and Alabama's relatively early participation in the Super Tuesday primaries hold the most promise for the state to exert influence in shaping presidential politics. In 2016, Alabama Democrats exerted more influence in presidential politics through the primary system than they are able to either in general elections or through state governance. Republicans fully control the executive and judicial branches and exert supermajority control in the legislature. The only Democrats to appear on the ballot in a statewide race during the 2016 election were at the federal level. In contested races, Democratic candidates in Alabama may expect to garner roughly a third of cast votes.

The state has returned to a fully one-party system as the Democratic Party has imploded, removing any further opportunities for it to function as a meaningful opposition party. In any functional two-party system, the leadership meltdowns of the Republicans in each branch of state government would serve as an ideal catalyst for Democratic resurgence; however, the weakness of the Alabama Democratic Party and the apparent lack of willingness among voters to tie the dysfunction to the GOP will likely keep Alabama a one-party state.

The current lack of two-party competition harks back to the environment that V. O. Key analyzed seven decades ago. While no clear factional cleavages are present within the Republican Party in Alabama, its dysfunction is apparent in the disintegration within the institutions of government and the familiar use of the court system to fight political battles that cannot be fought at the ballot box. Meanwhile, a virtually nonexistent minority party persists but is ineffective as the Democrats hover along eerily familiar fault lines of racial control. For as long as each party engages in cannibalizing itself from within and one-party politics is the norm, Alabama politics may prove the old adage that what's old is new again.

4

Georgia

A Swing State That Didn't Swing

Charles S. Bullock III

During the 2016 campaign season, pundits reclassified Georgia from a solidly Republican state to a toss-up state. The state last enjoyed competitive status in 1996 when Bob Dole defeated Bill Clinton by 1.2 percentage points. Georgia had not voted Democratic for president since 1992 when, thanks to Ross Perot, who attracted more than three hundred thousand votes, Clinton won by fewer than fourteen thousand votes, making it the most hotly contested state in the nation.

With the new century, the Peach State returned to the GOP fold where it had been in 1984 and 1988. Republican success, which had been largely confined to presidential and, in the 1990s, congressional contests, expanded up and down the ballot. Sonny Perdue became the first Republican governor in 130 years, and Republicans took the state senate in 2002. Two years later, following court-imposed redistricting, Republicans won the state house.[1] No nonincumbent Democrat has won a statewide office since 1998, and after 2010 Republicans held every statewide position.

Despite the persistent string of GOP triumphs, Democrats saw a chance for Hillary Clinton to win the Peach State as her husband had a quarter century earlier. The hope rested on the state's changing demographics. Of the fourteen states that *RealClearPolitics* rated as battle-grounds during 2016, Georgia had the largest African American elector-ate (30 percent) and the greatest concentration of minority voters (40 percent). This marked a dramatic shift from 1996, when whites cast 77.5 percent of Georgia's votes.[2] If Republicans continued to attract little sup-port from minorities, at some point white votes would become too few for victory. Adding to the GOP predicament, young voters have joined minorities in favoring Democratic candidates. Those who gaze at the stars, polls, and demographics agreed that Georgia was edging toward the precipice of realignment.

Even though Democrats lost Georgia in 2012, in sifting through the results, they found the first tangible prospects for reversing fortunes. Barack Obama lost Georgia by less than 8 percentage points. Of the states that voted for Mitt Romney, only North Carolina gave him a smaller margin.

The Democratic Party hit bottom in 2013 when the state chair resigned during an investigation into $2 million he stole from his law firm's clients.[3] The first tentative step toward renewal began in 2014 when Democrats fielded a ticket headed by heirs bearing two of the state's best-known polit-ical names. Michelle Nunn sought to reclaim the Senate seat her father Sam held from 1972 to 1997, and Pres. Jimmy Carter's grandson Jason challenged Gov. Nathan Deal. These two big names succeeded in rais-ing funds across the nation and, unlike the hapless Democrats four years earlier, matched their GOP opponents in terms of television ads, mail-outs and volunteers. Democrats vote at lower rates than Republicans in midterm elections, so despite a well-known and generously funded ticket, Democrats came up empty-handed, although the Nunn vote did break 45 percent.

How Competitive?

Surveys conducted in the wake of the parties' national conventions gave Democrats hope. Several polls showed Clinton ahead in Georgia, with JMC Analytics putting her up by 7 points and others registering a tie. In early August, the *RealClearPolitics* average had her leading by 1.5 points. For the first time in years, national and even some international media paid attention to Georgia. But as the excitement generated by the Democratic convention and the image of Trump's boorish treatment of a gold-star Muslim family that had endorsed Clinton faded, the billion-aire regained the lead. Seven polls of likely voters conducted between

September 9 and September 22 showed Trump ahead by 2 to 7 points with an average of 4.6 points. Georgia then fell off the pollsters' radar, not to be revisited until ten days into October.

RealClearPolitics reported a dozen Georgia surveys during the last four weeks of the campaign. Trump led all of these, although after the release of the infamous *Access Hollywood* tape, a widely-reported *Atlanta Journal-Constitution* poll showed only a 2-point advantage. Rather than converging as polls often do as Election Day draws nigh, two of the last samples before the election produced differing results. In the wake of FBI director James Comey's announcement that the agency would be sifting through 650,000 emails on a computer shared by top Clinton confidant Huma Abedin and her ex-husband, the disgraced former member of Congress Anthony Weiner, SurveyUSA had Trump ahead by 7 points with 49 percent to Clinton's 42 percent. However, a sample completed four days later by NBC and the *Wall Street Journal* found a statistical dead heat in which Trump was up by 1 percentage point. Two polls done in the first days of November had Trump ahead by 2 and 4 points, respectively. The final *RealClearPolitics* average showed Trump leading by 49.2 to 44.4 percent.

Results showing a horse race underway stimulated increased media attention but did not prompt Hillary Clinton to campaign in Georgia after February, although her husband dropped in for a fundraiser.[4] Nor did Democrats make a major media buy or send in ground troops.[5] As the Clinton campaign was focused elsewhere, the Trump team also largely ignored the state, although Ivanka Trump and her half-sister Tiffany Trump campaigned for a day in the Atlanta suburbs in late October.[6] Donald last visited Georgia in June, but Mike Pence came to Atlanta in August.

Early in the fall, Atlanta mayor Kasim Reed called on the Clinton campaign to invest $8–$15 million in a full-court press to win the Peach State.[7] The mayor expressed no preference about whether the money would go to mobilizing minority voters or to television advertising. Had Clinton continued to coast to victory and expanded the scope of her efforts, as she briefly did when she thought a landslide victory within her grasp following the *Access Hollywood* tape and before the Comey letter, she might have invested resources in Georgia. That Georgia did not become a Democratic priority in the campaign's closing days may have been due, at least in part, to the lackluster Democratic Senate candidate, a topic discussed later. Clinton gave greater attention to swing states like Arizona, Florida, and North Carolina that had hot Senate races that she hoped to impact.

Results

A degree of suspense surrounded the outcome in Georgia on election night as the networks hesitated to award the state's electoral vote. Both Florida and North Carolina, traditional swing states and ones Trump had to win, were called before Georgia. Once all votes were counted, Georgia would perform in line with the last *RealClearPolitics* average, with Trump winning by 5.2 percentage points. The billionaire would carry the Peach State 51.1 to 45.9 percent, so why the delay? DeKalb County, which has the fourth largest electorate, reported late, and analysts wanted to see whether this Democratic stronghold could propel Clinton to victory.[8] As anticipated, DeKalb, with an electorate more than 60 percent nonwhite, went heavily for Clinton, who received 80.4 percent of its votes (251,370)—but not heavily enough to offset Trump's showing elsewhere in the state.

Trump's Georgia margin equaled John McCain's advantage over Barack Obama eight years earlier, making it one of the narrowest Republican triumphs in a statewide contest in a decade. As table 4.1 shows, Mitt Romney's 2012 margin was 50 percent larger than Trump's. From another perspective, Trump's vote share was the second smallest among Republicans in the last decade. He performed 1 to 2 points below most of the other Republicans who faced the most successful Democrats.[9] Clinton's vote share was the largest achieved by a Democrat in a statewide contest since 2008 and slightly better than the one President Obama managed in his reelection bid.

What would it have taken for Clinton to break the string of GOP successes and win Georgia? The broad outlines of the Democratic path to victory became public knowledge in 2014 when a staffer inadvertently posted online the strategy memo a consultant had prepared for Michelle Nunn's Senate campaign.[10] If African Americans cast 30 percent of the votes, then Nunn needed 30 percent of the white vote to win. In 2014, the black vote came close to hitting the Nunn target when blacks cast 28.7 percent of the state's votes, with 90 percent choosing the Democrat. Nunn and Carter came up woefully short in seeking white support. The usual gender gap appeared among white voters when the exit poll showed that males were loath to vote Democratic, giving Nunn just 19 percent. Since more white males than females turned out, Nunn needed 40 percent from white women to reach the goal of 30 percent white support. She got 27 percent.

Table 4.1. Strongest Democratic Performances in Recent Elections

Year	Office	Republican	Vote (%)	Democrat	Vote (%)
2016	President	Trump	51.1	Clinton	45.9
2014	Senator	Perdue	52.9	Nunn	45.2
2012	President	Romney	53.3	Obama	45.5
2010	Atty. Gen.	Olens	52.9	Hodges	43.6
2008	President	McCain	52.2	Obama	47.0
2008	Senator	Chambliss	49.9	Martin	46.8

Source: Georgia Secretary of State, http://sos.ga.gov/index.php/elections.

Enthusiastic black support would be crucial for Clinton, and it largely came through for her. Even in the absence of Obama's charisma and his special connection to the black electorate, African American voters turned out for Clinton. The official count done by Georgia's secretary of state shows the black share of the vote at 27.6 percent, 2 points below black turnout in Obama's elections.[11] Clinton received strong black support but was short of the near unanimity enjoyed by Obama. As shown in table 4.2, she received 89 percent of the black vote, significantly less than the 98 percent that Obama polled in 2008 and slightly less than Nunn's 92 percent and Jason Carter's 90 percent.[12] The 2016 exit poll does not provide separate estimates for Latino or Asian American support, but minorities other than African Americans also favored Clinton, giving her 63 percent of their votes.

Like the Democratic candidates of 2014, Clinton lost Georgia because of her inability to make inroads among whites, who cast 61 percent of the state's votes. She performed even worse than the 2014 Democrats, managing just 21 percent of the white vote, down from Carter's 25 percent and Nunn's 23 percent. Given that black turnout would be lower than what Obama had attracted, Clinton, like Nunn, needed at least 30 percent of the white vote to win. The gender gap persisted, with Clinton losing by 80 to 16 percent among white men and performing 10 points better among white women.

Nationally, as in Georgia, Clinton was expected to lose the white vote, but some analysts anticipated she would perform relatively well among more highly educated white women. Across the nation, college-educated white women rallied to the Wellesley alumna, giving her 51 percent of their votes. But in Georgia, this cohort showed little interest

Table 4.2. Georgia Presidential Election Exit Poll Results, 2016

	Share of Vote	Trump (R)	Clinton (D)
Race			
White	60	75	21
Black	30	9	89
Other	10	36	63
Gender			
Male	45	60	37
Female	55	43	54
Party			
Democrat	34	5	94
Republican	36	94	4
Independent	30	52	41
Age			
18–29 years	18	33	63
30–44 years	28	44	51
45–64 years	38	57	41
65+ years	16	67	31
White evangelical			
Yes	34	92	5
No	66	31	66
Region			
Atlanta	18	22	76
Atlanta suburbs	28	46	50
North	19	69	28
Central	19	55	42
South	16	65	32

Source: National Election Pool, "Exit Poll: Georgia," November 23, 2016, http://edition.cnn.com/election/results/exit-polls/georgia/president.

Note: All table entries are percentages.

in making a woman commander in chief, rejecting Clinton by a margin of 63 to 34 percent.

Despite struggling to attract white women, with backing of minority women Clinton won Georgia's female vote by 11 points. She lost men by 23 points, and the magnitude of Trump's advantage among men more than compensated for men's lower rates of poll attendance. The lower rates at which black men participated contributed to the gender turnout difference. Going into the general election, black women registrants outnumbered black men by almost 50 percent.[13]

White evangelicals are the core constituency for the Georgia GOP, and in 2016 they constituted 34 percent of the electorate. They proved themselves Trump's strongest supporters. The thrice-married billionaire won the evangelical vote by an astonishing 92 to 5 percent. Trump outperformed Sen. David Perdue, who attracted 86 percent of white evangelicals in 2014, and Gov. Nathan Deal, who managed 82 percent. Strong social pressures mobilized in some congregations, urging members to support Trump and ignore what might be seen as his unchristian behavior. A woman reluctant to support Trump told a *Time* reporter that members of her Sunday school class screamed at her, and a fellow parishioner warned that to oppose Trump was to be in league with the devil.[14] Those willing to overlook Trump's attitudes toward women and his lack of biblical knowledge explained that they supported him because he opposes abortion and would appoint conservative judges.[15] Since white evangelicals were both more cohesive and more numerous than African Americans, who are Democrats' core constituency, the white evangelical vote more than offset black support for Clinton.

Despite coming up short once again in Georgia, Democrats could take heart in their success among young voters. Table 4.2 shows that 63 percent of the youngest cohort favored Clinton. The former senator also won among voters thirty to forty-four years old, although the margin here was just 7 points. In contrast, senior citizens broke for Trump by more than two to one. They were slightly outnumbered by their grandchildren, as the under-thirty cohort provided more votes for Clinton than the oldest group gave Trump. If millennials remain in the Democratic Party as they age and are joined by newer entrants into the electorate, the future looks promising for Democrats. The ranks of the young are destined to grow, as is Georgia's minority population, forming what Ronald Brownstein has called the coalition of the ascendant.[16]

The exit poll showed Republicans with a thin 2 percent advantage over Democrats in party loyalty. With each candidate attracting 94 percent of his or her party's members, the decisive push for Trump came from independents, who cast 30 percent of the vote. Table 4.2 shows that independents broke for Trump by 52 to 41 percent.

In winning 45.9 percent of the vote, Clinton tapped into the parts of Georgia that have remained loyal to Democrats for president and statewide offices. As in other states, she won the core urban counties of the state's major cities—Atlanta, Athens, Augusta, Columbus, Macon, and Savannah. She won cities with populations greater than fifty thousand by 68 to 29 percent. A majority of Clinton's Georgia votes came from the state's four largest counties and Clayton County, metropolitan Atlanta's sixth largest county. The Atlanta metropolitan area's twenty-nine counties include several rural ones, but Clinton carried the entire metropolitan area by 52 to 44 percent.

Clinton outperformed Obama in the Atlanta area, attracting more votes than the president did in 2012 in seventeen counties.[17] In 2004, only three Atlanta-area counties voted for John Kerry. Obama expanded the Democratic enclave to six counties in 2008. Six years later, a seventh county voted for Nunn and Carter. Clinton enlarged the blue island by adding the state's second and third most populous counties, besting Trump by 19,164 votes in Gwinnett and 7,209 votes in Cobb. Gwinnett's electorate may be majority minority, and it currently boasts the state's largest Latino concentration.[18] Trump's threats to deport those without papers may have spurred the county's Latinos to turn out and provide Clinton's victory margin. Clinton's win in Cobb was especially surprising. Just days before the election, GOP activists hoped to win big in what reporters characterized as "this heavily conservative county."[19] When it is compared with the congressional results, Cobb's Clinton vote may have been more a rejection of Trump than an embrace of the donkey as suggested. Sen. Johnny Isakson won Cobb by 35,398 votes, and the Sixth Congressional District, which contains much of Cobb, enthusiastically supported the GOP incumbent. Ironically, Trump lost Cobb despite his daughters' campaigning there in late October.

Six congressional districts lie wholly within metropolitan Atlanta. African American Democrats represent three of the districts, while white Republicans serve the other three. Clinton won the three majority-black districts overwhelmingly, receiving more votes and having larger margins than Obama had four years earlier. She also did well in the GOP districts; two that had given Mitt Romney a combined 129,580-vote margin found Trump far less appetizing, going for him by fewer than 5,000 votes in the Sixth District and less than 18,000 in the Seventh District. The rejection was limited to Trump. As shown in table 4.3, Tom Price, Trump's choice to head the Department of Health and Human Services, coasted to reelection with 61.7 percent, and Rob Woodall took 60.4 percent in the Seventh District.

Also voting Democratic was a necklace of rural counties strung across the middle of the state, the remnants of the historic Black Belt, counties with many African Americans. Of sixteen rural counties that voted for Clinton, all are in the Black Belt except for one, a coastal county that had rice-growing plantations before the Civil War.

In contrast to the 30 counties that voted for Clinton, Trump carried 129 counties. His most enthusiastic support came in 23 small-to-medium counties (only one had more than twenty-five thousand voters), all of which honored him with more than 80 percent of their votes, and three, with more than 88 percent. Much of Trump's strongest support came in north Georgia, an area that includes several mountainous counties. In all likelihood, more than 90 percent of white men in some of these counties, which have few minority registrants, voted for Trump.

Turnout

Prior to the election, many commentators fretted that, confronted with the two most unpopular candidates to ever receive major-party nominations, turnout might decline. These concerns did not prevent participation in Georgia from setting a record of 4,165,405 votes, more than 231,000 above the 2008 figure. However, abstention from the presidential choices increased in 2016 as 2.7 percent of voters did not select a candidate; 0.3 percent had skipped over the presidential options in 2008 and 2012.

Groups concerned about minority participation have filed multiple suits claiming that Georgia officials were not sufficiently committed to facilitating minority voting.[20] The results that showed minorities accounted for 39 percent of the electorate belie those claims. Statewide registration rose by more than 82,000 over 2012 because of heightened minority interest. African American registration rose by 7.8 percent, while Latinos increased their ranks by 44.3 percent and Asian American numbers rose by 50.0 percent. White registrations declined. Secretary of State Brian Kemp pointed proudly to steps taken to facilitate registration, which can now be done online using an internet browser or an application on a smart phone, in addition to more traditional methods.

Presidential Primary

Georgia's Secretary of State Brian Kemp took the lead in promoting what became known as the "SEC Primary," taking its name from the overlap between states holding primaries on Super Tuesday and states with universities whose sports teams compete in the Southeastern Conference. Kemp sought to resurrect the Super Tuesday of 1988 when all southern states held presidential primaries in early March.[21] The SEC Primary was frontloaded, taking place on March 1, the first available date.

Donald Trump did well across the region and scored a plurality in Georgia with 38.8 percent of the vote. Despite having the support of none of the state's top GOP officeholders, he finished 14.4 percentage points ahead of his nearest rival. Marco Rubio and Ted Cruz came in second and third, respectively, separated from each other by a margin of eleven thousand votes.

Of Georgia's seventy-six delegates to the national convention, each of the fourteen congressional districts awarded two to the district winner, and the runner-up received one delegate. Rubio concentrated his efforts in the Atlanta area and won two districts. Trump won the other twelve, with Rubio finishing second in three and Cruz in the other nine.

Georgia was one of the states in which Cruz operatives sought to overcome losses at the ballot box by having a sophisticated ground game at the district conventions, which selected the delegates for Cleveland. Cruz supporters, hoping that the nomination process in Cleveland would extend beyond the first roll call, snared most of the district seats won by Trump in the hope that, having honored their legal obligation to support Trump, these delegates would rally to Cruz in later rounds.[22] This ultimately made no difference, however, since Trump secured enough delegates to assure nomination before the Republican National Convention convened.

On the Democratic side, Clinton won every congressional district. Her weakest performance, 58.8 percent, came in the Ninth District, which, based on the Cook Partisan Voting Index, is Georgia's most Republican district.[23] Bernie Sanders's strength in the Ninth District underscores that his antiestablishment message held some of the same appeal as Trump's critiques. Clinton registered her greatest strength diagonally across the state in southwest Georgia's majority-black Second District with 84.2 percent of the vote. Statewide, she won 71.3 percent of the vote.

Other Contests

Georgia, like most southern states, elects statewide constitutional officers at the midterm. In 2016, senior senator Johnny Isakson sought a third term. The only other statewide contest involved a seat on the Georgia Public Service Commission, where incumbent Tim Echols coasted to victory over a Libertarian challenger since Democrats failed to field a candidate.

Isakson has spent his adult life in public service, having won election to both chambers of the Georgia General Assembly and the US House of Representatives before going to the Senate. Democrats, eager to begin rebuilding their party, desperately wanted to challenge Isakson, but several individuals with a degree of name recognition, including the minister at the church once led by Martin Luther King Jr., declined. Unknown investment advisor Jim Barksdale finally picked up the gauntlet. An advantage Barksdale offered was that he could fund his own campaign, and he spent more than $3 million of his own money in the futile effort.[24] But self-funding could not compete with the fund-raising power of a popular two-term incumbent. By mid-October, Isakson had outspent Barksdale by two to one, having invested almost $10 million in his reelection bid.[25] Barksdale had little success in attracting support from industry, while Isakson reported 23 entities that contributed at least $20,000.[26]

One of the challenges confronted by Barksdale was that Isakson is probably the state's most popular politician. He is one of the increasingly rare officeholders with bipartisan appeal. Throughout his eighteen years in the state legislature, Isakson languished as a member of the minority party, which forced him to build bridges with Democrats if he hoped to have any policy successes. His bipartisan efforts paid dividends in 2016 when he received campaign contributions from Democratic former senator Sam Nunn and Georgia's last Democratic governor, Roy Barnes. Sitting representative David Scott, a Democrat who had served with Isakson in the general assembly and the US House, endorsed the Republican.[27]

Isakson took the Barksdale challenge seriously and mounted an extensive television advertising campaign. His ads did not attack Barksdale but instead stressed how he had served Georgians in a nonpartisan manner. One ad featured an African American mother who met with Isakson when her daughter, a disabled air force veteran, encountered difficulties in getting support from the Veterans Administration to pay for college. In another ad, a mother whose daughter was murdered while serving in the

Peace Corps thanked Isakson for his concern and for pushing legislation to protect others like her daughter. The Peace Corps mother ended her statement by noting that she was a lifelong Democrat but appreciated having Johnny Isakson as her senator.

Barksdale, wearing what became his signature, a touring cap, to make the point that neither hats nor many other products are now made in Georgia, criticized Isakson's support of trade legislation. He also tried to get on the outsider bandwagon driven by Trump by stressing that unlike Isakson, he, Barksdale, was not a politician. The challenger never succeeded in getting traction with the electorate. He finished with 41.0 percent of the vote; Isakson swept to a third term with 54.7 percent.

Isakson ran 3.6 percentage points ahead of Trump. The senator also won the three counties in metropolitan Atlanta that most recently showed signs of going Democratic and that voted for Clinton. Although the Senate contest attracted some two hundred thousand fewer voters than the presidential election, Isakson led Trump by forty-six thousand votes. The lower participation in the Senate election demonstrates that in Georgia there was not a substantial constituency that refused to vote for either Trump or Clinton but that went to the polls to register preferences in down-ticket contests.

With the 2014 defeat of John Barrow, the last white Democrat from a Deep South state, Georgia's ten Republican and four Democratic members of Congress all have safe districts. As reported in table 4.3, every incumbent polled at least 60 percent. Five incumbents escaped opposition, including two GOP freshmen. Indicating how uncompetitive Georgia districts are, the Republican won the one open seat with more than two-thirds of the vote.

Most members of the Georgia General Assembly have seats as safe as those of the members of Congress, so the election produced little change in the legislature. Democrats did, however, claw back a few seats, reclaiming a state senate seat lost in a special election and picking up two Democratic-leaning districts so that the GOP again failed to attain a supermajority in the lower chamber.

Conclusion

Georgia remained Republican. Donald Trump won Georgia by 5.2 percentage points, a margin greater than in five other states. Trump's vote margin was almost identical to the victories of Senator Perdue and Governor

Table 4.3. Georgia Federal Election Results, 2016

Office	Candidates	Rep. (%)	Dem. (%)	Lib. (%)	Votes (#)
President	**Trump** (R) vs. Clinton (D)	51.7	45.9	3.1	4,092,373
US Senate	**Isakson** (R) vs. Barksdale (D)	54.8	41.0	4.2	3,897,792
US House					
First District	**Carter** (R)	100.0	—	—	210,243
Second District	Duke (R) vs. **Bishop** (D)	38.8	61.2	—	242,599
Third District	Ferguson (R) vs. Pendley (D)	68.4	31.7	—	303,187
Fourth District	Armendariz (R) vs. **Johnson** (D)	24.3	75.7	—	290,739
Fifth District	Bell (R) vs. Lewis (D)	15.6	84.4	—	300,549
Sixth District	**Price** (R) vs. Stooksbury (D)	61.7	38.3	—	326,005
Seventh District	**Woodall** (R) vs. Malik (D)	60.4	39.6	—	288,301
Eighth District	A. **Scott** (R) vs. Harris (D)	67.6	32.4	—	257,208
Ninth District	**Collins** (R)	100.0	—	—	256,535
Tenth District	**Hice** (R)	100.0	—	—	243,725
Eleventh District	**Loudermilk** (R) vs. Wilson (D)	67.4	32.6	—	323,318
Twelfth District	**Allen** (R) vs. McCracken (D)	61.6	38.4	—	258,912
Thirteenth District	D. **Scott** (D)	—	100.0	—	252,833
Fourteenth District	**Graves** (R)	100.0	—	—	216,743

Source: Georgia Secretary of State, http://sos.ga.gov/index.php/elections.

Note: Boldface indicates incumbency.

Deal in 2012. All three Republicans beat their opponents with approximately one hundred thousand fewer votes than Romney beat Obama with. Clearly, before Democrats can win statewide in Georgia, they need to find an additional two hundred thousand votes.

How can they make up the deficit? Democrats do not answer with one voice. Stacey Abrams, minority leader in the house and an African American, wants to register an additional eight hundred thousand minority Georgians and encourage higher rates of turnout among minorities. Others, like former governor Roy Barnes and Jason Carter, see the path to victory running in appealing to working-class whites and addressing their economic concerns.[28] Regardless of the approach favored, Democrats agree that a union of young whites and minorities will at some point constitute a majority that will push Republicans out of the statewide offices they currently dominate. But 2016 was not the year.

5

Louisiana

Trump Wins Big on the Bayou

Robert E. Hogan

Introduction

While elements of the 2016 presidential race departed from past campaigns in many fundamental ways, it is remarkable how closely the results resembled those of recent contests in the Pelican State. The Republican nominee Donald Trump won the state with 58.1 percent of the vote to Hillary Clinton's 38.4 percent. The two-party vote margin favoring Trump was 20.3, which was only slightly higher than Republican candidate margins in recent elections (17.5 in 2012 and 18.9 in 2008).[1] While these aggregated results are quite similar to past elections, there are some differences in voter responses that are worth noting. As the analysis will demonstrate, voters in some parts of the state responded more favorably to Trump than to recent Republican nominees for president. These gains indicate that Trump's brand of campaign rhetoric and issue positions resonated well among Louisiana's dominant electoral coalition. This suggests that the GOP is likely to remain a powerful force in the state's politics for the foreseeable future.

Brief History

Like many southern states, Louisiana's political landscape has undergone dramatic changes over the past several decades as white voter sentiment shifted away from the Democrats and towards the Republican Party.[2] While the GOP had some early successes at the state level in presidential politics (Dwight Eisenhower in 1956 and Barry Goldwater in 1964), it was not until the 1970s that Republicans established a sustained electoral presence. Louisiana elected its first Republican to the US House of Representatives in 1972 and its first Republican governor in 1979 (David Treen won both positions). As table 5.1 shows, support for Republican candidates has grown steadily since 1980 for various offices. At the beginning of this period, Republican candidates for the US Senate received very limited support, and only two of the state's eight US House members were Republicans (25 percent of the delegation). In the early 1980s, the GOP presence in the state legislature was minimal. However, Republican fortunes began to change, and a steady rise in support for the party's candidates can be observed across the time period. In recent years, the pace of this change has accelerated. Republicans currently hold all but one of the state's six US House seats (83.4 percent), and since the 2014 election, both US Senate seats. Their advantage in the legislature is now quite large—they hold 64.1 percent of state senate seats and 58.1 percent of state house seats.

Given such strong support for Republican candidates, one might assume that Democrats would have little chance of capturing statewide office in Louisiana, but in the 2015 run-off election for governor, Democrat John Bel Edwards soundly defeated Republican US senator David Vitter. While this was certainly an encouraging sign for the state's Democratic Party, it is important to note that the circumstances surrounding the Democratic victory were atypical. Throughout the campaign, Sen. David Vitter was dogged by questions concerning his involvement with a prostitute in the so-called DC Madam scandal. The issue dated from 2007, so many believed he had successfully weathered the controversy, especially given his reelection victory in 2010. Yet relentless attacks from his opponents in conjunction with assistance provided by outside political action committees kept the matter alive. During the runoff, his Democratic rival skillfully exploited the issue and defeated Vitter by a margin of 56 to 44 percent.[3] While certainly a positive development for the state's flagging Democratic Party, the results can only be interpreted as a consequence of unique circumstances that are not likely to be repeated. Overall, the GOP remains the dominant party in statewide elections.

Primary Elections

Louisiana voters were probably more attuned to the presidential primary season than usual, given that the state's governor became a declared candidate for the presidency in June of 2015.[4] Bobby Jindal's ambition for higher office was well known, and speculation had swirled about his candidacy since 2012. But in the crowded Republican field, Jindal had difficulty gaining traction. A number of fellow contenders were occupying the conservative ideological space that Jindal had long cultivated. Moreover, the diminished economic conditions of the state made the policies

Table 5.1. Rising Support for the GOP in Louisiana, 1980–2016

Year	Vote for president	Vote for US Senate	US House seats	Vote for governor	State senate seats	State house seats
1980	51.2	0.0	25.0	50.3	9.5	0.0
1982			25.0			
1984	60.8	9.0	25.0	36.3	10.5	2.6
1986		47.2	37.5			
1988	54.3		50.0	18.6	16.2	12.8
1990		43.5	50.0			
1992	41.0	8.0	42.9	38.8	15.2	15.4
1994			42.9			
1996	40.4	49.8	42.9	63.5	26.6	33.8
1998		31.6	71.4			
2000	52.6		71.4	62.2	29.5	33.3
2002		48.3	57.1			
2004	56.7	51.0	71.4	48.1	38.5	35.2
2006			71.4			
2008	58.6	45.7	85.7	53.8	35.9	41.0
2010		56.6	85.7			
2012	57.8		83.4	65.8	61.5	55.2
2014		55.9	83.4			
2016	58.1	60.7	83.4	43.9	64.1	58.1

Source: "Find Results and Statistics," Louisiana Secretary of State, https://goo.gl/7mz3Rz.

Note: All table entries are percentages. For president and US Senate, percentages are of the two-party vote; for governor, percentages are of the total vote. Governors and state legislators are elected every four years, and results are noted in the year following their election. For US House, state senate, and state house, entries represent the percentage of seats won by Republicans.

he championed during his two-term governorship less marketable to a national audience. Low poll numbers and sluggish fundraising led him to suspend his campaign in mid-November, weeks before the first nomination contests.[5]

In anticipation of a competitive presidential nomination, the Louisiana legislature in 2014 moved the state's presidential primaries up two weeks in the election calendar to Saturday, March 5.[6] This date was just five days after Super Tuesday (also referred to as the "SEC Primary") when the largest number of delegates of the nomination season would be chosen. On the heels of this major contest, the primaries in Louisiana and the elections in four additional states (Kansas, Kentucky, Maine, and Nebraska) were collectively dubbed "Super Saturday." For the Democrats, performance in the primary determined the allocation of fifty-one of the fifty-nine delegates to the national convention (eight of the delegates were superdelegates and were unpledged). For the Republicans, primary results were used for allocating its forty-six delegates based on district and statewide vote totals.[7]

Given its position earlier in the calendar and the fact that both nominations were far from being decided, Louisiana received a fair amount of attention from the presidential contenders. Early visits focused on shoring up support from key party officials and fundraising in the state's major urban centers of New Orleans and Baton Rouge. Nearly all the major candidates for both the Democratic and Republican nominations made at least one appearance in the state. However, in the weeks leading up to the March 5 primary, it was mostly the Republicans who visited. One of the largest campaign events of the season was a rally for Trump in Baton Rouge on February 11. It was attended by an overflow crowd estimated at nearly ten thousand and received significant coverage from both local and national media outlets.[8] On the eve of the campaign, both Donald Trump and Ted Cruz held spirited rallies in the New Orleans area. Trump's event in particular received significant media attention because of the presence of protesters, crowd chants, and the candidate's familiar taunting of his opponents, in which he called them "Little Marco" and "Lyin' Ted."[9]

While Louisiana uses an open election system or "jungle primary" for electing nearly all state and local officials, its presidential primaries are restricted to party registrants. In 2016, 311,776 voters took part in the Democratic primaries, while 301,241 participated in the Republican primaries. The primary results are reported in table 5.2. While it may seem remarkable that turnout was higher for Democrats in this

Republican-leaning state, it is important to understand that Democratic registrants outnumbered Republican registrants by a wide margin (45.5 percent Democrats, 28.7 percent Republicans, and 25.7 percent other party or "no party"). This means that turnout was actually much higher for Republicans than for Democrats (35.9 percent compared to 23.5 percent).[10] It is notable that Republican turnout was higher in 2016 than in either 2012 (24.0 percent) or 2008 (22.7 percent). Such high levels of participation, particularly in the GOP primary, reflected an enthusiastic electorate and a large field of candidates drawing support from across the party's various ideological and geographic divisions.[11]

Hillary Clinton won a very large majority of votes in the Democratic primary. Her 71.1 percent over Bernie Sanders's 23.2 percent was a decisive victory. Clinton bested Sanders in all but two of the state's sixty-four parishes (parishes are Louisiana's equivalent to counties). While she outperformed him in all four major regions of the state, her support was higher in the state's north-central parishes and its Florida parishes (located east of the Mississippi River). In the Republican primary, the race was more competitive, but Donald Trump came out on top with 41.5 percent, followed closely by Ted Cruz with 37.8 percent. Marco Rubio's 11.2 percent put him in third place, and John Kasich followed with 6.4 percent. Trump's strongest support in the state was in the Acadiana region (southwestern parishes) and in the greater New Orleans area. Overall, he beat Cruz in all but seventeen of the state's parishes. Cruz's support was highest in the northern portions of the state, which

Table 5.2. Louisiana Presidential Primary Results, 2016

	Votes (#)	Vote (%)
Democratic Primary		
Hillary Clinton	221,733	71.1
Bernie Sanders	72,276	23.2
Republican Primary		
Donald Trump	124,854	41.5
Ted Cruz	113,968	37.8
Marco Rubio	33,813	11.2
John Kasich	19,359	6.4

Source: Louisiana Secretary of State.

Note: The eight additional candidates for the Democratic nomination and the ten additional candidates for the Republican nomination attracted less than three percent of the vote each and are not included in the table.

contained high concentrations of evangelical Protestant voters. These were the same areas where social conservatives Rick Santorum and Mike Huckabee had drawn their strongest support in previous contests for the Republican nomination (in 2008 and 2012, respectively).[12]

When the votes were counted and delegates apportioned, Clinton ended up with thirty-seven delegates to Sanders's seventeen. Once the additional eight unpledged delegates (superdelegates) were added at the convention, Clinton's total expanded to 45.[13] On the Republican side, the delegate counts immediately following the primary stood at eighteen for Trump, eighteen for Cruz, and five for Rubio. However, a controversy erupted several days later when Marco Rubio suspended his campaign. Trump's supporters openly worried that Rubio's five delegates that were now up for grabs might be persuaded to support Cruz. The prospects of seeing Trump receive fewer delegates than Cruz after having won more primary votes did not sit well among Trump supporters. Trump himself called the situation "unfair" and threatened legal action.[14] The controversy faded as Trump's chances of securing the nomination looked increasingly certain. In early May following Trump's overwhelming victory in the Indiana primary, the five Rubio delegates (along with two of the state's five unpledged delegates) announced their support for Trump.[15]

General Election Campaign

Given its history as a reliably red state in recent presidential elections, one might expect that neither major party would give much attention to Louisiana. But a catastrophic flood in the Baton Rouge metropolitan area in mid-August drew Louisiana into the national spotlight, and with it, its role in the presidential election. As the extent of the crisis began to unfold (it would become the costliest natural disaster to hit the United States since Hurricane Sandy in 2012), state leaders began calling on Washington for assistance.[16] President Obama declared the flooding to be a major disaster and directed FEMA assistance to the area. However, the president did not make immediate plans to tour the devastation, choosing instead to remain with his family on vacation on Martha's Vineyard. The president's delayed response in visiting raised the ire of Republicans including Donald Trump, who made plans to bring his own assistance to the devastated region. On August 19, Trump arrived in Louisiana with his running mate, Mike Pence, to tour the flood damage, meet with victims and distribute supplies he had donated. The event attracted national media attention and allowed Trump to showcase his compassionate side while casting himself in a presidential role.[17] Footage of Trump helping distribute donated items to flood victims was used in a commercial aired in selected states later in the fall campaign.

For the rest of the general election campaign, however, Louisiana voters mainly watched events unfold through news media accounts, television commercials, and social media. The lopsided support for Trump made Louisiana an easy flyover state for both campaigns. Election polls showed Trump consistently ahead throughout the campaign. During the last three months, reputable surveys showed Trump holding a double-digit lead on average (polls indicated his lead was anywhere between 7 and 33 points).[18] While both political parties conducted their traditional get-out-the-vote operations, many volunteers directed efforts to other states where the polls indicated the race to be much closer. Both the state Democratic and Republican Parties coordinated volunteer efforts to make phone calls to voters in swing states. Some activists from each of the parties even traveled to Florida to assist in door-to-door canvassing.[19]

Louisiana residents played an important supporting role in the presidential season through their financial contributions to candidates seeking the presidency. Reports made available through the Federal Election Commission show that citizens in Louisiana contributed approximately $7.49 million during the 2015–2016 period. Given the political inclinations of the state's voters, it is not surprising that the total contributed to Republican candidates ($5.12 million) was about double the amount contributed to Democrats ($2.34 million). Given the highly competitive nature of the primaries for both parties, Louisiana voters contributed to various presidential candidates. However, the bulk of the funding ultimately went to the nominees of the major parties. Clinton and Trump each received contributions totaling approximately $2 million each ($1.97 million for Clinton and $2.06 million for Trump).[20]

Slightly more than two-thirds of registered voters turned out to vote for president in Louisiana (67.8 percent). As table 5.3 indicates, this level of participation was very similar to turnout four years earlier (67.9 percent). Participation varied by racial category, with whites turning out at rates higher (71.5 percent) than blacks (62.0 percent) or voters categorized as "other" (56.5 percent). The gap between blacks and whites was much higher than four years ago, which was due in large measure to the diminished turnout among blacks (over a 5 percent drop). Such a reduction, no doubt, reflected the ticket's lack of President Obama, whose candidacy had spurred turnout among African Americans. Looking at differences by gender, one sees that women voted at higher rates than men (by a margin of 69.9 to 65.3 percent). In spite of the fact that a woman was at the top of the Democratic ticket, turnout among women actually diminished slightly from 2012.

There were large differences in voter participation by party registration. Turnout was nearly 10 points higher for Republicans than Democrats, a pattern also observed in 2012. However, it is interesting to note that while turnout among Democrats decreased from 2012 to 2016 (moving from 69.8 percent down to 68.0 percent), among Republicans it increased (moving from 76.4 to 78.0 percent). Breaking the party categories down by race, one sees that it was among black Democrats that the largest drop in turnout occurred, falling from 70.9 percent in 2012 to 66.6 percent in 2016. For white Democrats, there was a small uptick in turnout from 69.3 percent to 70.6 percent. An increase was also observed for white Republicans (77.6 percent to 79.2 percent), while for black

Table 5.3. Voter Turnout in Louisiana Presidential Elections in 2012 and 2016

	2012	2016
Total	67.9	67.8
Race		
White	69.4	71.5
Black	67.2	62.0
Other	52.9	56.5
Gender		
Men	65.2	65.3
Women	70.2	69.9
Affiliation		
Democrats	69.8	68.0
Republicans	76.4	78.0
Unaffiliated / Other Parties	54.7	55.6
Race and Affiliation		
White Democrats	69.3	70.6
Black Democrats	70.9	66.6
White Republicans	77.6	79.2
Black Republicans	54.3	51.0

Source: Louisiana Secretary of State.

Note: All table entries are percentages.

Republicans, turnout fell from 54.3 percent to 51.0 percent (note that only about 2.5 percent of Republican registrants are black).

Table 5.4 displays the number of votes received by each major party candidate along with the percentage of the two-party vote won by the Republican nominees in both 2012 and 2016. Overall, Donald Trump received 1,178,638 votes to Hillary Clinton's 780,154 votes. Trump's vote total was widely reported to be the highest number of votes any candidate had received for any office in the state's history.[21] It constituted a two-party vote percentage of 60.2 percent, which was an improvement over Romney's two-party vote percentage of 58.8 percent. When looking across the four regions of the state, some differences in candidate support emerge. Trump did best in the Acadiana region (67.0 percent) and in the north-central area of the state (64.0 percent) while performing poorly in comparison to Clinton only in the Greater New Orleans parishes (48.9 percent). This was also the only one of the four regions where Trump underperformed in comparison to Romney in 2012.[22]

Voter Support in General Elections

One way to assess voting in Louisiana's presidential election is to examine individual survey responses of voters. Here we rely on publicly available data from a reputable polling firm that surveyed voters in late October.[23] The results provided in table 5.5 show the distribution of several relevant characteristics by support for Trump and Clinton: political party, race, age, and gender.

Table 5.4. Louisiana Votes for President in 2012 and 2016

Region	2012			2016		
	Romney votes (#)	Obama votes (#)	Romney two-party vote (%)	Trump votes (#)	Clinton votes (#)	Trump two-party vote (%)
Greater New Orleans	230,234	231,492	49.9	232,742	243,690	48.9
Acadiana	409,254	230,988	63.9	430,673	211,990	67.0
Florida Parishes	192,376	145,164	57.0	191,455	142,184	57.4
North-central	320,398	201,497	61.4	323,768	182,290	64.0
Statewide	1,152,262	809,141	58.8	1,178,638	780,154	60.2

Source: Louisiana Secretary of State.

Research indicates that party identification plays a major role in shaping voter decisions in elections, and national exit polling data in 2016 supported this claim. In 2016, for example, 89 percent of Democrats supported Clinton, while 90 percent of Republicans supported Trump.[24] However, it is also true that partisanship has generally been less helpful in explaining voting patterns in southern states. For Democratic identifiers, and registrants in particular, we know that many of them voted for Democrats at the state and local levels but support Republicans for president. For example, a poll in Louisiana in 2012 showed that approximately 94 percent of registered Republicans supported Mitt Romney, but only about 59 percent of Democrats supported President Obama.[25] Did we see a similar pattern in 2016?

The results in table 5.5 indicate that there were major differences in the levels of support Democratic and Republican registrants had for their party's nominee. Whereas 91.6 percent of Republican registrants supported Trump, only 61.3 percent of Democratic registrants supported Clinton. Only 2.1 percent of Republicans registrants supported Clinton, while 22.4 percent of Democratic registrants supported Trump. These results are very consistent with the findings from the 2012 poll cited above showing that many Democrats were willing to cast ballots for a Republican in presidential elections.

But what about voters who were registered neither as Democrats nor Republicans? Voters who registered as unaffiliated or with a minor party comprised a progressively larger portion of the electorate in Louisiana. In 2012 these voters supported Mitt Romney over President Obama by a margin of two to one (61 percent compared to 29 percent).[26] The results from 2016 demonstrated a very similar pattern. Among voters who were unaffiliated (or registered with a minor party), Trump received more than twice the support that Clinton received (approximately 52 to 23 percent).

Race is another factor associated with candidate support, and in the last presidential election the connection was quite strong. Poll results from Louisiana indicated that approximately 88 percent of African Americans supported President Obama, while 79 percent of white supporters backed Romney.[27] In 2016 we again found race had a strong association with voting. Of white voters, 68.1 percent supported Trump, while 19.7 percent supported Clinton. Meanwhile, 72.8 percent of black voters supported Clinton, and 6.5 percent supported Trump. The differences between 2012 and 2016 indicate that a sizeable number of black voters were less supportive of Clinton than of Obama. Also, a sizeable number of white voters were more supportive of Clinton than of Obama.

Age is another factor associated with voting, and national exit polls indicated younger voters favored Clinton while older voters favored Trump. For example, eighteen- to twenty-nine-year-olds nationally supported Clinton over Trump by a 55 to 37 percent margin.[28] In Louisiana, support for Clinton does not appear to have been higher among younger voters. While the results were not completely comparable to the national exit polls (the categories for age were different in the two polls), we see in table 5.5 that younger voters in Louisiana in 2016 were not more likely to support Clinton over Trump. They were actually more likely to favor Trump than Clinton, and nearly one in five (19.5 percent) indicated support for Gary Johnson or another candidate. For the most part, these results indicate that age did not play a major role in shaping candidate choice between the Republican and Democratic nominees.

Finally, what role did gender have on the election support? National exit polls in 2016 indicated that Clinton was favored by women (by 54 to 42 percent), while Trump was favored by men by a similar margin (53 to 41 percent).[29] The results in table 5.5 indicate that in Louisiana, too, there was a gender gap. While both men and women favored Trump over Clinton, the margin among men was much higher (56.2 to 28.5 percent) than the margin among women (45.2 to 40.6 percent).

Overall, then, the results of these survey responses demonstrated that voter behavior among the categories of voters was not too distinct from what we observed in national surveys. These patterns were also in keeping with how voters had cast ballots in previous presidential elections in the state. Race, gender, and especially political party registration were shown to be strongly associated with voter choice.

Recent analyses indicate that a key to Trump's win was support he received from less-educated white voters living in rural areas.[30] Multivariate analyses of nationwide surveys indicate that additional factors such as racial resentment also help explain support for Trump.[31] One recent study suggests that similar sets of factors were at play in Louisiana.[32] Here, an aggregate-level analysis of the state's parishes made it possible to explore whether such factors were at work in the state's elections. Specifically, the focus was on the electoral advances made by Republicans in 2016 in comparison to gains by Republicans in previous presidential elections. Was increased support for the GOP nominee in 2016 concentrated in areas with large proportions of whites with low levels of education? Was support for Trump significantly higher in rural areas? Finally, did Trump do better in places where a higher proportion of voters were likely to harbor attitudes of racial resentment?

Table 5.5. Poll Results of Likely Voters in Louisiana

	Trump	Clinton	Other	Don't know*
Base support	50.1	35.1	6.8	7.9
Party registration				
Democrat	22.4	61.3	5.6	10.7
Republican	91.6	2.1	4.8	1.4
No party / Other	51.5	22.7	13.7	12.1
Race				
White / Other	68.1	19.7	6.8	5.5
Black	6.5	72.8	6.8	13.9
Age				
Under 35 years	49.1	22.6	19.5	8.8
35–49 years	50.2	31.6	8.3	9.9
50–64 years	52.9	38.7	3.1	5.2
Over 64 years	47.3	41.2	2.9	8.5
Gender				
Men	56.2	28.5	7.2	8.1
Women	45.2	40.6	6.4	7.8

Source: Southern Media and Opinion Research, Inc., October 2016, https://goo.gl/KZDTEi.

*The "don't know" category also includes those who "won't say."

Table 5.6 explores these possibilities by examining the percentage increase in Republican support (from 2012 to 2016) at the parish level across three sets of variables. The percentage of less-educated whites is measured as percentage of white voters with no college education (using five-year American Community Survey data).[33] Percentage of rural voters is based on the US census designation (2010). Racial resentment attitudes are gauged using the parish-wide percentage of the vote received in the 1991 governor's race by former Ku Klux Klan grand wizard David Duke. The parishes are divided into thirds based on relative values of the variables (low, medium, and high) to see how Republican support varies. In addition, a correlation coefficient is provided. To discern whether gains in support for the GOP are unique to changes from 2012 to 2016 or are part of a general pattern, two additional sets of changes over time are also examined (2008 to 2012, and 2004 to 2008).

Looking at the first row of table 5.6, we find that GOP support at the parish level improved from 2012 to 2016 in parishes where there were fewer whites with no college (bottom third) by 1.04 percentage points. In the middle third of parishes, support for the GOP increased by 3.33 percentage points, while for the top third of parishes, Republican percentage-point gains moved 4.19 points. A correlation coefficient indicates that the percentage of non-college-educated whites and the percentage change in GOP support is correlated at .80 ($p < .001$). Such differences indicate that Trump's improvement in Romney's performance was quite strong in those parishes where white voters with no college comprised a larger proportion of the population.

Among parishes with large rural populations, a similar pattern emerges. For the third with the least-rural populations, Trump's level of support was an improvement over Romney by 1.66 percentage points. For parishes in the top third, however, the change was approximately 3.57. The correlation coefficient between Republican change and percentage of rural population was also fairly strong, at .47 percent ($p < .001$). Finally, the indicator of racial resentment, 1991 support for David Duke, also appears to have been related to improvements in GOP support in 2016. Whereas parishes that fall in the bottom third of percentage support for Duke had an improvement of only 2.24 in GOP support, those at the high end saw an improvement of 3.40. The correlation coefficient of .37 demonstrates a fair level of association between these two variables ($p < .01$).

So far, these results demonstrate that increased support for the GOP presidential candidate in 2016 was very strong in parishes with high concentrations of white voters without college degrees. In rural parishes and in those where voters gave high support to David Duke back in 1991, gains were observed in support for Trump over 2012 levels of support for Romney. These findings are consistent with the sources of Trump's success in other parts of the country. A key question, however, is whether improvements in GOP success were unique to the Trump candidacy or part of an ongoing trend in the state. To make this determination, table 5.6 also provides analyses of the two previous presidential elections: 2004 to 2008, and 2008 to 2012. In both periods examined, GOP increases were indeed greater in rural parishes and in those with high concentrations of whites without college degrees. However, the size of the correlation coefficients (and their corresponding levels of statistical significance) indicates that these relationships were much stronger for the gains made from 2012 to 2016. For example, the correlation coefficient for whites with no college for 2012–16 is 0.80 but only .21 for 2008–12 and .49 for the 2004–08 period. Similarly, the rural population correlation is .47 for the 2012–16 period but only .30 for 2008–12 and .19 for the 2004–08 period. As for David Duke support, the association is positive for the 2004–08 period but is actually negative for the 2008–12 period (neither is statistically significant). Again, the size of the correlation coefficient for the 2012–16 period is much stronger (nearly double the size of the 2004–08 period) and statistically significant. In combination, these aggregate findings suggest that while the Republican gains were indeed part of a trend, these trends accelerated in 2016. Areas of the state with heavy concentrations of the voter characteristics described above responded more favorably to Trump's campaign in 2016 than they did to Republican nominees in previous years.

Other Elections

Louisiana elects state executive officials and legislators to four-year terms in odd-numbered years (the last being in 2015). This means that congressional elections were the only major offices on the ballot. Due to the large number of seats being vacated by incumbents, voters in 2016 had a rare opportunity to send a large cohort of new representatives to Washington. In fact, more than one-third of the congressional delegation contests were open elections (one US Senate seat and two of the state's six US House seats). The US Senate seat became open after the state's senior senator, David Vitter, announced that he would not seek another term after losing a bid for governor in 2015. Consequently, two congressmen announced their intentions to run for Vitter's senate seat.

As one might expect, the senate race attracted significant voter attention when twenty-four candidates qualified to run. Due to the growing strength of the GOP in state-level elections, a number of prominent Republicans entered the race, including Rep. Charles Boustany of the Third District, Rep. John Fleming of the Fourth District, and state treasurer John Kennedy. Among the Democrats, two major contenders were Louisiana public service commissioner Foster Campbell and New Orleans attorney Caroline Fayard. Given the political experience and financial connections of the candidate pool, significant amounts of funding were raised and spent (nearly $26 million by the candidates themselves, not including outside spending).[34] Under Louisiana's open-election system, all candidates regardless of party run against one another in a first-round election, and a runoff is set only if no candidate receives a majority. In the end, it was Republican John Kennedy (25.0 percent) and Democrat Foster Campbell (17.5 percent) who made it to the runoff (Republican Boustany came in a close third with 15.4 percent). The campaign for the December 10 election generated far less attention than the first round of elections (turnout was only 29.5 percent). Kennedy's campaign capitalized on his steadfast support for president-elect Donald Trump, enabling him to trounce Campbell by a margin of 60.7 to 39.3 percent.[35]

In the elections for the US House seats, four of the six incumbent representatives (three Republicans and one Democrat) faced minimal

Table 5.6. Sources of Republican Gains in Parish-Level Presidential Elections, 2008–2016

Characteristic	2012–16			
	Low	Med	High	Correlation
Whites with no college	1.04	3.33	4.19	.80d
Rural population	1.66	3.33	3.57	.47d
1991 David Duke vote	2.24	2.93	3.40	.37c
	2008–12			
	Low	Med	High	Correlation
Whites with no college	−.80	−.77	1.17	.21a
Rural population	−1.38	.70	.21	.30c
1991 David Duke vote	.47	−.38	−.50	−.10
	2004–08			
	Low	Med	High	Correlation
Whites with no college	−.31	2.03	5.59	.49d
Rural population	1.09	3.16	3.00	.19
1991 David Duke vote	1.76	2.61	2.91	.19

Source: Election data are from the Louisiana Secretary of State. Parish statistics are from the US Bureau of the Census and the American Community Survey five-year average (2008–12).

Note: The table displays the percentage-point change at the parish level in two-party support for Republican presidential candidates over the previous presidential election. Pearson correlation coefficients indicate the relationships between these percentage-point changes from one period to the next and each factor of the three factors: whites with no college, percentage of the population living in rural areas, and percentage support for David Duke for governor in 1991.

[a]$p < .10$

[b]$p < .05$

[c]$p < .01$

[d]$p < .001$

opposition, defeating their opponents soundly without the need for a runoff. However, in the two open-seat contests, competition was fierce between a number of well-financed candidates. When the final votes were tallied following the December 10 runoff, two new Republican congressmen were elected. Overall, the 2016 elections were highly competitive, but the partisan distribution of the delegation remained unchanged. As for effects on the presidential election, the large number of Republican candidates seeking these congressional seats probably contributed to the high turnout among Republicans and unaffiliated voters.

Conclusion

Despite the unconventional nature of the candidates and the campaigns they waged, the overall outcome of the presidential election in Louisiana did not differ markedly from previous years. The Republican nominee won a significantly higher percentage of the vote in comparison to his Democratic opponent, and the margin of victory was only slightly larger than in recent elections. The distribution of the votes across the state's major regions was also similar to past elections, and factors such as partisanship and race continued to shape the voting patterns observed. However, looking closely at parish-level results, one does see that certain segments of the electorate responded more favorably to Donald Trump's candidacy than to recent Republican nominees. In 2016, Republican gains were stronger in rural areas containing high concentrations of non-college-educated whites and where voters had previously provided greater electoral support to David Duke. Given the issue positions and rhetoric used by Trump over the course of his campaign, these patterns of voter support make sense. Overall, one might say that Trump's campaign could be viewed as a catalyst for Republican gains. This may portend an acceleration in the movement toward greater GOP dominance that has been underway in the state for some time. These findings suggest that Louisiana is likely to remain a state favorable to Republican presidential candidates for years to come.

6

Mississippi

Republican Dominance Confirmed

Stephen D. Shaffer and David A. Breaux

Political Context

Mississippi Republicans entered the 2016 election season in the most dominant position since the post–Civil War Reconstruction era. Not since the 1976 election of Georgian Jimmy Carter as president had the state voted for a Democrat for President, and not since the final reelection of Democratic senator John C. Stennis in 1982 had the state backed a Democrat for either of the state's US Senate seats, as Thad Cochran earned his seventh senate election victory in 2014, and Roger Wicker succeeded Trent Lott, who had replaced Stennis in 1988. After the 2010 national GOP tsunami cost Democrats two US House incumbents, Democrats were reduced to only one of the state's four US House seats, the majority-black Delta district held by Bennie Thompson since 1993. Even in state-level elections were Republicans dominant, as Phil Bryant in the 2015 state elections became the second consecutive GOP governor (following Haley Barbour) to win reelection. Republicans also maintained control of six of the seven other statewide offices, a feat inaugurated in the Barbour 2007 reelection year (Democrats retained only the attorney general position with Jim Hood, first elected in 2003). A final coup for the state GOP was retention of control of both state legislative chambers, a more recent party breakthrough accomplished in 2011.

The 2014 federal elections in Mississippi illustrated how the real electoral battles were now taking place within the dominant Republican Party's primary, as seventy-six-year-old senator Thad Cochran faced the political fight of his life in the GOP primary against conservative state senator Chris McDaniel, who modeled himself after Texas senator Ted Cruz. Blasting the incumbent for spending too much federal money and increasing the debt ceiling, McDaniel charged that Cochran had "been in Washington so long, he's forgotten his Mississippi conservative values."[1] Cochran stressed that his senior position on the Senate Appropriations Committee had helped fund Mississippi's university and agricultural research and protect the state's military bases.

Aggressively campaigning across the state, McDaniel shocked the political establishment by leading the first primary with 49.5 percent of the vote to Cochran's 49.0 percent, with a minor candidate forcing a runoff race. Cochran supporters immediately became energized, and the senator personally campaigned across the state. Republican leaders in Washington and in Mississippi urged a Cochran vote to help ensure the GOP could capture the Senate (for the first time since 2006), and many state African American leaders praised Cochran's support for some programs that benefited minorities. In the face of McDaniel's call for fiscal responsibility and an end to states' addiction to federal money, the chairs of all three of the state's public education bodies (those for elementary and secondary schools, community colleges, and universities) pleaded for Cochran's return to the US Senate. Cochran's forces managed to reverse their initial first primary deficit with a narrow 51 percent runoff victory, prompting McDaniel to spend months on court challenges over allegedly illegal Democratic crossover votes in the GOP runoff. By contrast, November was a cakewalk for Republicans as Cochran polished off Democratic former congressman Travis Childers with a 60 percent landslide, and US House incumbents Alan Nunnelee, Steven Palazzo, and Gregg Harper earned landslides of 68 percent or higher (as did Democrat Bennie Thompson).

The 2015 state elections underscored this dominant Republicanism in Mississippi. The GOP not only swept all statewide offices (except attorney general) but also gained a 60 percent supermajority in both legislative chambers with thirty-two senators (to twenty Democratic senators) and seventy-four representatives (to forty-eight Democratic representatives).

Governor Bryant successfully embraced the popular issue of economic development as he attended business openings and expansions throughout the state, including in the northern cities of Baldwyn, Burnsville, Columbus, Ecru, Guntown, New Albany, Pontotoc, Starkville, Verona, and West Point. Other Republican officeholders were also positively associated with nondivisive issues, as state treasurer Lynn Fitch touted her office's provision of online resources teaching financial literacy to schoolchildren, Secretary of State Delbert Hosemann promoted election reform measures and publicized ten photo identifications permissible under the state voter ID law, and insurance commissioner Mike Chaney earned praise for working to ensure that all residents would have access to insurance exchanges under the Affordable Care Act. Fitch and Chaney were reelected without any Democratic opponent, while all other incumbent Republican statewide officers achieved landslides of over 60 percent of the vote (Democrat Jim Hood won a 55 percent reelection victory). Democratic futility was reflected in their gubernatorial nominee, Robert Gray, a truck driver who admitted that he had been too busy to even vote in the party primary. Gray presumably won because his name was listed first on the ballot, and his two opponents also lacked name visibility and any previous elected-office experience.

Republicans proceeded to flex their muscles during the 2016 state legislative session. GOP Speaker of the House Philip Gunn maintained the state's bipartisan power-sharing tradition, but seeking to advance more conservative legislation, he reduced the number of Democratic committee chairs to only two (African American Democrats chaired the Energy Committee and the Youth and Family Affairs Committee), while Republicans chaired the other forty-two committees. Lt. Gov. Tate Reeves continued to pursue a more bipartisan approach to committee chairmanships in the senate, appointing eight African American Democrats, five white Democrats, and twenty-five Republicans as chairs. Frustrated house Democrats sometimes resorted to delaying tactics to protest Republican actions during the sessions on issues including a judicial redistricting bill, a proposal to transfer control of Jackson's airport to a regional board, and a GOP-led tax cut and resulting budget cuts. Another controversial GOP action was House Bill 1523—a "religious freedom" law that permitted government workers and businesses to deny services to gay customers because of their religious values. Much of the state's business community, including the powerful Mississippi Economic Council and the Mississippi Manufacturers Association, had opposed the bill, arguing that it violated most businesses' own corporate policies and might harm state economic development efforts, and the American Civil Liberties Union and Human Rights Campaign promptly denounced the measure.[2]

While almost nobody expected the state to be competitive in the presidential race, Mississippi has become so Republican that it has emerged as a real player within the party, and GOP hopefuls repeatedly have visited the state and relied on state officeholders to assist the party's presidential and congressional chances in other states. The Democratic Party's hope of becoming more electorally competitive in 2016 rested on capitalizing on some progressive public discontent with recent legislative actions and possible public discontent with the eventual GOP nominee.

Mississippi's Impact on National Party Politics: Primary Season

Fully two years before the election, GOP hopefuls appeared to be testing the waters in Mississippi. In August 2014, New Jersey governor Chris Christie, chair of the Republican Governors Association, visited Biloxi to thank Mississippi's first responders who had helped New Jersey after Hurricane Sandy hit it. Two months later, Rick Santorum spoke in Ridgeland at a fundraiser for his Patriot Voices political action committee (which was striving to elect a GOP senate majority), and Rick Perry spoke at Governor Bryant's annual Energy Summit in Jackson to tout unleashing the nation's oil and gas exports. In December, Bobby Jindal attended a Gulfport fundraiser for Lieutenant Governor Reeves' reelection campaign, and Rand Paul expressed his libertarian views (which included criticizing the war on drugs as creating an unfair incarceration impact on minorities and helping fuel "overly aggressive" police tactics) at the state GOP's Victory Lunch fundraiser.[3]

Republican presidential politics accelerated in 2015. In January, Mitt Romney tested the waters at a Global Lecture Series event at Mississippi State University, before making his final decision to not be a candidate. Ben Carson related how religion and a mother who stressed reading and writing helped him grow up in impoverished Detroit and stressed his pro-life message at a pregnancy clinic fundraiser in Tupelo in February.[4] Before even officially announcing his candidacy, Jeb Bush spoke in April at Governor Bryant's signing ceremony for a bill that provided vouchers for parents of children with special needs, a bill modeled on the former Florida governor's own program and backed by his Foundation for Excellence in Education. Chris Christie's speech in May at a party fundraiser was overshadowed by press questions about the indictment of his former aides in the Bridgegate lane closure scandal. At a July fundraiser for state house Republicans, Marco Rubio explained how he had lived the American dream, which was made possible by limited government and free enterprise, and urged that young people make the right choices (get educated, employed, and married, in that order).[5] From the bed of a pickup truck in a restaurant parking lot in Tupelo in August, Ted Cruz fired up a crowd of hundreds by promising to rescind Obama's "illegal and unconstitutional" executive orders, to investigate Planned Parenthood, to get rid of the "catastrophic" Iran deal, and to "stop the persecution of religious liberty."[6] Bush made a brief speech for the tail-gating crowd in Starkville before the annual Egg Bowl (the football rivalry between University of Mississippi and Mississippi State University) and attended a Jackson fundraiser. Meanwhile, John Kasich had been collecting some impressive endorsements that included Rep. Gregg Harper, former senator Trent Lott, and former governor Kirk Fordice's chief of staff Andy Taggart. Other endorsements included Senator Cochran for Bush, state senator Chris McDaniel for Cruz, former GOP state chair Arnie Hederman for Rubio, and retired federal judge Charles Pickering (father of former congressman Chip Pickering) for Carson.[7] Reflecting his non-establishment insurgency, Trump's campaign was endorsed by a handful of state legislators lacking statewide constituencies.

Republican presidential politics hit a peak just before the March primary as three of the top candidates visited the Magnolia State. Over 13,500 Trump supporters overfilled Biloxi's Mississippi Coast Coliseum in January, praising his lack of "political correctness" as the political outsider ranted about "how crooked the system is" and "how crooked these reporters are" and argued that Hillary Clinton "should be in jail" and should not even "be allowed to run."[8] By contrast, though many state officials and political observers praised Kasich as having "character" and "competence" and demonstrating "effective leadership," he drew a crowd of only hundreds at a Gulfport town hall meeting.[9] After speaking at an early March fundraiser for Hinds and Rankin County GOP committees, Kasich was endorsed by the Jackson *Clarion-Ledger* as being "principled and pragmatic" and having a track record of "actual conservative governing," while the major state newspaper blasted Trump as being a "narcissist" who "appealed to the lowest common denominator" and provided "a despicable example of leadership."[10] Cruz made a last minute stop at a Florence restaurant to speak to several hundred supporters, earning a late endorsement by Governor Bryant.[11] Drawing nearly ten thousand people at a rally at Madison Central High School's gym and football stadium the night before the election, Trump drew cheers when speaking about building a wall, supporting the Second Amendment, and halting the "chipping away" of Christianity, and he decried the "jobs that are being lost" in Mississippi, promising that when he brought "our jobs back" he wouldn't be "forgetting Mississippi."[12]

Trump's economic and outsider messages garnered some notable last-minute backing. Wirt Yerger III, son of one of the state's modern GOP founders, argued that "our country needs a businessman" and that "our government should be basically by the people and for the people, not for the politicians."[13] Charles Evers, brother of slain civil rights leader Medgar Evers, backed Trump because "he's a businessman" and "jobs are badly needed in Mississippi."[14] Backing conservative Ted Cruz, American Family Association president Tim Wildmon lamented Trump's likely win in Mississippi, labeling Trump the "new Daniel Boone: The rippin'est roarin'est fightin'est man the frontier ever knew," with supporters "willing to accept his boorish, often childish, behavior in exchange for a chance to reach the castle with their pitchforks."[15]

In contrast to the exciting GOP presidential campaign, national Democrats made little effort in the Magnolia State. Congressman Thompson and Jackson mayor Tony Yarber both endorsed Hillary Clinton, but Clinton's greatest personal outreach to Mississippians was to comment about the problem of lead in the drinking supplies of cities like Jackson (while campaigning in New Hampshire). Bill Clinton did speak at Jackson State University, calling Hillary a "change agent" who would help reduce student debt.[16] Understandably, on primary day, the Republican presidential primary drew 416,270 votes, compared to only 227,164 for the Democrats. Trump won a 47 percent plurality to Cruz's 36 percent and Kasich's 9 percent, while Clinton won a smashing 82 percent over Bernie Sanders's 17 percent in the smaller Democratic primary. Ideology was a major dividing line in the state GOP primary, as Cruz outpolled Trump by 51 to 41 percent among the 47 percent of exit poll voters who described themselves as "very conservative," while Trump beat Cruz by more than a two to one margin among the 52 percent who called themselves "somewhat conservative" or "moderate."[17] Clinton won landslides in every demographic group, with Sanders breaking the 30 percent mark only among those under thirty, white college graduates, and independents voting in the Democratic primary.[18]

The General Election: Setting the National Campaign Agenda

Mississippi Republicans proceeded to set the national GOP theme by quickly unifying behind the Trump candidacy, while national Democrats continued to virtually ignore the Magnolia State. Former national GOP chair during the 1994 election tsunami and former governor Haley Barbour addressed a stunned party establishment in a *USA Today* interview by explaining that many Republican voters were "mad as hell" and wanted "to send Washington the bird" and concluding that "Donald Trump is the greatest manifestation of a gigantic middle finger that I've ever seen."[19] Speaking at the Mississippi College scholarship banquet in late March, Rudy Giuliani pointed out that Trump was "a strong man" who understood how our "strongest economy in the world" could "use economic warfare" to achieve such goals as Iranian sanctions.[20] By early May GOP unity was largely accomplished: Chris McDaniel admitted that the Trump and Cruz campaigns were "two sides to the same coin . . . a reaction to an establishment that we insist has to be changed," Governor Bryant explained that "as a conservative" he found "the possibility of a Clinton victory . . . unacceptable," and Senator Cochran proclaimed that straight-ticket Republicanism was the best way to ensure "individual liberty, strong national defense, secure borders and effective governance."[21] A very different vision of America and its priorities came from First Lady Michelle Obama's commencement speech at Jackson State University when she stressed the importance of civil rights and standing "side by side with all of our neighbors—straight, gay, lesbian, bisexual, transgender, Muslim, Jew, Christian, Hindu, immigrant, Native American."[22]

A unity theme, fueled by prominent Mississippians, marked the national Republican convention. Delegates boosted the Trump-Pence ticket, with Governor Bryant praising Pence as "a strong conservative leader in Congress" and "one of the nation's leading Republican governors," and Congressman Harper contrasting Trump's "broad base of support" with Clinton's appearance of being "above the law."[23] Illustrating the state party's importance to the national party, state treasurer Lynn Fitch and Secretary of State Delbert Hosemann both served on the party platform committee, and House Speaker Paul Ryan keynoted the Mississippi delegation's breakfast. Senator Wicker, as chair of the National Republican Senatorial Committee, addressed the convention, blasting Clinton as having "a dangerous record on national security" and a "lifetime of scandals and lies."[24] By contrast, the state Democratic delegation to their national convention experienced more divisiveness: some Clinton delegates related how they were verbally abused by Sanders supporters, and at least one delegate expressed disappointment with Clinton ignoring Mississippi.[25]

The Trump campaign, on the other hand, courted Mississippi voters, with Donald Trump and his son Donald J. Trump Jr. making high profile speeches before Labor Day. Trump Jr. courted the blue-collar working class at the Neshoba County Fair by explaining that his father had taken him "at a very young age on job sites, on construction sites" to learn from "not Ph.D.s, not MBAs, but people who had doctorates in common sense."[26] As the crowd chanted "Trump, Trump, Trump" and "U-S-A," he recounted how his father had "given the people of this country who have been left in the dust a voice again," and he explained that "it's my father vs. a machine, my father vs. Hollywood and my father vs. the media."[27] Speaking to thousands at the Mississippi Coliseum in Jackson, Donald Trump blasted Clinton as "a bigot who sees people of color only as votes, not as people" and appealed for the vote of people of color by asking, "What do you have to lose by trying something new?"[28] Trump then turned the podium over to Nigel Farage, a leader of Brexit, the successful British movement to exit the European Union. Farage drew a parallel between Brexit and the Trump movement, proclaiming that "you can go out, you can beat the pollsters, you can beat the commentators, you can beat Washington, and you'll do it by doing what we did for Brexit in Britain" and concluding, "If I was an American citizen, I wouldn't vote for Hillary Clinton if you paid me."[29]

Mississippi Republican activists effectively stayed on target despite Trump's Twitter distractions. Reacting to stories of Trump allegedly groping and kissing women, Governor Bryant wrote a fundraising email and Senator Wicker spoke at a Tupelo pro-Trump rally reminding voters about the importance of Supreme Court appointments, with Wicker stressing protecting gun rights and repealing the Affordable Care Act and Bryant stressing the importance of preventing more "leftist judges who will take every opportunity to 'legislate from the bench.'"[30] At the annual Mississippi Economic Council's Hobnob Mississippi at the Mississippi Coliseum, the overweight Haley Barbour observed that "Hillary Clinton being the candidate for change would be like me being the spokesman for Weight Watchers," while state GOP chair Joe Nosef claimed that to vote for Clinton, one would have to believe "that government is too small," "that taxes are too low," and that "we can't do any better than we're doing now."[31]

In the face of national Democrats' choice to write off the state for financial support and candidate appearances, the Clinton campaign received very little publicity except for expressions of public support by Congressman Thompson. One other positive effort was the activism of the Oktibbeha County Democratic Party, fueled by students at Mississippi State University, as they repeatedly publicized the location and hours of their local party headquarters and its voter registration aids. Veteran state columnist Bill Minor did point out Clinton's strengths, crediting her "longtime dedication to children's education and health" that would "mean a great deal to this poor state in lifting us off the bottom."[32] Millsaps College history professor Robert S. McElvaine blasted Trump as the "the most dangerous, the most unstable, the most un-American, and the least qualified person ever to come this close to the presidency of the country we love."[33]

The congressional election campaigns were largely invisible, especially after the party primaries. First District congressman Trent Kelly, an Iraqi war veteran, had won a special election in 2015 after Nunnelee's death. Kelly quickly worked to serve his constituents, holding open houses to meet them, serving on the Agriculture Committee (important to his rural north Mississippi district), and building congressional relationships that included such Democrats as Bennie Thompson (who worked with him to protect the state's catfish industry). Kelly faced a candidate from the Tea Party wing in the GOP primary, newcomer Paul Clever, who blasted runaway spending and the federal deficit and accused the freshman congressman of backing an omnibus spending bill that did not block Planned Parenthood funding.[34] Third District congressman Gregg Harper, well known in his district for his constituency service of attracting federal funds and speaking to numerous community organizations, was challenged by a second Tea Party candidate, Jimmy Giles, who pledged to "oppose all Muslimification of our United States," asserted that "butchering babies is an abomination in the eyes of God," and urged voters to "vote for the two Rebels, Trump and Giles" in order to "MAKE AMERICA GREAT AGAIN!"[35] Unlike the more competitive Tea Party challenges to incumbents Nunnelee and Palazzo in 2012, four years later Republicans Kelly and Harper polished off their right wing challengers, both winning 89 percent of the GOP vote (Palazzo, representing the Fourth District, was renominated without opposition).

Congressmen Thompson and Palazzo were also well known for fighting for their constituents' interests. In addition to speaking to community groups, honoring the state's veterans, and attending new business groundbreakings, Thompson successfully worked to remove Confederate "symbols of hatred and bigotry . . . that seek to divide us" from the grounds of the US House of Representatives, including the state flag of Mississippi, which featured the Confederate emblem.[36] Palazzo was known for working with fellow Mississippi senators and congressmen of both parties to reduce burdensome federal regulations on small housing agencies in small towns and to prevent the air force from reducing the mission of Keesler Air Force Base.[37] All four general election campaigns were described as so "low-key" with so few public appearances and so little spending by challengers that only one had filed any campaign spending report with the Federal Election Commission by late October. Democrat Mark Gladney, a retiree, reported collecting nearly $50,742, while Palazzo collected $721,203.[38]

Election Results and Analysis

The Magnolia State continued a streak it had begun in 1980 of voting Republican for president as Trump won 57.9 percent of the vote to Clinton's 40.1 percent (see table 6.1). Mississippi continued to be one of the most Republican states in the nation as Trump's percentage of the two-party vote was about 10 percent higher than it was nationally. The 2016 election results in the Magnolia State were therefore in line with the high level of presidential Republicanism that began in 1992, when Mississippi began to consistently exhibit an 8 to 10 percent margin of greater Republicanism than the nation as a whole.

We turn to aggregate data by county to provide some insight into these results, given the absence of exit poll data for Mississippi and the temporary discontinuation of the statewide Mississippi Poll project (in the face of sinking response rates and suspected sampling problems with discontented voters).[39] Our unit of analysis is the county, the dependent variable is Trump's percentage of the two-party vote, and the independent variables are census data on the racial composition of each county and attitudinal data on each county drawn from the pooled Mississippi Polls from 2002 through 2014. These attitudinal variables include party identification, abortion views, economic issue attitudes (a scale of agree-disagree items on health care and jobs), and racial issues (combining affirmative action and minority aid items). The aggregate-level relationships among these attitudinal items, using the county as the unit of analysis, were quite consistent, including the directions of the relationships and even their strengths when measured at the individual levels in each year of the Mississippi Poll to minimize the ecological fallacy possibility (see table 6.2).[40]

Mississippi presidential voting patterns are amazingly stable over time. The Pearson correlation by county of the Republican share of the two-party presidential vote between 2016 and 2012 was a remarkable .996. Race was most highly correlated with the Trump vote (–.977), with

Table 6.1. Election Returns in Mississippi Federal Elections, 2016

Candidate (party)	Vote (%)	Votes (#)
President		
Hillary Clinton / Tim Kaine (Democratic)	40.1	485,131
Donald J. Trump / Michael Pence (Republican)	57.9	700,714
Darrell Castle / Scott N. Bradley (Constitution)	0.3	3,987
Roque "Rocky" De La Fuente / Michael Steinberg (American Delta)	0.1	644
Jim Hedges / Bill Bayes (Prohibition)	0.1	715
Gary Johnson / Bill Weld (Libertarian)	1.2	14,435
Jill Stein / Ajamu Baraka (Green)	0.3	3,731
Total presidential vote	100.0	1,209,357
US House of Representatives		
First District		
Trent Kelly (Republican)*	68.7	206,455
Jacob Owens (Democratic)	27.9	83,947
Cathy L. Toole (Reform)	1.3	3,840
Chase Wilson (Libertarian)	2.1	6,180
Total district vote	100.0	300,422
Second District		
John Bouie II (Republican)	29.2	83,542
Bennie G. Thompson (Democratic)*	67.1	192,343
Johnny McLeod (Reform)	1.3	3,823
Troy Ray (Independent)	2.4	6,918
Total district vote	100.0	286,626
Third District		
Gregg Harper (Republican)*	66.2	209,490
Dennis C. Quinn (Democratic)	30.4	96,101
Roger I. Gerrard (Veterans)	2.7	8,696
Lajena Sheets (Reform)	0.7	2,158
Total district vote	100.0	316,445
Fourth District		
Mark Gladney (Democratic)	27.8	77,505
Steven Palazzo (Republican)*	65.0	181,323
Richard Blake McCluskey (Libertarian)	5.3	14,687
Shawn O'Hara (Reform)	1.9	5,264
Total district vote	100.0	278,779

Note: Results are complete but uncertified.

Source: Mississippi Secretary of State, accessed November 25, 2016, https://goo.gl/4JtBMG.

*Incumbent.

Table 6.2. Correlation Coefficients and Regression Results for County-Level Presidential Election Results

Predictors	Correlation coefficient	Unstandardized B-score	Std. error	Beta	t-score	Statistcial significance
Black percentage of county	−.977**	−.009	.000	−.955	−33.344	.000***
Party identification	.601**	.013	.009	.052	1.404	.164
Abortion attitudes	−.275*	−.025	.010	−.059	−2.533	.013*
Economic issue attitudes	.175	−.018	.009	−.049	−1.903	.061
Racial issue attitudes	.469**	−.008	.012	−.023	−.644	.522

Note: Adjusted R^2 = .960

*p < .05

**p < .01

***p < .001

heavily black counties being least likely to vote for him. Party identification was second in importance (.601), as counties that were more Republican were most likely to vote for him. Racial issues were third in importance (.469), with conservative racial attitudes being correlated to a Trump vote. And abortion views were fourth in importance (−.275) as more pro-choice counties were least likely to back him. The economic scale was not statistically significant in these bivariate analyses. However, when all of these predictors were placed into one multiple regression equation, all of them were statistically insignificant except for race and abortion. Furthermore, the standardized regression coefficient (Beta) for race was −.955, compared to a modest −.059 for abortion. The adjusted R-squared for the multiple regression equation was an incredible 96 percent!

Republican Donald Trump won an average of 78 percent of the vote in the twenty-one counties where African Americans made up 25 percent or less of the population, and he averaged 62 percent of the vote in the thirty-six counties with a black presence of 26 to 49 percent. However, in the twenty-five counties where African Americans comprised a majority, Trump earned an average of only 33 percent. Majority black counties were so loyal to the Democratic presidential nominee that Clinton outpolled Trump in every one of these counties, winning all thirteen Delta counties (near the Mississippi River in the northwest of the state), the four black-majority Natchez District counties (along the Mississippi River in the southwest), and the other eight black-majority counties in other regions of the state (southern Piney Woods, Hills, and Black Prairie areas). Unfortunately for the Democrats, Clinton won only two white-majority counties—Oktibbeha County, which has a strong local Democratic organization and a major research university (Mississippi State University), and Marshall County.

In addition to losing so many white voters, national Democrats may have made the problem even worse by virtually ignoring the state, possibly contributing to the dip in turnout in comparison to 2012. The average drop in Democratic votes across the eighty-two counties was 949, compared to only 122 for Republicans. The turnout decline was especially evident in black-majority counties, where Democratic votes dropped an average of 1,275. Democratic votes also declined by an average of 870 in counties that were 26 to 49 percent black and decreased by an average of 696 in counties with fewer African Americans. By contrast, Republican votes dipped in more modest numbers (318 in black-majority counties and 141 in 25 to 49 percent black counties) or even increased slightly (by an average of 143 in counties with populations less than 26 percent black).

The observations of two state columnists suggest some attitudinal reasons for why so many Mississippians (usually white) have abandoned the Democratic Party. One cited a host of ideological issues such as the size of government and abortion and then concluded that, given a choice between "the jerk and the crook," he'd choose "the jerk," since he at least had "real world business experience" and the Clintons were too associated with the "corruption of our political process."[41] Another columnist blasted the Clinton mindset of viewing Trump supporters as a "basket of deplorables . . . racist, sexist, homophobic, xenophobic, Islamophobic" and concluded that the "establishment politicians like Hillary and elite media that support her are 'full of hypocrisy and lawlessness.'"[42]

In the congressional elections, incumbency triumphed yet again, as it has in nearly every modern election except for the 2010 GOP tsunami that claimed two Democratic incumbents. Republicans Trent Kelly, Gregg Harper, and Steven Palazzo and Democrat Bennie Thompson all earned at least 65 percent of the general election vote. When the multiple regression analysis was repeated with the Republican percentage of the two-party House vote as the dependent variable, and incumbency was measured by party of the incumbent (four counties that were split between two congressional districts were omitted from this county-level analysis) added to the attitudinal predictors, three statistically significant regression coefficients were found (see table 6.3). Race was most important with a Beta of –.746, showing that more extensively African American counties were less likely to vote Republican. Incumbency was second in importance with a Beta of .282: counties represented by a Republican were more likely to vote Republican for Congress than counties represented by the only Democratic representative, Bennie Thompson). Abortion was third in importance with a Beta of –.049, showing that more pro-choice counties were less likely to vote Republican. These results suggest that many voters in the three white-majority districts are quite comfortable with Republicans posting conservative roll-call voting records and that many voters in the one black-majority district are quite comfortable with a Democrat posting a liberal roll-call voting record, provided that their representatives, regardless of party or ideology, diligently pursue constituency services for all groups of voters.

Table 6.3. Regression Results for County-Level Congressional Election Results

Predictors	Unstandard-ized B-score	Std. error	Beta	t-score	Statistical significance
Party of House incumbent	.131	.014	.282	9.405	.000***
Black percent-age of county	–.008	.000	–.746	–22.330	.000***
Party identifi-cation	.006	.010	.024	.632	.529
Abortion attitudes	–.023	.011	–.049	–2.073	.042*
Economic issue attitudes	–.016	.010	–.039	–1.524	.132
Racial issue attitudes	.008	.014	.022	.625	.534

Note: Adjusted R^2 = .962

*$p < .05$

**$p < .01$

***$p < .001$

A New Dominant Party in the Magnolia State

Given the ideological chasm between the two national parties, winning a more conservative state like Mississippi will likely remain a long shot for national Democrats. The typical Mississippi voter tends to view Democratic presidential candidates as "somewhat liberal" and Republican candidates as "somewhat conservative," while their own ideological views are nearly identical to their perception of those of the Republican nominees.[43]

Given the strong relationship between race and ideology, this ideological split between the parties has also produced a huge racial gulf between the two parties in Mississippi. Consequently, Mississippi has not voted Democratic for president since 1976 and has not voted Democratic for the US Senate since 1982. Democrats retain greater hope for electoral victories in other offices when matching them with more ideologically inclusive candidates, such as a Gene Taylor for the US House or a Jim Hood for a statewide office such as attorney general.

A fascinating development is how Mississippi has fully flipped from a solid Democratic state sixty years ago to a very strong Republican state today; the state now produces prominent Republican officeholders who help to set the national agenda. Former governor and Republican National Convention chair Haley Barbour stressed that Trump was the candidate of change when he joked that voters were so angry that they would flip a big middle finger at Washington and that Clinton could no more stand for change than Barbour himself could represent Weight Watchers. Gov. Phil Bryant not only campaigned for Trump in Florida and other states but also met Brexit leader Nigel Farage at the Republican National Convention, inviting him to visit Mississippi during a Trump event, which effectively reinforced a vital antiestablishment, antipolling campaign theme. Sen. Roger Wicker not only chaired the National Republican Senatorial Committee but also defied the odds by defending twenty-four GOP seats to ensure that his party retained control of the senate. On multiple occasions, Republican US House members and Sen. Thad Cochran successfully fended off spirited challenges from their party's Tea Party wing, and Cochran then assumed the chairmanship of the powerful Appropriations Committee. Mississippi remains a politically fascinating state that provides many important lessons for political observers, even in this new era of a dominant Republican Party.

7

South Carolina

It's All About the Primary

Cole Blease Graham Jr. and Scott E. Buchanan

Electoral Traditions

In 2012, Mitt Romney won the Palmetto State with 54.6 percent of the vote. As the 2016 presidential election approached, one Democratic-leaning polling group suggested that Donald J. Trump might be in trouble among Republican voters.[1] However, when the votes were actually cast and counted, Trump won 54.9 percent of the vote. What is even more significant, though, is that Hillary Clinton won 40.8 percent of the vote, in comparison to the 44 percent that President Obama had won in 2012. In other words, South Carolina saw a noticeable number of Democrats who did not support Secretary Clinton at the same level as President Obama. In fact, Clinton's performance illustrates the Democratic Party's long decline in strength in the Palmetto State. Democrats likely wonder how much longer this prolonged decline will continue. This chapter might offer little consolation for the long-suffering Democrats.

For significant periods, one party has dominated South Carolina politics. Once one of the most thoroughly Democratic states in the country, in the twenty-first century, South Carolina has been one of the most loyally Republican states. Democrats first dominated the landscape from the end of Reconstruction until the 1960s. After a period of transition from the 1960s to the early 1990s, since 1995, the Republican Party has been dominant. Across time and regardless of party, political winners have traditionally had agricultural roots. One industry, textiles, was dominant until the transition to a more diversified manufacturing base including automobile and aircraft assembly and distribution centers for consumer products. A politics of sameness has been reinforced by conservative social and fiscal values throughout the state's post–Civil War history.

What political change there has been has typically been triggered by white political rage. One example is white reaction to post–Civil War Reconstruction as precursor to the installation of legalized, state-based racial segregation in the 1890s. Another is negative white reaction to national civil rights policies in the 1960s that spurred the growth of the contemporary state Republican Party. After some internal accommodation of national civil rights policies, more recently, the Tea Party rage against liberalism in Washington and within the GOP has had an influence, particularly in promoting conservative preferences in fiscal and social policy.

Changing Partisan Divisions

The transition from Democratic to Republican dominance in South Carolina took more than a century. After Reconstruction, Democrats enjoyed back-to-back victories. Republicans, after all, had been the party of Lincoln, and it was the strife of Reconstruction that led most white Carolinians to favor Democratic presidential candidates, even if they sometimes were undesirable in other respects. During this time, African Americans who would have favored the GOP as the party supporting their interests, along with the few whites who opposed the Democrats, were excluded systematically from the electorate. Consequently, white Democrats dominated state politics until the national civil rights revolution in the 1960s.

Except for the 1876 presidential election, the national Democratic Party tended to dismiss South Carolina's Electoral College vote as irrelevant. Large waves of immigrants in other parts of the country during the late nineteenth and early twentieth centuries also became Democrats because of the party's support for labor unions. The growing opposition by national Democrats to racial segregation weakened the party's attractiveness to many white South Carolinians. National Democrats really did not need South Carolina's vote to win presidential elections. For the first four decades of the twentieth century, popular elections in South Carolina continued to be won by Democrats—at least in name—from statewide candidates all the way to local ones.

South Carolina Democrats began to give way in their support for the national party by backing the ticket of the States' Rights Democratic Party, or "Dixiecrats," in 1948. The Dixiecrats stridently opposed the national Democratic Party's support for civil rights policies. The Dixiecrats were led by South Carolina's Strom Thurmond as their candidate for president. Some evidence suggests that white South Carolinians' voting patterns were in flux throughout the 1950s and early 1960s.[2] Although not a Dixiecrat, favorite son Jimmy Byrnes added more energy to South Carolina's falling out with national Democrats. Byrnes had served in the US House and Senate, as "assistant president" to Franklin D. Roosevelt, and ultimately as secretary of state. He had also been a US Supreme Court justice for a time in the 1940s. Despite his extensive service and experience in all three branches of government, Byrnes found himself on the outs with national Democrats in 1944 as he opposed major party policies, especially on civil rights. When Byrnes's name was floated for nomination as Roosevelt's running mate in 1944, nonsouthern delegates within the Democratic Party balked, resulting in Harry Truman's nomination for the vice presidency.[3]

Late in his political career, Byrnes won election as governor and worked mightily in 1952 to get a Republican, Dwight Eisenhower, elected President. Byrnes invited Eisenhower to address a large crowd in front of the state capitol. Nevertheless, loyal Democrats continued to prevail in South Carolina. Illinois senator Adlai Stevenson won South Carolina's Electoral College slate in 1952 and 1956. Massachusetts senator John F. Kennedy won the state in 1960, albeit with a narrower margin, defeating Richard Nixon by only ten thousand votes. Republican success in South Carolina began when Arizona senator Barry Goldwater carried South Carolina in the 1964 presidential election. Only once since then, in 1976, has a Democrat, Georgia governor Jimmy Carter, won the state's electoral vote.[4]

In 1980, Gov. Carroll Campbell and his political operative, Lee Atwater, supported Ronald Reagan and led the effort to stop former Texas governor John Connally's bid for the Republican presidential nomination early in the primary campaign. Despite spending millions, Connally lost the South Carolina primary thoroughly, even though he had the support of Sen. Strom Thurmond and the first contemporary

Republican governor, James Edwards. Reagan's primary victory in South Carolina and his successful national election gave rise to South Carolina's reputation as first in the South. From 1980 until 2008, the winner of South Carolina's first-in-the-South primary went on to win the Republican presidential nomination.[5]

The Current Political Landscape

Statewide election results since 1980 show at least three distinct internal political regions with varying degrees of Republican interests and influence.[6] First is Upstate, representing approximately 33 percent of the state's population, where Republicans tend to emphasize social issues such as social services reform and freedom of religion. Republican support for independent, local decisions regarding schools or local determination of social policy is higher there than in other parts of the state. Greenville is the largest county in this region, with about 490,000 residents.

Next, Midlands Republicans tend to focus on national defense, especially the prospect of base closings. The area is home to major military facilities such as Fort Jackson and Shaw Air Force Base, as well as the Savannah River Project near Aiken and the headquarters of the National Guard and many state law enforcement agencies around Columbia. About 39 percent of the state's residents live here, making it the most populated of the three regions. However, that population tends to be concentrated in three large urban areas, making the many rural counties between these cities sparsely populated by comparison. With 407,000 residents, Richland is the largest county in the Midlands, followed by Aiken with 166,000 residents and Florence with 139,000.

Democrats compete more strongly with Republicans in the Midlands because of a larger African American population. The state's Black Belt, made up of counties with a majority-black population, lies in two crescent-shaped slices across the state, originating in Marlboro County on the northeastern border with North Carolina, that spread above and below Columbia to the Savannah River. About one-half of the state's counties are included in these slices, but they include only about 15 percent of the population. Many of these counties have large proportions of minority voters, and many of them lost population between 2010 and 2015, according to estimates from the Bureau of the Census.

Another 28 percent of the population is in the Lowcountry, where Republicans are more libertarian than in other regions. They are attracted to the Republican agenda of lower taxes and smaller government. Charleston

County's 390,000 citizens are the core here, followed by Horry County with 309,000, Berkeley County with 203,000 and Beaufort County with 180,000. The Lowcountry is the fastest growing section of the state, which is in part due to industrial development by companies like Boeing and Volvo in the Charleston area. The other reason is the area has become popular with retirees. Both trends have had the net effect of strengthening the Republicans' hand in the region.[7]

Party Identification

Since the 1980s, party identification in the Palmetto State has become decidedly more Republican among whites, with blacks remaining over-whelmingly Democratic. The South Carolina State Survey included polit-ical identification questions in biannual surveys between fall 1989 and fall 2006. There were thirty-six survey periods, each with an average of 837 respondents, and the research objective in this series of studies was partisan identification.[8] The average findings showed Republican support at 45.3 percent and Democratic support at 43.4 percent, with independent identifiers making up the rest of voters.

In September 2016, the Winthrop Poll found the partisan leanings of the state becoming even more Republican in recent years. In that poll, 47 percent of likely voters were Republican, while only 38 percent of respondents stated that they were Democrats. The remaining 16 percent stated that they were either independent (11 percent) or "other."[9] In the last few decades, the percentage of voters who identify themselves as Republicans has increased, while the number of independents has been decreasing. Election results, especially on the state level, suggest that Republicans have had more success in swaying independent voters than Democrats. If past elections are any indication, it is the centuries-old socially and fiscally conservative views of South Carolinians that makes the difference in statewide electoral outcomes.

The Democratic Primary

Unlike four years ago, both parties had contested presidential primaries in South Carolina in 2016. Throughout 2015, most political observers thought that the Republican primary would be much more interesting than the Democratic primary. However, the insurgent campaign of Bernie Sanders actually created the potential for an interesting Democratic pri-mary. Meanwhile, the Republicans saw as many as seventeen declared candidates at one point in the 2016 election cycle, though most GOP candidates did not spend much, if any, time in the Palmetto State. Despite the fact that South Carolina is not a battleground state in the general election, it is an important state for both parties in the nominating process as it is the first occasion that candidates face southern voters.

In late 2015, it appeared that Hillary Clinton was the sure favorite for the nomination and that the South Carolina Democratic Party primary would be a dull affair. Clinton failed, however, to emerge as the frontrunner after the Iowa caucus and the New Hampshire primary. Indeed, she barely won Iowa by 0.2 percent of the vote and decisively lost New Hampshire by 22 percent. Surprisingly, Clinton's frontrunner status began to hinge upon how she performed in South Carolina. In fact, Clinton's loss in New Hampshire began to lead to some defections from Clinton to Sanders among South Carolina Democrats. While most state Democratic leaders endorsed Clinton, a handful of black Democratic state legislators endorsed Bernie Sanders.[10] This led to more media exposure on the Democratic primary in the state than was first anticipated.

When the Democratic primary was held on February 27, 2016, it turned out that Hillary Clinton's campaign had little outward reason to worry. Once the ballots were cast, Clinton won all forty-six counties in the state. Statewide, she trounced Sanders, winning 73 percent of the vote to Sanders's 26 percent. According to exit polls conducted in the state, Clinton won overwhelmingly in almost every demographic group except two: voters under thirty years old and white males of any age. The problem for Sanders, though, was that these two groups made up very small percentages of the overall primary turnout. As has become the case in the state over the last generation, black voters were the overwhelming majority in the Democratic presidential primary. In 2016, black voters accounted for approximately 61 percent of all Democratic voters, while white voters accounted for 35 percent.

Similarly, Hillary Clinton did well among all Democratic voters on issue positions important to South Carolina Democrats. When voters were asked about which candidate quality mattered the most to them, though, Clinton showed some signs of weakness. While this did not affect her victory in the primary, it did spell potential trouble for her in other states and ultimately on the national level. Clinton was markedly in the lead among voters who were the most concerned about electability in the general election and among those voters who wished to see Obama-era policies continue. However, she had trouble among voters who were the most concerned with honesty and integrity and among those voters who

Table 7.1. South Carolina Democratic Nominating Primary Exit Poll, February 27, 2016

	Clinton	Sanders
Demographics		
Male (39% of respondents)	68	32
Female (61%)	79	21
White (35%)	54	46
Black (61%)	86	14
17–44 years old (35%)	63	37
45+ years old (65%)	81	19
Issues		
Health care (21%)	79	21
Economy (44%)	75	25
Terrorism (10%)	82	17
Income inequality (21%)	63	37
Candidate Quality		
Electability (12%)	82	18
Honesty (23%)	51	49
Cares aboutpeople like me (31%)	68	31
Continue Obama policies (74%)	81	19
More liberal (21%)	45	55

Source: National Election Pool, "South Carolina Exit Polls," *New York Times*, February 27, 2016, accessed November 27, 2016, https://goo.gl/SOsqAa.

Note: All table entries are percentages.

felt that the next president should be more progressive. In the end, these voters were in the minority of all voters in the South Carolina primary.[11]

In an examination of statewide returns, Clinton's overwhelming victory makes it difficult initially to determine trends on the county level. After deeper digging, though, an interesting trend begins to emerge: Hillary Clinton handily won the majority-black counties of the state. In fact, she racked up victories in some counties of nearly 90 percent of the vote. Simultaneously, Sanders did better in the urban counties and those rural counties with higher white votes—though he failed to win any county. Overall, Sanders lost by narrower margins as the share of white population of a county increased. This pointed toward a trend that manifested itself across the South, where Hillary Clinton performed overwhelmingly well among black voters. Part of this can be attributed to the popularity of former President Bill Clinton among black Americans.

In sum, South Carolina was on the front line of Clinton's southern firewall that ultimately helped deliver the nomination for her. Still, troubling signs did exist that seemed to go unnoticed at the time. In 2016, total turnout in the Democratic primary was only 12.5 percent of registered voters. In the last competitive Democratic primary, the one in 2008, turnout was 23 percent, and Barack Obama won more votes in an eight-candidate field than Clinton did in 2016. Quite simply, the excitement among black voters in South Carolina did not exist in 2016 as it had in the 2008 presidential primary.

The Republican Primary

For Republicans in South Carolina, the presidential primary presented a chance to return to the role of first in the South and predictor of the eventual Republican nominee. In fact, state Republicans were anxious to see if the primary would return to form and correctly predict the eventual Republican nominee. Alternatively, would the state's primary winner lose the eventual nomination, as Newt Gingrich had in 2012? In the lead-up to the 2012 primary, most state Republican leaders, including Gov. Nikki Haley, endorsed Mitt Romney. Thus, the picks of state leaders, which historically were not always predictive, was also being closely watched in 2016.

Enter Donald J. Trump in a surprising rise through the Republican nominating field in 2015. Despite losing in Iowa, Trump scored an impressive win in New Hampshire as the Republican field headed south in February. In the lead-up to the state's primary, Sen. Lindsey Graham suspended his campaign, freeing state Republicans to endorse other candidates. In early February, Sen. Tim Scott endorsed Marco Rubio, and two weeks later Gov. Nikki Haley followed suit by endorsing Rubio. Republican officeholders were not united, though. In January, Lt. Gov. Henry McMaster surprised many Republicans by endorsing Donald Trump. Two state legislators, Jim Merrill and Mike Ryhal, endorsed Trump, as did former lieutenant governor Andre Bauer.[12] Headed into the primary on February 20, Republican leaders were as divided as the Republican field. As it turned out, Republican voters were not nearly as divided.

In a statewide result that looked eerily similar to 2012, when Newt Gingrich had surprised the political world, Donald Trump shocked the political establishment by winning a solid victory of 32.5 percent in a six-candidate field. Marco Rubio, who had been endorsed by most statewide Republicans, came in second with 22.4 percent of the vote. Ted Cruz was right behind Rubio with 22.3 percent of the vote. The remaining 22.7 percent of the vote was almost evenly split between Jeb Bush, John Kasich, and Ben Carson, in that order. Despite placing second, Rubio was barely ahead of Cruz, a showing that was a sign of weakness because it was his third loss in as many contests. When he first announced in 2015, Rubio was seen by many as a frontrunner for the nomination. However, his faltering performance in Iowa and New Hampshire placed him in a precarious position. With his failure to win the first-in-the-South primary, Rubio's candidacy was called into serious question, though he stayed in the contest until failing to win his home state of Florida.

The big story in the state's primary, though, was Donald Trump. After winning a solid victory in New Hampshire, all eyes were on the New York billionaire to see how he would fare among Southern Republicans. As it turned out, Trump did quite well. En route to victory, Trump won forty-four of the forty-six counties in the state, losing only Richland County (Columbia) and Charleston County. Despite losing these two counties to Marco Rubio, Trump came in a close second in both counties, highlighting his support among nontraditional Republicans. In fact, Trump arguably helped to drive up Republican turnout in the primary. In 2012, total turnout in the contested Republican primary had been 603,770. Four years later, turnout in the primary was 740,881, an increase of 20.39 percent.

Exit poll results illustrate the nature of Trump's victory. Leading in virtually every category, he won among men by a 36 to 22 percent margin over Marco Rubio, and Trump did surprisingly well among women, beating Rubio by a margin of 29 to 23 percent. Demographically speaking, Trump led in virtually all categories. In fact, one of the big questions for Trump was how he would perform among the Republicans' large evangelical Christian base. In 2012, Newt Gingrich had won handily among the state's evangelical Republicans, and Romney had won among those Republicans who did not consider themselves evangelical Christians. In 2016, Trump performed consistently, winning 33 percent of evangelicals to Ted Cruz's 27 percent. Among non-evangelicals, Trump beat Rubio by a 30 to 27 percent margin. The only group where Trump failed to have clear support was among younger voters, who split almost evenly between Trump, Cruz, and Rubio. Older voters, though, preferred Trump by a clear 35 to 22 percent margin over Rubio. While a bit speculative,

Table 7.2. South Carolina Republican Nominating Primary Exit Poll, February 20, 2016

	Trump	Rubio	Cruz	Kasich	Bush	Carson
Demographics						
Male (51% of respondents)	36	22	22	7	7	7
Female (49%)	29	23	22	9	9	8
White (96%)	33	22	22	8	8	7
Black (1%)	—	—	—	—	—	—
17–44 years old (27%)	26	25	26	8	4	10
45+ years old (73%)	35	22	21	7	9	6
Evangelical Christian (72%)	33	22	27	5	7	7
Not evangelical Christian (28%)	30	22	13	19	9	5
Issues						
Immigration (21%)	51	11	25	3	3	7
Economy (29%)	36	24	15	13	7	6
Terrorism (32%)	31	23	25	5	9	7
Government spending (26%)	25	25	25	8	9	8
Candidate quality						
Electability (15%)	21	47	17	7	6	2
Shares my values (37%)	8	27	34	10	10	11
Tells it like it is (16%)	78	3	8	4	4	4
Can bring needed change (31%)	45	16	19	7	8	6

Source: "South Carolina Exit Polls," *National Election Pool*, February 20, 2016, accessed November 27, 2016, https://goo.gl/cQF6hi.

Note: All table entries are percentages.

one hypothesis is that Trump was doing better among older white voters who wanted to see a change from the status quo in Washington, DC.

On the issues, Trump resonated well with the voters. Exit poll data found that the threat of terrorism was the most important issue to Republicans, followed by the economy, government spending, and immigration. Trump was the favorite of Republican voters on all issues except government spending, where he tied with Rubio and Cruz. Unsurprisingly, for those voters for whom curtailing immigration was the most important, Trump was the overwhelming choice, preferred 51 to 25 percent over Ted Cruz. In terms of which quality voters were seeking in the candidates, Trump split these evenly between his opponents. He clearly won among voters who wanted a blunt and outspoken candidate who would change the political system. However, he was not the favored choice for those voters who were seeking a candidate who shared their values, losing to Ted Cruz. Interestingly, Republican voters who were the most concerned about electability were not impressed by Trump and thought that Marco Rubio had the best chance of defeating Hillary Clinton in November.[13]

Much like Hillary Clinton's performance in the Democratic primary, Trump's solid victory across the state makes discussing statewide trends a bit challenging. What is immediately noticeable is that Marco Rubio, the favored candidate of the state's Republican establishment, carried both Columbia and Charleston. This is not a surprise, as most Republicans in Columbia and Charleston tend to be more oriented towards the business and political elite of the state. What is a bit surprising is how well Trump did in Beaufort, Greenville, and Horry Counties, which are also associated with Republican elites. In rural South Carolina, Trump was the overwhelming favorite of Republican voters. Given the substance of Trump's rhetoric and issue positions, this is not altogether surprising.

The General Election Campaign

In 2012, Republican candidate Mitt Romney defeated Democratic incumbent Barack Obama in South Carolina by 10.47 percentage points. Given South Carolina's entrenched Republicanism, outside polling groups largely ignored the state. While one Democratic-leaning polling group, Public Policy Polling, suggested Trump had only a 2 percent lead over Hillary Clinton in August, a Republican pollster found Trump with a 15-point lead in September. Two other unaffiliated pollsters found Trump with a 4-point lead in the late summer and early fall.[14] However, no other polls were conducted prior to Election Day. In the end, the Trafalgar Group poll, a Republican polling group, turned out to be the closest to reality. Trump defeated Clinton by 54.9 to 40.8 percent—a difference of 14.1 percent. In fact, Trump performed better than any Republican nominee since George W. Bush in 2004. In this way, South Carolina was much like the rest of the nation, where Trump's support was much deeper and stronger than most pollsters were suggesting. Unfortunately, no exit poll data exists from the general election, but broad trends can be detected by examining the vote totals in the state.

Simply put, the 2016 presidential election revealed the continuing strength of the GOP in South Carolina. Indeed, the Republicans displayed even greater strength than they had in the last presidential election. In the Upstate region, Trump had his strongest showing where he won that eleven-county region by a 63.8 to 32.4 percent margin. If one considers 60 percent of the vote to be a landslide, then Trump's victory in the Upstate was overwhelming. This is all the more impressive when considering that the Upstate is more heavily populated by white evangelical Christians than any other region of the state. After the early October allegations of Trump's self-proclaimed "locker room talk" about women, one might have logically wondered how Trump would do among evangelical Christians. Based upon the results here, it seems not to have fazed them. Perhaps the dislike of Hillary Clinton was more motivating for these voters than any negative feelings towards Donald Trump.

In fact, Trump's margin was 1 percent higher than Mitt Romney's performance in the region in 2012. Pickens County, where the vote was nearly three to one for Trump (73.8 percent to 26.1 percent), maintained its position as the most Republican county in the state in presidential voting. Trump's dominance is not entirely surprising, given the Upstate counties' dominant white majorities and expanding industrial and commercial activities. Overall, voter turnout in the Upstate was 69.1 percent, higher than the other two regions of the state.

The Midlands has been the most competitive region for the Democrats in South Carolina over the last generation. However, Democratic support has not been evenly distributed throughout the twenty-six-county region. An accurate assessment of the area is that it is a predominately rural region with large minority populations in the more rural areas and large white populations in the areas of Aiken, Lexington County (a suburban county outside of Columbia), and Florence. These areas are the source of Republican strength, especially in Aiken and Lexington Counties, and Democrats do well among minority voters in both Columbia and the

Table 7.3. South Carolina by Region and County Turnout Rate in the 2016 General Election

Regions and counties	Trump (%)	Clinton (%)	Others (%)	Total votes (#)	Total vote (%)*	Turnout (%)
Upstate						
Pickens	**73.8**	21.1	5.0	49,941	2.3	71.9
Abbeville	**62.7**	34.7	2.6	10,880	0.5	70.9
Union	**58.3**	39.1	2.6	12,217	0.6	69.5
Greenville	**59.4**	34.6	6.0	217,378	10.2	69.5
York	**58.4**	36.3	5.3	115,269	5.4	69.0
Upstate totals	**63.8**	32.4	3.8	705,739	33.2	69.1
Midlands						
McCormick	**50.8**	47.5	1.6	5,285	0.2	74.5
Saluda	**64.5**	32.9	2.6	8,664	0.4	73.3
Newberry	**59.6**	37.0	3.4	17,004	0.8	72.3
Fairfield	35.7	**61.6**	2.6	11,401	0.5	71.8
Lancaster	**60.9**	35.5	3.6	39,321	1.9	71.7
Midlands totals	48.0	**49.3**	2.7	806,293	37.9	67.5
Lowcountry						
Georgetown	**55.0**	42.0	3.0	32,051	1.5	74.9
Beaufort	**54.7**	40.9	4.4	79,571	3.7	71.1
Colleton	**52.7**	44.2	3.1	17,438	0.8	69.0
Berkeley	**56.1**	38.6	5.3	80,188	3.8	68.0
Williamsburg	32.3	**66.1**	1.6	15,181	0.7	67.0
Lowcountry totals	**51.4**	44.7	3.9	611,552	28.8	67.5
Urban counties (26)	**55.9**	40.2	3.9	1,778,412	83.7	68.3
Rural counties (20)	48.0	**49.7**	2.3	345,172	16.2	66.8

Source: Calculated by the authors from data on the South Carolina State Election Commission website, https://goo.gl/ddHU.

Note: Winning percentages are in boldface. Totals have been rounded and may not always add to 100 percent. The configuration of counties by region used by the authors in the analysis is devised using a composite of various internal regional configurations.

*Each percentage in this column represents the percentage of the total number of votes cast in the county or region as a proportion of all votes cast in the state.

rural counties. This is evidenced by Hillary Clinton's victory in the region overall by a 49.3 to 48.0 percent margin. However, Clinton's slim margin of victory in the region highlighted problems for her with the Democratic base. Black voters did not turn out in the same numbers as they did for Barack Obama in 2008 and 2012. While Trump won fourteen Midlands counties, he lost the remainder of the region by large margins. For the most part, this was because of large margins of victory for Clinton in majority-black counties and in Richland County, the largest urban county in the region.

The Lowcountry has been a majority Republican region, like the Upstate. Yet, the Lowcountry is more heavily populated by economic conservatives, as compared to the social conservatives of the Upstate. With a more racially diverse population, the Lowcountry is solidly Republican but not as overwhelmingly Republican as the Upstate. Still, Trump performed well in the region, winning by nearly 7 percent. Much as she had in the Midlands, Clinton did better in the less-populated majority-black counties, but Trump won solid victories of around 55 percent in the more densely population urban and suburban counties associated with the Charleston, Beaufort, and Myrtle Beach areas. Voter turnout in both the Midlands and the Lowcountry was at 67.5 percent.

Table 7.3 also demonstrates Trump's and Clinton's support in rural and urban counties. While Clinton won the state's twenty rural counties, she only won by 1.7 points. This was a much closer margin than recent election cycles, where the rural areas with higher concentrations of minority voters are usually solid victories for Democrats. What is especially noticeable about all three regions, though, is the amount of support for Trump among rural white voters. In fact, rural counties were leading the way in all three regions in levels of turnout. Simply put, Trump resonated with many rural white voters, helping him either to win rural counties or, failing that, to be more competitive in some rural counties than in the past several election cycles. Without trying, in the absence of exit poll data, to be too definitive in describing the motivations of these voters, it is safe to say that something about the Trump persona resonated.

Whether it was immigration, "draining the Swamp," opposition to Clinton, or just political incorrectness, many rural white South Carolinians found the New York mogul appealing despite the world of difference separating him from them. In fact, Trump performed at historic levels in some rural South Carolina counties. One such example was McCormick County. Richard Nixon in 1972 was the last Republican presidential nominee to carry the county. While Trump was winning the county, Democrats were being swept into all the county-level offices. In fact, Republicans did not even field candidates for those county level offices, further highlighting the extraordinary nature of Trump's victory. Nor was McCormick County an isolated case. Dillon County had not gone Republican in nearly two generations. However, Trump was running ahead of Clinton until the last absentee ballots were counted, allowing Clinton to eke out a victory.

At the same time, however, the state's twenty-six urban counties were not as excited about Trump. While Trump still won the urban and suburban counties that typically vote Republican, he won by narrower margins. While many rural counties saw high levels of voter turnout, many urban counties saw slight decreases in voter turnout in comparison to recent election cycles. One hypothesis is that Republicans in these urban areas were not as impressed with Trump's rhetoric, nor did his protectionist economic message play as well with voters who had been benefiting in many cases from global trade.

Down the ballot, Republicans continued their electoral successes. Voters were asked to choose someone to serve in the US Senate for another six-year term. In 2012, Sen. Jim DeMint resigned in early December 2012 to become the new head of the Heritage Foundation. In mid-December Governor Haley appointed First District Republican congressman Tim Scott to replace DeMint. In accordance with South Carolina law, Scott faced the voters in a 2014 special election, which he easily won. In 2016, voters overwhelmingly voted to return Scott, the first black US senator from a southern state since the Reconstruction era, to Washington for a full six-year term. In a sign of Scott's popularity, he won over 60 percent of the vote—the highest vote total of any statewide Republican in 2016. The US House delegation, in which the GOP has a six-to-one advantage, remains solidly Republican.

Conclusion

South Carolina has often been a key player in national politics, especially since it initiated in 1980 its first-in-the-South presidential nominating primary. All eventual Republican presidential nominees between 1980 and 2008 won the South Carolina primary. That streak ended in 2012 with Newt Gingrich's victory in the state's primary and with Mitt Romney's nomination as the GOP presidential candidate. Donald Trump restored South Carolina's streak in 2016 and perhaps South Carolina's significance as the first-in-the-South presidential nominating primary.

Table 7.4. Results of 2016 South Carolina Presidential and Congressional Elections

Candidate (party)	Vote (%)	Votes (#)
President		
Donald Trump / Mike Pence (R)	54.94	1,155,389
Hillary Clinton / Tim Kaine (D)	40.67	855,373
Gary Johnson / Bill Weld (L)	2.34	49,204
Evan McMullin / Nathan Johnson (I)	1.00	21,016
Jill Stein / Ajamu Baraka (G)	0.62	13,034
Darrell Castle / Scott Bradley (C)	0.27	5,765
Peter Skewes / Michael Lacy (A)	0.15	3,246
Total		2,103,027
US Senate		
Tim Scott (R)*	60.57	1,241,609
Thomas Dixon (D/WFM/G)	36.93	757,022
Bill Bledsoe (L/C)	1.83	37,482
Michael "Rebel" Scarborough (A)	0.58	11,923
Write-in	0.09	1,857
Total		2,049,893
US House		
First District		
Mark Sanford (R)*	58.56	190,410
Dimitri Cherny (D/WFM/G)	36.83	119,779
Michael Grier Jr. (L)	3.57	11,614
Albert Travison (A)	0.85	2,774
Write-in	0.18	593
Total		325,170
Second District		
Joe Wilson (R)*	60.25	183,746
Arik Bjorn (D/G)	35.89	109,452
Eddie McCain (A)	3.75	11,444
Write-in	0.12	354
Total		304,996
Third District		
Jeff Duncan (R)	72.84	196,325
Hosea Cleveland (D)	27.06	72,933
Write-in	0.10	282
Total		269,540
Fourth District		
Trey Gowdy (R)	67.19	198,648
Chris Fedalei (D)	31.01	91,676

Table 7.4. (continued)

Candidate (party)	Vote (%)	Votes (#)
Michael Chandler (C)	1.73	5,103
Write-in	0.08	243
Total		295,670
Fifth District		
Mick Mulvaney (R)	59.22	161,669
Fran Person (D)	38.74	105,772
Rudy Barnes Jr. (A)	1.97	5,338
Write-in	0.06	177
Total		273,006
Sixth District		
James E. "Jim" Clyburn (D)	70.09	177,947
Laura Sterling (R)	27.61	70,099
Rich Piotrowski (L)	1.23	3,131
Prince Charles Mallory (G)	0.98	2,499
Write-in	0.09	225
Total		253,901
Seventh District		
Tom Rice (R)	60.96	176,468
Mal Hyman (D/WFM/G)	38.95	112,744
Write-in	0.09	251
Total		289,463

Source: Calculated by the authors from data on the South Carolina State Election Commission website, https://goo.gl/ddHU.

Observers debate the lasting political impact of working-class whites who supported Trump in such large numbers. In South Carolina, working-class whites, especially males, have identified with the Republican Party in varying degrees since the 1970s. The increased white support for Trump in 2016 suggests at least enhanced GOP preference in South Carolina. What may weaken GOP support within the state is the extent to which Trump delivers on his promises. If he does not, another Trump-like candidate may emerge to win the loyalty of the white working class in the future.

In future general elections, South Carolina politics will turn on the question whether South Carolina Republicans can maintain their dominance. Enjoying safe margins of 55 percent or more in virtually all elections, Republicans currently have a commanding position, including majorities in the general assembly, the governorship, all statewide elected officers, both US Senate seats, and a majority in the House delegation (six Republicans to one Democrat).

Democrats, by comparison, seem competitive only in a few general assembly races. In most cases, Democratic success is assured only when legislative districts feature majority-black electorates. There was some past hope for a broad, statewide Democratic resurgence when Jim Hodges defeated an incumbent Republican governor, David Beasley, in 1998 by over eighty-seven thousand votes, a 53 to 45 percent victory. Mark Sanford soon reversed the Democrats' reawakening by taking the governorship away from the incumbent Hodges by sixty-four thousand votes in 2002. Sanford ran without significant opposition in 2006. Nikki Haley's election as governor in 2010 and 2014 continued the Republican control of the governor's office.

Today, there is virtually no statewide lineup of Democrats to challenge the Republicans. A few Democratic challengers run statewide, without any real hope of victory, seemingly just to maintain the honor of the party and the two-party system. Candidates from the Midlands, especially Democrats, typically do not fare well statewide. There seems to be a "Do not cross" line for Democrats preventing political success in the Upstate, the most supportive region for Republicans. The Lowcountry has significant independent, conservative, and even libertarian leanings, and does not offer an inherent advantage to a statewide Democratic candidate.

The task for Republicans is to keep Democrats on the defensive and maintain as many noncompetitive statewide and local races as possible. Barring any destructive state factions or third-party splinter groups, a future GOP November vote count for president may be projected to start at 50 percent and slowly improve as votes are counted to a winning share of 55 percent or more. If President Trump delivers, the starting point in the next presidential election may even be 55 percent or more. The November tally in the governor's race in even years with no presidential election may not be as high, but it should be at least close to 55 percent. The major glitch may be a destructive Republican statewide nominating primary that reduces turnout or generates protest candidates. Currently, in the absence of an elected governor following the appointment of Gov. Nikki Haley as ambassador to the United Nations, the Republican gubernatorial nomination in 2018 may become testy as it draws various GOP contenders. Despite the departure of the Fifth District member of Congress, Mick Mulvaney, to become Office of Management and Budget director in the Trump administration, the strong Republican congressional delegation will continue to draw on a broad statewide, but locally focused, Republican base.

By comparison, the Democrats seem to have only vague choices for a gubernatorial candidate and do not claim to have a pipeline of potential statewide candidates under development. The established levels of Republican representation in the general assembly seem as solid as the granite mass in Caesars Head State Park. Democrats face challenges, not only in the general assembly but statewide, reminiscent of the twists and turns, rises and falls of the rocky nineteenth-century Jones Gap Toll Road near Caesars Head. Given these static conditions, South Carolina's main contribution to presidential politics will continue to rotate around the Republican presidential primary.

III

Elections in the Rim South

8

Arkansas

Trump Is a Natural for the Natural State

Jay Barth and Janine A. Parry

While Arkansans have voted consistently for Republican presidents since 1980 (when Bill Clinton was not the Democratic nominee), those elections remained competitive until recently because of the continued strength of Democrats at the state level.[1] The wholesale rejection in 2008 of Sen. Barack Obama by the state's white rural swing voters, however, ushered in a series of blowouts. Sen. John McCain earned 59 percent of the state's vote that year, followed by Gov. Mitt Romney with 61 percent in 2012. In the latter contest, the Democratic incumbent, so popular nationally, won only a handful of counties in the Arkansas Delta and urban Pulaski County (Little Rock). Most startling for the state's Democrats, Romney ran up his largest margins in the rural swing counties that historically have been so determinative.[2]

Beyond these suddenly decisive presidential contests in 2008 and 2012, a more fundamental realignment occurred in Arkansas during the Obama era. Indeed, no state political party in the modern era has experienced a more precipitous decline than Arkansas's Democrats during this period. Going into the 2010 election cycle, the Democratic Party of Arkansas controlled every statewide elected position, maintained solid majorities in both houses of the Arkansas General Assembly, and held five of six positions in the state congressional delegation. Just six years later, that balance of power has been upended, with Republicans now boasting every statewide post and all members of the state's Washington, DC, delegation. Republicans have also achieved a supermajority in the Arkansas House of Representatives as a result of the 2016 election (and two subsequent party switches by Democratic legislators). Donald Trump's extraordinary appeal in the rural quadrants of Arkansas—adding to the rejection of national Democrats associated with President Obama—helped propel Arkansas Republicans to these new heights.

Despite the absence of any real campaigning in the state and the easiness of the win for the Republican nominee, Arkansas still played an outsized role in the 2016 election. Attacks on Trump's character, behavior and statements were the dominant theme of the Clinton campaign, but the key subtheme of Hillary Clinton's general election campaign was her lifetime of service. As many of the key moments in that career of service occurred during her nearly two decades in public life in Arkansas, Arkansas was featured prominently. Still, neither that fact—nor the fact that numerous Arkansans who were central to the Clinton campaign were eager to return to a second Clinton administration—mattered a lick as another national Democrat was demolished in this suddenly and stunningly red state.

The Primary Season

The ascendancy of the GOP in the state's politics set the stage for the state to matter more than ever in the nomination battle on the Republican side. Consequently, during its 2015 session, the general assembly voted to move the state's traditional late May contest so the state could participate in the so-called SEC Primary scheduled for March 1. Initially, the state GOP's dream of candidate visits and campaign spending in the state was stymied because of Mike Huckabee's candidacy. When the former Arkansas governor announced another bid for president in May 2015 in his hometown of Hope, most high-profile Arkansas Republican officeholders lined up behind him. The stances of these state GOP elites and Huckabee's having gained more than 60 percent of the Arkansas primary vote in his 2008 run for president limited other candidates' inroads into the state before the Iowa caucuses.[3]

Still, indicative of Huckabee's distance from Arkansas temporally (he had left the governorship in 2007) and physically (he had relocated to Florida at the start of the decade), a handful of state legislators representative of the post-Huckabee wave of Republicanism in the state announced support for other candidates.[4] Several of those candidates made brief stops in the state during 2015, including an appearance by Donald Trump as the keynote speaker at the state GOP's annual Reagan-Rockefeller Dinner in July. A ticket sale surge forced a change of venue for the Hot Springs event, and his hour-long remarks included many of the phrases that would become commonly known in the year and a half to follow. Specifically, he targeted Hillary Clinton for having "deserted Arkansas" and declared emphatically that the "last thing we need is another Bush."[5] By Arkansas's November 2015 filing deadline, thirteen GOP candidates had paid the $25,000 filing fee, to the benefit of the state GOP coffers.

Huckabee's departure from the race, following a miserable ninth-place showing in the Iowa caucuses he had won in 2008, opened the floodgates for the leading candidates to invest time and money in Arkansas.[6] Even before Huckabee's February exit, Trump had scheduled a rally at Little Rock's Barton Coliseum that took place two days after Iowa's event. Approximately six thousand Trump acolytes, spectacle seekers, and scattered protestors turned out for what was a classic Trump rally in style and content.[7] (Paula Jones, who accused Bill Clinton of sexual harassment, was photographed greeting Trump at the rally; she would return to the story in the fall campaign.[8]) In the lead-up to the March 1 primary, Trump was joined by Texas senator Ted Cruz and Florida senator Marco Rubio in contesting the state vigorously. Throughout the second half of February, each made appearances in Little Rock or in northwest Arkansas.

The three candidates represented the three major branches of the contemporary Arkansas GOP.[9] Rubio received the endorsements of most high-ranking state elected officials—including Gov. Asa Hutchinson and the leaders of both chambers of the Arkansas General Assembly—and others in the state GOP establishment. Cruz, on the other hand, was arguably the best fit for the mix of Tea Party adherents and evangelicals who had fueled the GOP rise in the Obama era; many of those activists came on board for Cruz. Finally, while receiving little warmth from party elites of any stripe (indeed, Governor Hutchinson became a harsh critic of Trump, saying his "words are frightening" in a national interview just before the "SEC Primary"), Trump showed the same ability he had shown in other states to bring into the GOP primary disaffected independents who rarely participated in primaries.[10]

The geographical patterns of the votes received across the state by Rubio, Cruz, and Trump on March 1 illustrate these factional divides.

Rubio only won two counties—Pulaski and Benton—but this success in the two largest (and the two wealthiest) counties in the state equated to nearly a quarter of the overall primary vote (24.8 percent). Cruz showed success in the suburban counties around Little Rock, the handful of exurban counties across the state, and those counties closest to the Texas border, gaining him just over 30 percent of the electorate.

Yet it was Trump's success across the entire state, particularly in rural counties where voters had shied away from GOP primary participation before his arrival on the scene, that won the day. In 2008, the most recent comparable primary, just under 230,000 voters had participated in the Republican selection process (fueled, of course, by Huckabee's candidacy that year) (see table 8.1). In 2016, 410,920 voters took part in the GOP primary, and a disproportionate amount of that increase came from outside of the traditional GOP enclaves of Northwest Arkansas and the Little Rock metropolitan area. A good example is Polk County, a rural county on the western border of the state. There, a 148 percent increase in turnout from 2008 to 2016 emerged (nearly double the already impressive statewide increase), and Trump earned over 40 percent of those votes. Ironically, considering his origins in an America so culturally disconnected from rural Arkansas, it was grassroots strength in these isolated counties that pushed Donald Trump to a first-place finish on the March 1 primary with just under one-third of the vote.

The results from the primary vote showed a dramatic reversal from one recent pattern in Arkansas elections: the decline in primary voting in general in the state.[11] At the same time, the results showed a further acceleration of a second trend: the relative growth in participation in the GOP primary as compared to the Democratic primary. The decidedly less vibrant battle in Arkansas between Clinton and Vermont senator Bernie Sanders helped promote this decrease in Democratic primary participation.

In her 2008 nomination contest with Barack Obama, Clinton won over 70 percent of the vote in the Arkansas primary, her strongest performance anywhere in the country. Her history in the state along with that recent success limited any real Arkansas contest between her and Bernie Sanders. Clinton came to the state to headline the state's Jefferson-Jackson Dinner in the summer of 2015, addressing two thousand attendees and helping sustain the budget of the state party. Even then, her strongest supporters were conscious of the general-election challenges in the state. Out of office only six months, former governor Mike Beebe, the last of Arkansas's high-profile Democrats for the foreseeable future, said "it'll be

Table 8.1. Primary Voter Turnout in Arkansas in Presidential Election Years, 1976–2016

Year	Democratic primary	Republican primary
1976	525,968	22,797
1980	415,406	8,177
1984	492,321	19,040
1988	497,506	68,305
1992	502,130	52,297
1996	300,389	42,814
2000	246,900	44,573
2004	256,848	38,363
2008*	315,322	229,665
2012	162,647	152,360
2016	221,020	410,920

Source: Arkansas Secretary of State, https://goo.gl/9FP9O5.

*Arkansas made an earlier bid to increase its significance in the nominating process in 2008, moving its primary from May to February. Participation levels in the state nearly doubled those of previous years. This also proved significant because it separated voters' national partisan preferences from the overwhelming number of local contests in which Republican candidates had not, to date, appeared or were not competitive. The resulting opportunity for voter targeting undoubtedly played a role in the party's growth since that time.

an uphill battle" for Clinton to win its electoral votes.[12] She followed up with a September 2015 visit that combined a public audience at Philander Smith University—a historically black university in Little Rock—with a $2700-per-person fundraiser. Before a thousand supporters at Philander Smith, Clinton recounted her time in Arkansas and reiterated her commitment to the state, saying, "I can tell you this: When I'm president, Arkansas will be on my mind every single day."[13] In addition, while no formal Clinton campaign operation established itself in the state, there was a rebirth of the Arkansas Travelers program that sent Arkansans to other key states at their own expense to tout their Clinton's attributes, as had been the case in 1992 for her husband and in 2008 for her own candidacy.

Sanders himself never made an appearance in the state, ceding it to Clinton entirely. (Maryland governor Martin O'Malley did campaign for a state senate candidate in 2014 and returned to hold an event with only twenty people at Philander Smith University, the Arkansas Democratic

Black Caucus Christmas Gala, and a fundraiser for his presidential campaign in early December 2015.)[14] The Sanders camp did open two offices (an official office in Little Rock and a volunteer-run office in Fayetteville), had six paid staffers in the state ahead of March 1, and had a social media presence in the state.

The absence of an energetic approach by either Democrat led to a predictable result. Clinton won two-thirds of the votes in the Arkansas primary. Although this was not as strong a position for Clinton as she had in other southern states with larger African American populations, she took seventy-three of the state's seventy-five counties. Still, the real challenge for Clinton was obvious to anyone watching: while she remained strong with the Democratic stalwarts, the majority of the long-blue state had turned ruby-red.

The General Election Campaign

Because the outcome in Arkansas was never in any real doubt, the general election action there was also limited. That said, the state was front and center for much of the fall campaign, as the Clinton campaign emphasized her work on children's issues while in the state as evidence of her commitment to public service. On the other hand, particularly while under attack for his own treatment of women, Donald Trump brought to the forefront a different side of Clinton's Arkansas years: the allegedly abusive treatment of several Arkansas women by Bill Clinton—and by his wife.

Only two campaign appearances by candidates or spouses occurred in Arkansas during the general election campaign—both on the Democratic side. After Clinton had the nomination in hand, former president Bill Clinton followed his wife's lead from the prior year in headlining the Democratic Party of Arkansas's Jefferson-Jackson Dinner (the last to bear that name).[15] There, he gave a meandering speech in which he insisted it was necessary for the Democratic Party to contrast itself with Republicans on bread-and-butter economic issues, both to gain votes and to live up to the core values of the party. As Clinton summed up his argument: "We've got to do a better job of explaining to people that we're in it for them and that anybody that spends all their time trying to keep you mad at somebody else is not really your friend. . . . They want your vote, not a better life for you."[16] Following Clinton's November 8 defeat, many cited the absence of a clear economic argument from her campaign as a reason for her weakness in the Upper Midwest and in Coal

Country.[17] Democratic vice presidential candidate Tim Kaine appeared briefly in Little Rock in late August, stopping by to officially open the Clinton Little Rock headquarters en route to a fundraiser. At the headquarters, Kaine expressed his typical optimism in touting his running mate's chances in Arkansas, saying, "This is a state where person-to-person contact matters and people know Hillary Clinton."[18]

While she never made a stop in the state during 2016 as the general election date approached, Arkansas remained omnipresent in Hillary Clinton's campaign. The 2016 Democratic National Convention was a celebration of her lifetime of service, and much of it focused on her time as Arkansas's first lady. In recounting "the best darn change-maker I ever met in my entire life," Bill Clinton recounted in great detail Hillary's work in the state—from organizations she founded to programs she brought to the state to her work in reforming the state's educational system.[19] To provide handy visuals to accompany these remembrances of her Arkansas years, the Arkansas delegation was front and center at the convention, and Saline County teacher Dustin Parsons appeared as a speaker on the stage to highlight the impact of the educational reforms in Arkansas.[20]

The campaign's focus on her Arkansas years did not stop at the convention. Her fall advertising push used Arkansas examples to demonstrate her lifetime of dedication to children and family issues, and Clinton herself made overt references to her Arkansas experience in the final presidential debate both in expressing her understanding of American gun culture and in contrasting herself with Trump. "In the 1980s, I was working to reform the schools in Arkansas," she said. "He was borrowing $14 million from his father to start his businesses."[21]

While the Clinton campaign's version of her time in Arkansas emphasized her work and accomplishments, her opponents focused on a different version of those years. In the lead-up to the second debate with Trump that occurred just after Trump's infamous *Access Hollywood* videotape came to light, the Republican nominee brought forward two women from the Clinton years in Arkansas—Paula Jones and Juanita Broaddrick—who renewed their allegations of sexual abuse by Bill Clinton (and, in the case of Broaddrick, a heavy-handed effort by Hillary Clinton to maintain her silence) and a rape victim whose rapist was represented by Hillary Clinton as a court-appointed defense attorney. The woman, Kathy Shelton, said, "At 12 years old, Hillary put me through something you would never put a 12-year old through. . . . Now she's laughing on tape saying she knows they [carried out the rape]."[22] Whether

Clinton had indeed laughed at the rape victim received some attention in the state; Roy Reed, the longtime journalist who had conducted the interview in question over three decades earlier, characterized the laugh as one of exasperation with the unprofessional actions of local law enforcement, not one targeted at the victim.[23]

Despite their coolness to Trump during the primary campaign, Arkansas's GOP leaders and activists united behind him once it became clear Trump would be the GOP nominee. Their loyalty (at least compared to others in the party from across the nation) was rewarded with a series of appearances by Arkansas elected officials at the Republican National Convention in July. Former governor Huckabee, Governor Hutchinson, Sen. Tom Cotton, and Atty. Gen. Leslie Rutledge all took the stage to tout Trump. Rutledge criticized Clinton, saying, "Sometimes Hillary Clinton speaks with a New York accent. Sometimes an Arkansas accent. But, y'all, this is what a real Arkansas woman sounds like."[24] As the fall campaign continued, Rutledge would become a regular media surrogate for the Trump campaign.

In addition to the Clintons themselves, a number of Arkansans also were deeply involved in the Clinton campaign. Particularly prominent in this group were Adrienne Elrod, director of strategic communications for Clinton after beginning the campaign cycle at Correct the Record (a super PAC built to respond rapidly to attacks on Clinton); Craig Smith, who headed up the Ready for Hillary super PAC that preceded her candidacy and was in a leadership role on the Clinton Florida campaign down the home stretch; and Greg Hale, the campaign's director of production.[25] Working collaboratively with the Clinton campaign, the volunteer Arkansas Travelers were active throughout the campaign, often visiting smaller towns in parts of swing states similar to Arkansas in terms of their cultural conservatism. The Travelers' primary task was to engage in direct voter contact through door-to-door interactions and phone calls to tell of their longstanding personal connection with Clinton.[26]

Similarly, Clinton's deep connections in Arkansas with individuals used to giving political money to Democrats paid off as she received campaign donations from Arkansans totaling $2.4 million. This swamped Trump's take in the state as his campaign gained just over $800,000 during that year.[27] However, Clinton's advantage was countered by one donation to the Trump super PAC—$2 million from Little Rock's Ronald Cameron, owner of the Mountaire Corporation (the nation's sixth-largest poultry company), who had been the major super PAC backer of Mike Huckabee during his failed campaign.[28] While the Trump campaign showed little formal organization in the state, the enthusiasm for his candidacy showed itself in ad hoc pro-Trump billboards and farm implements painted with "Trump for President" in fields across the state. It was those actions rather than the actions of political professionals that showed the depth of the Trump movement in Arkansas.

The Outcome

The fact that Arkansas again cast its six Electoral College votes for the Republican nominee in 2016 surprised no one. Statewide polls stretching back into 2015 had revealed a double-digit lead for the generic Republican (against a generic Democrat and against Clinton specifically), and from September of 2016 forward, the average projected margin of victory among all polls exceeded 20 points, approaching the actual margin of 23.7 (see table 8.2). Indeed, Trump's vote share was higher in only eight other states. These included many of Arkansas's low-density and southern peers, including Wyoming and West Virginia (68 percent), Kentucky (66 percent), Oklahoma (65 percent), North Dakota (63 percent), Alabama and South Dakota (62 percent), and Tennessee (61 percent).[29] It is particularly telling to examine the Republican vote share in 2016 in comparison to 2012. Although both the final vote share and the statewide margin of victory for Republicans exactly matched that of 2012, Donald Trump increased his party's share in the state's most rural US House districts (the First and the Fourth Districts) while incurring losses that were modest compared to Mitt Romney's in the state's urban areas (the Second and Third Districts).[30] The complete results of the presidential and congressional elections are in table 8.3.

The explanation for this dueling force lies in a fact noted above: that statewide elections in Arkansas are decided by a large collection of rural swing counties identified by political scientist Diane Blair in the 1980s.[31] Most of these counties—disproportionally white and rural—have been experiencing population stagnation, if not decline, for decades. They cut a diagonal swath from the southwest to the northeast and long have demonstrated a propensity to "swing" between Republican candidates and Democratic candidates, depending on the central issues—economic or cultural. For three consecutive election cycles—in presidential politics—we have watched these counties swing emphatically Republican. In 2008 and 2012 in particular, we argued that it was voters in these counties who felt most culturally disconnected from Barack Obama.[32] Table 8.4 provides evidence of still another burst—indeed, a

Table 8.2. Selected Polls in Arkansas, Presidential Race 2016

Poll and Polling Dates	Trump	Clinton	Margin
Arkansas Poll (University of Arkansas), Oct. 18–Oct. 25	58	31	27
Talk Business & Politics / Hendrix College poll, Oct. 21	56	33	23
Talk Business & Politics / Hendrix College poll, Sept. 15–Sept. 17	55	34	21
Emerson College poll, Sept. 9–Sept. 13	57	29	28
Talk Business & Politics / Hendrix College poll, June 21	47	36	11

Sources: The Arkansas Poll, https://goo.gl/uXInjm; *Talk Business & Politics* / Hendrix College poll, https://goo.gl/Qw9q6N. More polling results available from *RealClearPolitics*, https://goo.gl/10yYJK.

Note: All table entries are percentages.

larger one—of GOP support in these communities. While the statewide average for the Republican candidate was 60.6 percent in both 2012 and 2016, the rural swing counties that had given Romney 65.7 percent in 2012 gave Trump 69.0 percent in 2016, a gap of more than 8 points from the statewide average. Conversely, counties with bigger (and more diverse populations) showed less enthusiasm for Trump than they had for Romney. Trump's vote share, for example, declined about 6 points in Benton and Washington Counties and nearly 5 points in Pulaski.

Social and Demographic Factors

Of course, regional differences alone do not explain Arkansas's third consecutive presidential rout. Hampered again by the reduction of state-level exit polling to just twenty-eight states [33] exclusive of Arkansas, we turn to an examination of the University of Arkansas's annual pre-election Arkansas Poll, which is presented in table 8.5.[34] Overall, the GOP candidate of 2016 maintained (or saw only small downturns in) support from members of nearly every demographic category, while significantly improving vote share among the young, the poor, and—in keeping with nationwide patterns—white women.

Table 8.3. Results of the 2016 Arkansas Presidential and Congressional Elections

Candidate (party)	Vote percentage (2012 party vote)	Vote total (2012 party vote)
President		
Donald Trump / Mike Pence (R)	60.6 (60.6)	684, 872 (647,744)
Hillary Clinton / Tim Kaine (D)	33.7 (36.9)	380,494 (394,409)
Gary Johnson / Bill Weld (L)	2.6 (1.5)	29,829 (16,276)
Evan McMullin / Nathan Johnson (BFA)	1.2 (—)	13,255 (—)
Jill Stein / Ajamu Baraka (G)	0.8 (0.9)	9,473 (9,305)
US Senate		
John Boozman (R)[a]	59.8 (44.1b)	661,984 (458,036b)
Conner Eldridge (D)	36.2 (55.9b)	400,602 (580,973b)
Frank Gilbert (L)	4.0 (—)	43,866 (—)
US House of Representatives		
First District		
Rick Crawford (R)[a]	76.3 (56.2)	183,866 (138,800)
(no candidate) (D)	— (39.1)	— (96,601)
Mark West (L)	23.7 (2.6)	57,181 (6,427)
Second District		
French Hill (R)[a]	58.3 (55.2)	176,472 (158,175)
Dianne Curry (D)	36.8 (39.5)	111,347 (113,156)
Chris Hayes (L)	4. 7 (2.3)	14,342 (6,701)
Third District		
Steve Womack (R)[a]	77.3 (75.9)	217, 192 (186,467)
Steve Isaacson (L)	22.7 (8.1)	63, 715 (19,875)
Fourth District		
Bruce Westerman (R)[a]	74.9 (59.5)	182,885 (154,149)
(no candidate) (D)	— (36.7)	— (95,013)
Kerry Hicks (L)	25.1 (1.9)	61,274 (4,984)

Source: Arkansas Secretary of State, https://goo.gl/9FP9O5.

[a]Incumbent.

[b]Totals for 2004, the last time Arkansas hosted a competitive US Senate race in the same year as the presidential contest.

Table 8.4. Republican Vote in Arkansas by County, 2008, 2012, and 2016

County	2008	2012	2016	Change 2012–16	Change 2008–12	Change 2008–16	Black pop., 2010
Arkansas	60.0	60.0	61.6	1.6	0.0	1.6	24.5
Ashley	62.3	61.4	66.0	4.6	−0.9	4.6	27.8
Baxter	64.3	70.8	74.3	3.5	6.5	3.5	0.3
Benton	67.2	69.0	62.9	−6.1	1.8	−6.1	1.1
Boone	68.3	72.5	75.9	3.4	4.2	3.4	0.3
Bradley	56.1	58.4	59.2	0.8	2.3	0.8	28.2
Calhoun	65.9	67.1	68.6	1.5	1.2	1.5	23.2
Carroll	57.5	60.2	63.1	2.9	2.7	2.9	0.3
Chicot	40.3	38.3	41.1	2.8	−2.0	2.8	53.9
Clark	50.7	51.7	51.7	0.0	1.0	0.0	22.3
Clay	55.0	63.1	63.0	−0.1	8.1	−0.1	0.3
Cleburne	70.2	74.6	78.3	3.7	4.4	3.7	0.5
Cleveland	69.9	70.8	73.4	2.6	0.9	2.6	13.5
Columbia	61.1	61.2	61.4	0.2	0.2	0.2	36.6
Conway	57.6	58.4	61.2	2.8	0.8	2.8	12.5
Craighead	61.0	64.2	64.4	0.2	3.2	0.2	9.7
Crawford	71.5	73.6	74.3	0.7	2.1	0.7	1.1
Crittenden	41.9	41.9	43.7	1.8	0.0	1.8	49.4
Cross	61.6	63.9	66.7	2.8	2.3	2.8	23.4
Dallas	53.0	54.0	54.4	0.4	1.0	0.4	40.7
Desha	43.3	42.9	45.0	2.1	−0.4	2.1	46.8
Drew	58.4	58.6	60.2	1.6	0.2	1.6	27.5
Faulkner	62.9	64.5	61.8	−2.7	2.6	−2.7	9.3
Franklin	68.1	70.8	74.4	3.6	2.7	3.6	0.7
Fulton	57.8	65.2	72.7	7.5	7.4	7.5	0.3
Garland	61.2	63.9	64.0	0.1	2.7	0.1	7.9
Grant	73.9	74.5	74.7	0.2	0.6	0.2	3.1
Greene	63.0	65.9 ·	73.5	7.6	2.9	7.6	0.3
Hempstead	58.1	61.9	62.5	0.6	3.8	0.6	29.1
Hot Spring	60.3	63.0	68.5	5.5	2.7	5.5	10.2
Howard	61.1	64.8	67.5	2.7	3.7	2.7	20.7
Independence	67.1	70.4	73.0	2.6	3.3	2.6	2.1
Izard	61.2	67.7	74.2	6.5	6.5	6.5	1.5
Jackson	55.9	57.5	63.3	5.8	1.6	5.8	19.4
Jefferson	36.0	34.8	35.7	0.9	−1.2	0.9	51.9
Johnson	60.1	62.5	66.8	4.3	2.4	4.3	1.8
Lafayette	58.1	58.5	61.5	3.0	0.4	3.0	36.1
Lawrence	57.6	63.8	71.5	7.7	6.2	7.7	0.7
Lee	38.7	37.4	40.7	3.3	−1.3	3.3	57.2
Lincoln	57.1	59.0	64.2	5.2	1.9	5.2	32.9
Little River	63.0	67.0	68.3	1.3	4.0	1.3	21.2
Logan	67.7	69.3	72.5	3.2	1.6	3.2	1.3
Lonoke	72.7	74.2	73.7	−0.5	1.5	−0.5	6.5

Table 8.4. (continued)

County	2008	2012	2016	Change 2012–16	Change 2008–12	Change 2008–16	Black pop., 2010
Madison	62.8	64.9	72.0	7.1	2.1	7.1	0.2
Marion	63.2	67.7	74.9	7.2	4.5	7.2	0.3
Miller	65.8	69.3	70.2	0.9	3.5	0.9	23.4
Mississippi	49.9	49.4	53.4	4.0	−0.5	4.0	34.1
Monroe	50.9	49.1	50.4	1.3	−1.8	1.3	39.3
Montgomery	**65.3**	**69.9**	**74.1**	**4.2**	**4.6**	**4.2**	**0.6**
Nevada	56.7	59.0	61.7	2.7	2.3	2.7	32.7
Newton	67.0	68.5	76.6	8.1	1.5	8.1	0.2
Ouachita	**53.9**	**53.5**	**53.9**	**0.4**	**−0.4**	**0.4**	**40.2**
Perry	**64.2**	**65.5**	**69.9**	**4.4**	**1.3**	**4.4**	**2.0**
Phillips	34.5	32.8	35.2	2.4	−1.7	2.4	61.4
Pike	**68.8**	**75.2**	**79.1**	**3.9**	**6.4**	**3.9**	**3.9**
Poinsett	**61.8**	**65.8**	**59.1**	**−6.7**	**4.0**	**−6.7**	**7.4**
Polk	71.3	77.0	80.4	3.4	5.7	3.4	0.3
Pope	70.9	72.2	72.1	−0.1	1.3	−0.1	3.0
Prairie	**65.8**	**68.6**	**72.8**	**4.2**	**2.8**	**4.2**	**14.5**
Pulaski	43.5	43.3	38.4	−4.9	−0.2	−4.9	34.0
Randolph	**57.2**	**62.1**	**70.7**	**8.6**	**4.9**	**8.6**	**1.2**
Saline	69.4	70.0	68.2	−1.8	0.6	−1.8	50.5
Scott	**69.9**	**72.3**	**78.3**	**6.0**	**2.4**	**6.0**	**3.2**
Searcy	70.9	73.1	79.3	6.2	2.2	6.2	0.5
Sebastian	66.3	67.3	65.2	−2.1	1.0	−2.1	0.2
Sevier	68.3	72.4	71.8	−0.6	3.9	−0.6	6.3
Sharp	62.5	67.6	74.6	7.0	5.1	7.0	4.4
St. Francis	41.7	40.3	43.0	2.7	−1.4	2.7	0.9
Stone	**66.4**	**70.5**	**73.3**	**2.8**	**4.1**	**2.8**	**0.3**
Union	62.2	62.3	62.1	−0.2	0.1	−0.2	33.0
Van Buren	63.8	67.9	75.6	7.7	4.1	7.7	0.5
Washington	55.5	56.3	50.8	−5.5	0.8	−5.5	2.7
White	**72.2**	**75.5**	**75.3**	**−0.2**	**3.3**	**−0.2**	**4.0**
Woodruff	43.7	49.9	52.4	2.5	6.2	2.5	28.7
Yell	**63.1**	**67.7**	**71.6**	**3.9**	**4.6**	**3.9**	**1.5**
Avg. (all counties)	60.1	62.6	64.8	2.4	2.3	4.7	na
Avg. (RSC)	**62.6**	**65.7**	**69.0**	**3.3**	**3.1**	**6.3**	**na**
Statewide vote	58.7	60.6	60.6	0.0	−1.9	1.9	na

Source: Data compiled by the authors from the official website of the Arkansas Secretary of State, https://goo.gl/9FP9O5. See also US Bureau of the Census's American FactFinder, https://goo.gl/IzIVZU.

Note: All table entries are percentages. Boldface denotes Blair's "rural swing counties" (RSC).

Ethnicity, Income, and Age

The multiethnic coalition that brought President Obama to power nationally is not of sufficient size to wield influence in Arkansas's statewide elections. Black voters, the largest state's largest minority group, compose only about 10 percent of the electorate (and just under 16 percent of the population), and the Latino presence remains small. The support of 60 percent or more awarded to Trump by the whites who dominate the state's demographic landscape consequently wins the day. The patterns again proved equally predictable with respect to income and age, with Clinton trailing Trump in nearly every category except the very poor.

Gender

The election of 2016 nationwide put a spotlight on the strong support of white women for the GOP candidate. This was strongly evident in Arkansas, with more than two-thirds of those voters selecting Trump, barely outpacing his support among white males. This marked a reversal of 2012 with respect to the state's gender gap, which usually matches or approaches the gap recorded nationally. For example, in 2012, Arkansas men of all ethnicities had preferred Romney over Obama by 12 points more than Arkansas women of all ethnicities. In 2016, the gender gap collapsed.

Other Social and Demographic Factors

Support for Trump was robust among the three-quarters of Arkansans who consider themselves born-again or evangelical Christians; as in 2012, nearly two-thirds of this group reported support for the Republican. With respect to educational attainment, although not all analyses are shown in the interest of space, Trump earned strong support among likely voters at nearly every level. His support fell considerably as attainment rose (from, for example, 66 percent among those with "some college" to 50 percent of those with a graduate degree), but his support still outpaced Clinton's. The marriage gap remained as significant in Arkansas as elsewhere, with two-thirds of married respondents preferring the Republican candidate but just 40 percent of singles preferring him.

Political Factors

Partisanship

In just three election cycles (2010, 2012, and 2014), Arkansas voters appear finally to have experienced the partisan realignment most of their southern peers experienced decades earlier. As in 2012, however, the shift remained subtle at the individual level. In the last decade, the proportion of Arkansas Poll respondents identifying as either generically Democrat or generically Republican has not much changed save a modest, but relatively steady, contraction in the size of the Democratic share. The more important change has been among the state's always-robust proportion of self-identified independents who in 2010 took a hard right turn and have not looked back.[35] This has bearing on the party identification data featured in table 8.5. As in 2012, Arkansas's partisans voted for their party's nominee at rates consistent with those seen nationwide. Partisan defectors, even in an unusual election cycle, were few.

Issues

With respect to specific issues, the economy once again proved to be the "most pressing issue or problem in Arkansas today" among Arkansas Poll respondents, and Trump earned the strong support of this group. The former First Lady, who spearheaded significant education reform in the state in the 1980s, was the choice only among those for whom education was of greatest significance.

Turnout

Turnout among registered Arkansas voters statewide was about as predicted at 64.7 percent (see table 8.6). The distribution of this participation, however, merits attention. About half of the state's total population (see table 8.7) remains concentrated into just ten counties. As in elections past, turnout and vote preference varied in these ten. The booming suburban communities of Saline and Benton Counties, for example, not only exceeded the statewide turnout average by 6 and 3 percentage points, respectively, but again posted healthier-than-average margins for the Republican nominee. (Indeed, the Saline County vote spread was 69 to 25; in high-growth White County, it was 75 to 19.) Heavily African American Jefferson County, in contrast, again threw its still-substantial

Table 8.5. Poll Results of Arkansas Voters, 2016

Characteristic	Trump	Clinton	GOP 2012
Party identification			
Democrat	10	89	13
Republican	94	4	96
Independent	62	29	67
Most important problem*			
Economy	65	31	65
Education	46	48	40
Health care	54	41	47
Crime	51	47	—
Taxes	72	28	57
Politicians	67	28	—
White evangelical / born again			
Yes	65	32	65
No	48	48	55
Gender			
Men	60	33	71
Women	59	39	59
White men	64	29	71
White women	67	31	62
Race			
White	65	30	66
Black	4	96	3
Age			
18–29 years	56	28	44
30–44 years	61	37	61
45–64 years	60	34	61
65+ years	60	38	60
Income			
Under $7,500	45	48	28
$7,501–$15,000	56	41	42
$15,001–$25,000	60	38	57
$25,001–$35,000	55	39	56
$35,001–$50,000	67	30	65
$50,001–$75,000	52	42	65
$75,001–$100,000	60	32	58
$100,001 or more	72	26	77
Size of community			
Urban	42	54	57
Suburban	66	26	63
Small town	65	31	58
Rural	67	30	61
Vote for medical marijuana			
Yes	52	45	50
No	67	27	77

Source: The Arkansas Poll, 2016, accessed November 8, 2016, https://goo.gl/DzpIrN.

Note: All table entries are percentages.

*The Arkansas Poll allows respondents to direct the "most important problem" categories, so comparability is lost between years on some issues.

Table 8.6. General Election Voter Turnout in Arkansas, 1972–2016

Year	Turnout (%) of reg. voters
1972	69 (g)
1976	71 (g)
1980	77 (g)
1984	76 (g)
1988	69 (p)
1992	72 (p)
1996	65 (p)
2000	59 (p)
2004	64 (p)
2008	65 (p)
2012	67 (p)
2016	65 (p)

Source: Data compiled from the official website of the Arkansas Secretary of State and from various volumes of *America Votes* (Washington, DC: Congressional Quarterly).

Note: Voter turnout figures are based on gubernatorial voting (g) or presidential voting (p) depending on the highest turnout race of the year. After shifting from two- to four-year terms in 1986, Arkansas gubernatorial elections are no longer held in presidential years.

weight to the Democrat but suffered a post-Obama decline in turnout, rendering its preferences irrelevant in Arkansas's rising Republican tide.

Other Election Races

Down the ballot, this increasingly baked-in Republicanism was shown in two ways: the absence of high-quality Democratic challengers to engage in contests with Republican incumbents, and the strong support in the handful of elections that were contested. The highest profile of those races was Sen. John Boozman's reelection to his second term in the US Senate. Former federal prosecutor Conner Eldridge, in his first race for elective office, was never able to gain traction against Boozman aside from national attention that came from his cutting-edge attack on Boozman in May 2016 for his support of Trump. In a web ad that received national play, the Eldridge campaign strung together a litany of Trump's crude comments regarding women and charged Boozman with standing idly by in allowing the "sexual harasser" to become his party's standard bearer.[36] Following the release of the *Access Hollywood* tape

Table 8.7. Registered-Voter Turnout and Presidential Vote in the Ten Most Populous Arkansas Counties, 2016

County	Total pop., 2010 (2000)	% pop. change, 2000–2010 (1990–2000)	% turnout, 2016 (2012)	% Rep. vote, 2016 (2012)	% Dem. vote, 2016 (2012)
Pulaski	373,911 (361,474)	3.4 (3.4)	65.5 (67.5)	38.3 (43.3)	56.1 (54.8)
Benton	203,107 (153,406)	50.0 (57.3)	67.8 (68.7)	62.9 (69.0)	28.9 (28.6)
Washington	191,292 (157,715)	21.3 (39.1)	64.0 (66.2)	50.7 (56.3)	40.8 (40.1)
Sebastian	121,766 (115,071)	5.8 (15.5)	60.9 (63.8)	65.3 (67.3)	27.6 (30.2)
Faulkner	104,865 (86,014)	21.9 (43.3)	64.2 (61.8)	61.8 (64.5)	30.8 (32.9)
Garland	96,371 (88,068)	9.4 (20.0)	63.1 (65.5)	63.9 (63.9)	30.2 (33.9)
Saline	96,212 (83,529)	15.5 (30.1)	70.5 (71.3)	68.8 (70.0)	25.4 (27.3)
Craighead	91,552 (82,148)	11.4 (19.1)	60.4 (57.0)	64.4 (64.2)	29.6 (33.2)
Jefferson	78,986 (84,278)	−6.3 (−1.4)	61.5 (69.0)	35.7 (34.8)	60.9 (63.8)
White	73,441 (67,410)	8.9 (22.6)	65.7 (56.8)	75.3 (75.5)	18.5 (21.7)

Source: Data compiled from the US Bureau of the Census and the official website of the Arkansas Secretary of State.

in the fall, Eldridge returned to this line of attack but was never able to establish his own identity in the race against the mild-mannered—and still relatively unknown—senior senator.

In three of the state's four congressional districts, Arkansas Democrats were unable to even field an opponent to GOP incumbents (a breathtaking reversal of the events of 2008), leaving only Libertarian candidates to contest the races. Dianne Curry did carry the Democrat banner in the state's Second Congressional District but was swamped in the suburban counties around Little Rock, winning only a slight majority in Pulaski County—home of both herself and incumbent French Hill.

Finally, at the state legislative level, Republicans swept almost all contested races, moving them close to supermajority status (75 percent) in each house of the general assembly. A series of party switches in the state house following the election allowed Republicans to surge above that threshold as they went into the 2017 legislative session, sealing the GOP's unprecedented dominance of state government.

Still, as is normal, Arkansas's voters again showed contradictory behavior as they voted on a medical marijuana amendment to the state's constitution (a competing act was struck from the ballot only weeks before the election by the Arkansas Supreme Court). While voting for a host of socially conservative candidates at every level of government, voters solidly supported the legalization of the medical use of marijuana. Voters in counties where Trump did worst in the state—those with higher percentages of nonwhite voters and those with higher levels of well-educated voters—were strongest in their support of the measure, but—as shown in table 8.5—even a slight majority of Trump voters in the state supported allowing individuals with a series of medical conditions access to regulated marijuana.

Conclusion

The 2016 election—a Republican rout up and down the ballot—sealed the tomb of a southern Democratic Party that until 2010 had managed not only to remain competitive but indeed to dominate state elections. As the rural swing counties veered right and stayed there in 2010, 2012, and 2014, Arkansas Democrats found themselves where their Republican counterparts had spent more than a century: so maligned they could not even field high-quality candidates to contest most races. Although a handful of Democratic Pollyannas, mostly from outside the state, speculated that the national Democrats' nomination of a quasi-hometown girl would put the state's Electoral College votes back up for grabs, it did not come to pass. Instead, the Republican standard-bearer—Donald Trump—stimulated another large increase in Republican primary participation and then played a central role in maintaining the rightward tilt of the state's large proportion of independents. Outside of a smattering of local races in a handful of urban and diverse counties, Arkansas Democrats are in for some lean years.

9

Florida

Old South Electoral Strategy Trumps the Newest Southern Politics

Jonathan Knuckey and Aubrey Jewett

The 2016 presidential election once more reaffirmed Florida as the ultimate bellwether state. The Sunshine State has now also picked the national winner in the prior six presidential elections, a feat matched only by Ohio. Indeed, since World War II, Florida has only failed to pick the national winner twice, in 1960 and 1992. Donald Trump's narrow victory over Hillary Clinton—by a little more than a single percentage point—also meant that Florida was the most competitive southern state in 2016. Nationally, Florida ranked behind only Wisconsin, Michigan, New Hampshire, and Pennsylvania in terms of the winning candidate's margin of victory. Most conventional wisdom suggested that, while plausible paths existed for Clinton to accumulate 270 Electoral College votes without Florida, a victory there would cut off Trump's ability to win an Electoral College majority. To that end, it is unsurprising that both campaigns devoted more resources to Florida, in terms of both campaign expenditure and visits by the presidential and vice presidential candidates, than to any other state in 2016.

Florida also featured prominently during the presidential primary season in 2016. Hillary Clinton's overwhelming victory over Bernie Sanders helped strengthen her grip on the Democratic presidential nomination. On the Republican side, two favorite-son candidates, former governor Jeb Bush and US senator Marco Rubio, were considered to be serious candidates for the GOP nomination. Bush's candidacy, however, failed to even survive until his home-state primary, while Trump's convincing victory in the primary was responsible for Rubio's departure from the race. Rubio, however, would return to run for the US Senate seat he had planned to vacate in an effort to secure the Republican majority in the US Senate, ultimately winning a closely fought election in which he prevailed over the Democratic nominee, Rep. Patrick Murphy. And while Florida Democrats picked up a handful of congressional and state legislative seats, the congressional delegation and Florida House of Representatives and Senate remained under firm GOP control.

This chapter places the 2016 election in Florida in the context of a series of presidential elections dating back to 1992 that saw the Sunshine State evolve from a Republican stronghold at the presidential level to the mostly hotly contested swing state.[1] Not since 1996 has the winning candidate in Florida won by more than 5 percentage points, when Bill Clinton carried the state by 5.7 percentage points. Moreover, on only two occasions since 1996 has the winning candidate won with over 50 percent of the vote. George W. Bush won 52 percent in 2004, and Barack Obama won 51 percent in 2008. Indeed, since 1996, the average margin of victory in Florida for the presidential winner was about 2.9 percentage points; the next closest was Ohio with 3.9 percentage points. To place Florida's competitiveness in presidential elections in perspective, the average margin of victory for the winner (the average of state averages, including Washington, DC) over that same span was 16.1 percentage points. Following the close 2016 election, the average margin of victory in Florida has now dropped to 2.6 percent, compared to 4.7 percent for Ohio.

Despite the closeness of recent presidential elections in Florida, and despite opinion polls persistently characterizing Florida as a toss-up state, Trump's victory over Clinton might still be considered something of an upset. After all, Trump's anti-immigration rhetoric, beginning on the day he announced his candidacy for the presidency when he referred to Mexican immigrants as "rapists,"[2] seemed destined to mobilize Latinos in the state against him, meaning that he would need an even larger share of the white vote than Mitt Romney had received in 2012. Indeed, there was a surge in Latino voter registration in Florida.[3] However, Trump's counter-mobilization of the white electorate, especially in exurban and rural areas of Florida, ultimately enabled him to eke out a narrow victory. The ability to replicate Trump's winning formula in future elections, however, will be tempered by long-term demographic change in Florida that is still likely to favor the Democratic Party. Ultimately, the 2016 presidential election in Florida might be viewed as the last gasp of an Old South electoral strategy—appealing almost exclusively to a white electoral base—as opposed to one in which the Republican Party appeals to the diversity and pluralism that now defines Florida's electorate, making it the leading exemplar of the "Newest" South.

Political Context

Party Registration

Figure 9.1 displays party registration over time in Florida, showing the increasing competitiveness of the state. Republicans have gained ground on Democrats since the 1970s, but Democrats have always held, and continue to hold, a small lead. Because of population growth, the number of registered voters has increased steadily, but since the 1990s, the percentage of Republicans and Democrats has actually been in slow decline, and voters registered with no party affiliation or with minor parties have soared from about 9 percent to almost 27 percent. This large and fast-growing pool of "other" voters has contributed to the competitiveness and tendency to swing in Florida elections. Barack Obama helped to mobilize Democrats in 2008 and their lead actually increased slightly for the first time in decades (to about 4.5 points). However, between 2012 and 2016, the percent of Floridians registered as Democrats declined, and Republicans held steady, so that by the time of the 2016 general election, Republicans had pulled to within 2.5 points: Democrats were at 37.9 percent; Republicans, 35.4 percent; and other affiliations, 26.7 percent. Overall, the party registration of Floridians helps to explain why recent elections for major statewide offices have been so competitive. Indeed, in the past twenty years, the winning candidate in the presidential, gubernatorial, or US Senate election received over 55 percent of the vote on only five occasions.[4]

2014 Midterm Elections: A Republican Sweep

While the 2014 gubernatorial election was competitive, Republicans dominated the 2014 midterm campaign in Florida. Republicans swept

Figure 9.1. Florida Voter Registration, 1972 to 2016

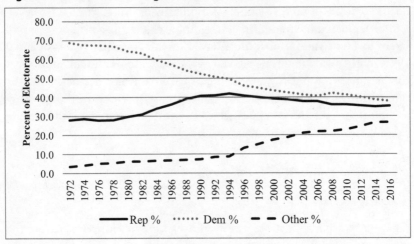

Source: "Voter Registration Statistics," Division of Elections, Florida Department of State, accessed December 21, 2016, https://goo.gl/dWKDEi.

the four statewide executive branch contests, increased their margin in the state legislature, and maintained a large lead in the congressional delegation.[5] GOP victories can generally be explained by Republicans' success in fielding more and better candidates, raising more money, and spending more money as well as depressed Democratic turnout for the off-year election in the second term of Pres. Barack Obama.

The gubernatorial election saw Gov. Rick Scott hold on for a second term, narrowly defeating former governor Charlie Crist by 48.1 to 47.1 percent. The race featured a relatively unpopular incumbent; Scott never attained 50 percent popularity in any poll during his first term, and he faced a former Republican governor who had switched party registration twice in less than four years. Used to projecting a staunchly conservative ideology, Scott had an election year conversion on a number of issues to moderate his image (higher spending for education, support for Medicaid expansion under the Affordable Care Act, and more protection for the environment), raised and spent twice as much as Crist on political advertising (including political parties and outside groups), and attacked Crist repeatedly for being a slick, flip-flopping political clone of Obama. The attacks worked and helped lower Crist's popularity below 50 percent. Moreover, many progressives expressed concerns that Crist was not really a Democrat and could not be trusted to pursue liberal policies if elected. Ultimately, the Democratic coalition that reelected Obama in

Florida failed to mobilize for Crist. Turnout among those thirty years old and younger, single white women, and minorities was lower than it had been in 2012.

While the governor's race was close, most other 2014 Sunshine State contests were not. All three GOP Cabinet officers achieved reelection by more than 55 percent: Atty. Gen. Pam Bondi, chief financial officer Jeff Atwater, and agricultural commissioner Adam Putnam. Republicans gained seven seats in the state house to take a lead of eighty-one to thirty-nine and maintained their solid advantage of twenty-six to fourteen in the state senate. The congressional delegation remained in favor of Republicans at seventeen to ten for the second election in a row, although Democrats had been behind by nineteen to six in 2010 and so could take some solace in at least consolidating the gains they made in 2012 after redistricting.

The Nomination Contests

Unlike in 2008 and 2012, when Florida held early presidential primaries in January, the 2016 presidential primary was scheduled for March 15, two weeks after the first multistate contests of Super Tuesday on March 1. While the Democratic primary utilized proportional representation for allocating delegates, as mandated by national party rules, the use of the winner-take-all method by the Republican Party meant that the winner of the Florida GOP primary would be at a great advantage in accumulating delegates. The Republican state party chairman, Blaise Ingoglia, acknowledged that this gave the Sunshine State a big say in the nomination process: "The road to the White House runs through Florida. This now confirms that the road to the Republican nomination for President will run through Florida as well."[6]

The Republican Primary: Trump Triumphs over Favorite Sons

When state Republicans set the date and winner-take-all rules for the Florida GOP presidential primary, they assumed they were enhancing the prospects of former Florida governor Jeb Bush or current US senator Marco Rubio to secure the nomination. However, Bush performed so poorly that he dropped out before the Florida primary, and when Rubio lost his home state, he suspended his campaign. Much to the chagrin of the Republican establishment and the "Never Trump" movement, Trump's strong showing in Florida entitled him to all ninety-nine delegates (this third-largest of all states was behind only Texas in the South), enhanced his status as the GOP frontrunner, increased his momentum going into the remaining contests, and began to make his nomination look almost inevitable.

Jeb Bush, a successful and popular two-term governor of Florida from 1999 to 2007, raised over $150 million dollars for his presidential primary battle, created an impressive campaign organization, received numerous endorsements from high-profile establishment Republicans, and was in first place in most poll averages calculated from January through June 2015.[7] Despite these promising early signs (highlighted frequently by his staff and designed to produce "shock and awe" in his opponents), Bush's Republican presidential primary campaign ended after a dismal fourth place finish in the South Carolina primary. Bush's poor performance can be accounted for by several factors: Bush fatigue (Republicans were simply tired of the Bush brand); his position as the establishment candidate in a cycle that favored outsiders; an overreliance on traditional media like television advertisements; his appearance as "rusty" and lacking enthusiasm on the campaign trail ("low-energy Jeb" as Trump labeled him); the failure to realize that Trump was a real threat and to formulate an effective response to his candidacy; and the impression that he was out of step or outdated in his campaign stances (especially on illegal immigration and the Common Core).[8]

Donald Trump had not only surged nationally but was also beating both Bush and Rubio in Florida polls from August 2015 onward. When Bush dropped out of the race, Rubio hoped that he would be able to take the lead away from Trump in Florida as the remaining favorite-son candidate. While Rubio did gain ground in Florida polls in late February and early March, he was never able to pull closer to Trump than 15 percentage points as Trump also surged after Jeb Bush left the race.[9] Ultimately, Trump won the Florida Republican presidential primary with 45.7 percent of the vote, and Rubio placed in a distant second at 27 percent. After losing his home state by over four hundred thousand votes, Rubio suspended his campaign. The two other major alternatives to Trump both won their respective home-state primaries. John Kasich won Ohio the same day Rubio lost Florida, and Ted Cruz won Texas two weeks earlier on Super Tuesday.

Why did Rubio do so poorly with Republicans in his home state, losing every county except Miami-Dade and nearly every demographic group except Latinos? Explanations include the following: Rubio's efforts on comprehensive immigration reform upset hard-liners who thought he was offering amnesty and reformers who blamed him for failing and giving up. He decided to retaliate with personal attacks against Donald Trump, including the infamous reference to Trump's "small hands" with the unstated, but suggestive, correlation that might have with Trump's "manhood." He was unable to distinguish himself from the large pack of establishment Republicans (including Florida's own Jeb Bush) vying to become the main alternative to Trump.[10] This was ironic because Rubio was a candidate who had been able to win a contested Republican primary for a US Senate seat from Florida in 2010 by running as an outsider, despite having held public office for more than a decade at the local and state level, including as Speaker of the Florida House of Representatives. Yet, he was viewed as part of the Republican establishment by 2016 and lost to Trump, who really was a political outsider.

The Democratic Primary: A Clinton Landslide

There was little suspense about the outcome of the Democratic primary election. Polls showed consistent leads in the state for Hillary Clinton over Bernie Sanders, with Clinton's support often recorded at over 60 percent and Sanders struggling to break 35 percent.[11] Moreover, Clinton's sweep of South Carolina and other southern states on Super Tuesday, based on overwhelming support among minorities and older voters, indicated that Florida would be favorable territory. The fact that Florida used a closed primary also prevented Sanders from using his strength among independents. Indeed, Sanders appeared to write off devoting time and campaign resources to Florida, only making his first campaign visit to the state just one week ahead of the primary, which coincided with a debate at Miami Dade College on March 9.[12]

Overall, 1.7 million votes were cast in the Democratic primary, which was approximately the same number as in 2008.[13] The result was as expected, with Clinton winning 64 percent of the vote to Sanders's 33 percent, sweeping all but nine of sixty-seven counties, all of which were sparsely populated counties in northern Florida.[14] This enabled Clinton to make a net gain of 68 pledged delegates, winning 141 to Sanders's 73. Exit polls reveal the breadth and depth of Clinton's support; she won not only a large share of the African American and Latino vote, (81 and 68 percent, respectively), but also 53 percent of the white vote. Sanders won among two groups that had been favorable toward him in previous primaries, those aged under thirty (64 to 35 percent) and white men (52 to 45 percent), although even among these groups, his margins over Clinton did not match those found in earlier contests.

The General Election

Florida seemed destined to play a pivotal role in the general election. While there appeared to be multiple paths to 270 Electoral College votes for Clinton, even without winning Florida, the conventional wisdom was that a victory in the Sunshine State would almost certainly close off any path Trump had of reaching the necessary 270 votes. Accordingly, Florida was the most visited state by both campaigns in 2016, hosting thirty-six events for the Clinton-Kaine ticket and thirty-five for the Trump-Pence ticket. In total, this was fifteen more events than there were in the next most frequently visited state, North Carolina.[15] At the same time, more campaign expenditure was devoted to Florida than any other state.[16]

The campaign in Florida, as was the case nationally, presented contrasting approaches. In the immediate post-convention period, the Clinton campaign sought to deliver a decisive blow to Trump in Florida, arguably in an effort to lock down the state early and thus make it difficult for Trump to recover. This was demonstrated by money spent on television advertising by the Clinton campaign and its allies, most notably the super PAC Priorities USA, through the middle of August, a period during which the Trump campaign had not run any commercials. Furthermore, this advantage in TV advertising was complemented by the organizational superiority of the Clinton campaign over the Trump campaign in Florida; the Clinton campaign opened fourteen offices across the state, while Trump opened just one, the campaign's state headquarters in Sarasota. By contrast, Trump placed greater emphasis on mass rallies and on his ties to a state where he considered himself a part-time resident, spending much of the time at his Mar-a-Lago estate in Palm Beach.[17]

The intense campaigning in Florida was briefly put on hiatus by the approach of Hurricane Matthew, which threatened Florida's Atlantic coast in the first week of October and made landfall on October 8. This led to the voter registration deadline being extended by one week to October 18 by a federal judge after the Florida Democratic Party filed a lawsuit requesting extra time for voters to register. Initially, Gov. Rick Scott—who also served as head of Rebuilding America Now, a pro-Trump super PAC—had refused to extend the registration period, noting that "everybody has had a lot of time to register."[18]

A major part of a campaign in Florida is mobilizing voters during the early voting period, with both campaigns essentially banking support ahead of election day. Early voting was available in Florida from October 29 to November 5, although supervisors of elections in individual counties could begin as early as October 24 and end on November 6 if they wished.[19] Around two-thirds of the total electorate voted in this early voting period. Most encouraging for the Clinton campaign was the surge in Latino early voting in comparison to 2012,[20] although it was tempered by lower rates of African American early voting than four years earlier.[21]

The final ten days of campaigning was dominated by the political bombshell dropped on October 28 by FBI director James Comey, who announced that the agency was investigating whether additional emails sent by Clinton via a private server contained classified material. On November 6, two days before the election, Comey made a second announcement that none of the new emails discovered contained any classified information, and many were, in fact, duplicates of previous emails that had been investigated.[22] Given that this late development might have swayed voters, especially in battleground states, the final week of campaigning saw the presidential and vice presidential candidates of both parties return to Florida on several occasions. Between them, Clinton and Kaine appeared in Florida over three days for seven separate campaign events. Additionally, an important surrogate for Clinton in the final push for votes was President Obama, who had already campaigned in Florida for the Democratic ticket on three occasions in October. Obama returned for two further events in the final week of the campaign, including November 6, the last day of early voting in many counties and traditionally a day that is important in efforts to mobilize African American voters. The day is known as "Souls to the Polls" because many voters visit the polls after morning church services.[23] The Republican ticket devoted more time to Florida in the final week of campaigning, perhaps realizing that it trailed, albeit narrowly, in most of the final polls of Florida. Between them, Trump and Pence spent all but one day from October 31 through the day before the election campaigning in Florida.

Despite the attention lavished upon Florida, and despite a series of campaign events that all had the potential to change the dynamics of the race in the swing state—including the presidential debates, questions about Clinton's health when she was suffering from pneumonia, Trump's lewd remarks about women and subsequent allegations of his behavior toward women, and the FBI intervention—polls continued to show stability in the race. Indeed, as shown in table 9.1, the final poll average showed that the race had ended largely where it had started: a narrow Clinton lead. Florida—once more—appeared too close to call.

Table 9.1. Florida Presidential Election Polls, January–November 2016

Month	Clinton	Trump	Clinton margin
January	43.5	42.7	0.8
February	43.8	42.0	1.8
March	43.8	41.7	2.1
April	44.0	41.2	2.8
May	44.1	41.0	3.1
June	43.0	39.6	3.4
July	43.3	40.5	2.8
August	44.5	41.7	2.8
September	45.1	43.2	1.9
October	46.0	42.5	3.5
November	46.8	45.0	1.8

Source: HuffPost Pollster, "2016 Florida President: Trump vs. Clinton," *Huffington Post*, accessed 21 Dec 2016, https://goo.gl/uXGeaC.

Note: All table entries are percentages. Monthly percentages, except for November, are the poll average on the first day of each month. November data are from the final poll average taken on November 7.

Results and Analysis

As table 9.2 shows, Trump carried Florida's twenty-nine Electoral College votes, winning 4,617,886 votes (48.6 percent) to Clinton's 4,504,975 (47.4 percent). Trump received 1 percent less than Mitt Romney had in 2012, while Clinton's vote was down by just over 2 percent from that of Barack Obama. Only the 2000 and 2012 elections had closer percentage margins of victory than the 2016 election's 1.2 percent. Moreover, Florida delivered the closest result of any southern state in 2016, and nationally it ranked as the fifth-closest state in terms of percentage victory margin, behind Michigan, New Hampshire, Wisconsin and Pennsylvania. For the sixth consecutive election, Florida voted for the winning presidential candidate. Despite preelection predictions to the contrary, Florida did not ultimately prove to be the decisive state in the outcome of the election, because of Trump's victories in the Rust Belt states of Michigan, Ohio, Pennsylvania, and Wisconsin.

Florida voter turnout based on the voting-eligible population was 65.6 percent, which was an increase from 2012 of a little over a 2 percent but a drop from the 67.1 percent turnout in 2008.[24] Overall, over

Table 9.2. Results of 2016 Florida Presidential, US Senate, and Selected US House Elections

Candidate (party)	Vote (%)	Votes (#)
President		
Donald Trump / Mike Pence (R)	48.6	4,617,886
Hillary Clinton / Tim Kaine (D)	47.4	4,504,975
Gary Johnson / Bill Weld (L)	2.2	207,043
Jill Stein / Ajamu Baraka (G)	0.7	64,399
Other candidates and write-ins	0.3	107,314
Total		950,1617
US Senate		
Marco Rubio (R)*	52.0	4,835,191
Patrick Murphy (D)	44.3	4,122,088
Paul Stanton (L)	2.1	196,956
Others	1.6	147,585
Total		9,301,820
US House of Representatives		
First District		
Matt Gaetz (R)	69.1	255,107
Steven Specht (D)	30.9	114,079
Total		369,186
Second District		
Neal Dunn (R)	67.3	231,163
Walter Dartland (D)	29.9	102,801
Total		343,362
Fourth District		
John Rutherford (R)	70.2	287,509
David E. Bruderly (D)	27.6	113,088
Total		409,662
Fifth District		
Al Lawson (D)	64.2	194,549
Glo Smith (R)	35.8	108,325
Total		302,874
Seventh District		
Stephanie Murphy (D)	51.5	182,039
John Mica (R)*	48.5	171,583
Total		353,655
Ninth District		
Darren Soto (D)	57.5	195,311
Wayne Liebnitzky (R)	42.5	144,450
Total		339,761

Table 9.2. (continued)

Candidate (party)	Vote (%)	Votes (#)
Tenth District		
Val Demings (D)	64.9	198,491
Thuy Lowe (R)	35.1	107,498
Total		305,989
Thirteenth District		
Charlie Crist (D)	51.9	184,693
David Jolly (R)*	48.1	171,149
Total		355,842
Eighteenth District		
Brian Mast (R)	53.6	201,488
Randy Perkins (D)	43.1	161,918
Total		375,918
Nineteenth District		
Francis Rooney (R)	65.9	239,225
Robert Neeld (D)	34.1	123,812
Total		363,166
Twenty-Sixth District		
Carlos Curbelo (R)*	53.0	148,547
Joe Garcia (D)	41.2	115,493
Total		280,542
Twenty-Seventh District		
Ileana Ros-Lehtinen (R)*	54.9	157,917
Scott Fuhrman (D)	45.1	129,760
Total		287,677

Source: "Florida Election Watch," Division of Elections, Florida Department of State, accessed December 21, 2016, https://goo.gl/MK1lir.

Note: Minor-party candidate votes are excluded from US House election results. R = Republican Party; D = Democratic Party; L = Libertarian Party; G = Green Party. Congressional results are for districts that were open-seat contests, for those in which the incumbent was defeated, and for those in which the winning incumbent received less than 55 percent.

*Incumbent.

9.5 million votes were cast in Florida, an 11.2 percent increase in total votes cast from 2012. This was the second largest percentage increase, behind Arizona, in votes cast of any battleground state, and among all states only Texas and Oregon had a higher percentage increase.[25] If the presidential election result was somewhat unexpected, it was not attributable to the failure of Democrats to turn out. Clinton actually won more votes in 2016 than Obama had in 2012, posting an increase of 6.3

percent in the total Democratic vote cast. However, Trump increased the Republican votes cast by 10.9 percent from the number received by Romney in 2012.

The geographic patterns evident in the county-by-county vote comported to a now familiar pattern evident in statewide elections.[26] There was an almost perfect relationship between the vote for Trump in 2016 and the vote for Romney in 2012 (Pearson r = .97), suggesting that Trump's victory was the result of overperforming in traditionally Republican counties rather than making substantial inroads into support in Democratic strongholds. Indeed, just four of Florida's sixty-seven counties that were carried by Obama in 2012 switched to Trump in 2016: Indian River, Jefferson, Monroe, and Pinellas. However, counties moved in a different partisan direction relative to 2012. A pro-Trump movement was evident in forty-eight counties, and in nineteen of these counties, the increase in the vote for Trump exceeded 5 percent. However, in nineteen other counties, Trump's support was lower than that received by Romney in 2012, although in none of these counties was the decline in the vote for Trump greater than 5 percent.[27]

Election outcomes in Florida are frequently decided by the seven "mega" counties, the most populous counties, which account for almost half of the statewide electorate. Table 9.3 shows how these counties have moved toward the Democrats over the past twenty years. Indeed, in 2016, Clinton was largely successful in mobilizing the Democratic vote in these counties. Although she received a slightly lower vote percentage across these counties (57.9 percent) in comparison to Obama in 2012 (58.2 percent), the larger number of votes cast in 2016 yielded a larger net advantage in total votes for Clinton. She actually had a larger percentage lead in Miami-Dade and Orange Counties, the latter registering the largest pro-Democratic movement of any county in Florida compared to 2012. Clinton also ran closer to Trump than Obama did to Romney in Duval County, historically the most Republican of the seven most populous counties. Only Pinellas County switched party columns, as a 5 percent Obama victory in 2012 was overturned into a 1 percent Trump victory in 2016. Overall, from an analysis of the mega counties, it is easy to understand why Democrats were initially optimistic about carrying Florida.

However, Trump was able to offset Clinton's large vote advantage from these counties in the rest of the state. Outside of the mega counties, Trump garnered a 961,934-vote advantage over Clinton, over 300,000 votes more than Romney's advantage over Obama in 2012. While the

Table 9.3. Partisan Change in Florida's Seven "Mega" Counties in Presidential Elections, 1996–2016

	1996	2000	2004	2008	2012	2016
	Winning party and margin of victory (%)					
County						
Miami-Dade	D +19	D +7	D +6	D +16	D +24	D +29
Broward	D +35	D +36	D +35	D +35	D +35	D +35
Palm Beach	D +24	D +27	D +21	D +23	D +17	D +15
Hillsborough	D +3	R +3	R +7	D +7	D +7	D +7
Pinellas	D +9	D +4	R +0.1	D +8	D +5	R +1
Orange	R +0.2	D +2	D +0.2	D +19	D +19	D + 24
Duval	R +6	R +16	R +16	R +2	R +3	R +1
	Totals for seven counties					
Avg. Dem. vote (%)	54.8	54.6	53.4	58.1	58.2	57.9
Net Dem. vote advantage (#)	+407,652	+331,928	+281,400	+682,524	+707,248	+849,023
Share (%) of total statewide votes cast	49.5	49.3	48.8	48.2	48.5	48.2

Note: Cell entries show the winning party and the percentage-point margin of victory.

Source: Compiled by the authors from data obtained from "Florida Election Watch," Division of Elections, Florida Department of State, accessed December 21, 2016, https://goo.gl/XKdB7N.

divide between urban Florida and the rest of the state represents a pre-existing cleavage underlying party support, it was one that grew wider in 2016 and ultimately delivered a narrow victory to Trump.

Exit Poll Analysis: Demographic and Political Characteristics

Table 9.4 displays the 2016 and 2012 Florida exit poll results for a variety of demographic and political characteristics, allowing for an understanding at the individual level of how a narrow Democratic victory in 2012 became a narrow Republican victory in 2016.[28] Compared to 2012, the 2016 Florida electorate was more male, slightly younger, less white, a little more educated, somewhat wealthier, less religious, less Democratic, and less moderate. And overall in 2016, Trump beat Clinton among voters who were male, middle-aged or older, white Anglo, Cuban, college attendees or graduates, middle- or upper-income, Republican or independent, and conservative and among those who made their decision in the last week of the election.

Table 9.4. Florida Presidential Exit Poll Results: Demographic and Political Characteristics

Category	2016			2012		
	Electorate	Clinton	Trump	Electorate	Obama	Romney
Gender						
Men	47	43	52	45	46	52
Women	53	50	46	55	53	46
Age						
18–29 years	17	54	36	16	66	32
30–44 years	23	54	39	23	52	46
45–64 years	38	43	56	37	48	52
65+ years	21	40	57	24	41	58
Race						
White (non-Latino)	62	32	64	67	37	61
African American	14	84	8	13	95	4
Latino	18	62	35	17	60	39
Race and Gender						
White men	29	28	67	30	33	65
White women	33	36	60	37	41	58
African American men	6	81	10	6	94	5
African American women	8	87	6	8	96	4
Latino men	8	60	36	7	58	40
Latino women	10	63	34	9	61	38
Ethnicity						
Cuban	6	41	54	6	49	47
Non-Cuban Latino	10	71	26	9	66	34
Education						
High school or less	18	51	46	22	55	44
Some college	30	45	49	30	49	50
College degree	36	42	54	32	46	52
Postgrad. degree	16	56	39	16	53	46
Income						
Under $30,000	20	56	38	21	61	37
$30,000–$49,999	19	51	46	25	57	43
$50,000–$99,999	32	45	52	31	44	54
$100,000–$199,999	21	42	54	16	45	55
Religion						
Protestant or other Christian	49	38	60	51	42	58
Catholic	25	44	54	23	47	52
Jewish	4	—	—	5	66	30
Another religion	6	64	34	6	68	28
No religion	17	58	32	15	72	26

Table 9.4. (continued)

Category	2016			2012		
	Electorate	Clinton	Trump	Electorate	Obama	Romney
Geography (Urbanism)						
Urban	46	53	41	27	56	44
Suburban	45	43	53	60	51	48
Rural	9	36	61	13	35	64
Party						
Democrats	32	90	8	35	90	9
Republicans	33	8	89	33	8	92
Independents	34	43	47	33	50	47
Ideology						
Liberal	25	81	14	22	86	13
Moderate	38	51	43	43	53	46
Conservative	36	17	79	35	20	78
Timing of vote decision						
Within the last week	11	38	55	8	57	43
Before that	88	49	48	89	52	47

Sources: "2016 Florida President Exit Poll," Fox News, accessed December 21, 2016, https://goo.gl/zDbbxa; "2016 Florida Exit Poll," CNN, accessed December 21, 2016, https://goo.gl/Nxvt2L; "2012 Florida President Exit Poll," CNN, accessed December 21, 2016, https://goo.gl/TwNnFp.

Note: All table entries are percentages.

Florida voters exhibited a gender gap in 2016, with men being more likely to vote for Trump and women more likely to vote for Clinton. However, compared to 2012, men made up 2 percent more of the electorate in 2016 (47 percent in 2016 to 45 percent in 2012). Further, the gender gap favored Trump in 2016 rather than Obama, as it had in 2012. Trump had a 9-point lead among men and only lost the vote of women by 4 points (in 2012 Obama had lost men by 6 points but had won women by 7 points). And when looking at race and gender, Trump won white men by almost 40 points (by 67 to 28 percent) and white women by 24 points (by 60 to 36 percent), improving on Romney's edge by 7 points among both groups. Thus, Trump's behavior towards, and comments about, women evidently had no effect in spurring a larger female turnout in opposition to his candidacy.

The 2016 Florida electorate was a little younger than the 2012 electorate. Senior voters were down about 3 percentage points, and Trump won the sixty-five-and-older vote by the same margin as Romney had in 2012: 17 points. While younger voters aged eighteen to twenty-nine made up 1 percent more of the electorate, Clinton did 12 points worse than Obama had among this group, Trump did 3 points better than Romney had, and a much higher percentage of younger voters went for a third-party candidate or did not vote for president. There was little change in the size of the electorate between thirty and sixty-four years old or in their voting preferences. Overall, Clinton could not take advantage of the fact that the Florida electorate actually skewed younger because many younger voters chose third parties (7 percent) or no candidate at all (3 percent) rather than support the Democratic nominee.

Florida voters were more racially and ethnically diverse in 2016 than they had been in 2012, with white non-Latinos making up 62 percent (a drop of 5 points) and African Americans and Latinos making up 14 and 18 percent, respectively (an increase of 1 percent for both groups). However, Trump won white voters by 32 points (up from 24 points in 2012) and lost the African American vote by a smaller margin than Romney had in 2012. Trump won 8 percent of African American voters (doubling Romney's total against Obama). Clinton carried the Latino vote by a larger margin than Obama had (winning by 27 points to Obama's 21 points). However, even among this demographic, Trump did slightly better than preelection polls of Florida Latino voters suggested he would.[29] Trump actually won the Cuban vote in Florida by a wide margin (54 to 41 percent), whereas in 2012, Obama had won the Cuban vote by 2 percent. Ominously for the GOP, however, Trump lost the non-Cuban vote by a margin of 71 to 26 percent, which is an 8-point drop from Romney's percentage in 2012. In summary, Trump won a larger share of the diminishing white Florida electorate and did marginally better among African Americans, and that was just enough to offset his losses in the growing Latino community.

Trump's larger victory among whites has several possible explanations. Trump's rhetoric against illegal immigrants and Islamic terrorists and in support of the police and "America First" economic nationalism can be viewed as an effort to appeal to white voters. Furthermore, it has been argued that, during the Obama presidency, there was a "racial spillover" effect priming white racial attitudes for any policy, attitude, or political figure associated with President Obama.[30] Given that Hillary Clinton closely associated herself with Obama, and given Obama's enthusiastic campaigning for her, racial resentment may loom large in explaining why Trump was able to win the largest share of the white vote in a presidential election in Florida since 1988.[31]

Trump's better showing among African Americans probably occurred as a confluence of two factors. First, a decline in support was likely for any white Democratic candidate, given the increase in the level of support given to the first African American president. Thus, this likely was a reversion back to a level of African American support for a Republican that was normal, although still somewhat lower than the 13 percent that George W. Bush received in 2004. Second, Trump did slightly better among African American men, winning 10 percent of the vote, which was double the share received by Romney on 2012. On the other hand, Trump's vote among African American women only increased by 2 percent relative to that of Romney. Overall, almost one in five African American men voted for a candidate other than Clinton or did not vote for any presidential candidate. Had the vote of African American men resembled that of African American women—as was the case in 2012—the election result might have been even closer.

Finally, Trump's larger loss among Latinos overall was expected given Trump's comments concerning Mexican immigrants, building a border wall, and deporting illegal immigrants. Conversely, Trump's better-than-expected showing among Cuban voters reminds us that Latinos are not a monolithic block, and different ethnic subgroups have different interests. It appeared that Trump better mobilized the traditional Republican loyalties of Cubans in Miami, where attitudes on immigration and economic issues might have aligned more strongly with those of Trump. Finally, Cuban Republican Marco Rubio's relatively comfortable 8-point victory in his US Senate race may have provided some reverse coattails for Trump in the Cuban community.

In terms of social class (education and income), college graduates made up 4 percent more of the electorate in 2016, while voters earning $30,000 to $49,999 fell by 6 points, and those making more than $100,000 increased by 5 points. Although Trump lost among voters with a high school education or less by 5 points, he did better relative to 2012 in every educational group except for postgraduates, which Clinton won by 17 points (Obama had won that group by just 7 points). Among income groups, the biggest changes occurred among voters earning less than $50,000. Although Clinton won these voters, Trump closed the 2012 gap by between 6 and 9 percentage points. Trump did particularly well among the white working class (whites without a college degree, a grouping not shown in the table), winning by 66 percent to Clinton's 30 percent and by even more among white men without a college degree: 70 to 25 percent.

In terms of religion, Trump won both Protestants and Catholics and won them each by a larger margin than Romney had in 2012. In terms of geography, Trump won suburban voters by 10 points and rural voters by 25 points, while Clinton won urban voters by 12 points.[32]

Political party affiliation and ideology also shed light on voting decisions. Democrats made up 3 points less of the electorate than in 2012 (falling from 35 to 32 percent), and so while Clinton's margin among Democrats was almost identical to Obama's (90 percent support), fewer Democrats actually showed up to the polls, indicating an enthusiasm or organizational get-out-the-vote gap in comparison to 2012. Trump did slightly worse among Republicans than Romney had (89 versus 92 percent support). The biggest difference occurred among independents: in 2012 Obama beat Romney by 50 to 47 percent among voters with no party preference, while in 2016 Trump beat Clinton by 47 to 43 percent. A much higher percentage of independents did not cast a vote for president or voted for a third-party candidate in 2016 (10 percent) than in 2012 (just 3 percent).

Liberals made up a greater percentage of the 2016 electorate (up 3 points) while moderates dropped by 5 points. Clinton could not take advantage of the surge in liberal turnout, receiving 5 percentage points fewer than Obama among that group (81 to Obama's 86 percent). Since Trump's percentage was almost identical to Romney's among this group, it seems that about 5 percent of liberals chose a third-party candidate or did not choose any candidate for president in 2016 (versus just 1 percent in 2012). Clinton won moderates by about 8 percent (roughly the same as the 2012 margin), while Trump won conservatives by 62 percent (slightly higher than Romney's 58 percent share).

Finally, the timing of a voter's decision is instructive as well. Eighty-eight percent of voters decided on their choice before the last week of the 2016 election, and Clinton won that group by a razor thin margin of 49 to 48 percent. However, 11 percent of voters made up their mind within the last week of the election in 2016, while just 8 percent had in 2012. And in 2016, late deciders broke heavily for Trump by a 55 to 38 percent margin. Conversely, in 2012, late deciders broke for Obama by a 57 to 43 percent margin. Were late deciders in 2016 influenced by the FBI announcement concerning the reopening of the Clinton email investigation? Or were late deciders struggling until the last minute with whether or not they should take a chance on Trump? For whatever the reason, late deciders were decisive in Trump's victory over Clinton in 2016 and equally decisive in Romney's loss to Obama in 2012.

Exit Poll Analysis: Issues and Candidate Images

Table 9.5 displays Florida exit poll results for a variety of issue and candidate image questions. Overall, almost 50 percent of voters in the Sunshine State thought the economy was the number one issue facing the country, 40 percent were looking for a candidate who could bring about needed change, and both these criteria favored Trump. In addition, a slight majority of Florida voters had unfavorable views of both candidates, but a higher percentage of voters with misgivings about Trump were still willing to support him.

The economy was listed as the most important issue facing the country by 48 percent of voters, and they favored Clinton over Trump by 49 to 46 percent. However, when asked who would better handle the economy, voters picked Trump by 50 to 44 percent, and almost all (96 percent) of these voters supported Trump. On the issue of trade, 39 percent of voters felt trade created more US jobs, while 34 percent thought they took away US jobs. People who thought trade was beneficial supported Clinton by 58 to 37 percent, while those who thought it had a negative effect supported Trump by a whopping 70 to 28 percent margin.

The second most important issue was terrorism (listed by 26 percent), and those voters supported Trump by 55 to 43 percent. Foreign policy voters (12 percent of the electorate) favored Clinton strongly by 66 to 30 percent. Finally, 10 percent of voters listed immigration as the most important issue, and those voters went strongly for Trump (by 66 to 30 percent). Seventy percent of voters thought that illegal immigrants should be offered a chance to apply for legal status, and those voters supported Clinton by 62 to 33 percent. Conversely, 23 percent thought that illegal immigrants should be deported, 92 percent of whom voted for Trump. Voters were fairly evenly split on their opinion of the fairness of the criminal justice system, with 45 percent stating that it treats all people fairly and 42 percent stating that it treats African Americans unfairly. Trump received support from 69 percent of those who thought the system was fair, and Clinton received the exact same percentage of support from those who thought the system was unfair. Finally, 66 percent of voters thought that global warming is a serious problem and supported Clinton over Trump by a margin of 61 to 35 points. The 31 percent of voters who did not think it is a serious problem overwhelmingly supported Trump (by 87 to 13 percent).

The most important candidate quality, selected by 40 percent of Sunshine State voters, was the ability to bring about change. Voters looking

Table 9.5. Florida Presidential Exit Poll Results: Issues and Candidate Characteristics

Category	Electorate	Clinton	Trump
What is the most important issue facing the country?			
Foreign policy	12	66	30
Immigration	10	30	69
Economy	48	49	46
Terrorism	26	43	55
Who would better handle the economy?			
Hillary Clinton	44	85	11
Donald Trump	50	1	96
Illegal immigrants working in the US should be			
Offered a chance to apply for legal status	70	62	33
Deported to the country they came from	23	5	92
Overall, trade with other countries			
Creates more US jobs	39	58	37
Takes away US jobs	34	28	70
The country's criminal justice system			
Treats all people fairly	45	27	69
Treats African Americans unfairly	42	69	26
Is climate change / global warming a serious problem?			
Yes	66	61	35
No	31	13	87
Which candidate quality mattered most in your voting decision?			
Cares about people like me	16	63	32
Can bring needed change	40	13	85
Has the right experience	21	88	8
Has good judgment	18	63	31
What is your opinion of Hillary Clinton?			
Favorable	45	96	2
Unfavorable	53	7	90
What is your opinion of Donald Trump?			
Favorable	41	4	96
Unfavorable	57	80	15

Table 9.5.(continued)

Category	Electorate	Clinton	Trump
Are the presidential candidates honest and trustworthy?			
Only Clinton	31	98	1
Only Trump	35	1	98
Neither	25	47	41
Do the candidates have the temperament to serve effectively?			
Only Clinton	47	92	4
Only Trump	35	2	98
Neither	9	14	67
Does Clinton's private email use while secretary of state bother you?			
A lot or some	63	23	70
Not much or not at all	35	89	9
Does Trump's treatment of women bother you?			
A lot or some	66	66	26
Not much or not at all	32	7	91

Source: "2016 Florida President Exit Poll," Fox News, accessed December 21, 2016, https://goo.gl/zDbbxa; "2016 Florida President Exit Poll," CNN, accessed December 21, 2016, https://goo.gl/Nxvt2L.

Note: All table entries are percentages.

for change supported Trump by a wide margin (85 to 13 percent). In contrast, voters looking for experience (21 percent of the electorate) supported Clinton by an even greater margin (88 to 8 percent). Eighteen percent of voters thought good judgment mattered most, while 16 percent were looking for someone who cares. Clinton won the support of 63 percent of voters in both these categories.

A majority of voters had unfavorable views of Hillary Clinton and Donald Trump (53 and 57 percent respectively), indicating a classic case of voters having to select from the lesser of two evils. But Trump was the lesser evil for a larger percentage, as 15 percent of voters supported the Republican nominee even though they had an unfavorable view of him, while just 7 percent of voters supported Clinton even when they had an unfavorable view of her. Only 31 percent of voters rated Clinton as honest and trustworthy, while a slightly higher 35 percent thought the same of Trump (25 percent of voters said neither candidate was honest or trustworthy). In terms of temperament, Clinton had a large lead, as 47 percent of voters said she had the temperament to serve effectively, while just 35 percent felt that way about Trump. Finally, Clinton's use of private email while secretary of state bothered 63 percent of voters a lot or some, while 66 percent of voters were bothered a lot or some by Trump's treatment of women.

US Senate, US House, and State Legislative Elections

Florida Republicans did extremely well in the 2016 US Senate and state legislative races, dashing Democratic hopes for major pickups. After dropping out of the Republican presidential primary, Marco Rubio decided to run for reelection in the Senate, and ultimately won by a relatively comfortable margin 52 to 44.3 percent over Rep. Patrick Murphy. And while Florida Democrats picked up a handful of seats, the GOP remained in firm control of the congressional delegation and both chambers of the state legislature.

When the cycle began, Democrats had high hopes for a senate pickup and thought Florida might help them regain the majority in the US Senate. Senator Rubio announced he was running for the GOP presidential nomination and would not seek his senate seat even if he failed in his bid to capture the nomination. Several quality Republican candidates filed to run, including the lieutenant governor, two congressmen, and two wealthy businessmen. Moderate, two-term member of the US House of Representatives Patrick Murphy was favored by the Democratic establishment over liberal firebrand Rep. Alan Grayson. When Grayson's campaign self-destructed under a series of ethical and personal scandals, the path seemed clear for Murphy, who maintained an early lead in the polls against all of the Republican challengers, who were struggling to gain name recognition in a crowded primary field. The national and Florida GOP establishment pleaded with Rubio to get back in the race, believing he was the only person who could save the seat. When Rubio decided to run for reelection after all, most of his Republican opponents dropped out of the race and Rubio cruised to victory in the primary.

The general election was presumed to be competitive and was listed as one of the toss-up senate contests by most rating organizations. Murphy attacked Rubio for missing numerous senate votes while running for president, and Rubio counterattacked, pointing out that Murphy had been named one of the least effective congressional representatives in the country. In the end, however, Rubio maintained a consistent 3- to 5-point lead in the polls throughout the cycle and ended up winning by a comfortable margin, 52 to 44 percent, as Murphy's promised outside money was redirected to more competitive races in other states over the last few weeks of the campaign. In addition to being outspent, Murphy proved to be a relatively weak campaigner and questions about his resume padding and lack of accomplishments in Congress turned voters off. Rubio's name recognition, resurgent campaign energy, and ability to convince skeptical voters that he actually intended to serve as a senator if he won all contributed to Rubio's win. Finally, of course, Rubio's Cuban identity and condemnation of Trump's language and policy towards Latinos and immigration helped him immensely with Cuban and other Latino voters and in the end helped him achieve a relatively comfortable margin of victory. Rubio outpolled Donald Trump in Florida and may have provided some reverse coattails to help Trump win the state. Exit polls showed that Rubio outpolled Trump in almost every demographic and, most importantly, received much higher support from Latinos (48 percent) and Cubans (68 percent), which may help explain why Trump did better than expected with these groups.

The political environment for down-ticket races received a jolt when the Florida Supreme Court required the districts for all twenty-seven US congressional seats and all forty state senate seats be redrawn for the 2016 elections to comply with the Fair District Amendments added by voters to the Florida Constitution earlier in the decade (state house seats were deemed to comply without redrawing).[33] The new maps largely eliminated partisan and incumbent gerrymandering, created many open seat races, and actually gave Democrats a registration lead in the majority of congressional and senate districts. Further Democratic turnout typically surges in Florida during presidential election years after declining in the midterm. Thus, Florida Democrats expected to make major gains, possibly even taking the majority of the forty-member senate and twenty-seven-member delegation. Florida even had four competitive congressional races, the most of any state. However, in the end, Democrats managed a net gain of only one congressional seat, leaving the Republicans with a sixteen-to-eleven lead in the congressional delegation. While they did not result in significant partisan change, the newly drawn congressional districts did result in large turnover, with ten new members out of twenty-seven, and in increased diversity, including four African Americans, four Latinos (including Darren Soto, the first Puerto Rican representative from Florida), and an Asian American (Stephanie Murphy, the first Asian American member from Florida and the first Vietnamese American female member in US history). Former governor Charlie Crist also finally resurrected his political career—now as a Democrat—after two defeats for statewide office, unseating Republican incumbent David Jolly. In the state senate, the Democrats also made a net gain of just a single seat, with the Republicans continuing to hold a solid twenty-five-to-fifteen advantage. While Democrats did not expect to compete for the state house majority, since they entered the cycle with a forty-two-seat deficit in a 120-member body, they did think they would do better than the two-seat gain they achieved. When the votes were counted, the GOP still held a commanding lead of seventy-nine to forty-one in the lower chamber.

While statewide contests in Florida are often competitive—the last two gubernatorial and presidential races were each decided by about 1 percent—district-based races have not been very competitive since the late 1990s. Florida Democrats had long complained that Republican gerrymandering was the prime reason for their failure to win more seats in the Florida congressional delegation and legislature. While gerrymandering may have played a role, the 2016 results make clear that Florida Democrats need to focus on strengthening their state party organization, fielding more and better candidates, raising larger sums of money, and rethinking their message if they want to be more competitive in congressional and legislative races.

Conclusion: GOP Wins 2016 Battle, But A "Blue" Future Looms

Florida lived up to its reputation as the premier battleground state in the 2016 presidential election. Trump's victory also confirmed a pattern, consistent with recent statewide election results in the Sunshine State, in which two equally matched party coalitions go head to head, with one prevailing narrowly. However, one development in 2016 was unexpected: Florida was not the state that decided the outcome of the election. Indeed, whereas Florida was vital to George W. Bush's victories in 2000 and 2004, Trump could have lost Florida and still won a majority in the Electoral College.

Future statewide elections for the most visible political offices in Florida are likely to remain intensely competitive. The 2018 midterm elections will feature an open race for governor as the current two-term incumbent, Rick Scott, is term-limited. Scott, however, has expressed interest in a bid for the US Senate seat currently held by three-term incumbent Bill Nelson, who is one of just three southern Democrats remaining in the Senate.[34] Such a match would inevitably be one of the marquee US

Senate contests of 2018, and likely one of the most expensive elections of the entire cycle. Of course, in 2018 the Republican Party will face a political environment it has not encountered in twelve years: the headwinds of a midterm election during a Republican presidency. The elections in Florida, as well as elsewhere, will inevitably be tied to the approval ratings of Donald Trump at the midpoint of his first term in office.

Looking further ahead to the 2020 presidential election, Florida will loom large in the political calculus of both parties. Indeed, for the Democrats, the 2016 result indicates that Florida has gone from being a luxury—Bill Clinton in 1996 and Barack Obama in 2008 and 2012 could have still been elected without carrying the state—to being an essential part of the path to 270 Electoral College votes. Carrying Florida's twenty-nine electoral votes will partially act as a hedge for the Democrats to compensate for two swing states, Iowa and Ohio, which are trending more Republican. These two states have twenty-four Electoral College votes between them, and Trump carried both quite decidedly, with a margin of 9 percent in Iowa and 8 percent in Ohio. Indeed, Florida may become part of an evolving Democratic road to the White House that shifts from a Rust Belt strategy to place greater emphasis on high-growth and racially diverse Sun Belt states, which also include Arizona, Georgia, North Carolina, and eventually Texas. Of course, if one adds Florida to Clinton's Electoral College vote tally, one has to add just one of the other close states won by Trump in 2016—Michigan, Pennsylvania, or Wisconsin—to reach a majority.

We concluded our analysis of the results of the 2012 presidential election in Florida by noting that "it may have been the last election in which a Republican strategy of assembling a coalition based on 60 percent of the white vote could have a chance of winning."[35] This claim was based on the assumption that Florida's electorate was becoming less white. Indeed, in 2016 whites were a smaller share of the electorate than in 2012. However, Trump compensated for this by winning an even larger share of the white vote than Romney. History may ultimately record the 2016 election in Florida as representing the high-water mark of a Republican electoral coalition in Florida that essentially relies on securing landslide support among whites to win elections. This is underscored by figure 9.2, which shows the very different racial composition of each party's vote in Florida. The fact that Trump won Florida with an overwhelmingly white vote—a strategy consonant with the politics of the Old South—does little to allow the GOP to adapt to an electorate that is a leading indicator of politics in the "Newest" South, one which

Figure 9.2. Racial Composition of the Trump and Clinton 2016 Presidential Vote in Florida

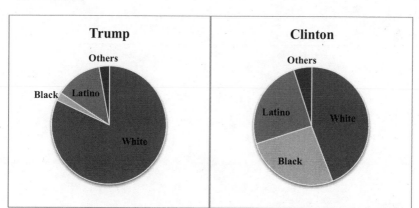

Source: Calculated by the authors from "Florida President Exit Poll," *CNN Politics,* 2016, accessed 21 Dec 2016, https://goo.gl/Nxvt2L.

Note: Segments in pie charts shows show the contribution of each racial group to the vote total of each candidate.

is becoming more multiracial and less white. Indeed, in winning Florida, and the presidency, a Trump-branded GOP is almost certainly unlikely to conduct the same type of post-election analysis that took place after defeat in 2012, which highlighted the need to appeal beyond its core base of white support.[36]

Ultimately, there is little evidence from the analysis of either county-level voting returns or exit polls in Florida that the Republican Party is in any better position to appeal to minorities, younger voters, women, or urban residents than it was four years ago. The 2016 presidential election in Florida may, in the final analysis, be more of a Trump speed bump on a road where demographic change in the state will still favor the Democrats, should recent population and political trends continue.

10

North Carolina

Up and Down the Tar Heel Political Roller Coaster

J. Michael Bitzer and Charles Prysby

In the last decade, North Carolina elections have resembled a roller-coaster ride: a series of ups and downs combined with wild turns. This stands in contrast to the previous decade or so, which resembled a train ride on a flat, straight track. Throughout the 1990s and into the twenty-first century, elections in North Carolina followed a predictable script. Republicans won the presidential elections, usually by comfortable margins; even in 1992 and 1996, the years that Bill Clinton carried four southern states in his election victories, North Carolina remained in the Republican column. Republican success in presidential elections carried over to congressional elections. From 1994 through 2004, Republicans won five of the six US Senate elections held during this time, and they won a majority of the US House seats in every election year except 1996, when the two parties split the House seats evenly. However, Republican success in federal elections was not accompanied by success in state elections, as Democrats won all the gubernatorial elections and maintained majority control of both houses of the state legislature during this time, save for a brief period in the 1990s when the Republican managed to win a slight majority of house seats. In sum, from 1992 to 2004, the North Carolina political map was consistently colored red on the federal level and blue on the state level.[1] The contrast in outcomes for federal and state elections during this time is particularly remarkable when we consider that North Carolina is one of the minority of states that hold their major state elections in presidential election years.

The old pattern of election outcomes disintegrated in the middle of the first decade of the twenty-first century. Table 10.1 shows the results for federal and state elections in presidential election years from 1992 through 2016. The stable pattern described above is clearly shown in the data for 1992–2004. Then the roller coaster ride begins. In 2008, Democrats swept the table, not only winning the gubernatorial and state legislative elections but also the presidential election, the US Senate seat, and over 60 percent of the US House seats in the state.[2] Four years later, just the opposite pattern appeared: Republicans won the presidential, congressional, gubernatorial, and state legislative elections.[3] In 2016, the GOP was almost as successful, but they lost the gubernatorial election because of specific issues discussed later in this chapter.

This chapter examines the 2016 election in North Carolina. We attempt to describe and explain what happened in that election and to discuss the recent changes in the political character of the state. We also hope to provide some indication of future political prospects in North Carolina. Of course, political developments in North Carolina reflect

Table 10.1. North Carolina Election Results, Presidential Years, 1992–2016

	1992	1996	2000	2004	2008	2012	2016
National elections							
Presidential vote	50.5	52.5	56.5	56.2	49.8	51.0	51.9
US Senate vote	52.2	53.4	—	52.3	45.6	—	53.0
US House vote	48.4	54.4	60.0	51.2	45.3	49.1	53.3
US House seats won	33.3	50.0	58.3	53.8	38.5	69.2	76.9
State elections							
Gubernatorial vote	45.1	43.3	47.1	43.5	48.3	55.8	49.9
State senate seats won	22.0	42.0	30.0	42.0	40.0	64.0	70.0
State house seats won	34.4	50.8	48.3	47.5	43.3	64.2	61.7

Source: Computed from data obtained from the North Carolina Board of Elections.

Note: Vote percentages are the Republican percentage of the major-party vote. Other figures are the Republican percentage of seats won. No US Senate election occurred in 2000 or 2012.

national political developments, so we intend to bring those factors into our discussion.

The Presidential Primary

North Carolina has traditionally scheduled its primary elections, including the presidential primary, for early May. In most years, the presidential nomination contests have been effectively decided by that time, and the North Carolina primary has had little impact on the nomination contests. There were a few exceptions to this pattern. In 1976, the state held its presidential primary in late March, and Ronald Reagan's victory in the Republican primary after a series of defeats in earlier contests helped to keep his campaign alive, which allowed him to continue on to win several more primaries.[4] While Gerald Ford ultimately prevailed and won the Republican nomination, the challenge from Reagan weakened Ford for the general election, which he lost in a close contest to Jimmy Carter. In 1980, however, the state moved its primary back to May, thereby diminishing the influence of the state in the nomination process. The state legislature did move the presidential primary up to March in 1988, when it joined with other southern states in an attempt to create what would amount to a largely regional primary, nicknamed "Super Tuesday," which supposedly would give more moderate southern Democrats more influence in choosing their party's nominees.[5] That attempt failed as the favored southern candidate, Al Gore, did not do as well as expected on Super Tuesday. Michael Dukakis, the governor of Massachusetts, won both Florida and Texas, the two largest southern states, and went on win the Democratic nomination, but he then failed to win a single southern state in the general election, which he lost to George H. W. Bush. The state returned to its May primary date for subsequent years, sometimes talking about moving the date up but never doing so.

Among the reasons for keeping the May date was the fact that holding a presidential primary in March and a separate state primary in May would cost more, and March was considered to be too far ahead of the general election for the state primaries. With the May primary date, the state had little influence on the presidential nominations in most years. However, in 2008, the Democratic presidential nomination contest between Barack Obama and Hillary Clinton was still undecided in early May, and Obama's victory in the North Carolina primary helped him to secure the nomination, demonstrating that it was possible for the state to be influential, even if this would be an atypical occurrence.[6] In 2016, the state legislature, concerned that the heavy frontloading of presidential primaries and caucuses was making North Carolina even less relevant, moved all of its primaries to March 15, although the US House primaries then had to be moved to June because a court challenge to the districts could not be resolved in time.[7]

Even with this change, about one-half of the states had already held their presidential primary or caucus by the time of the North Carolina primary. About one-third of the Democratic delegates and one-half of the Republican delegates had been selected. Both Donald Trump and Hillary Clinton came into North Carolina with clear leads in their nomination contests, but neither had locked up the nomination. Each left North Carolina with a larger lead. Trump won about 40 percent of the vote, slightly more than the 37 percent that Ted Cruz received, which gave Trump twenty-nine delegates and Cruz twenty-seven. Clinton did even better: she won almost 55 percent of the vote to Sanders's 41 percent, which gave her sixty delegates and Sanders forty-seven. The move to March gave North Carolina a modest influence on the presidential nominations, more than it otherwise would have had.

While each party had over 1.1 million votes cast in each of the semi-closed primaries (unaffiliated registered voters could select either major party primary to participate in), Republicans attracted more registered unaffiliated voters (27 percent of the total GOP ballots) than did the Democratic primary (only 20 percent of all Democratic ballots). The composition of both parties' primary electorates tended to reflect the state's registration patterns; voters in the Republican primary were overwhelmingly white (96 percent), while voters in the Democratic primary were 57 percent white and 37 percent black. Only 20 percent of the Republican primary voters were under the age of forty, while over one-quarter (26 percent) of the Democratic primary voters were under the age of forty. Even though more women are registered voters in North Carolina, the Republican primary saw a nearly even split among women and men, while women made up 60 percent of the Democratic primary electorate.

The other major primary contests were for the congressional races, especially the US Senate election, with incumbent Richard Burr winning renomination, but with only 61 percent of the GOP primary vote; challenger Greg Brannon, a former 2014 US Senate candidate, secured a quarter of the vote. In the Democratic US Senate primary, former state representative Deborah Ross secured 62 percent of the vote, defeating four other Democrats vying to take on Burr. In the June primaries,

Republicans George Holding and Renee Ellmers were double-bunked in the Second District following the revisions to the congressional districts. Holding defeated Ellmers by 53 to 23 percent, with Greg Brannon (who had earlier sought to deny Richard Burr's renomination) garnering 23 percent. In the newly created and open-seat Thirteenth Congressional District, seventeen Republicans and five Democrats vied for their party's nomination: the victorious Republican won with only 20 percent of the vote (6,340 actual votes), while the Democratic candidate won with 26 percent (4,709 votes). The other closely watched congressional primaries in North Carolina centered around Mecklenburg County. The first was the Ninth Congressional District's Republican contest, which saw incumbent Robert Pittenger win renomination by only 134 votes in a three-way race. The Twelfth Congressional District's Democratic primary saw incumbent Alma Adams, whose residency was in Greensboro but who moved to Charlotte after the reconfigured district was placed solely within Mecklenburg, hold back strong challenges from two state legislators who were well-known in Charlotte.

The Presidential Election

The expectation was that North Carolina would be a very competitive state for the 2016 presidential election. Both Clinton and Trump identified the state as one that they could win. All of the pundits listed North Carolina as a battleground state. Preelection polls showed the same thing. The election outcome did not match these predictions. Trump carried the state with almost 52 percent of the two-party vote. The unexpectedly high vote percentage for Trump reflected in large part the fact that Trump did better nationally than many analysts expected. Table 10.2 shows the presidential vote in North Carolina in comparison to the national vote for elections from 1992 to 2016. In 2016, the state was 3 percentage points more Republican than the nation, which was not much different from its position in 2008 or 2012. Prior to 2008, North Carolina was considerably more Republican than the nation. From 1992 through 2004, it was between 4 and 7 points more Republican, a difference large enough to ensure that the state would go Republican even in years when the Democratic presidential candidate was winning nationally. Now the state is only slightly more Republican than the nation, making it a likely battleground state in any year when the Democratic candidate is running slightly ahead in the national polls.

Table 10.2. Presidential Vote in North Carolina and the Nation, 1992–2016

	1992	1996	2000	2004	2008	2012	2016
NC	50.5	52.5	56.5	56.2	49.8	51.0	51.9
Nation	46.5	45.4	49.7	51.4	46.6	48.5	48.9
NC vs. nation	+4.0	+7.1	+6.8	+4.8	+3.2	+2.5	+3.0

Source: Computed from data in *America Votes*, various editions, the North Carolina Board of Elections website, and the *New York Times* 2016 elections website.

Note: Entries are the Republican percentage of the two-party vote for president. The last row gives the difference between the Republican vote in North Carolina and in the nation.

Population changes have contributed to the growing politically competitive character of North Carolina politics. The growth of major urban areas is one important change for the state; in 2016, half of the votes came from twelve of the state's hundred counties. The high growth urban areas in the state, such as the Raleigh-Durham and Charlotte metropolitan areas, have attracted younger and more educated voters from outside of the state, and these newcomers are more liberal and Democratic than older state natives.[8] The urban areas of the state were once disproportionately Republican in voting, but they are now areas of Democratic strength. A look at some of the most heavily populated counties illustrates this fact: Clinton carried Mecklenburg County (home to Charlotte) with 65 percent of the two-party vote, Wake County (Raleigh) with 60 percent, Guilford County (Greensboro) with 60 percent, Buncombe County (Asheville) with 57 percent, and Forsyth County (Winston-Salem) with 55 percent. This pattern extends beyond the largest cities in the state. Clinton won 55 percent of the vote in the nineteen urban counties, while Trump won 64 percent of the vote in the twenty-four suburban counties and 59 percent in the fifty-seven rural counties.[9]

Generational change also has contributed to political change in the state. In the nation as a whole, millennials are the most liberal generation and the most likely to vote Democratic, and this pattern carries over to North Carolina as well.[10] As older voters, who are more conservative and more Republican, are being replaced by younger voters, the state has shifted in a Democratic direction, at least in presidential elections. Millennials were 30 percent of registered voters in 2016, a number almost equal to the 32 percent who were baby boomers.[11] Generational change is intertwined with change in the racial and ethnic composition of the state, as younger voters are more likely to be minority group members: only 60 percent of registered millennial voters are non-Latino whites. White voters are a slightly smaller share of the electorate than they were a decade ago, and since Republicans do poorly among minority voters, this shift also has helped the Democrats.

The exit poll data from North Carolina illustrate these patterns. Table 10.3 shows the relationships of various demographic characteristics to the vote in the presidential, senatorial, and gubernatorial elections. Only the vote for the Republican candidates for these offices—Donald Trump, Richard Burr, and Pat McCrory—is shown, but the minor-party vote was small, so most of the vote that did not go to the Republican candidates went to the Democrats. As the data in the table show, age differences were sharp: Trump received 60 percent of the vote of those sixty-five and older but only 35 percent of the vote of those under thirty, and a similar difference exist for the other two offices. Racial differences were stark as well: Trump won 63 percent of the white vote but only 40 percent of the Latino vote and just 8 percent of the black vote. Exit poll data not included in the table show that Trump did about 10 percentage points better among those who were born in North Carolina than among those who moved to the state. All of these relationships are consistent with the above interpretation of why North Carolina is more competitive in presidential elections than it had been a decade ago.

Other demographic factors were related to the vote in the usual fashion. There was some speculation that white evangelical voters, who normally are strongly Republican, might not find Trump as appealing as most Republican candidates, but they wound up voting by over 80 percent for him. The 2016 North Carolina exit poll did not ask about church attendance, but data from 2012 show that those who attend regularly are more Republican, and there is every reason to believe that this was the case in 2016, especially because the national exit poll asked about church attendance and found that Trump received 53 percent of the vote from the roughly one-half of voters who attended church at least monthly but just 39 percent from those who attended less frequently.[12] Trump, like past Republican presidential candidates, did better among men and among married voters; the gender gap was larger than normal, but that seems unsurprising considering that the Democratic candidate was a woman and that Trump faced allegations about his treatment of women, which was highlighted by a video recording that showed him boasting about groping women, a recording that was released late in the campaign and was the subject of intense questioning in the second debate.

Table 10.3. North Carolina Voting by Selected Demographic and Social Variables, 2016

Political Orientation	Trump	Burr	McCrory
Race			
White (70)	63	64	62
Black (20)	8	9	12
Latino (5)	40	49	35
Religion			
White evangelical (38)	81	81	77
Other (62)	32	34	30
Education			
College degree (50)	48	50	47
Some college (32)	52	51	50
No college (18)	54	55	54
Income			
Under $50,000 (38)	38	40	39
$50,000–$100,000 (32)	50	51	49
Over $100,000 (30)	60	63	58
Gender			
Men (46)	56	58	55
Women (54)	45	46	45
Marital status			
Married (61)	59	60	57
Not married (39)	38	40	37
Age			
Under 30 years (18)	35	40	36
30–44 years (26)	46	47	46
45–64 years (38)	55	55	54
Over 64 years (18)	60	60	59

Source: National Election Pool, North Carolina Exit Poll, 2016.

Note: Entries are the percentage of voters who voted for the Republican presidential, senatorial, and gubernatorial candidates (Trump, Burr, and McCrory). The figures in parentheses indicate the percentage of all respondents in that category. For example, the data for race indicate that 70 percent of the voters were whites in 2016 and that 63 percent of whites voted for Trump.

The relationship between socioeconomic status and voting is interesting. Trump did much better among those with higher incomes. His share of the vote among those with incomes over $100,000 was over 20 points higher than his share of the vote among those with incomes under $50,000. That seems consistent with the traditional pattern of Republicans appealing more to those of higher socioeconomic status. However, Trump did his best among those with no college education and his worst among those with a college degree, which seems inconsistent with the relationship between income and the vote. Discussions of Trump's support in the national media portrayed him as doing better among white working-class voters, who usually were defined as those without a college degree. While the association between education and the presidential vote in table 10.3 supports this interpretation, the relationship between income and the vote does not. Also, income and education are related in the same manner to the vote for Richard Burr and Pat McCrory, the Republican candidates for the US Senate and North Carolina governorship, respectively, which undercuts the argument that Trump appealed to white working-class voters more than did typical Republican candidates. Furthermore, the relationship between income and voting in 2012 was weaker than it was in 2016: Mitt Romney did about 10 points better among those with incomes over $100,000 than he did among those with incomes under $50,000, in comparison to the 22-point difference for Trump.[13] Trump ran better than Romney among high income voters and worse among low income voters, which does not support the argument that Trump had a particularly strong appeal to working-class white voters in North Carolina.

An analysis of demographic factors takes us only so far. Ultimately, voting is determined by attitudes, not by demographic or social characteristics. Table 10.4 shows the relationship between voting and selected political attitudes. Voting was strongly aligned with party affiliation: over 90 percent of Republicans voted for Trump and over 90 percent of Democrats voted for Clinton. This strong relationship reflects voting patterns in the current era of high partisan polarization.[14] The ideological differences between the two parties are large, and images of the opposing party are extremely negative. The result is that both Democrats and Republicans are extremely reluctant to defect and vote for a candidate of the opposite party. Republican votes were not sufficient for Trump's victory, of course, so his ability to win a majority of the vote of independents, who were about one-third of the electorate, was critical to his success.[15]

Table 10.4. North Carolina Voting by Selected Political Orientations, 2016

	Vote		
Political orientation	Trump	Burr	McCrory
Party identification			
Democrats (35)	8	10	9
Independents (33)	53	53	53
Republicans (31)	94	96	92
Ideology			
Liberal (22)	9	8	8
Moderate (35)	37	40	38
Conservative (43)	83	83	81
Feelings toward the federal government			
Satisfied or enthusiastic (25)	13	17	15
Dissatisfied or angry (75)	62	64	57
Approval of Obama as president			
Approve (51)	9	12	12
Disapprove (49)	93	92	90
Effects of international trade			
Takes away US jobs (39)	70	69	69
Does not affect jobs (14)	28	30	32
Creates US jobs (38)	35	35	36
Policy toward illegal immigrants			
Should offer legal status (69)	36	37	38
Should deport to home country (25)	80	76	76
Perceptions of groups in the US			
Whites are favored (33)	14	12	16
No group is favored (33)	51	51	50
Minorities are favored (26)	90	87	86

Source: National Election Pool, North Carolina Exit Poll, 2016.

Note: Entries are the percentage of voters who voted for the Republican presidential, senatorial, and gubernatorial candidates (Trump, Burr, and McCrory). The figures in parentheses indicate the percentage of all respondents in that category. For example, the data for party identification indicate that 35 percent of the voters were Democrats in 2016 and that 8 percent of them voted for Trump.

Trump emphasized several issues in his campaign. Two of the more controversial issues involved trade and immigration policies. Trump argued that existing trade policy had cost the US millions of manufacturing jobs, a situation that he promised to reverse. He also proposed a harsher immigration policy, including building a wall along the Mexican border. The exit poll contained questions dealing with both of these issues, and the results show that the vote for Trump was strongly related to attitudes on these issues. Those who thought that international trade cost the US jobs voted heavily for Trump, while those who thought otherwise voted heavily for Clinton. Those who thought that illegal immigrants should be deported voted heavily for Trump, while those who favored offering them some sort of legal status voted heavily for Clinton. There were other issues in the campaign, such as health care, but the exit poll did not include questions on all of the relevant issues, so we can only speculate about how they may have influenced voting behavior, especially among the more volatile group of independent voters. The exit poll data show that the one-half of the electorate that disapproved of Obama's handling of the presidency voted overwhelmingly for Trump, and this suggests that those who largely opposed Obama's major initiatives and accomplishments, such as the Affordable Care Act, were motivated to vote for the Republican candidate.

Throughout the campaign, Democrats accused Trump of exacerbating racial divisions and playing on racial fears. One question in the exit poll indicates that such attitudes influenced the vote. Trump did extremely well among the one-fourth of voters who thought that minority groups were favored in the United States. However, attitudes on race-related issues have long been a relevant factor in voting behavior in North Carolina, as in the South as a whole, so there may be nothing unusual in this relationship.[16] Furthermore, Trump received a slight majority of the votes of those who thought that neither whites nor minorities received special favor, which suggests that his appeal rested on much more than racial resentment.

Candidate character traits played a much greater role in the 2016 than did issues of public policy. Not surprisingly, perceptions of the character traits of the candidates were strongly related to the vote, as the data in table 10.5 show. Overall, opinions of the personal qualities of the candidates were negative, but we can compare evaluations of the two candidates on several character traits to see which candidate had a relative advantage on each trait.[17] Trump was judged to be slightly more honest than Clinton, but Clinton had an advantage on being qualified to be president and on having the right temperament to be president. While this might appear to give Clinton an overall advantage on character traits, the data in table 10.5 show that there is an interesting aspect to the relationships between assessments of each trait and the vote. As we might expect, those who saw Clinton in favorable terms and Trump in unfavorable terms voted almost entirely for Clinton, and those who gave Trump a favorable evaluation and Clinton an unfavorable one voted almost entirely for Trump. The interesting group are those voters who gave both candidates an unfavorable evaluation on a given trait (hardly any voters gave both candidates a favorable evaluation on any of the traits): they did not split their vote fairly evenly; instead, they voted heavily for Trump.

Table 10.5. Presidential Vote by Assessments of Candidate Character Traits

	Vote	
	Clinton	Trump
Who is honest?		
Only Clinton (35)	100	0
Only Trump (38)	1	99
Neither one (21)	36	48
Who is qualified to be president?		
Only Clinton (45)	96	2
Only Trump (40)	2	98
Neither one (10)	14	67
Who has the right temperament to be president?		
Only Clinton (47)	96	3
Only Trump (36)	1	99
Neither one (11)	4	75
Favorable assessments of the candidates		
Only Clinton (41)	98	1
Only Trump (40)	1	98
Neither (16)	26	62

Source: National Election Pool, North Carolina Exit Poll, 2016.

Note: Entries are the percentage of voters in the specified category who voted for Clinton or Trump. The figures in parentheses indicate the percentage of all respondents in that category. For example, the data for which candidate is honest indicate that 35 percent of the voters thought that only Trump was honest, 99 percent of them voted for him, and 1 percent voted for Clinton. The percentages do not always add up to 100 percent because the vote for minor-party candidates is not shown.

The same pattern exists in responses to the question about voters' overall opinions of each candidate, a question that presumably captures both assessments of candidate character traits and evaluations of the candidates on public policy issues. Asked whether they had a favorable or unfavorable opinion of each candidate, 41 percent indicated they had a favorable opinion of Clinton, and 40 percent, of Trump. When we examine how people voted by how they responded to this question, we see that nearly all of the 41 percent who saw only Clinton as favorable voted for her, and the same was true of the 40 percent who felt that way toward Trump. However, the 16 percent who had an unfavorable evaluation of both candidates did not divide evenly; instead, they broke heavily for Trump, by 62 to 26 percent, with the remainder voting for another candidate.

Trump won North Carolina in large part because he won the vote of independents and of those who had unfavorable views of both candidates. One possible reason for Trump's ability to do this is that these voters found him appealing because he was an outsider who railed against the system. A combination of strong distrust of the federal government combined with intense dissatisfaction with Washington politics may have made a candidate like Trump more successful in 2016 than would have been the case in previous presidential elections. Trust in government has been on the decline in North Carolina: a 2015 poll found that only one-third of the electorate trusted the government to do what was right at least half of the time; six years earlier, a majority felt that way.[18] The exit poll data showed that three-quarters of North Carolina voters were either "dissatisfied" or "angry" about the federal government, and Trump received 62 percent of the vote of that group. Polling data show that voters saw Trump as much more likely to bring about real change in Washington. Exactly what change voters were thinking of when they said that is unclear, but they may have felt that the intense partisan bickering, continued partisan gridlock, and increasingly hostile partisan tone made the federal government unable to deal with problems that they were concerned about. For many independent voters, a vote for Trump may have been a repudiation of the leadership of both parties and even of the system as a whole.

Turnout patterns also contributed to Trump's victory. Overall turnout was the same in 2016 as it had been in 2012; in both years, 64.8 percent of the eligible electorate (i.e., citizens who were old enough to vote and not disqualified by a felony conviction) cast a ballot.[19] However, the 2016 electorate was slightly less black and Democratic. Black voters were

23 percent of those who voted in 2012, and other nonwhite voters were 5 percent of the electorate.[20] The 2016 electorate was again 28 percent nonwhite, but the share of black voters dropped to 21 percent, while all other races increased to 7 percent.[21] While the overall nonwhite percentage of the state's electorate stayed the same, the decrease in black voters, who generally vote Democratic 90 percent of the time, most likely hurt Clinton's performance in the state.

The composition of the electorate by party registration also was more favorable to the GOP in 2016 than it was in 2012: 33 percent of those who voted in 2016 were registered Republicans, 39 percent registered Democrats, and 27 percent unaffiliated voters; the comparable figures for 2012 were 33 percent Republican, 44 percent Democratic, and 23 percent unaffiliated.[22] The shift from 2012 to 2016 in the partisan composition of those who voted was produced by changes in both the composition of those who were registered to vote and the turnout rates of registered Democrats, Republicans, and unaffiliated voters. The share of registered voters who were Democrats declined from 44 percent in 2012 to 40 percent in 2016, and the turnout rate of this group also declined from 70 percent in 2012 to 68 percent in 2016; the opposite was the case for Republicans during this time period as they maintained their share of registered voters and improved their turnout from 73 percent to 75 percent.[23] The turnout improvement among Republicans occurred even though the Trump campaign put forth a minimal campaign effort in the state, forcing the state GOP to carry out get-out-the-vote activity on its own. Meanwhile, the Clinton campaign attempted to duplicate what Obama had done in the previous presidential elections by creating thirty-three field offices and staffing them with several hundred employees and about forty thousand volunteers.[24]

Congressional Elections

Like the presidential election, the US Senate election was projected to be highly competitive. The incumbent, Republican Richard Burr, was identified by Democrats as one of a number of vulnerable Republican senators up for election in 2016. Democrats hoped that enough of these incumbents could be defeated to return them to majority control in the Senate. Although the North Carolina seat was seen as winnable, the Democrats were unable to attract a high-profile candidate such as a former member of Congress or one of their statewide elected officials. Atty. Gen. Roy Cooper, who would have been a strong candidate, for example, chose to run for governor instead, and former US senator Kay Hagan decided against running. The Democratic nominee, former state senator Deborah Ross, lacked statewide recognition, but she nevertheless was regarded as a sufficiently able candidate. Other members of the state legislature had successfully run for the US Senate in recent years: as a state senator, Hagan had defeated incumbent Republican senator Elizabeth Dole in 2008, and she was in turn defeated in 2014 by Tom Tillis, the Republican state house speaker. Democratic hopes for Ross were based on the expectation that the other two Republicans at the top of the ticket, Trump and Governor McCrory, would have a difficult time winning and that their lack of success would hurt Burr. Although the *Cook Political Report* rated all three races as toss-ups, most analysts thought that Burr had the best chance of the three to win, and that assessment proved to be accurate as Burr won more votes than did either Trump or McCrory.

Spending on the election was heavy, as it was in the other highly competitive US Senate races in the nation. Burr and Ross each spent around $14 million, but that sum was dwarfed by the $60 million in outside spending.[25] It is difficult to determine exactly how much of the outside spending was on behalf of each candidate—the figures reported by the Center for Responsive Politics do not indicate the political leanings of every organization that spent money in the campaign—but there was heavy outside spending on both sides. Much of the outside spending went for attack ads, and the campaign took on a very negative tone. Republican ads attacked Ross for being too liberal, citing her prior position as head of the state chapter of the American Civil Liberties Union and claiming that she took radical positions, including being on the side of sex offenders, among other things. Democrats painted Burr as a Washington insider who put the interests of big-money donors first and also argued that he used his position in the Senate for personal financial benefit. Democrats also criticized Burr for his staunch support for Trump, including his refusal to disavow some of Trump's controversial statements.

The election outcome was not as close as most observers expected. Burr won with 53 percent of the two-party vote. His victory probably was the result of two factors. First, although Burr did not have a high approval rating, he had an amiable manner and was not prone to controversial or inflammatory statements, making it more difficult to effectively attack him. Burr's low approval rating undoubtedly stemmed more from his lack of visibility and from general dissatisfaction with Congress than from dislike of him in particular. Second, Democratic hopes for a Ross victory depended on 2016 being a good year for Democrats generally. As the national results showed, that proved not to be the case, and Burr was just one of several supposedly vulnerable Republican senators who won reelection.

While the Senate race was expected to be highly competitive, the US House races were not, and that expectation was confirmed. There were no close races and no unexpected winners. Republicans won ten of the thirteen seats despite winning only 53 percent of the total vote. The mismatch between the division of the vote and the division of the seats is a result of the redistricting plan drawn up by the Republican-controlled state legislature after the 2010 census. The GOP created three very heavily Democratic districts, two of which were also heavily black districts, and ten districts that were moderately strong Republican districts, but not so strong as to waste too many Republican votes. That plan, used in the 2012 and 2014 elections, was successfully challenged in the federal courts, thus requiring the legislature to draw up a new plan for 2016.[26] However, the new plan continued to accomplish the same Republican goal of distributing Republican votes more efficiently than Democratic votes. In 2016, six of the Republican winners received less than 60 percent of the vote. All three Democratic representatives won over two-thirds of the vote. Only one Republican won by that much.

The current district lines stand in contrast to the district lines drawn after the 2000 census. That plan, drawn up by a Democratic-controlled state legislature, created several very competitive seats, along with a few safe seats for each party. A good measure of the underlying partisanship of the districts is the vote percentage that went for John McCain in the 2008 presidential election (he received about 50 percent of the statewide vote). That measure shows that the district plan in use from 2002 through 2010 had five districts with an underlying Republican strength that was between 47 and 55, making them very competitive districts. Four districts were heavily Republican (i.e., a MCain vote over 60 percent) and four were heavily Democratic (i.e., a McCain vote less than 40 percent). This district plan produced outcomes where the share of the vote won by a party matched the share of seats won fairly well. For example, Republican congressional candidates won 51 percent of the vote and 54 percent of the seats in 2004, 47 percent of the vote and 46 percent of the seats in 2006, and 45 percent of the vote and 38 percent of the seats in 2008. Furthermore, there was significant turnover in party control in a number of the competitive seats during this decade, including the defeat of several incumbents.

State Elections

Republicans were quite successful in state elections as well, with one glaring exception: Gov. Pat McCrory was defeated in his reelection bid by Roy Cooper, the incumbent Democratic attorney general, in a hard-fought and closely contested election. In the end, Cooper beat McCrory by a little over ten thousand votes out of 4.7 million cast. McCrory gained the dubious distinction of being the first governor in the state to lose a reelection attempt since the state laws were changed in the late 1970s to allow for a second gubernatorial term. McCrory's defeat stands in contrast to Republican success in the other statewide races. Republicans controlled three of the nine North Carolina Council of State offices (lieutenant governor, commissioner of labor, and commissioner of agriculture) going into the 2016 election. Afterwards, Republicans claimed six of the nine offices, including that of lieutenant governor, the race for which was a rematch from 2012 between incumbent Republican Dan Forrest and Democrat Linda Coleman. Along with Republican incumbents being reelected as commissioner of agriculture and commissioner of labor, Republicans won the offices of commissioner of labor, superintendent of public instruction, and treasurer from the Democrats, while Democrats held on to the offices of attorney general, auditor, and secretary of state. In the nine state-wide contests, long-time Republican incumbents secured double-digit victories, while the contests for auditor and attorney general were narrowly decided (for auditor by less one-tenth of a percentage point and for attorney general by a half point).[27]

McCrory's inability to win reelection even though Republican candidates were doing well in other statewide races, from president down to the Council of State offices, can be attributed to his role as the point person for defending some controversial pieces of legislation, most notably the Public Facilities Privacy and Security Act, commonly known as "House Bill 2." This controversial piece of legislation came out of a special session regarding a nondiscrimination ordinance passed by the City of Charlotte. In February, 2016, the Charlotte City Council amended the city's anti-discrimination ordinance to prohibit places of public accommodation, including businesses, from discriminating on the basis of sexual orientation, gender identity, or gender expression. The last component, gender expression, garnered the most attention at the time by allowing transgender people to use public bathrooms corresponding to their gender identities.[28] Even with public warnings by the governor against enacting such provisions[29] (which had been considered and defeated by the Charlotte

City Council the previous year), the ordinance became the focus of a second special legislative session in March called by Republican legislative leaders to create a uniform state policy for single-sex multiple-occupancy bathrooms and for employment practices. The resulting law required individuals to use single-sex multiple-occupancy public bathrooms and changing facilities in government buildings, including public schools, that corresponded to their biological sex, as documented on their birth certificate. The legislation, often identified as the state's "bathroom bill," also included provisions preempting any local government from adopting minimum-wage requirements or other employment or compensation requirements, and it created a statewide definition of nondiscrimination that did not include sexual orientation or veteran status. The last provision prevented local governments from enacting the type of nondiscrimination law that the City of Charlotte had adopted. Introduced and considered in one day, the legislation passed the state house when all Republicans (except one) and eleven Democrats voted for it, and it passed the senate when all Republican senators voted for it after Democratic senators walked out of the chamber. Governor McCrory signed the legislation that evening.[30]

Public outcry over the legislation dominated the state's politics, accompanied by national headlines and actions against the state, including cancellations by businesses of job expansions in the state, boycotts and cancellations by performers such as Bruce Springsteen and Pearl Jam, and even a travel advisory issued by the British government to its LGBT citizens on traveling to the state. The National Basketball Association pulled its All-Star Game from Charlotte, the National Collegiate Athletic Association pulled its championship games from the state, and the Atlantic Coast Conference, a league born in North Carolina, moved its championship games from the state as well.[31] The controversial legislation only deepened the belief that the state was becoming polarized between urban interests and those of the rest of the state, the more so as the legislature was dominated by rural Republicans. Governor McCrory defended the legislation in the face of all the criticism and controversy, while his opponent, Atty. Gen. Roy Cooper, called for repeal of the law and repeatedly used the issue on the campaign trail, emphasizing the economic costs to the state.

House Bill 2 was not the only controversial law enacted by the Republican-controlled general assembly. The redistricting plans adopted for the 2012 US House, discussed earlier, and for the state legislature were criticized as egregiously gerrymandered and were challenged in the courts. Stronger restrictions on abortion were enacted. Republicans placed a constitutional amendment defining marriage as between one man and one woman before the voters in the May 2012 primary election; the amendment passed with 60 percent of the vote.[32] After the 2012 elections, which gave Republicans complete control of state government, the party continued its agenda to reshape the state into its political image, but this was not without further controversy or challenges. Beginning with the 2013 long session, the state's chapter of the National Association for the Advancement of Colored People and other liberal and Democratic-aligned groups held a series of protest rallies, named "Moral Mondays," against Republican legislative action, most notably on changes to the state's unemployment policies, education, teacher pay, and abortion laws. Following the 2014 election, Republicans continued their conservative agenda on election laws, environmental regulation reforms, firearm laws, unemployment insurance reforms, recusal for local officials in performing same-sex marriages, and taxes. One of the most controversial legislative actions taken by Republicans was their omnibus election reform bill, the 2013 Voter Information Verification Act (VIVA). VIVA created several important changes to North Carolina election law: it decreased the number of days (but not hours) of early voting, required voters to show a government-issued photo ID to vote, ended straight-ticket voting, changed mail-in absentee ballot requests, and ended same-day registration and voting. VIVA went into effect with the 2014 election, except for the voter ID provision, which was slated to begin in 2016. VIVA was challenged in court, and while a federal district court found no legal issues with the law, a three-judge panel on the US Court of Appeals for the Fourth Circuit found the law unconstitutional in July 2016, finding that the legislature's "discriminatory intent" infringed upon African American voters' rights "with almost surgical precision."[33] Therefore, VIVA did not go into effect for the 2016 election.

All of the controversial legislation enacted by the Republican state legislature, especially House Bill 2 and VIVA, appeared to hurt McCrory. He presented himself as a moderate Republican in his successful 2012 election as governor, but he was now placed in the position of having to defend some very conservative legislation, legislation that often lacked majority support in the population. House Bill 2, for example, was opposed by two-thirds of the voters, according to the exit poll, and only about one-third of this group voted for McCrory. The result was that his vote percentage was about 2 percentage points behind most of the other statewide Republican candidates, including Trump, who certainly had his share of controversies to deal with. The only statewide Republican candidate to do worse than McCrory was the one who ran against a strong Democratic incumbent for secretary of state.

In state legislative elections, Republicans solidified their hold on the North Carolina General Assembly, winning 70 percent of the state senate seats (a pick-up of one seat) and 61.7 percent of the state house seats (Democrats picked up three Republican and one unaffiliated seats, but Republicans picked up 3 Democratic seats). The seat totals were well above what Republicans won in their cumulative state vote: house Republicans received 52 percent of the state vote, while senate Republicans received 55 percent of the state vote. What was notable in the 2016 legislative contests was that 70 out of the 170 seats in the General Assembly went uncontested: thirty-seven Republicans and thirty-three Democrats had no opposing candidate in the general election.[34] The high percentage of uncontested seats and the ability of the GOP to win a high percentage of seats with a more modest share of the vote can be explained by the district lines for the state legislative seats that were drawn by the Republicans after they took control of the legislature in the 2010 election. As we discussed earlier, regarding the drawing of congressional districts, Republicans attempted to maximize their votes by packing Democrats into a small number of seats, by creating some very heavily black seats, and by creating as many fairly safe Republican seats as possible. Because most Republican state legislators held seats that were reasonably safe, they were not hurt by the controversies over House Bill 2, VIVA, or other legislative acts in the way that McCrory was.

Conclusion

Many studies of North Carolina's modern political history have focused on the tale of two states. In the mid-twentieth century, noted southern politics scholar V. O. Key described the state as a "progressive plutocracy,"[35] while at the beginning of the twenty-first century, Paul Luebke described Tar Heel politics as a battle between modernizers and traditionalists in the state's political and economic factions.[36] Rob Christensen, a long-time political reporter for the Raleigh *News & Observer*, contended that the state's politics were a "paradox" where neither political party or ideology could rest easily.[37] In his 2014 study, Tom Eamon contended that conflicts over race, the strengthening and polarization of two-party politics, the fierce competitiveness of elections, and the effects of individual politicians shape the state's political environment.[38] As noted at the beginning of the chapter, North Carolina was long seen in the divided political hues of federal red and state blue.

Since 2008, however, North Carolina's politics can only be described as intensely partisan and competitive. The 2016 elections demonstrate a continuing divide between the parties in statewide contests, and while congressional and state legislative elections were overwhelmingly one-sided in terms of seats won, the overall partisan division of the vote was much closer. With the tectonic shifts brought about by an ever-more-urbanized state, the generational sea change between baby boomers and millennial voters, and the increasing influence of in-migration, the Tar Heel state will continue to see its politics divided and polarized, and it is likely to be mentioned in the same breath as Ohio and Florida in future presidential elections. While the 2016 elections show a state that leans slightly right of center, North Carolina's politics will likely mirror shifts in the nation's politics, and the state will experience the wild ride of a political roller coaster.

11

Tennessee

From Crump to Trump

Vaughn May

In a 2005 piece titled "Southern Culture: On the Skids?," sociologist John Shelton Reed contended that Tennessee had a compelling case for being the most culturally representative state in the entire South. Reed, one of the region's most perceptive analysts, cited a number of markers in music, sport, and religion, stretching from Memphis's Beale Street to Nashville's Grand Ole Opry and Bristol's Motor Speedway.[1] A survey of southerners almost a decade later showcased a similar dynamic: when asked, "Which states are in the South?," southerners ranked Tennessee behind only the Deep South states in terms of the percentage of respondents who believed that the state deserved the southern label.[2]

Politically speaking, few observers would disagree with the proposition that Tennessee shares many of the traditionalistic characteristics that define the region's culture, including a commitment to limited government, an abiding affection for low taxes, and a deep suspicion of political reform efforts.[3] And, to the degree that rising levels of Republican support are signs of southern identification, an update by Reed might include mounds of political data. Gallup poll numbers from 2015, for example, placed Tennessee in the "solidly Republican" camp—a category defined by the Republican Party possessing at least a 10 percentage-point identification advantage over the Democratic Party. Tellingly, two Deep South states, Alabama and South Carolina, were the only two states of the old Confederacy to rank higher than Tennessee in their Republican identification.[4]

To longtime observers of the state's history, some of this data might appear puzzling, especially for those who have characterized Tennessee as a "somewhat reluctant southern state," and for whom grouping Tennessee with Deep South states is not familiar academic territory.[5] For these scholars, Tennessee is southern, but perhaps not *that* southern, certainly distinct from its Deep South sisters geographically, culturally, politically, and economically. David Woodard, for instance, offered the label of "emergent state" to Tennessee, noting its comparative racial moderation and the success of a creative urban class, especially when compared to the traditional political cultures of states such as Mississippi and Alabama.[6] Others have suggested that a robust progressive strain in its politics separated it from the rest of the old Confederacy on policy issues, including a "non-southern" approach to capital punishment.[7]

The story of the 2016 presidential election belies Tennessee's competitive electoral dynamics and the ideological push-pull of the state's political history. Indeed, GOP dominance in 2016 was so entrenched at every level that a newcomer to Tennessee politics might not be aware that the state featured a robustly competitive party system just two decades earlier. This chapter examines Tennessee's turn to the right, the ascendance of the conservative wing of the Republican Party, and the attendant rise of Donald Trump as a major political force.

A History of Two-Party Competition

The political diversity on display in the state has long been a staple of the literature on Tennessee politics. In his seminal work *Southern Politics in State and Nation*, V. O. Key noted various "coalitions and combinations that struggle for control of the state," which were grounded in vast geographical and historical differences among the state's subregions.[8] In the broadest of outlines, east Tennessee was the home of Mountain Republicanism, while Democratic bastions dominated middle and west Tennessee. Within the Democratic Party, scholars pointed to factional fights between E. H. Crump's political machine in Memphis and anti-Crump forces scattered across the state.[9] Crump cut a fearsome figure in Tennessee politics, skillfully using his political patronage to dominate both gubernatorial and legislative elections.[10]

As was the case elsewhere in the South in the early twentieth century, Democrats dominated most elections; the GOP was unlikely to inspire statewide victories or "put the fear in the hearts of Democrats."[11] Tennessee Republicans could, however, take solace in their control of two congressional districts as well as their role in fostering moderately competitive national elections. GOP strength was at least formidable enough that Key could label Tennessee as one of the only three states in the South where Republicans "approximate the reality of a political party."[12]

In the five decades spanning 1950 to 2000, both conservative and liberal ideologues could find something to cheer in the Volunteer State. In the 1950s and 1960s, Democratic officeholders such as Sen. Estes Kefauver, Sen. Al Gore Sr., and Gov. Frank Clement pushed for a number of progressive reforms statewide and made splashes on the national scene. Jack Bass and Walter Devries labeled them as a "trio whose combined potential of personality, youth, and talent was unmatched in the South."[13] By the end of the 1970 campaign season, however, Republicans were ascendant statewide with a talented trio of their own. Howard Baker Jr. won a Senate seat in 1966, followed by William Brock in 1970. Winfield Dunn won Tennessee's governor seat in 1970, the first Republican to hold that seat in fifty years. Democrats got some measure of revenge in the post-Watergate decade as Ray Blanton was elected governor in 1974, Jim Sasser won Bill Brock's Senate seat in 1976, and Al Gore Jr. captured the other Senate seat vacated by Howard Baker in 1984.

That Tennesseans were open to the entreaties of both parties is perhaps most evident at the gubernatorial level. From 1979 to the present, the parties have leapfrogged one another in power, with all five governors serving eight-year stints. If any patterns hold among the last five state executives—Republican Lamar Alexander (1979–86), Democrat Ned McWherter (1987–95), Republican Don Sundquist (1995–2003), Democrat Phil Bredesen (2003–11) and Republican Bill Haslam (2011 to the present)—all of the winning candidates promised competent government, exhibited a moderate pragmatism once in office, and eventually came to be despised by the ideological wings of their respective parties.

Competition was evident at the presidential level as well. In the century stretching from 1900 to 2000, Democratic candidates earned a plurality or majority in fifteen contests, while Republican candidates scored a plurality or majority in eleven contests. Even during the era of the Solid South, glimmers of Republican success were evident. Tennessee held the distinction of being the first state from the former Confederacy since Reconstruction to vote for a Republican—Warren Harding—in 1920, and it later joined four peripheral South states in throwing its electoral weight to Herbert Hoover in 1928. In 1944, Republican Thomas Dewey received almost 40 percent of Tennessee's votes, the highest percentage of any state in the old Confederacy.[14]

The real sustained Republican breakthrough at the presidential level in Tennessee was Dwight Eisenhower's campaigns. Eisenhower's wins in 1952 and 1956 signaled that the GOP brand had some clout beyond the East and was appealing to the state's burgeoning middle class.[15] Beginning in 1952, Tennessee's electoral vote would be in the Republican column in twelve of the next sixteen presidential elections. Tennesseans gave the Democratic candidate a majority or plurality of their vote four times: for Lyndon Johnson in 1964 (55.5 percent of the vote), for Jimmy Carter in 1976 (55.9 percent), and for Bill Clinton in 1992 (47.1 percent) and in 1996 (48.0 percent). The pattern was clear: although the GOP was emerging as the preferred choice, a southerner at the top of the ticket boded well for Democratic chances in Tennessee.

The presidential election of 2000 shattered that theory. Native son Al Gore Jr.'s defeat in Tennessee—he lost to George W. Bush by a margin of about 4 percentage points or a little more than eighty thousand votes–has been subjected to a tremendous amount of academic scrutiny. Some have placed blame on Gore's ineffectual campaign strategies, particularly his unwillingness to use Bill Clinton in Tennessee's growing urban centers.[16] Others cite Gore's particularly poor performance in the Appalachian counties in east Tennessee, where he carried only thirteen of fifty counties. In this interpretation, Gore's perceived radical environmentalism and other significant cultural issues, specifically Tennesseans' support for gun rights, figure heavily in his loss.[17]

The Volunteer State, then, has offered fertile terrain for Republicans and Democrats, progressives and conservatives. As late as 1998, one scholar convincingly compared the two state parties to two champion prizefighters, each one punching and counterpunching in successive elections.[18] Unfortunately for Democrats, the beginning of the twenty-first century marked a new political era, one in which the prizefight became much more lopsided. And the one aberration from this pattern—Democratic governor Phil Bredesen—would be the exception that proved the rule. The skillful GOP fusion of free-market economics and evangelical social concerns was a combination that would be very difficult for most liberal candidates to overcome, and this dynamic would soon become very evident in the electoral results at both the national and state levels.

2000–2014: Republican Fusionism Achieved

Frank Meyer's notion of "fusionism" was grounded in the idea that free-market libertarians and conservative traditionalists could build common ground on a wide range of political fundamentals, from a rejection of the centralized power of the state to their devotion to Western civilization and the Constitution.[19] And some evidence exists that the modern South has embraced this phenomenon: empirical studies have found strong evidence tying evangelicalism to Tea Party support in the region.[20] Whether the tensions between the two groups can be managed as part of a coherent political force is the subject of fierce debate. On election days in Tennessee, however, the case appears settled: the twin engines of free-market economics and evangelical politics are powering the Republican Party to unprecedented heights.

Tax Revolts and Evangelical Politics

"If they could manage this sneak attack on the pocketbooks of unsuspecting Tennesseans, this would rival the genius of the Great Train Robbery," notes colorful pundit Phil Valentine in his chronicle of the pressure-packed debates over a state income tax in legislative sessions from 2000 to 2002.[21] Valentine, a popular conservative voice on Nashville's talk radio circuit, was one of the leading voices against the resurrection of the income tax and a major player in its eventual defeat. Valentine's story begins on an odd note: in the fall of 1999, Republican governor Don Sundquist had astonished many political observers by proposing a state income tax to address state budgetary woes. This action, which represented a reversal of the governor's previous campaign pledges, ensured that the tax debate would occupy a central place in future legislative sessions. Few, however, would have predicted the fireworks that were to follow.

The legislative sessions from 2000 to 2002 were the most intense in the state's modern political history, featuring angry horn-honking protesters, state troopers in riot gear, legislative maneuvering, and votes so scrutinized that some legislators apparently collapsed from the weightiness of the decision.[22] The ultimate defeat of the income tax in May of 2002 was close—the tax failed by only four votes in the house[23]—but the political fallout heralded a culture that would be hostile to future income tax proposals no matter their iteration. Critics branded the anti-tax protesters as an Astroturf movement funded by the ultrarich and cited the income tax's application to a small segment of earners, but even scholars sympathetic to the tax proposal conceded that a more broad-based, "populist anti-tax furor" was at play.[24] Going forward, the idea of a state income tax became political poison for politicians of both parties. This sentiment was underscored nicely by Gov. Phil Bredesen, who had won office in 2002 in no small part because of anti-Sundquist outrage. Bredesen, often described by left-wing media as a "quasi-Republican," noted that a state could not have "Massachusetts services and Tennessee taxes" and that it was clear that Tennesseans preferred the latter.[25]

Tennessee's commitment to free market ideology is matched by its fervent religious traditions. Indeed, the state's high level of religiosity has received a great deal of attention from scholars who sought to understand its politics. The cultural markers are certainly there: Tennessee serves as the headquarters to an interesting medley of faith denominations stretched across its borders, including the Southern Baptist Convention (Nashville), the Cumberland Presbyterians (Cordova), and the Church of God (Cleveland), among others. The flowering of these denominations fostered other opportunities in the areas of education, publishing, and music.[26]

Given a state so infused with religion, politicians have been predictably comfortable talking about their respective faith walks. What might be more surprising is that politicians of all ideological stripes, not just conservatives, have used religious rhetoric in ways that showcased their policy priorities. Sekou Franklin's discussion of former Tennessee governor Frank Clement illuminates how Clement's evangelical style was an integral part of his progressive outlook on social welfare policies, particularly criminal justice reform.[27]

In the current political context, however, the description used to label Clement—"a Godly man in his extroverted fashion"[28]—appears apropos to the political right rather than the political left. Recent legislative sessions have featured robust tussles over legislation with keenly Christian overtones, including debates over the Bible as the official book of Tennessee, as well as fierce debates over the policy implications of religious liberty bills. Tennessee is home to a unique law allowing licensed counselors to refer elsewhere clients whose "goals, outcomes, or behaviors" clash with the counselors' sincerely held principles," a provision derided by the American Counseling Association as a "hate bill" that adversely impacts the state's LGBT community.[29] Outside of sessions, the political rhetoric of the state's leaders has reinforced the idea that Christianity is under attack: Republican legislator and former Lt. Gov. Ron Ramsey, in response to a mass shooting in Oregon, indicated in a Facebook post that Christians should arm themselves, noting, "Whether the perpetrators are motivated by aggressive secularism, jihadist extremism, or racial supremacy, their targets remain the same: Christians and defenders of the West."[30]

The state's robust support for free-market politics and evangelical Christianity were soon reflected in the electoral results, both at the presidential level and below. The tight margins on display in the 2000 presidential race—the last time Tennessee could plausibly be labeled a battleground state—would not be repeated in subsequent elections. In 2004, Bush bested John Kerry with almost 57 percent of the state's votes, a figure that McCain matched in his victory over Obama in 2008. In 2012, the margin grew even larger as Romney won a staggering 59.5 percent to Obama's 39.8 percent.

At the congressional level, both US Senate seats have remained safely under Republican control, and in the 2010 House elections, Tennessee voters flipped the delegation in the House from five-to-four Democratic to seven-to-two Republican. The lone congressional Democrats to survive the carnage resided in the state's urban enclaves: Steve Cohen in the Ninth District (Memphis) and Jim Cooper in the Fifth District (Nashville). At the state level, recent election cycles have brought relentlessly bad news for the Democrats and featured new milestones for the state's GOP. In 2008, Republicans won both houses of the state legislature for the first time since the 1860s. In 2012, the GOP expanded their totals in the state legislature to encompass a two-thirds majority in both houses, leading one scholar to pronounce that "the Democratic Party's grass roots are parched."[31]

The elections of 2014 offered some glimpses of hope for Democrats, but these were soon dashed. Scandal-ridden Republican congressman Scott DesJarlais initially appeared vulnerable but managed to demolish Democrat Lenda Sherrell in the general election. US senator Lamar Alexander faced a strong challenge from erstwhile Tea Partier Joe Carr, but any Democratic hopes that Alexander would be damaged goods in a general election were put to rest by Alexander's commanding victory over Gordon Ball in November.

The GOP further solidified its dominance in state legislative races. Reeling senate Democrats lost two more seats in the midterm, shrinking their total caucus to five in a body of thirty-three senators. House Democrats lost two seats as well; Republicans increased their total in the ninety-nine-member house from seventy-one to seventy-three. Even more dispiriting for Tennessee's progressives, and perhaps the culminating moment for fusionism, was the 2014 ballot measure result. Amendment 1, a measure that furnished legislators more flexibility to regulate abortion rights, passed with 53 percent of the vote, despite pro-Amendment 1 forces being outspent by three to one by anti-Amendment 1 forces in the month before the election.[32] The other ideologically charged amendment on the ballot—Amendment 3, which codified in the state constitution that the state legislature cannot enact an income tax—passed easily with two-thirds support. The passage of both amendments reaffirmed that cultural conservatism and libertarian economics could exist happily side-by-side on Election Day.

2014–2016: Preparing for Trump

A GOP operative working in a lab would be hard pressed to design a harsher landscape for a Democratic presidential candidate than what Tennessee offered in 2016. But in a crowded field of GOP nominees, which Republican would stand out? In the months leading up to Super Tuesday, some clues signaled that Tennessee's political terrain would be conducive to a Trump candidacy.

In retrospect, the 2014 Senate primary between Lamar Alexander and his primary challengers presaged the rise of an antiestablishment candidate. Alexander, armed with almost unanimous establishment support and an immense money advantage over his primary challengers, did not crack the 50 percent mark and won by just 9 points over second-place finisher Joe Carr, "a low water mark" for an incumbent in a GOP primary against a Tea Party insurgent derided by many as running an amateurish campaign.[33] Moreover, the rhetorical animus directed at the federal government in the 2015 and 2016 Tennessee General Assembly sessions suggested that the state political leaders had at least one eye on Washington, DC, during legislative deliberations. It became clear fairly quickly that the GOP's ascendant conservative wing would not brook any policy that had the slightest whiff of the Obama administration, even if the policy had significant support from the GOP establishment. The issue of Insure Tennessee serves as exhibit A in this case.

In November 2014, fresh from his landslide victory, Governor Haslam introduced Insure Tennessee, a policy designed to furnish coverage for Tennesseans who did not qualify for TennCare (the state Medicaid program) or who were unable to purchase insurance through the Affordable Care Act. Haslam was careful to emphasize that his proposal was not simply Tennessee's version of Medicaid expansion and that Tennessee's hospitals had committed to subsidize any potential increase in costs, thus freeing Tennesseans from any new tax increases.[34] Haslam was also careful to use rhetorical touchstones that might be pleasing to conservatives, highlighting the free-market aspects of the plan and its emphasis on personal responsibility. Supporters of Insure Tennessee could be forgiven for cautious optimism given that a constellation of forces seemed to be aligned in their favor: Haslam was a well-liked governor eager to leave his mark on public policy, public opinion polls registered moderate support for the legislation, and large swaths of the business community—particularly hospital executives—came out in full force to back it.[35]

It soon became clear, however, that a tortuous path would await the policy's deliberations.

Haslam called for a special session of the general assembly to debate the merits of Insure Tennessee. Opponents of the bill contended it was simply another variation of the costly Medicaid expansion occurring in other states; in casting a no vote, Senator Roberts noted that Tennessee had "no written guarantee with the federal government that we could end Insure Tennessee and go back to TennCare."[36] Supporters of the bill made a number of interlocking arguments stressing potential economic benefits, the likelihood of job growth in the health care industry, and the moral obligation to take care of the state's working poor.[37] In significant ways, the debate over Insure Tennessee mirrored the income tax debates that had happened over a decade earlier: a center-right governor proposed a contentious policy that would rely on moderate Republicans and significant numbers of Democrats for its passage. The denouement in this case, however, was far less dramatic. Insure Tennessee met a resounding defeat, killed by two senate committees, never even making it to the floor of the Tennessee Senate or House of Representatives for deliberation.[38] It was a defeat so thorough that Haslam seemed unwilling to spend his political currency on the issue in 2016. The debate over Insure Tennessee also highlighted an important political reality for the kind of insurgent campaign Trump offered: not only was the Democratic brand badly damaged in the Volunteer State, establishment Republicans who expressed willingness to collaborate on Democrat-supported legislation would also be considered suspect by a large contingent of Tennessee's voters.

Presidential Primary in Tennessee

In the lead-up to Super Tuesday, the state's rising prominence in Republican circles was on display, with journalists singling out the state's expansive media markets, its large delegate counts, and its ideological diversity.[39] The party's frontrunners on the Republican side seemed to understand this point as well. Ted Cruz, Donald Trump, Marco Rubio, and Ben Carson made several stops across the state in 2015, with Cruz in particular showcasing a well-organized and extensive campaign infrastructure.[40] At a December rally in Nashville, Cruz fed red meat to the audience, attacking Obama's national security, immigration, and gun policies. Referring to the tragedy in Chattanooga months earlier in which Islamic terrorist Muhammad Youssef Abdulazeez committed drive-by shootings at two military installations, Cruz promised new laws designed to allow soldiers to carry weapons, noting, "What that means is the next time a Jihadist shows up at a recruiting center in Chattanooga, he's going to encounter the business end of firearms wielded by a dozen Marines."[41]

The antiestablishment mood on display at the national level matched the mood in Tennessee. A November 2015 poll found Carson in the lead and the only candidate of either party who received positive favorability ratings.[42] Carson's fade on the national scene mirrored his fade in Tennessee. Four days before the Iowa caucus, another poll revealed that Trump had jumped convincingly ahead of the pack, becoming the favorite of a third of Republican registered voters and the surprising leader among independents.[43] Two days before Super Tuesday, Trump had a commanding double-digit lead in Tennessee, almost matching the total favorability share of his two closest rivals.[44]

Trump's deep support in the state was reflected in the raucous crowds that greeted him during multiple visits to Tennessee, and his incendiary rhetoric found receptive ears among Tennessee voters as well as among some of the state's political leaders. In response to Trump's call for banning Muslim immigration, Republican state senator Mae Beavers expressed her unqualified support, noting that "it's about protecting our own, protecting our country."[45] In some cases, politicians escalated the rhetoric: in response to the debate over Syrian refugees, GOP caucus chairman Glen Casada argued, "We need to gather (Syrian refugees) up and politely take them back to the ICE center and say, 'They're not coming to Tennessee, they're yours.'"[46]

To be sure, a considerable number of elected officials expressed unease with Trump's candidacy, and several dismissed his rhetoric outright. GOP chairman Ryan Haynes roundly condemned Trump's comments on Muslim immigration, and as Super Tuesday approached, it was clear that voter affection for Trump was not matched by support from the political elite. Cruz led the way in endorsements, snagging the support of twenty state lawmakers, while Rubio hauled in the biggest fish, earning endorsements from both Governor Haslam and Senator Alexander, both of whom stressed his electability and issued dire warnings about a possible Trump takeover of the GOP.[47] The organizational dynamics mirrored those elsewhere: the Cruz campaign featured a strong ground game, a television ad blitz, and a special role for evangelical pastors, who doubled as campaign chairmen.[48]

On the Democratic side, there was very little appetite for an insurgent candidacy: Hillary Clinton led comfortably in the polls throughout the primary season, and Bernie Sanders apparently recognized this reality by not appearing at a campaign rally in the state. Clinton held rallies in both Nashville and Memphis in November and complemented her personal appearances with ad buys in the bigger media markets. Two days before Super Tuesday, Clinton returned to Tennessee, reiterated her support for the Affordable Care Act, and urged Tennessee's lawmakers to reconsider Medicaid expansion.[49]

Primary Results

The state of Tennessee offered a desirable prize on March 1. With fifty-eight delegates at stake for the Republicans and seventy-six at stake for the Democrats, Tennessee ranked behind only Georgia and Texas in delegate numbers on Super Tuesday. Record-breaking early primary voting numbers suggested a preternatural amount of interest as well. Befitting the state's turn to the right, Republicans appeared to be especially energized, outnumbering Democratic voters by two to one.[50] Election Day results mirrored the late polls: Trump won comfortably with almost 39 percent of the vote, followed by Cruz with 24.7 percent and Rubio with 21.2 percent. Observers looking to tease out major differences in the grand divisions in the state would search in vain: Trump won every county in both east and west Tennessee and lost only in one middle Tennessee county (Williamson) to Rubio by a slim margin. Ted Cruz emerged from Super Tuesday clearly ensconced in second place, beating Rubio in all but seven counties. Rubio supporters could take heart that he met the 20 percent threshold for earning delegates, but he still finished a distant third with nine, behind Cruz with fourteen and Trump with thirty-one.

In line with scholarship that contends that Trump drew disproportionate support from economically depressed communities, I performed a linear regression comparing county unemployment rates at the time of the primary with Trump's vote share, and found a somewhat strong linear relationship (multiple R = .560) between the two variables. Journalistic accounts of rural communities reinforce the narrative that Trump did especially well in Tennessee's impoverished rural areas, where free-trade policies have devastated blue-collar manufacturing.[51]

But to paint Trump as solely a savior for working-class whites understates his appeal in Tennessee. Table 11.1 compares Trump to his two closest Republican rivals across various demographic categories. According to CNN exit polls, Trump won a plurality of voters in virtually every income and age category, including women (38 percent), men (43 percent), high school graduates (51 percent), college graduates (36 percent), upper-income voters (36 percent), and independents (40 percent).[52]

Comparing Trump with the winners of the last two Republican primaries—Mike Huckabee in 2008 and Rick Santorum in 2012—further illustrates his appeal. In terms of vote percentage, Trump outperformed Huckabee in eighty-three of ninety-five Tennessee counties (87 percent of counties) and outperformed Santorum in seventy-six of ninety-five Tennessee counties (80 percent of counties). Table 11.2 displays Trump's victory in terms of raw vote totals, percentage totals, and the number of counties in which he exceeded 40 percent. Cracking the 40 percent threshold in over four-fifths of the state's counties was no mean feat for a political novice saddled with the task of fending off several experienced candidates. And although all three Republican winners won multicandidate elections against quality challengers, only Trump was faced with a relentlessly negative ad blitz timed to derail his front-runner status.

Table 11.1. Tennessee Presidential Primary Exit Polls, 2016

	Total	Women	Men	High-school or less	College degree	Earning at least $100,000	Independents
Trump	38.9	38	43	51	36	36	40
Cruz	24.7	23	26	22	27	26	21
Rubio	21.2	23	18	15	24	26	24
Clinton	66.1	70	64	77	59	72	45
Sanders	32.4	29	35	23	40	27	54

Sources: "Tennessee Exit Polls: Republican," *CNN Politics*, http://www.cnn.com/election/primaries/polls/tn/Rep; "Tennessee Exit Polls: Democrat," *CNN Politics*, http://www.cnn.com/election/primaries/polls/nh/Dem.

Note: All table entries are percentages. Republican candidate totals may not add up to 100 percent, as other party candidates are omitted.

Table 11.2. Tennessee Republican Primary Results, 2008–2016

	Trump, 2016	Santorum, 2012	Huckabee, 2008
Votes (#)	332,702	205,809	190,904
Vote (%)	39	37	34
Counties won (#)	94	91	69
Counties exceeding 40% threshold (#)	78	52	36

Sources: "2008 Tennessee Primary Results," *CNN Politics*, http://www.cnn.com/ ELECTION/2008/primaries/results/state/#TN; "2012 Tennessee Primary Results," *CNN Politics*, http://www.cnn.com/election/2012/primaries/state/tn/; "2016 Tennessee Primary Results," *CNN Politics*, http://www.cnn.com/election/primaries/states/tn.

In the Democratic primary, Hillary Clinton breezed to victory with 66.1 percent of the vote, winning ninety-two of the state's ninety-five counties. Sanders won a majority in only three sparsely populated counties on or near Tennessee's eastern border. Table 11.1 showcases Clinton's dominance across various demographic categories—she won a majority of women (70 percent), men (64 percent), college graduates (59 percent), high school graduates (77 percent), and upper-income earners (72 percent). Only among self-identified independents did Sanders narrowly outperform Clinton (by 54 to 45 percent). Not included in table 11.1 is Clinton's substantial win with nonwhite voters (by 85 to 14 percent).[53] As a coda to the primary season, I examined Clinton's county margins along racial lines. In the ten counties with the largest African American populations, Clinton won at least 73 percent of the vote, including a remarkable 80.1 percent in Memphis's Shelby County. But to assume that Clinton's success was powered solely by African American votes would be a mistake: in the ten counties featuring the smallest African American populations, Clinton still performed exceptionally well, earning approximately 65 percent of votes cast. Sanders's supporters would be hard pressed to find a silver lining in Tennessee.

The General Election in Tennessee

The political "off-season" in Tennessee was relatively quiet. Most Republicans in the state quietly accepted Trump as the presumptive nominee and exhibited no appetite for abandoning the Republican standard-bearer, although some leading figures, including Governor Haslam and Senator Corker, indicated unease with his unorthodox campaigning. Corker, who had withheld his endorsement during the primaries, later agreed to advise

Trump on foreign policy issues.[54] The biggest Republican defection from the campaign occurred in mid-October when Haslam encouraged Trump to step aside when the latter's lewd comments about women surfaced in the now infamous *Access Hollywood* video.

The summer party conventions featured Tennesseans as prominent speakers. Conservative congresswoman Marsha Blackburn offered a full-throated endorsement of Trump just hours before his acceptance speech, and Democratic state legislator Raumesh Akbari pledged her support for Clinton. The convention also featured one other peculiar moment: anti-Islam firebrand and leader of the Dutch Party for Freedom Geert Wilders attended the convention as a guest of Tennessee Republicans, suggesting that antipathy to Islamic terrorism might be the glue that continues to fuse together the disparate wings of the party.[55]

The results in Tennessee on November 8 were decidedly undramatic, especially in comparison to the national political shockwaves generated by the state's neighbors.

No statewide elections or referenda dotted the ballot and none of the House races were remotely competitive. Table 11.3 offers a broad overview of the election results. Trump cruised to victory with 61.1 percent of the state's vote to Clinton's 34.9 percent, a win so complete that Trump's Tennessee vote margin ranked only behind Alabama among southern states. Clinton carried precisely the same four counties where Obama had prevailed in 2012. She coasted to victory in the state's two most populous counties—Shelby and Davidson—and squeaked by in two rural counties in west Tennessee that featured large African American populations. West Tennessee appears to be the only region of the state that is in play for both parties, but that is no doubt due to Memphis's disproportionate influence.

Given the state's lack of competition, Tennessee found itself paired with Massachusetts as one of the two most populous states in the country without network-sponsored exit polling.[56] Nevertheless, some interesting trends emerged in comparisons of 2016 with 2012. Table 11.3 indicates that Trump outperformed Romney statewide (by 61 percent to 59 percent) and outpaced him in the three grand divisions of the state. GOP fears of establishment Republicans staying home or crossing over to support the Democratic candidate never materialized. By contrast, Clinton lagged behind Obama statewide (by 35 percent to 39 percent) and registered, in each division of the state, the worst loss for a Democratic presidential nominee since George McGovern's woeful performance in 1972. Dejected state Democrats were left to ponder how low the political floor would sink.

Table 11.3. Tennessee Presidential Election Results, 2012–2016

	2016		2012	
	Trump	Clinton	Romney	Obama
Total votes (#)	1,517,402	867,110	1,460,238	959,439
Statewide (%)	61.1	34.9	59.0	39.0
East TN (%)	73.0	27.0	69.0	31.0
Middle TN (%)	63.0	37.0	60.0	40.0
West TN (%)	50.5	49.5	48.0	52.0

Sources: "2012 Tennessee Poll," CNN Politics, http://www.cnn.com/election/2012 / results/state/TN/; "2016 Tennessee Poll," CNN Politics, http://www.cnn.com/ election/ results/states/tennessee/president.

Down the ticket, the House incumbency advantage was alive and well: eight of the nine House members won handily, and the ninth candidate, Republican David Kustoff, breezed to victory in an open seat election in west Tennessee. No House incumbent received less than 62 percent of the vote, and the institutional split remained at seven to two in favor of the GOP. The predictive pattern is simple: expect Democrats to dominate in Nashville and Memphis but be routed elsewhere. At the state legislative level, Democratic vital signs went from serious to critical condition: the GOP picked up yet another house seat, raising its total to seventy-four in the ninety-nine-seat body. In the state senate, Republicans retained a margin of twenty-eight to five.

Conclusion

Although Tennessee's political culture has long exhibited a powerful conservatism, strong progressive and moderate voices—at least by southern standards—gave the state its reputation as an ideologically diverse battleground open to both parties. That dynamic has disappeared. Twenty years after Bill Clinton won the state with a 48 percent plurality and captured large sections of west and middle Tennessee, Hillary Clinton lost ninety-one of ninety-five counties to Donald Trump in a race that was never remotely competitive. In 1996, one could plausibly argue that Tennessee would follow the path of North Carolina or Virginia on Election Day. After 2016, the safe bet is to assume that the state's presidential elections will continue to track closely with its neighbors in Alabama and Mississippi. Tennessee is no longer a reluctant southern state.

12

The Great Red Wall of Texas

How Long Will It Stand?

Brian Arbour

The 2016 election produced one of the most shocking upsets in American political history. Again and again, political observers predicted the political demise of Donald Trump. But voters proved indifferent to Trump's transgressive behavior and lack of policy knowledge and decorum. Trump's own shamelessness and willingness to move forward seemed to overload the circuits of the media and many voters. The constant barrage of negative stories about Donald Trump seemed to constantly pass by, with few fully sticking to him. Questions about the accuracy of these stories seemed almost an afterthought after a few days.

As a result, Donald Trump won the 2016 election in large part because he won a vote share that looks like a normal Republican one. He overcame a series of seemingly disqualifying characteristics and a lack of long-term loyalty to the Republican Party and its ideals to win 89 percent of the votes of Republicans across the country, according to the exit polls conducted by the major television and cable news networks. Trump's ability to make himself acceptable to Republicans allowed him to win easily in traditionally red states. The largest of those is Texas.

Republicans have been on a long-term winning streak in the state of Texas. The Republican presidential nominee has not lost the state since

1976, and Republicans have not lost a race for any of the Lone Star State's twenty-seven statewide elected offices since 1998. The year 2016 proved to be more of the same. Donald Trump consolidated the Republican vote (he won Texas Republicans by a margin of 88 to 9 percent) and, as a result, won the state by a comfortable margin. While Texas did not feature a senate or governor's race in 2016, it did feature seven minor statewide races where the Republican nominees outpaced their Democratic opponents by 14.5 points, on average. Republicans held on to the state's one contested US House race (in the Twenty-Third District, where incumbent Will Hurd won by 48 to 47 percent over former representative Pete Gallego). In the state legislature, Republicans maintained their overwhelming majorities in both bodies (twenty to eleven in the state senate; ninety-five to fifty-five in the state house).

In short, Texas has been and continues to be a red state. Republicans win the state comfortably, and voters have consistently shown their approval of Republican governance of the state. Yet, the 2016 election shows some signs of blue cracks in the state's red wall. Hillary Clinton only trailed Trump by 9 percentage points, cutting nearly 6 points off Mitt Romney's margin in the state over Barack Obama in 2012.

Clinton made big gains over Barack Obama's 2012 vote share in the state's largest counties—15 points in Travis (Austin), 12 points in Harris (Houston), nearly 11 points in Dallas, 9 points in Bexar (San Antonio), and 7 points in Tarrant (Fort Worth). These Democratic gains came not only from the increased share of Latino and Asian American voters in each county but also from the ability of Clinton to gain votes among whites living in upscale urban precincts. These numbers indicate that Texas's big cities are transforming politically to look more and more like urban areas in the rest of the country—where socially liberal whites vote with working-class minority communities to create a strong political base for the Democratic Party. In urban Texas, local politics are becoming more similar to national politics, and that is good news in the long term for the Democrats.

The bad news for Democrats in Texas is that the state's suburbs do not behave like suburbs in the rest of the nation. The suburban counties that ring the state's five largest cities are reliably and strongly Republican. Trump won 61.0 percent of the vote there. When one combines that with the 61.5 percent of the vote that Trump won in rural and small-town Texas, one can see why Republicans win Texas so easily and why Republicans seem strong favorites to continue to win Texas in the 2018 statewide elections and, assuming their positions are held, in the 2020 presidential election. Even with all of his flaws, Donald Trump won land-slide shares outside of the state's large cities and won the state while investing few resources in it. The 2016 election results may provide some signs of hope for Democrats in Texas, but they also show that these hopes are still a long way from being realized.

This chapter examines Texas's role in the presidential nomination pro-cess, highlighting the campaign of Ted Cruz and his victory in his home-state primary. It then focuses on the general election campaign, noting the unsuccessful attempt of the Clinton campaign to feint the Trump campaign into expending resources defending the state. The chapter then discusses the election results and polling results from Texas, which demonstrate the conservative policy preferences of Texas voters. The chapter concluded by analyzing the hopeful signs for Democrats in the 2016 election results, highlighting their gains in urban Texas and examining how long it might take for Democrats to break through to overcome Republican dominance in the state.

Nomination Politics in Texas

Texas played a critical role in the 2012 nomination contest, as then gov-ernor Rick Perry quickly emerged as a serious challenger to presumptive favorite Mitt Romney and, just as quickly, receded after an inability to address his position on immigration and a series of gaffes.[1]

In 2016, Texas again played a crucial role in the Republican nomi-nation contest by supplying candidates from the state's deep Republican bench. Perry ran again, but his campaign received no support from Repub-lican donors, elected officials, or voters. Languishing in the polls and out of money, he dropped out of the race five months before the Iowa caucuses.[2]

Texas senator Ted Cruz proved a much longer-lasting part of the Republican primary contest. Cruz's ambitions for higher office were evi-dent from the moment of his upset victory in the US Senate primary in Texas in 2012. In the Senate, Cruz made high-profile stands against the Affordable Care Act, staging an all-night speech from the Senate floor to oppose the law, and being a key supporter of the government shutdown in 2013.[3]

Cruz announced his candidacy in March 2015 in a speech to stu-dents at Liberty University.[4] He worked to position himself on the right-most flank of the Republican electorate. He stayed steady in the polls throughout summer and the early fall, but started to make gains when

Ben Carson's support collapsed in November 2015. By late 2015, Cruz had risen to second in the polls behind Donald Trump, a position he would maintain throughout the rest of the nomination contest.[5]

Cruz won his home state primary on March 1, 2016, taking 44 percent of the vote and 104 of the 155 delegates at stake that night. Cruz also won contests in Oklahoma, Colorado, and Alaska that night, establishing him in second place behind Trump (who won that night in Virginia, Tennessee, Massachusetts, Georgia, Arkansas, and Alabama).[6]

But Cruz's success in his home state could not be replicated elsewhere. He was not able to consolidate the anti-Trump vote because of his ideological distance from moderate anti-Trumpers, the continuing presence of John Kasich in the race, and the clear ambivalence of the Republican establishment on supporting Cruz. After Trump's victory over Cruz in the Indiana primary, Cruz dropped out of the race.[7] Over the course of the race, Cruz had consolidated the support of the Texas's Republican establishment. Perry endorsed Cruz in January[8] and Greg Abbott a week before the Texas primary;[9] Lt. Gov. Dan Patrick, the Texas politician most in tune with right wing voters, endorsed Cruz in October 2015. As a result of their support for Cruz, Texans at first seemed to be less likely to hold important jobs in the first few years of the Trump administration. But the Trump administration offered an olive branch to Texas Republicans when they nominated Rick Perry for the symbolically important job of secretary of energy.[10]

On the Democratic side, Hillary Clinton easily won by 65 to 33 percent.[11] Sanders essentially conceded the state to Clinton, and the results show it. Sanders won only a handful of demographic groups in Texas—voters aged eighteen to twenty-nine, independents, those who had never voted in a previous Democratic primary, those who never attend church, and white men.[12] Clinton won among all other demographic groups in the state, and coasted to an easy victory.

General Election in Texas

Usually, most Texans experience the general election campaign for president as something that happens in other states. The Wesleyan Media Project reported that less than 15,000 of the 920,000 presidential broadcast television advertisements aired in a Texas media market. A healthy share of these aired in El Paso, whose media market includes parts of the state of New Mexico (including the city of Las Cruces), which was a potential swing state.[13]

The candidates paid little attention to the state except as a source of funds. Donald Trump held rallies in Houston and Dallas in June and Austin in August.[14] Trump reportedly would not do the work of going to fund-raising events unless he got to do a rally, no matter how little the effect of the rally on the goal of winning the election.[15] Trump made a fundraising swing through the state in mid-September and attended a rally organized by an anti-immigration group in Houston.[16] Clinton herself did not make an appearance in Texas, but vice presidential nominee Tim Kaine talked at organizing events in Austin in August[17] and in Houston in September in connection with fundraising events.[18]

As happens every four years, some Democrats made noises about a Democrat winning Texas. The Clinton campaign even opened up an office in Houston in mid-September,[19] and buoyed by a survey by the *Washington Post* and Survey Monkey that showed Clinton with a 1-point lead in the state,[20] there was enough smoke around the Texas results for the *New York Times* to headline the preelection article "Could Hillary Clinton Win Texas? Some Democrats Say Maybe."[21]

The best way to interpret the Clinton campaign's efforts in Texas is as a feint. They hoped that giving a little attention to the state would compel the Trump campaign to have to spend resources to defend the nation's largest red state. The efforts of the Clinton campaign in Texas were ultimately unsuccessful—the Trump campaign did not respond by spending money or time in Texas. But because the Clinton campaign used so few of the campaign's resources, it is unlikely that their small efforts in Texas cost them anything important in swing states.

Election Results

As has been the case for many cycles, it did not take long to call the state of Texas for the Republican presidential nominee. Donald Trump easily won the state, garnering 52.2 percent of the vote. Hillary Clinton won 43.2 percent of the vote, while third-party candidates took home 4.0 percent of the vote. Table 12.1 presents these results.

There was little action down the ballot. Neither of the state's US Senate seats were on the ball. The state featured only one contested US House race, as incumbent Republican Will Hurd held off former US representative Pete Gallego by 48.5 to 46.8 percent in the Twenty-Third District, which runs from the San Antonio suburbs along the Rio Grande to the exurbs of El Paso. None of the major statewide offices were on the ballot, but Republicans comfortably won an open seat race to the

Table 12.1. The Vote in Texas, 2012

	President	Twenty-Third Con- gressional District	Six contested court races
Republican	Donald Trump 4,685,047(52.2%)	Will Hurd (incumbent) 110,577 48.3%)	Average (54.9%)
Democrat	Hillary Clinton 3,877,868 (43.2%)	Pete Gallego 107,526 (47.0%)	Average (40.0%)

Source: Election results from the Texas Secretary of State.

Note: Texas held elections for three Texas Supreme Court seats and three seats on the Texas Court of Criminal Appeals. The fourth column averages the percentage of the vote received by the Republican and Democratic nominees.

Railroad Commission of Texas and all six of the statewide judicial races on the ballot. Table 12.1 shows the average vote share for each party in the court races.

Red Wall

Why did Trump win Texas? Trump was a Republican running in a Republican state. The network exit polls showed that 38 percent of the state's voters are Republicans, and only 29 percent are Democrats. In addition, 44 percent of Texas voters identify their ideology as conservative, while only 20 percent identify themselves as liberal. Much like previous Republican nominees, Trump was able to easily win the state of Texas with little effort because of its conservative and Republican nature. In addition, Trump won the state's independent voters by a 52 to 38 percent margin (previous Republican nominees have won Texas independents by similar margins).

Trump performed better in Texas across a wide variety of groups than he did nationally. In Texas, Trump lost women by only 2 points (by 49 to 47 percent), while he lost them nationally by a 54 to 42 percent margin. Trump won only 21 percent of minority voters nationally, but he won 29 percent of them in Texas. This was most notable among Latinos; Trump won 34 percent of Texas Latino voters, 5 points more than his national vote share.[22]

It is also notable that there was no "class inversion" in Texas. Journalist Ronald Brownstein identified an accelerated trend in 2016 where voters without a college degree were migrating to the Republicans and those who graduated college were trending Democratic.[23] In 2016, Clinton won college graduates nationally by a 52 to 42 percent margin, while Trump won voters who lacked a college degree by a 51 to 44 percent margin. That gap did not appear in Texas. Trump won college graduates by a 51 to 43 percent margin, and those without a college degree by a similar 53 to 43 percent margin. The ability of Texas Republicans to retain the loyalty of college graduates stands in contrast to other large states that Clinton easily won. For example, Clinton won college graduates by 65 to 30 percent in California, 64 to 33 percent in New York, and 58 to 36 percent in Illinois. As long as Texas Republicans retain the voting loyalty of highly educated Texas, they will continue to win the state by large margins.

A preelection poll from the *Texas Tribune* and the University of Texas at Austin showed the conservative policy preferences of Texas voters, which led to them to vote for the more conservative candidate on Election Day.[24] The poll found that more Texans supported deporting undocumented people than supported allowing them to stay in the country, and 50 percent of Texans agree with the position that the state should not accept Syrian refugees. Only 35 percent of Texans thought that women faced "a great deal" or "a lot" of discrimination, while 52 percent thought they only faced "a little" or "a moderate amount" of discrimination.

Polling results from both the exit poll and the poll by the University of Texas and the *Texas Tribune* showed that Texans were pleased with the way things are going in the state. While only 22 percent of respondents thought the nation is "on the right track," 42 percent of Texans thought their state was going in the right direction. Texans were broadly happy with the condition of the economy in their state—only 24 percent of Texans thought the economy was worse off than it had been a year before. This positive view of the state of Texas has led to a positive view of its leaders. This was shown not only in the election results and the continual support for Republican candidates but also in polling results. For example, 9 percent more Texans approved of the job Governor Abbott has done than disapprove.

Polling data also shows that campaign events worked to hinder Hillary Clinton's standing in the state, while they had little impact on Donald Trump's standing. For example, 49 percent of Texas voters said they were bothered by Hillary Clinton's use of a nongovernment email account. One analyst said that "there's one ideology that [Trump] does hold with sincerity and practices with unwavering fervor: misogyny." During the campaign, a video leaked showing Donald Trump bragging about regularly sexually assaulting women,[25] and a dozen women came forward to allege that Trump had groped them.[26] According to the exit polls, only 41 percent of Texas voters declared that Trump's treatment of women bothered them "a lot."[27]

Texas is a state with more Republicans than Democrats and more conservatives than liberals. It has conservative policy preferences, views its own state and economy in a positive light, and is pleased with the leadership it is receiving from its conservative Republican government. In short, it surprised no one when Texas went red in the 2016 election.

Hope for Democrats

Yet despite the easy and comfortable Republican victory, a closer look at the election returns and the exit polls shows that there are some reasons for optimism among Democrats. The election returns show that Trump won the state easily, marking the tenth straight presidential election in which the Lone Star State has gone red. But Trump's margin was reduced from that of Mitt Romney. Table 12.2 shows the vote share for Republican presidential nominees nationally and in the state. The right-hand column, titled Difference, is calculated by subtracting the margin in the Texas from the national margin. The number shows how much more Republican (positive values) or Democratic (negative values) the Texas electorate is compared to the national electorate.

In the 1950s and 1960s, Texas was more Democratic than the nation, but it moved toward the Republicans in the 1970s and 1980s. Starting in the 1996 election, Texas turned even further to the right. In the four elections between 2000 and 2012, the Republican nominee ran at least 10 points better in Texas than he did nationally. In the context of a seemingly steady rise of Republican voting in the state, 2016 stands out. Trump won 52.2 percent of the vote in the state, only 6.1 percent more than his national vote share. Hillary Clinton, for all of her flaws, cut the Republican margin in Texas by half.

What accounts for the trimmed Republican margin in the state? The exit polls show that Hillary Clinton won Texas voters under the age of forty. And she won voters under thirty in the state by a margin of 55 to 36 percent. That mirrors the 55 to 37 percent margin by which Clinton won young voters nationally. So, if young voters in Texas are behaving in the same way as young voters across the nation, then Democrats have a chance to build on that to achieve parity in Texas.

The exit polls also show that Clinton won majorities among minority voters in Texas, just as she did nationally. Clinton won 84 percent of

Table 12.2. Republican Vote Trend in Texas, 1948–2008

Year	Vote share of Rep. pres. nominee		Difference
	Texas	National	
1948	24.3	45.1	−20.8
1952	53.1	55.2	−2.1
1956	55.3	57.4	−2.1
1960	48.5	49.6	−1.0
1964	36.5	38.5	−2.0
1968	39.9	43.4	−3.6
1972	66.2	60.7	+5.5
1976	48.0	48.0	−0.1
1980	55.3	50.8	+4.5
1984	63.6	58.8	+4.8
1988	56.0	53.4	+2.6
1992	40.6	37.5	+3.1
1996	48.8	40.7	+8.0
2000	59.3	47.9	+11.4
2004	61.1	50.7	+10.4
2008	56.3	46.3	+10.0
2012	57.2	47.2	+10.0
2016	52.2	46.1	+6.1

Sources: Historical data from David Leip, "Dave Leip's Atlas of US Presidential Elections," http://uselectionatlas.org/. Data for 2016 from David Wasserman, Cook Political Report, http://cookpolitical.com/story/10174.

Note: All table entries are percentages.

African American Texans, 75 percent of Asian Americans in the state, and 61 percent of Latinos in the state. Combined, nonwhite voters made up 43 percent of the Texas electorate in 2016. The minority share of the Texas population and the Texas electorate is growing. The 43 percent nonwhite share was up from 37 percent in 2008 and 34 percent in 2004.[28]

Most of the gains that Clinton made over previous Democratic nominees were in urban Texas. Most notable were her gains in Harris County (Houston), which she won by 54 to 42 percent. In 2012, Barack Obama had eked out a 971-vote victory in the most populous county in the state. It was a similar story throughout the five largest counties in Texas. As table 12.3 shows, Clinton won these counties by 55 percent to Trump's 40 percent. She improved 11 points in the five biggest counties over Barack Obama's margin in 2012.

Table 12.3. Presidential Vote in Texas by Geographic Region

	2016 Election			2012 Electorate		
	Trump	Clinton	Share of electorate	Romney	Obama	Share of electorate
Statewide	52.4	43.3	—	57.2	41.4	—
Urban (five big cities)	40.3	55.1	42.2	47.3	51.1	42.7
Suburban	61.0	34.4	25.7	63.7	34.8	25.8
Rest of state	61.5	34.9	32.1	65.2	33.6	31.5

Source: Data from Texas Secretary of State. Calculations done by author.

Note: All table entries are percentages. The urban counties are Bexar (San Antonio), Dallas, Harris (Houston), Tarrant (Fort Worth), and Travis (Austin). Suburban counties are all those designated by the US Bureau of the Census as part of the Austin, Dallas–Fort Worth, Houston, or San Antonio metropolitan areas except for the urban counties listed above.

Table 12.3 may show some good signs for the Democrats, but it also shows why Republicans have won handily in Texas and why Republican candidates are the favorites to continue to win statewide elections. Republicans won in both the suburbs and the small towns and rural Texas by landslide margins.[29] Trump won the suburban counties that surround the state's five largest cities by a 61 to 34 percent margin, and he won the rest of the state's counties by a 62 to 35 percent margin. Clinton did make small gains in these two regions over Barack Obama's performance in 2012, but the landslide margins by which Trump won regions of the state outside of its biggest counties gave him a comfortable win on election night. In states where Democrats have won comfortably in recent years, they have done so because they were able to win suburban counties and to add them to their landslide margins in urban precincts. Until Texas Democrats can gain a significant number of votes in suburban counties, they will continue to languish without any victories.

Looking Ahead in Texas Politics

This chapter has argued that while the 2016 results provide some signs of hope for Texas Democrats, they also demonstrate that the state remains strongly Republican. Broadly speaking, Texas voters have conservative policy preferences and are relatively pleased with the actions of the conservatives who run the state. For all the gains that Hillary Clinton made in Texas's five urban counties, she made few gains in the suburban counties that ring the five urban counties or in the small towns and rural areas that make up the rest of the state. As long as Republicans maintain landslide levels in suburban and small-town Texas, they will continue to comfortably win elections in the state.

In 2018, first-term senator Ted Cruz and first-term governor Greg Abbott will both be up for reelection. As incumbent Republicans in a Republican state, they both enter the 2018 election cycle as substantial favorites to win reelection. Two potential pitfalls should cause worry for these politicians and their staffs. The first threat to both men is in the 2018 Republican primary, and each has his own individual set of worries.

For Cruz, his testy relationship with President Trump is key to determining his fate within the Republican primary. Cruz finished second in the 2016 Republican nominating contest in terms of votes and contests won, and Trump needlessly attacked Cruz's wife's physical appearance[30] and insinuated that Cruz's father was involved in the assassination of John F. Kennedy[31] (as with all Trump conspiracy theories, there is no evidence for this claim). At the Republican convention, Cruz did not directly endorse Trump but urged people to "vote your conscience."[32] No matter how bizarre, personal or insignificant the reasons for Trump's dislike of Cruz, they do create a negative mark for Cruz's political future. In addition, Cruz spent his first four years in Washington burnishing his own credentials to run for president, often by criticizing establishment politicians as insufficiently conservative. As a result, a number of establishment Republican figures are not fans of Cruz.[33] The *Texas Tribune* reported in November 2016 that no less a Texas Republican establishment figure than Rick Perry had encouraged Rep. Michael McCaul to challenge Cruz in the 2018 primary.[34] Cruz will have to spend substantial time and effort in 2017 mending fences with a party base enthralled by Donald Trump and a party establishment angered by his attacks on him.

For Abbott, his primary worry is Lt. Gov. Dan Patrick. Patrick is the definition of a colorful character—a Houston sportscaster turned failed restaurant owner turned successful right-wing talk radio host. Patrick was known for ratings stunts such as painting his body the Columbia blue of the Houston Oilers for a sportscast and having a vasectomy performed live on the radio.[35] In 2006, Patrick ran for state senate and crushed three experienced elected officials in the Republican primary. His bombastic personality, honed by hours on air, made him a star in the Texas legislature with Tea Party and other antiestablishment Republicans. In 2014, Patrick defeated incumbent David Dewhurst by 30 points in the Republican primary, and his popularity with the Republican base in the state has made him the most important figure in state politics in the legislative session of 2015.[36] Patrick has defeated establishment figures in Republican primaries and Abbott has behaved as governor as though he does not want to be Patrick's next victim. Abbott has signed bills pushed by Patrick and social conservatives to expand gun rights, defund Planned Parenthood, and protect pastors from having to perform same-sex weddings. Few thought these were Abbott's priorities when he took office.

Assuming they win the Republican nomination and advance to the 2018 general election, the fates of Abbott and Cruz are collectively tied to the popularity of Donald Trump, their party's president. Political scientists have long studied the midterm decline, in which the party of the president almost inevitably loses Senate seats and governor's chairs in midterm elections.[37] Presidential ratings often sag across time as presidents learn that pleasing people while making the hard choices of government is more difficult than making easy promises during a campaign.[38] Also, presidents often bring out new supporters in their initial run for office, but these occasional voters are less likely to turn out when their president is not on the ballot.[39] The midterm slumps of Barack Obama led to Republican US Senate victories in blue states such as Illinois and GOP victories in governors' races in Democratic bastions such as Maryland and Massachusetts. These trends bode ill for Abbott and Cruz. If President Trump's approval ratings are in the low forties, there is reason to think that even red-state politicians such as Cruz and Abbott might be in political trouble.

The midterm slump phenomenon, though, conflicts with the recent midterm-election trend of reduced turnout by Democrat-friendly demographics such as young voters and minorities. The 2016 electorate was 43 percent nonwhite and 19 percent under the age of 30. The midterm electorate in 2014 was 34 percent nonwhite and 14 percent under the age of 30. In short, the midterm electorate is much friendlier to Republicans and provides an extra cushion for Abbott and Cruz, or whoever wins the Republican nomination for these seats. In the Obama midterm elections, these two trends reinforced each other and led to substantial Republican victories in both 2010 and 2014 in Texas and across the nation. Under a Republican president, these trends will be in conflict, and it is unclear how they will interact in 2018.

What is clear is that the Republican nominees in 2018, whether Cruz or McCaul, Abbott or Patrick, will enter the general election as the favorite. That is the bad news for Texas Democrats. The good news is that for the first time in nearly two decades, there is clear evidence that the electorate is shifting in ways that advantage the Democrats. As the Latino and Asian American population share of the state increases, so do Democratic fortunes. While Democrats are not likely to win the state in 2018 or 2020, they can and should improve on their performance from recent elections by holding onto their gains among minority Texans. In 2016, Hillary Clinton won 69.5 percent of the two-party vote share of nonwhite Texans and 27.3 percent of the two-party vote share of white Texans. If Democrats maintain the same share of the vote from these two groups, they will outpace Republicans once the electorate is 55 percent nonwhite.

When will the electorate have enough nonwhites for Democrats to win the state of Texas? Table 12.4 examines trends in the racial composition of the Texas electorate over the twenty-first century, finding that the electorate in the state increases by approximately 3 percent each presidential election. If that trend continues, the state's electorate will be majority nonwhite voters by 2028. If the Democrats continue to win the same share of the white and nonwhite vote that Hillary Clinton did in 2016, then the Democratic nominee will win the state in 2032. Of course, the calculations presented in the table assume that everything stays constant

Table 12.4. Projected Presidential Vote Share in Texas Across Time

	White share of electorate	Nonwhite share of electorate	Republican vote share	Democratic vote share
2000	69	31	59	38
2004	66	34	61	38
2008	63	37	55	43
2012	60	40	57	41
2016	57	43	52	43
2020	54	46	53.3	46.7
2024	51	49	52.0	48.0
2028	48	52	50.8	49.2
2032	45	55	49.5	50.5

Sources: Vote share data from 2000, 2004, 2008, and 2016 from network exit polls conducted by Edison Media Research. Calculations from 2020 to 2032 by author, assuming that Democratic nominees win the same two-party share of the white (29.5 percent) and nonwhite (69.5 percent) parts of the Texas electorate that Hillary Clinton won in 2016.

Note: All table entries are percentages. Author estimates are in boldface. Vote share in 2012 and from 2020 to 2032 assumes the 3 percent quadrennial growth in the nonwhite share of the electorate continues in a linear fashion. Vote share data from 2000 to 2016 reflect actual election results.

across time. Democrats can accelerate this clock either by increasing the share of minority voters through registration and mobilization or by winning a greater share of the white vote in the state. The good news on that front for Democrats is that Donald Trump underperformed George W. Bush and John McCain among white voters in Texas. Of course, due to his many personal problems, Trump ran behind most other Republican officials in 2016. If a more acceptable Republican runs in the 2020s and wins a higher share of the white vote in the state, then the task becomes more difficult for Democrats, and the brass ring of a blue Texas is further away.

The results of the 2016 election provide Texas Democrats a glimmer of hope. For the first time in a generation, they made substantial gains at the presidential level in the state. Yet those gains still leave Texas Democrats a long way from even being competitive in the state and much farther from being able to win it. Texas is a red state and will be one for the foreseeable future.

13

Virginia

The Old Dominion Stands Out in Blue

John J. McGlennon and Jakob A. Deel

Introduction

The 2016 presidential election had far more than its share of surprises, and Virginia provided at least one in its combination of predictability and contrariness. Here was a state that had been reliably Republican for forty years prior to Barack Obama's elections extending its Democratic preference once more. This state had resisted the appeal of two Democratic presidents hailing from the South in earlier elections (three of which Jimmy Carter and Bill Clinton won nationally). The Old Dominion was the only state once part of the Confederacy to support Hillary Clinton, and her margin exceeded President Obama's 2012 edge as well (see table 13.1).

Initially, Virginia was expected to be the site of fierce combat in 2016, as it had been in the previous two national contests.[1] Both parties targeted its thirteen electoral votes and anticipated pouring financial, organizational, and candidate resources into the Commonwealth. It was routinely assigned to the "purple" states, neither firmly red nor blue, capable of switching sides on the basis of small moves among the electorate.[2]

Table 13.1. General Presidential Election Results in Virginia, 2016

Party	Candidate	Votes (#)	Vote (%)
Democrat	Hillary Clinton	1,981,473	49.75
Republican	Donald Trump	1,769,443	44.43
Libertarian	Gary Johnson	118,274	2.97
Independent	Evan McMullin	54,054	1.36
Green	Jill Stein	27,638	0.69

Source: Virginia State Board of Elections, https://goo.gl/AmcHws.

So what explained Virginia's sudden exit from these ranks, in the minds of many analysts, and its arrival on the list of Democratic locks? And is that characterization accurate, or was the 2016 outcome the result of the confluence of demography and personality?

Virginia's continuing movement toward the Democrats in presidential and other statewide contests in the twenty-first century was cited by many as a critical obstacle to Republicans seeking to regain the White House. It was argued that, as long as Democrats could compete for toss-up states like Florida, Ohio, and North Carolina, their narrow advantage in Virginia blocked GOP success. The Democrats could assemble an Electoral College majority by carrying the reliably Democratic states of the Northeast, West Coast, and industrial Midwest, and they could cement this unshakeable base using Virginia's electors.[3]

Public opinion polling from mid-2015 on suggested Democratic strength, especially against a potential Donald Trump candidacy for the Republicans. Clinton's close relationship with the Commonwealth's popular governor, Terry McAuliffe, and her eventual selection of the state's junior senator, Tim Kaine, as her running mate made the state seem impregnable as the fall campaign progressed.

Trump's challenges in the Old Dominion were evident throughout the year. Though he won a plurality in the primary, Trump consistently trailed Clinton in public opinion polls of the state. A last-ditch effort by Trump's campaign may have narrowed the gap between the two parties but in the end was not enough to capture the state. Before that point, the campaign appeared to have abandoned Virginia for more promising states.[4]

Without statewide offices at stake, and with odd-year contests for the state legislature, the remaining attention was focused on a handful of the eleven congressional districts. Several had been reconfigured as a result of a successful legal challenge to the congressional map drawn by state legislators. The US Supreme Court found the plan had unconstitutionally packed too many African Americans into one district in order to minimize their impact on the delegation.[5]

The Background

The presence of a Democratic-leaning Virginia in presidential elections is a recent phenomenon. Having supported only one Democratic presidential candidate between 1952 and 2004 (Lyndon Johnson, in 1964), Virginia might have seemed an unlikely battleground in the open 2008 presidential contest. However, in George W. Bush's narrow re-election, observers saw some interesting trends among the state's voters. Presaging a strong movement away from the GOP among college-educated voters in subsequent elections, suburban areas like Albemarle County and university towns moved to the Democrats, and Fairfax County, the state's largest population center, went blue for the first time in forty years.[6]

In both 2008 and 2012, the Old Dominion was a central focus of the election, as measured by campaign spending, presidential and surrogate visits, and grassroots organization. New configurations of the electorate emerged, with fast-growing, increasingly diverse metropolitan areas breaking for Democratic gubernatorial candidate Tim Kaine in 2005, senatorial candidates Jim Webb and Mark Warner in 2006 and 2008 respectively, and Obama in 2008. Only Bob McDonnell, the GOP governor elected in 2009, was able to overcome the Democratic tilt of the electorate. Though a landslide winner, McDonnell eventually would resign from office in the last year of his four-year term upon his conviction on corruption charges. Though the conviction was later overturned by the US Supreme Court, McDonnell's fall was precipitous, coming soon after he was a final candidate to become the vice presidential running mate of Mitt Romney.[7]

McDonnell's inclusion among the final three Romney options, along with the Romney campaign's choice to announce the selection of actual vice presidential nominee Paul Ryan in Norfolk, Virginia, underscored how critical the state seemed to GOP fortunes. Obama's victory for a second term was closer than his first in Virginia, as was true nationally. Tim Kaine succeeded Jim Webb in the US Senate in the same election.

Sterner tests faced the Democrats in 2013 and 2014. Former Democratic National Committee chair Terry McAuliffe overcame the three-decade-old tradition of Virginia's one-term-and-out gubernatorial elections—that the party winning the White House would lose the governor's mansion in the following odd-year election. By hanging on to a 2.5-point advantage over Atty. Gen. Ken Cuccinelli, McAuliffe broke the trend.

The 2014 elections, disastrous for Democrats nationwide, nearly claimed a victim in Sen. Mark Warner despite a high approval rating, a lopsided financial advantage, and late polling indicating a nearly 10-point advantage. Warner wound up holding on to his seat by a meager 17,000-vote margin out of 2.2 million ballots (as opposed to his two-to-one win in 2008), and these cliff-hanging contests created a sense of uncertainty as 2016 approached.

The major internal realignments that accompanied these trends came in stages: an initial movement by the suburban electorate toward the Democrats, a surge of participation among minority voters in the state's urban areas and young voters in college towns, and then, offsetting these gains, a tidal wave of support for the GOP among rural white voters. The 2016 election would show that these trends generally intensified.

Nomination Contests

The Virginia primaries for president fell on March 1, the middle of the primary and caucus calendar, but a point where the fields were already shaking out. With a cascade of contests surrounding Virginia's, the Commonwealth did not claim major attention. Still, the results demonstrated the divisions within each party and provided insight into the November contest.

Primaries

Democrats

Early expectations in the Democratic field were shaped by the belief that Hillary Clinton was the overwhelming favorite for the nomination. Clinton's dominance was exemplified by early polling that showed her with a 50-point lead among state Democrats until July of 2015. By March, the Democratic contest had narrowed to Hillary Clinton and Vermont senator Bernie Sanders.

Two candidates who might have been expected to have some appeal to Virginia Democrats had already exited the contest. The state's own senior senator, Jim Webb, the surprise winner over incumbent Republican George Allen in 2006, had just as surprisingly declined to seek a second term in 2012, and mystified his fellow partisans even more by announcing his candidacy for the White House in 2015. In his own extra-partisan way (he had served as navy secretary to Republican president Ronald Reagan and often criticized his own party's leaders as a senator), Webb suggested that he was best positioned to regain the support of the rural white hill-country voters of Appalachia. Ultimately, he withdrew from the contest, declaring that he was being marginalized by the national party and threatening to run as an independent.[8]

Martin O'Malley, the two-term former governor of Maryland, might have had some regional appeal, especially since his state and Virginia shared a media market in the vote-rich Washington, DC, metropolitan area. Seeking the mantle of a liberal alternative to Clinton and a fresh face to young voters eager for change, on paper O'Malley seemed to have significant potential. Unfortunately, this was not ballot paper, and after O'Malley had been humiliated in the Iowa and New Hampshire contests, he left the field.[9]

In other states, Senator Sanders drew strong support by emphasizing a left-leaning populist agenda. He found resonance among college students, liberals, and blue-collar Democrats in industrial states. Among rural voters in economically depressed areas, Sanders had some appeal as well. Yet Virginia posed a challenge, with its substantial minority population (a Sanders weakness). The state's dependence on the federal government for public employment and defense contracting also minimized the appeal of an "outsider" candidate.

In the end, Hillary Clinton won a landslide victory in Virginia, falling just short of a two-to-one margin, despite a narrowing margin in pre-primary polls. As figure 13.1 shows, Clinton's lead in the polls did decline as the race developed into a two-candidate contest. One mid-February poll by Christopher Newport University's Wason Center showed Clinton with only a 12-point lead over Sanders.[10] While this gap seemed daunting, the Sanders and Clinton campaigns must have both been cognizant of other states where the underdog had outperformed the final polls. In Michigan, an 18-point advantage in polling averages disappeared as Sanders finished barely ahead of Clinton.

The actual Virginia results produced one of Clinton's better showings. Though not record-breaking, turnout in the Democratic primary was strong, with over 785,000 votes being cast. This turnout was second only to the 2008 turnout, among Democratic primaries, and the third highest primary turnout for any party.[11]

Sanders lost every region of the state except for the Shenandoah Valley, a spine of mainly rural counties along the western side of the state.

Figure 13.1. Poll Support for Selected Candidates for the Democratic Nomination in Virginia, February 2015–February 2016

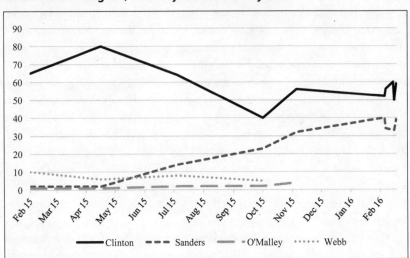

Source: RealClearPolitics, https://goo.gl/qyS9Sn.

His campaign effort was largely focused around college towns. He carried only sixteen cities and counties, including Charlottesville (University of Virginia), Blacksburg (Virginia Tech), Harrisonburg (James Madison University), and Radford (Radford University) and barely eked out a win in Williamsburg (College of William & Mary). His populist appeals, which propelled his success in other states, did not seem to resonate with the Commonwealth's white Democrats, and Sanders struggled to gain support among minority voters here as elsewhere. The attraction to an "outsider" promising to radically overhaul the national government would not seem to have been strong among Hampton Roads and Northern Virginia voters. Hampton Roads depends heavily on federal spending for defense, space, and science research, while Northern Virginia is home to large numbers of federal employees, contractors, and others who recognize themselves as part of the system being criticized.

Regionally, Clinton dominated in the vote-rich Northern Virginia and Hampton Roads communities. Minority voters undoubtedly propelled her in these racially and ethnically diverse areas, where she had her strongest performances. Sanders ran ahead in the relatively disadvantaged but ethnically homogenous Shenandoah Valley, a reflection of his success in other states whose rural areas fit that description, such as Michigan, Indiana, and West Virginia. As for the rest of the state, Clinton managed to run ahead comfortably in southwest and central Virginia. Turnout benefited Clinton, as the southwest–based Ninth Congressional District cast only thirty-three thousand primary votes, while the urban and minority voters in the Third and Eighth Districts turned out more than three times that number.

Republicans

The Republican field of 2016 reflected the lack of an obvious frontrunner to be the party's standard-bearer in the presidential contest. Although former Florida governor Jeb Bush had assembled a bevy of financial and political supporters, he did not deter challengers. Early public opinion showed him with a lead but with less than a quarter of the primary vote. As shown in figure 13.2, by the fall of 2015, he had slipped behind three other candidates and was shedding support quickly. New York developer Donald Trump, Florida senator Marco Rubio, and physician Ben Carson all moved up through the debate season, with Carson later dropping while Texas senator Ted Cruz joined the leaders of the pack. Bush proved to be a flawed messenger for the party, which was increasingly exhibiting disinterest in establishment figures and traditional center-right politics.

One Virginian did enter the fray for the GOP, though hardly anyone noticed. Former governor Jim Gilmore (1998–2002), had spent much of

Figure 13.2. Poll Support for Selected Candidates for the Republican Nomination in Virginia, February 2015–February 2016

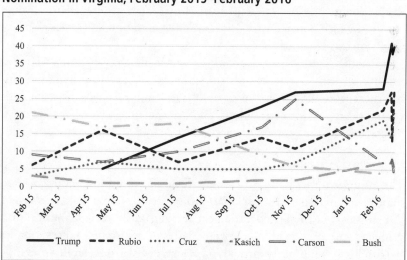

Source: *RealClearPolitics*, https://goo.gl/iLB6HD

his administration fighting with his own party's legislative majorities and lasted only one year as George W. Bush's Republican National Committee chair. He resigned under pressure when the GOP lost both Virginia and New Jersey gubernatorial elections in 2001. He had been humiliated in his 2008 US Senate contest, first by barely winning the GOP nomination against a gadfly state legislator, and then by losing the general election to his successor as governor, Mark Warner, by a 31 percent margin. Gilmore withdrew from the contest before the Virginia primary.[12]

The primary revealed a sharp divide in the state's GOP electorate. Though Trump won the plurality of the vote, Rubio trailed by less than 3 percent, winning nearly a third of the total. Texas senator Ted Cruz finished third with almost 17 percent, and Ohio governor John Kasich was fourth, with a bit less than 10 percent.

Relaxation of the rules for gaining a spot on the ballot allowed the GOP to avoid the embarrassment of 2012, when only Mitt Romney and Ron Paul were able to qualify, but the top four candidates' votes combined accounted for roughly 93 percent of the total. Regional patterns show that Trump and Cruz performed well in the more rural and western parts of the state, while Rubio dominated and Kasich exceeded his statewide percentage in the more urban and suburban communities. In the Southwest, where Trump came close to a majority of the primary vote, he and Cruz together won 70 percent or more in many communities. Conversely, in Northern Virginia communities, Rubio and Kasich finished with a similar combined vote. Participation was the lightest in the predominantly African American Third Congressional District, while the southwest's Ninth District produced two and one-half times as many GOP votes as Democratic ones.

Trump's victory in the primary revealed the challenge that he faced moving toward November. His strengths were evident in the now deep-red rural white counties and cities of the south and west, but his lack of support in larger metropolitan areas, especially in Northern Virginia, represented major barriers to success.

Primary Participation

The large GOP field and unsettled contest produced a turnout of more than 1.025 million votes, which broke the previous single party record of 986,203 cast in the Democratic primary of 2008. That Obama-Clinton primary still produced the largest share of registered voters casting ballots in a single party primary, 21.3 percent of registered voters, as opposed to the 19.5 percent of 2008. Since Virginia does not provide party registration of voters, the percentages represent the share of all registered voters in February of the primary year.

Turnout for both parties combined in 2016 did break the all-time combined primary record, as 34.4 percent of registered voters cast either a Republican or Democratic ballot. That topped the previous record of 2008, when the two-primary total represented 31.9 percent of registrants. In comparison, primary day in 2012 generated little interest, as no Democrat was challenging President Obama's reelection in Virginia, and the GOP voters had a choice of only Mitt Romney or former Texas congressman Ron Paul. The total of 265,000 voters that year constituted a mere 5.1 percent of the registered voters.

The Nominating Conventions

Republicans

While the primary results gave Trump a victory, his lack of organization and lack of support among party leaders became evident in the weeks following the vote. Conventions were held in each congressional district to elect delegates to the national convention, and while these delegates were technically bound to support Trump, in a number of instances the selected delegates actually favored Senator Cruz for the nomination. Although this did not ultimately affect Trump's ability to secure the party nomination, it produced a Virginia delegation to the Republican National Convention that was notably lacking in enthusiasm for the nominee.[13]

Throughout the four days of convention activity, Trump defied expectations. He showed up at the convention hall long before the traditional sightings of the nominee are expected, appearing through a theatrical smoke-machine silhouette more commonly seen at a professional wrestling extravaganza than at the traditionally staid and formal party convention. His moves seemed calculated to stir controversy, insult former rivals, or expose an outsized ego. In the end, the political pundits tended to critique the convention as poorly run, contentious, and a missed opportunity. Trump achieved the most important benefit of the conclave, however: he received a convention bounce of several points in his national public opinion poll standing. But no such bounce occurred in Virginia, and nothing in the convention itself suggested that Virginia was likely to shift from its pro-Clinton standing.

Ken Cuccinelli, the former attorney general and defeated 2013 gubernatorial candidate, was selected to lead the delegation in Cleveland despite his role as chief delegate-hunter for the Cruz campaign. He did not play a unifying role, instead proposing a change of rules which, had it been in place in 2016, would have aided Cruz and hampered Trump by restricting participation in primaries and caucuses to registered party members. When his motion was ruled to have failed on a voice vote and the convention chair refused to acknowledge a demand for a roll-call vote, Cuccinelli led a walkout from that day's convention activities.

Democrats

The Democratic convention would simply elevate Virginia's likelihood of backing the former secretary of state. Though Sanders supporters continued to express some dissatisfaction, they were not a major presence in the Old Dominion delegation.

On the Saturday preceding the convention, Clinton chose a rally in Florida to announce that Senator Kaine would be her running mate. With a live broadcast of the rally on national television, Kaine introduced himself with a highly personal speech, seamlessly moving from English to Spanish. This fluency resulted from a missionary trip to Honduras during a one year hiatus from Harvard Law School. The combination of the ability to communicate directly to a growing segment of the electorate in their native language and the ability to connect to his deep religious faith had served Kaine well in his previous elections and was widely praised in what was his true national debut (despite his having served as President Obama's Democratic National Committee chair from 2009 to 2012).[14]

Despite his former leadership of the party, Kaine was not widely known among the nation's electorate, and some party activists questioned his support for the Trans-Pacific Partnership trade deal and his commitment to abortion rights, gay marriage, and other issues. Some complained that he did little to reach out to the Sanders supporters who sought evidence that the Democrats would fight for a more populist economic agenda. In the end, however, Kaine's nomination occurred without controversy and helped cement the Virginia connection to the Clinton campaign.

Virginians played at least one other significant role at the Democrats' conclave. Charlottesville attorney Khizr Khan, with his wife Ghazala standing at his side, spoke movingly about the loss of their son, Humayun, a graduate of the University of Virginia who lost his life as a US Army captain in Iraq. Pakistani immigrants, the Khans were there to draw attention to Donald Trump's anti-Muslim rhetoric. When Mr. Khan pulled a copy of the US Constitution from his pocket and challenged Trump to read it to understand its inclusive principles, the convention erupted in applause, and the Khans became an instant phenomenon of the 2016 election.[15]

Fall Campaign

The fall campaign represented a significant regression to the mean for Virginia. After two presidential election cycles in the bull's-eye of the parties, suddenly the state slipped on the target list. Spending on television advertising was perhaps not as useful as in the past for tracking campaign prioritization. The Trump campaign in particular seemed to devote far less money to media ads than had been the trend. Partly, this was due to the significant amount of "free" media Trump received, as broadcast and cable news organizations found the unconventional and incendiary nature of Trump's campaign appearances to be ratings bonanzas.[16]

The general perception of both campaigns was that Virginia was probably off the table for Trump, and spending dropped precipitously in the Commonwealth. With the absence of a US Senate contest, overall spending was just a fraction of its level in the two previous presidential campaigns. Though Republicans denied that they were shifting resources to other battlegrounds like North Carolina, evidence seemed scant of an active GOP effort until the national tightening of the race and the final surge of campaign cash to Trump led to a late ad blitz.[17]

Campaign visits, on the other hand, saw Trump putting more effort into Virginia while the Democrats felt confident of victory. Hillary Clinton made no visits to Virginia between August 1 and November 1, while her running mate campaigned in his home state four times (including the vice presidential debate at Longwood University). Trump and Pence made thirteen visits to the state, including trips to two anchors of the evangelical movement, Pat Robertson's Regent University and Jerry Falwell's Liberty University. In both of these cases, Trump was probably primarily reaching out to a broader national audience, but he got the attention of Virginians nonetheless. The contrast in number of events nationally between Trump and Clinton was striking in the fall as he appeared at 85 to her 48.[18]

The main themes of the two campaigns, then, played out largely as they did nationally. Trump presented himself as the agent of change, threatening to disrupt business as usual in Washington and promising support for a socially conservative Supreme Court nominee, opposition to abortion, a restoration of industrial and coal jobs, and a comprehensive overhaul of immigration policies. He devoted equal time to berating Hillary Clinton as corrupt, dishonest, incompetent, and the ultimate personification of "the system."

Clinton argued, on the one hand, that she was best equipped to move forward with policies she believed most voters liked (such as protecting reproductive and civil rights, addressing climate change, and increasing college affordability), reshape policies in need of revision (the Affordable Care Act), and bring change to the targets of populist anger used effectively in rhetoric by Bernie Sanders (tax codes, trade deals, and financial markets). She gave at least equal weight, however, to the argument that Trump was totally unprepared for and unqualified to take on the presidential role.

These campaign themes resonated with the varied portions of Virginia's electorate, as they did throughout the nation. It was in the proportional impact of those various segments that we find the explanation for Virginia's countercyclical outcome in 2016.

Voting rights and participation became an issue during the year as both newly passed voter identification requirements passed by the Virginia General Assembly and efforts by Governor McAuliffe to restore voting rights to felons who had completed their sentences were challenged in court. Although not decided until after the election, in December a panel of the US Court of Appeals for the Fourth Circuit ruled unanimously that the law passed in 2013 requiring the presentation of photo identification at the polls was constitutional. Although a different panel of the same court had struck down a North Carolina voter ID law, in that case the court found evidence of specific intent to impose higher burdens on African Americans. The Virginia panel said the process and provisions of the law were more flexible and did not show evidence of discriminatory intent.[19]

Governor McAuliffe's action was an attempt to undermine Virginia's restrictions on voting by convicted felons even after their sentences are completed. The Commonwealth has required individual petitions by felons when their sentences are completed, leading to one of the highest rates of disenfranchisement of any state. While he and his predecessor, Republican governor Bob McDonnell, had restored rights individually to more than 30,000 petitioners in total, McAuliffe issued a blanket restoration to approximately 206,000 former felons so that they could be eligible to register and vote without further petition.

Republican legislative leaders protested the move and challenged it up to the Virginia Supreme Court, arguing that the governor only had the power to restore rights on a case-by-case basis after a petition, not on a universal basis without individual petition. On a four-to-three vote, the Virginia Supreme Court ruled that since no previous governor had attempted to utilize such power, it was not permissible. That left in limbo some thirteen thousand citizens who had registered between McAuliffe's April order and the supreme court's July decision. McAuliffe promptly set about individually approving those cases and promised to do the same with the nearly two-hundred thousand that remained.[20]

By the October 17 deadline, it was estimated that more than seventy thousand former felons had registered to vote in the Commonwealth as a result of the governor's actions, which were widely supported in public opinion polls.[21]

General Election

November 8, 2016, produced a record voter turnout in Virginia, despite the relatively limited attention paid to the state. The 3.983 million votes represented an increase over 2012 but a decrease from 2008. In the end, 2016 marked the second highest turnout rate among registered voters since the implementation of the National Voter Registration Act in 1996.

Hillary Clinton defeated Donald Trump by a margin of 5.4 percent (49.8 to 44.4 percent). The remaining vote was scattered among Libertarian Party candidate Gary Johnson (3.0 percent), Green Party candidate Jill Stein (0.7 percent), and independent Republican Evan McMullin (1.4 percent), with close to 1 percent of voters writing in a candidate.

Clinton's victory was at the low end of public opinion averages (displayed in figure 13.3), some of which showed her winning the Commonwealth by margins up to double digits. Still, the margin exceeded that of

Figure 13.3. Poll Support for Major Party Candidates in 2016 General Presidential Election in Virginia, June–November 2016

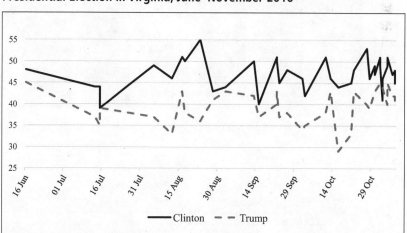

Source: *RealClearPolitics,* https://goo.gl/tAEKJS.

President Obama in 2012 by 1.5 percent of the vote. The outlines of the win followed Obama's victory, with deeper gaps between the parties in their areas of greatest strength.

As shown in figure 13.4, the vote-rich Northern Virginia and Hampton Roads regions delivered massive majorities for Clinton, as they had done for Obama. Clinton improved on Obama's dominant performance in Northern Virginia, while falling a little short in Hampton Roads, where African Americans comprise a large share of the vote. Trump dropped below thirty percent in each region, and fell significantly below Mitt Romney's showing in the fast-growing Washington suburbs of Northern Virginia.

Southwest Virginia, whose history of two-party competition had stretched back to the 1850s, saw the continuation of Democratic collapse as Clinton fell below 30 percent and Trump approached 70 percent. In fact, only two regions saw Trump outperform Romney: the hardscrabble farming and coal country of the southwest and the rural white

Figure 13.4. Support for Major-Party Candidates in 2016 and 2012 General Presidential Elections in Virginia by Region

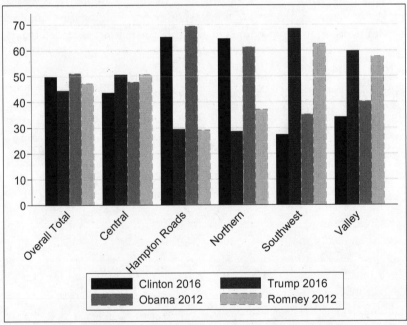

Source: Authors' calculations from Virginia State Board of Elections results, https://goo.gl/rEquZs.

Shenandoah Valley. Even where Clinton fell below Obama's percentages, Trump tended to lag behind Romney's vote share. This was the result of a somewhat higher minor-party vote, which ballooned from 1.6 percent to 5.1 percent between the two elections. With the bulk of that vote going to two Republican-leaning candidates (Johnson and McMullin), Trump was arguably more affected, especially in suburban areas.

The sample of communities shown in table 13.2 illustrates the trends discussed above. Fairfax County, the state's largest jurisdiction, saw Clinton run 5 percent higher than Obama with higher turnout than in 2012, and Trump fell below Romney's showing by 10 percent. The minor-party vote hit 8 percent there. In Arlington, the already overwhelmingly Democratic vote increased by 6.7 percent to more than three-quarters of the total and had higher levels of turnout, while the GOP vote share dropped by nearly 13 percent. Suburban Richmond voters in Henrico County improved the Democratic majority by 2.4 percent over 2012, while Republicans dropped 6.7 percent.

In Hampton Roads, cities with significant racial minorities that had rallied in unprecedented numbers for President Obama's two wins were slightly less supportive of Clinton, but she may have suffered from greater participation by the more blue-collar white voters preferring Trump in places like Newport News and Norfolk, as participation did increase here as well. Clinton's winning share dropped by a few percentage points in each city, while Trump came within a point of Romney's showing.

Though it still lagged behind other regions of the Commonwealth, southwest Virginia was the only region where turnout percentages equaled the 2008 level. All regions showed increases from 2012, but no other area hit the earlier mark. Still, the increased turnouts helped Trump as he saw his share of the total vote surge past Romney's vote in counties like Buchanan (+12.2 percent) and Dickenson (+14.7). Smaller but similar trends were seen in other southwest and valley communities.

Finally, the evidence from localities with major colleges or universities suggests a growing dominance by Democrats. Turnout rose in all four such communities, as shown in table 13.2, and the Democratic vote increased substantially in three. The outlier was Lynchburg, home of Jerry Falwell's Liberty University.

Despite carrying Virginia comfortably, Clinton's national Electoral College loss created disappointment for Virginia Democrats beyond their general dismay at losing the White House. The expectations of a Clinton win had set in motion a series of contingencies. With the Clinton win, it was suggested, Governor McAuliffe was likely to be called to serve in the

Table 13.2. Turnout and Candidate Support in Selected Localities in the 2016 Virginia General Presidential Election

	2016 Turnout	2012 Turnout	Democrats		Republicans	
			Clinton 2016	Obama 2012	Trump 2016	Romney 2012
Virginia overall	75.70	70.98	49.75	51.11	44.43	47.24
Northern Virginia						
Arlington	78.93	69.59	75.83	69.10	16.64	29.31
Alexandria	79.28	68.21	75.56	70.98	17.54	27.53
Fairfax	78.40	71.79	64.43	59.44	28.61	38.99
Loudon	68.69	75.78	55.06	51.52	38.21	47.03
Richmond and suburb						
Richmond City	78.90	73.08	78.58	77.68	15.09	20.51
Henrico	78.29	76.76	57.44	55.04	36.60	43.28
Chesterfield	79.22	76.07	45.97	45.38	48.22	53.11
Hampton Roads						
Hampton	71.49	68.37	66.34	70.60	28.75	28.02
Norfolk	75.92	66.76	68.39	71.89	25.85	26.54
Newport News	71.28	65.10	60.31	64.23	33.67	34.23
Southwest						
Buchanan	59.67	58.28	18.61	32.08	78.90	66.72
Tazewell	69.49	61.01	15.59	20.64	81.70	78.03
Dickenson	60.91	60.59	20.73	35.81	76.58	61.90
Floyd	77.60	72.93	28.57	35.73	65.75	61.12
Smyth	67.95	64.50	20.67	32.64	75.64	65.58
Grayson	70.98	67.15	19.31	29.04	76.76	67.42
Shenandoah Valley						
Rockbridge	78.00	70.93	32.50	40.17	61.88	57.95
Shenandoah	69.62	70.59	25.71	33.39	68.72	64.72
Warren	75.93	67.47	28.80	38.64	65.58	59.10
University towns						
Williamsburg	71.35	69.35	68.27	63.28	25.24	34.62
Harrisonburg	70.10	63.62	56.77	55.50	34.81	42.10
Charlottesville	70.28	65.87	79.68	75.72	13.17	22.22
Lynchburg	68.34	67.00	41.48	43.76	50.43	54.34

Source: Virginia Department of Elections, https://goo.gl/rEquZs.

Note: All table entries are percentages.

cabinet or some other high-level position, perhaps as secretary of commerce. If he were to leave office in his final year, Lt. Gov. Ralph Northam would be elevated and might then have the unique opportunity to seek a full term as governor while occupying the office.

If Tim Kaine were to become vice president, Governor McAuliffe would also have the opportunity to appoint a new senator to serve until a special election concurrent with the scheduled gubernatorial election in fall 2017. Early expectations focused on several representatives, but especially Rep. Bobby Scott, an African American serving his twenty-fourth year in the US House.[22] Scott's presence on the November ballot would also help encourage black voters, it was reasoned, helping the Democrats to retain the governor's mansion. Needless to say, those plans were abruptly halted on November 8.

So what accounts for the Virginia outcome of 2016? Why did this state seem to move counter to the national trend and become the only southern state to align with the Democrats? The most logical explanation comes from exit polling conducted during the election, which demonstrated the presence of groups in the electorate that made Virginia stand out from states that abandoned Democratic support, either longstanding or recent. Relevant portions of Virginia's exit poll data are summarized in table 13.3 below.

As Virginia has developed in recent decades, it has taken on characteristics that matched well with the profile of Democratic voters. To a largely suburban, affluent, and well-educated population, we can add a slightly larger-than-average minority share. The high proportion of African Americans in the minority cohort drive the vote even more heavily to the Democrats. The comparison of Virginia's exit polling to the national results reveals the subtle contrasts in electoral composition: more college and postgraduate degree holders, more affluence, fewer whites and more minorities, and more blacks than Latinos.

The skewing of highly educated voters toward Clinton and the Democrats was present at the national level but intensified in Virginia. Both the share of the electorate holding college degrees or more and their level of support for the Democratic nominee exceeded the national results. The support for Clinton among those earning more than $100,000 per year was particularly striking in the Commonwealth given the comparatively high number of wealthier voters. It is likely that much of that income is dependent in some way on federal government activity, making these voters less susceptible to the appeal of a candidate promising to be an agent of change. While she tied Trump nationally among voters

Table 13.3. Demographic Size and Support Patterns in 2016 General Presidential Election in Virginia and Nationally

Demographic	National			Virginia		
	Share of electorate	Clinton	Trump	Share of electorate	Clinton	Trump
Race						
White	71	37	57	67	35	59
Black	12	89	8	21	88	8
Latino	11	66	28	6	65	30
Age						
18–29 years	19	55	36	18	54	36
30–44 years	25	51	41	25	53	40
45–64 years	40	44	52	41	47	50
65+ years	16	45	52	16	45	52
Education						
High school or less	18	46	51	14	44	52
Some college	32	43	51	31	44	51
Bachelor's degree	32	49	44	31	51	44
Postgrad. degree	18	58	37	23	61	33
Income						
Below $50,000	36	53	41	30	53	41
$50–100,000	30	46	49	30	47	49
Above $100,000	34	47	47	40	51	44

Source: Exit poll data from the *Washington Post*, https://goo.gl/EFme51.

earning $100,000 or more, her Virginia margin with these voters was 7 percent.

Table 13.4 below displays more evidence for the importance of demographics (especially education and income) in determining Virginia's sway in the 2016 election. This table presents correlation coefficients between various locality characteristics and candidate support in the election. Higher percentages of college students and bachelor's-degree holders among a local population were positively related to Hillary Clinton's performance, while the same groups were related negatively to Donald Trump's support. Similarly, the relationship between support for Clinton and a locality's income was positive, while support for Trump seemed to decrease with higher incomes. In both of the cases above, the relationships were stronger than they had been in the 2012 election.

Congressional Elections

The campaigns for Virginia's eleven seats in the US House of Representatives took an unexpected turn more than two years before ballots were cast as a federal court ordered the state to redraw some of the district lines. Holding that state lawmakers had packed African American voters into one majority-black district (the Third District), the two-to-one decision set in motion a plan imposed by the judges that would create two districts with African American voting age populations in excess of 40 percent. The lower court ruling was upheld by the US Supreme Court, and elections were held under the new lines.[23]

The immediate casualty of the new map was Rep. Randy Forbes, an eight term Republican from the suburban Hampton Roads city of Chesapeake. Forbes's district went from one that had narrowly favored Mitt

Table 13.4. Correlations between Turnout and Candidate Support in the 2012 and 2016 General Presidential Election in Virginia Localities and Locality Characteristics

			Support			
	Turnout 2016	Turnout 2012	Clinton 2016	Trump 2016	Obama 2012	Romney 2012
Support for Obama 2012	−0.11	0.00	0.97	−0.95	1.00	−1.00
Support for Romney 2012	0.11	0.01	−0.97	0.95	−1.00	1.00
Increase in turnout since 2012	0.43	−0.17	−0.15	0.10	−0.18	0.17
African American population	−0.12	0.16	0.65	−0.59	0.71	−0.69
Latino population	0.02	−0.09	0.46	−0.49	0.39	−0.39
Population in college	−0.09	−0.21	0.40	−0.44	0.32	−0.34
College-educated population*	0.41	0.27	0.50	−0.55	0.33	−0.33
Median income	0.61	0.49	0.21	−0.26	0.08	−0.07

Sources: Authors' calculations based on data from Virginia Department of Elections, https://goo.gl/rEquZs; and US Bureau of the Census, https://goo.gl/m5p3kC.

*Percent of population whose highest level of education is at least a bachelor's degree.

Romney in 2012 to one that would have given Barack Obama more than 60 percent of the vote. Rep. Bobby Scott was returned in the Third District and joined by state senator A. Donald McEachin in the Fourth District.

The new map virtually assured change in the delegation, but the turnover potential increased when two Republicans announced their intentions to step down. Rep. Scott Rigell, representing the swing Second District based in Norfolk and Virginia Beach, decided that three terms was enough. The car dealer turned politician was somewhat unpredictable in his short tenure, sometimes supporting the Tea Party movement (voting against John Boehner's re-election as Speaker, for instance), and sometimes allying with Democrats on more progressive policies. Rigell often expressed his frustration with partisan gridlock, and his departure seemed to open a door for Forbes to return to the next Congress.

With the encouragement of Republican leaders in Washington and Virginia (including Rigell), Forbes announced his intention to run in the newly configured, slightly more Republican Second District. Forbes had endorsements, financial resources, and a powerful position on the House Armed Services Committee, vital to the area. He did not, however, live in the district, and a young member of the Virginia House of Delegates, former US Navy SEAL Scott Taylor, challenged Forbes and soundly defeated him in the June primary.

Rep. Robert Hurt, representing much of central Virginia, was a second Republican to choose voluntary retirement. Democrats made a serious effort at his open seat, but it was claimed by state senator Tom Garrett. The one seriously contested House race was in Northern Virginia, where freshman Republican Barbara Comstock faced headwinds from the Trump candidacy. In a race that was reported to have been the most expensive in the nation, a total of $22 million dollars were spent, with Comstock having to outpace Trump by more than 10 percentage points to defeat Democrat LuAnn Bennett.

No other congressional race finished with a margin below 10 percent, as two additional Democrats and four Republicans reclaimed their seats for another term. The delegation's partisan split changed from eight-to-three to seven-to-four Republican after the redistricting. Hillary Clinton led her ticket mates in eight of the eleven districts (one of them was uncontested by the Republicans), and Trump trailed all ten of his fellow GOP candidates. Results of Virginia's congressional elections, along with presidential results broken down by congressional district, are summarized in table 13.5 below.

Table 13.5. 2016 Presidential and Congressional General Election Results in Virginia by Congressional District, in percent

	President		House of Representatives	
	Clinton	Trump	Democrats	Republicans
State overall	49.75	44.43	49.17	48.74
First District, north-central	40.97	53.22	Matt Rowe	Rob Wittman
			36.61	59.86
Second District, Virginia Beach and Eastern Shore	45.03	48.47	Shaun Brown	Scott Taylor
			38.46	61.33
Third District, Hampton Roads	63.25	31.68	Bobby Scott	Marty Williams
			66.70	33.07
Fourth District, central, and Richmond suburbs	58.37	36.96	Donald McEachin	Mike Wade
			57.73	42.04
Fifth District, central	42.09	53.11	Jane Dittmar	Tom Garrett
			41.58	58.24
Sixth District, Shenandoah Valley	34.67	59.32	Kai Degner	Bob Goodlatte
			33.15	66.63
Seventh District, central, and Richmond suburbs	43.73	50.18	Eileen Bedell	David Brat
			42.24	57.51
Eighth District, north	72.42	20.58	Donald Beyer	Charles Hernick
			68.39	27.28
Ninth District, southwest	27.16	68.44	Derek Kitts	Morgan Griffith
			28.32	68.59
Tenth District, northern exurbs	51.57	41.75	LuAnn Bennett	Barbara Comstock
			46.92	52.69
Eleventh District, north	66.12	27.17	Gerry Connolly	None*
			87.88	—

Source: Virginia State Board of Elections, https://goo.gl/AmcHws and https://goo.gl/gnXzl3.

Note: All numerical table entries are percentages. The House of Representatives columns present election results under candidate names.

*The Republican Party fielded no candidate in the Eleventh Congressional District.

One other notable vote occurred in the election when voters soundly rejected an effort by the Republican-controlled general assembly to embed the state's right-to-work law in the constitution. The law prohibiting closed-shop unionization had been on Virginia's books for decades and was not likely to be repealed any time soon. Editorialists and others criticized the GOP for overreach and for attempting to clutter the Constitution for partisan gain, and voters took the highly unusual step of rejecting the amendment.

Summary and Conclusion

It seems evident that the alignment of Virginia's political leadership behind Hillary Clinton's campaign was a benefit to her success here. A long-time friend in the governorship who was looking to expand rather than contract voter participation, a popular home-state senator as a ticket-mate, and a perception of a pro-Democratic trend may have discouraged more serious efforts in the primary and general campaigns. Ultimately, however, the unique position of Virginia among the southern states is rooted in demographics.

A highly educated and affluent citizenry, with a significantly larger African American population than the country at large, pushed Virginia more firmly into the Democratic camp in 2016. The skepticism of radical populism among an electorate closely tied to the federal government made the Commonwealth even more inhospitable to Donald Trump's appeals. Finally, the rapid migration to Northern Virginia continues to shift the state's balance of power to a more urban, liberal electorate.

The 2016 results surely do not take Virginia into untouchable territory for future races. A candidate with more establishment credentials may well have put the state in play in this election and could again in the future. But the trends of demographic change make Virginia's Democratic lean seem likely to become a bit more solid over time.

Conclusion

The Long-Term Pitfalls of Trump's Southern Strategy

H. Gibbs Knotts

The South was very kind to Donald Trump. He won ten of eleven southern states in the 2016 general election, the most since George W. Bush swept the South in 2004. The region's hospitality extended to the primary contests as well. Trump won ten of the eleven southern primaries, and his impressive 10-point win over Ted Cruz and Marco Rubio in the South Carolina primary gave him momentum and catapulted his campaign toward the Republican nomination. Trump's only southern hiccup was his loss in Cruz's home state of Texas.

Trump acknowledged the important role the South played during his "thank you" tour following his November victory. He held a series of rallies in the crucial swing states of Ohio, Michigan, Wisconsin, Pennsylvania, and Florida. However, he ended his tour in deeply red Alabama. It was a homecoming of sorts for Trump, returning to the University of South Alabama's Ladd-Peebles Stadium, the site of a large primary rally in August 2015.[1] Trump began his remarks by telling the crowd that "this is where it all began" and noted, "Boy, did we do well in the South."[2]

While there is no disputing Trump's southern dominance, the reasons for his overwhelming success in the South are less clear. After all, he is a brash New York billionaire with few ties to the region. Moreover, Trump's appeal to evangelical Christian voters is particularly puzzling given his bombastic tone, aggressive style, and propensity for crudeness.

One theory posits that Trump fits within a long line of colorful politicians supported by the region. Some have noted that he has a "speaking style that recalls Southern politicians like 'Pitchfork' Ben Tillman and George C. Wallace."[3] Beyond style, the substance of Trump's remarks follows popular post–Civil War themes for southern whites. His "criticism of the federal government, attacks on illegal immigration, protests of foreign trade deals and pledges to bolster the military" cover familiar and well-travelled territory.[4] These campaign themes also recall Richard Nixon's Southern Strategy, in which he used law-and-order appeals to pull white voters, many of whom had supported Wallace in 1968, to the GOP.[5]

Others have pointed to an even darker side of Trump's appeal. His support from white nationalists and alt-right groups harkens back to the segregationist era. Trump's message was certainly less overt than early-twentieth-century South Carolina senator Ellison D. "Cotton Ed" Smith's mantra, "Cotton is king and white is supreme,"[6] but comparisons to southern demagogues were frequent during this election season. Historian Dan Carter penned a *New York Times* op-ed piece drawing a direct comparison between Wallace's racist appeals and Trump's rhetoric, arguing that "both George Wallace and Donald Trump are part of a long national history of scapegoating minorities: from Irish, Catholics, Asians, Eastern European immigrants and Jews to Muslims and Latino immigrants."[7] In an effort to provide historical context, Carter said, "During times of insecurity, a sizable minority of Americans has been drawn to forceful figures who confidently promise the destruction of all enemies, real and imagined, allowing Americans to return to a past that never existed."[8]

It is also likely that anti-Clinton sentiment, particularly in the South, served to trump concerns about Trump. Hillary Clinton was born in Illinois, the Land of Lincoln, and moved to Arkansas to marry her Yale Law School classmate, Bill Clinton. From the beginning, she challenged the region's traditional culture, famously keeping her maiden name after getting married. Historian Craig Shirley described the sentiment in Little Rock at the time, "Here she comes, the feminist from Wellesley and Yale."[9] Clinton's national favorability ratings have certainly ebbed and flowed (from a high of 67 percent in December 1998 to a low of 38 percent in July 2016),[10] but she has often generated particularly strong negative reactions among white southerners.

How did Donald Trump do so well in the South? This concluding chapter provides a broad view of the 2016 election in the region. To begin, the chapter highlights just how thoroughly the Republican Party has dominated the region's politics. Next, the chapter investigates the role of race in the 2016 election, focusing specifically on how racial context correlates with Trump's support. The chapter also explores the South's increasing urbanization, and the ways urbanization can impact the region's politics. Following this, the chapter investigates in-migration and population growth, and how these demographic changes help explain the 2016 election and southern politics more generally. Given the important role that educational attainment played in the 2016 election, the chapter also investigates the education gap in the 2016 election. Finally, the chapter ends with reflections on larger trends in southern politics and explores prospects for Republicans and Democrats in future contests.

A Republican Stronghold

Trump's 2016 victory is just the latest evidence of how thoroughly Republicans dominate southern politics. Following the 2016 elections, the GOP holds eight of eleven governorships after incumbent Republican Pat McCrory lost a close reelection bid to Democrat Roy Cooper in North Carolina.[11] Republicans also dominate the region's state legislatures, holding majorities in all chambers.[12]

Republican domination is evident at the federal level as well. Figure C.1 shows the growth of Republican office holding in the US House of Representatives and Senate in the eleven southern states between 1980 and 2016. Republicans were the minority party during the 1980s and early 1990s. Following the 1994 midterm elections, however, Republicans held majorities in the southern House and Senate delegations. Currently, Republicans hold 19 of 22 (86 percent) Senate seats in the South and 99 of 138 (72 percent) House seats.

Looking back at the seventeen presidential elections between 1952 and 2016, Republicans won the majority of southern states in eleven of these seventeen contests.[13] Republican domination in presidential politics has been even more impressive since 1980. Starting in 1980, Republicans have won the majority of southern states in each cycle, winning eleven of eleven southern states in 1984, 1988, 2000, and 2004.[14] The only other time all southern states went Republican was during Nixon's landslide victory in 1972.[15]

The 2016 contest could have been different, however. Trump's divisive rhetoric had the potential to alienate white evangelicals, perhaps the most important component of the southern Republican coalition.[16] Yet, national exit polls showed how strongly Trump was supported among this group, winning 80 percent of the white evangelical vote.[17] Political scientist Scott Huffmon explained the appeal by noting that "a lot of Southern evangelicals have looked hard at Trump and said, 'I wish he wasn't potty-mouthed. I wish he wasn't thrice-married, but I believe he

Figure C.1. Republican Congressional Success in the South

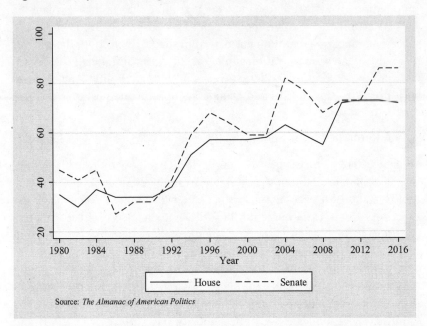

Source: *The Almanac of American Politics*

is going to fight for my Christian way of life, and having a strong fighter is important."[18]

In many ways, the 2016 results were similar to what occurred in the South in 2012. Figure C.2 compares support for Trump to support for Romney in the eleven southern states.[19] As you can see, the relationship between these two factors was positive and quite strong ($r = 0.94$, $p \leq$ .01).[20] In addition, most states were fairly close to the trend line. Trump outperformed Romney in six southern states: Alabama, Arkansas, Louisiana, Mississippi, South Carolina, and Tennessee. The most noteworthy jump in support occurred in Mississippi, where Trump received 57.9 percent of the vote compared to Romney's 55.5 percent.

It is also important to note the southern states where Trump underperformed Romney. He received a lower percentage of votes than Romney in Florida, Georgia, North Carolina, Texas, and Virginia. However, three of these states stand out in comparisons of support for Trump to support for Romney. Compared to 2012, Trump's support was down 2.9 percentage points in Georgia, 3.4 percentage points in Virginia, and 5.0 percentage points in Texas.

Figure C.2. Comparing Support for Romney in 2012 and Trump in 2016

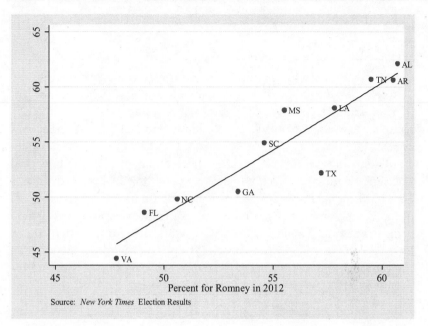

Source: *New York Times* Election Results

The Racial Divide

Race continues to be a dominant factor in southern politics. In a recent study, political scientist Trey Hood argued that "race is the largest dividing line between the Republican and Democratic Parties in the region, dwarfing the effects of religion and class."[21] Southern blacks and whites are ideologically polarized as well, with the plurality of southern whites identifying as conservative and an increasing percentage of southern blacks, particularly following Barack Obama's historic victory in 2008, identifying as liberal.[22]

National exit polls confirm the racial divide, with 8 percent of blacks voting for Trump compared to 57 percent of whites. Racial differences were even larger in the South. As an example, 8 percent of blacks voted for Trump in North Carolina, but 63 percent of whites did so. In Georgia, the gap between black and white support was even greater, with 9 percent of blacks voting for Trump and 75 percent of whites casting ballots for the New York billionaire.

Students of southern politics also know that the geographic makeup of an area can have an effect on voting patterns. The threat hypothesis posits, in part, that "whites engage in racial violence, resist desegregation, vote for racist candidates, and switch political parties partly in response to the threat that living among many blacks poses to their political and economic privilege."[23]

Figure C.3 compares the percentage of black population in southern states with support for Trump.[24] Overall, there is a weak relationship between the percentage of a state's population that is black and support for Trump ($r = 0.20$, NS). For comparison purposes, the correlation between percentage of black population and support for Romney was even smaller ($r = 0.03$, NS).

Trump did very well in three states (Alabama, Mississippi, and Louisiana) with large black population proportions. Georgia also has a high black population, but Trump received comparatively less support in the Peach State. Of particular note, Trump also received a very high percentage of the vote in Arkansas and Tennessee, two states with much lower percentages of African Americans. In sum, there was not a strong correlation between a southern state's racial makeup and support for Trump in 2016.

Figure C.3. Racial Context and Support for Trump

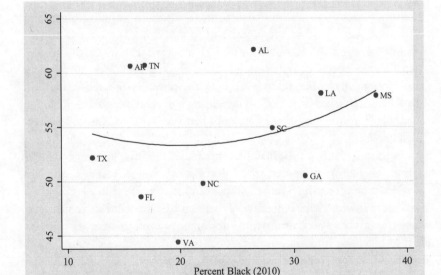

Sources: U.S. Census and *New York Times* Election Results

The Increasingly Urban South

Another big story of the 2016 election has been the urban-rural divide. Large cities went strongly for Clinton, while small towns and rural areas provided overwhelming support for Trump.[25] The divide between urban and rural America is certainly occurring in the South as well. While rural and small town North Carolina remains largely in the GOP column, cities and some suburbs, particularly near Research Triangle Park, support Democrats.[26] A similar pattern is emerging in Georgia, with the state getting redder the further one travels from the capital, Atlanta.[27]

One reason for the political divisions between urban and rural areas is what political scientist Katherine Cramer has labeled "rural resentment."[28] Initially, she focused on the political ascendency of Wisconsin's Republican governor, Scott Walker, arguing that people living in rural areas perceived that they were not getting the "power, resources, and respect" that they deserved.[29] The lessons from Wisconsin can be applied to the 2016 presidential contest as well. In a *Washington Post* op-ed shortly after the election, Cramer warned that labeling Trump's support as solely racism "is to ignore the key role of economic anxiety and resentment toward the white urban establishment."[30]

The South is a noteworthy place to investigate the urban-rural divide, particularly in light of the substantial urbanization in the postwar period. According to the 1950 US census, only 48 percent of southerners lived in urban areas, but this percentage has risen each decade.[31] By 2010, 77 percent of the South's population lived in urban areas. Moreover, most demographers expect urbanization to continue as millennials move to urban areas at high rates.[32]

As you can see in figure C.4, there was a strong negative relationship between percentage of urban population and percentage of support for Trump in the eleven southern states ($r = -0.65$, $p \leq .05$). Interestingly, this correlation was stronger than the correlation between support for Romney and percentage of urban population in the eleven southern states in 2012 ($r = -0.50$, NS).

Alabama, Tennessee, and Louisiana are the furthest above the trend line. Tennessee is a particularly interesting case, falling in the middle of southern states in percentage of urban population, but emerging as one of the states with the strongest support for Trump. Louisiana is also an outlier: 73 percent of residents living in urban areas, but there was also strong support for Trump (58 percent). North Carolina and Virginia are notably below the trend line. North Carolina is near the middle of

Figure C.4. Trump's Decreased Support in More Urban States

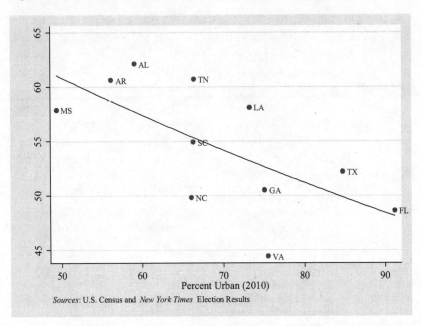

Sources: U.S. Census and *New York Times* Election Results

southern states in terms of its urban population proportion (66 percent), but it was a state with comparatively less support for Trump (50 percent). Virginia is the third most urban state in the region, but its support for Trump was the weakest.

Population Change as a Democratic Driver

Population change is also a key dynamic in southern politics. People continue to move to the region in pursuit of job opportunities, warmer weather, and lower taxes. Of course, some southern states have experienced more rapid population increases than others. According to the US census, Florida (+94 percent), Georgia (+78 percent), Texas (+78 percent), and North Carolina (+63 percent) grew at the highest rates between 1980 and 2010. In-migrants have led to increased support for Democratic presidential candidates, particularly when in-migrants come from the Northeast and Midwest.[33] States with the largest percentages of in-migrants from the Northeast (not including in-migrants from other southern states) are Virginia (52 percent), South Carolina (48 percent), North Carolina (46 percent), and Florida (46 percent).[34]

Figure C.5 shows the relationship between population change in southern states and support for Trump. As you can see, the relationship is strong and negative ($r = -0.72$, $p \leq .05$). This was stronger than the correlation between population change and support for Romney ($r = -0.60$, $p \leq .05$). Once again, Virginia was an outlier, with much less support for Trump than states with comparable population growth.

The Education Gap

One of the most-discussed factors in the 2016 election was education level. Journalist Nate Cohn argued that the election exposed "a new split between the beneficiaries of multicultural globalism and the working-class ethnonationalists who feel left behind economically and culturally."[35] He predicted that the division "wouldn't divide the country as much by region and religion, but more along the lines of urbanization and education." The national exit polls did, in fact, expose an education gap, with 52 percent of college graduates supporting Clinton and just 42 percent supporting Trump.

Figure C.5. Trump's Challenges in High-Growth States

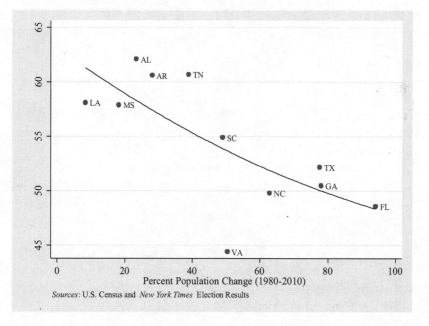

Sources: U.S. Census and *New York Times* Election Results

The story, at least at the individual level, appears to be slightly different in the South. In fact, there was not a consistent pattern among the six southern states with exit polling in 2016. Clinton won among college graduates in North Carolina (+1 percent), Georgia (+1 percent), and Virginia (+16 percent). But Trump won among college graduates in Florida (+3 percent), Texas (+8 percent), and South Carolina (+9 percent).

State-level educational attainment, however, is strongly correlated with state-level voting. Figure C.6 shows the relationship between the percent of the population with a college degree and support for Trump. The trend line highlights the strong negative relationship that exists between these two factors ($r = -0.87$, $p \leq .01$). By comparison, the correlation between state-level support for Romney and percentage of college-educated voters was negative but slightly smaller in magnitude ($r = -0.77$, $p \leq .01$).

The majority of southern states tracked closely to the trend line in figure C.6. Alabama and Tennessee supported Trump at higher levels than states with similar levels of educational attainment. Florida was a bit of an outlier as well, with lower support for Trump than states with similar levels of educational attainment.

Figure C.6. Trump's Challenges in More Educated States

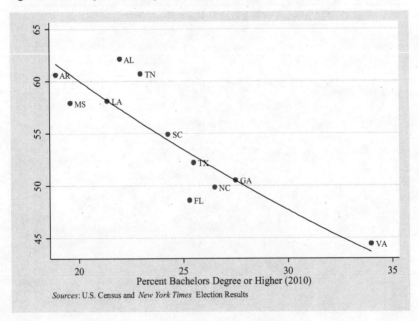

Sources: U.S. Census and *New York Times* Election Results

Conclusion

Trump's 2016 victory was certainly impressive. He performed better than both Romney and John McCain, winning every southern state except the Commonwealth of Virginia. Despite the convincing victory, however, longer term trends point to several areas of concern for the Republican Party.

Consider the GOP's "postmortem" following the 2012 presidential loss. The report highlighted several demographic trends that would make future Republican victories more challenging. In particular, the report called for increased outreach to women and minority voters.[36] South Carolina senator Lindsey Graham provided a similar warning in 2013, focusing particularly on the party's challenges with Latinos. Speaking on *Meet the Press*, Graham said, "We're in a demographic death spiral as a party and the only way we can get back in good graces with the Hispanic community in my view is to pass comprehensive immigration reform."[37]

Trump's victory will certainly lead some to question the conclusions of the GOP "postmortem." His backing among Latino voters was 8 percentage points higher than Romney's support, even with his anti-immigration rhetoric. However, the underlying fundamentals identified by the GOP report remain in place. Former Republican National Committee chair Reince Priebus conceded as much, telling *Face the Nation* that the report was "a prescription for the long term, not the short term."[38]

A number of other trends could become pitfalls for southern Republicans. Urbanization will continue to occur, and this dynamic is good for Democrats. In addition, the region's diversity will increase, particularly as a result of the continued growth of the South's Latino population. Though Trump did better than Romney among Latino voters, Democrats have an electoral advantage with this group. There is also a high likelihood that residents from outside the South will continue to move to the region. In many cases, particularly when in-migrants come from the Northeast and Midwest, these population changes benefit Democrats. Finally, it is likely that educational attainment will also increase, further advantaging Democrats.

A final piece of good news for Democrats can be found by considering the size of the states where Trump did the best. Trump won overwhelming victories (greater than 58 percent support) in Mississippi, Alabama, Louisiana, Arkansas, and Tennessee. However, these states account for just 25 percent (40 of 160) of the region's Electoral College votes. The election was much closer in the remaining six southern states (Florida, Georgia, North Carolina, South Carolina, Texas, and Virginia), and these states account for 75 percent of the South's Electoral College votes. Republicans can certainly celebrate, but they need to develop a new Southern Strategy to account for the inevitable demographics shifts in the region.

Notes

Introduction

1. Christopher Jones-Cruise, "Republicans Have Gained Strength in State Legislatures and Governorships," Voice of America, October 4, 2016, http://rslc.gop/blog/2016/10/04/republicans-have-gained-stength-in-state-legislatures-and-governorships/.

2. V. O. Key Jr., *Southern Politics in State and Nation* (New York: Alfred A. Knopf 1949).

3. Michael Hirsh, "Why George Washington Would Have Agreed with Donald Trump," *Politico*, May 5, 2016, http://www.politico.com/magazine/story/2016/05/founding-fathers-2016-donald-trump-america-first-foreign-policy-isolationist-213873.

4. David Sherfinski, "Donald Trump's Campaign: There Will Be a Physical Wall That Mexico Will Pay For," *Washington Times*, August 30, 2016, http://www.washingtontimes.com/news/2016/aug/30/donald-trump-campaign-there-will-be-physical-wall-/.

5. Reid J. Epstein and Colleen McCain Nelson, "Donald Trump Lays Out Protectionist Views in Trade Speech," *Wall Street Journal*, June 28, 2016, https://www.wsj.com/articles/donald-trump-lays-out-protectionist-views-in-trade-speech-1467145538.

6. Ivana Kottasova and Sonam Vashi, "Reality Check: Trump on NATO Countries Paying Their Fair Share," *CNN Politics*, July 27, 2016, http://www.cnn.com/2016/07/27/politics/donald-trump-nato-allies/.

7. Michael C. Randle, "Where in the World Would the South's Economy Be without Foreign Direct Investment?," *Southern Business Development*, Summer 2011, http://archive.sb-d.com/Features/MadeintheSouth2011/tabid/450/Default.aspx.

8. M. J. Lee and Dan Merica, "Clinton Slams Trump's 'Demagogic' Rhetoric on Terror," *CNN Politics*, September 20, 2016, http://www.cnn.com/2016/09/19/politics/hillary-clinton-donald-trump-terror-reaction/.

9. Josh Lederman, "Donald Trump May Support Gay Rights, But Does the Republican Party?," *PBS NewsHour*, July 21, 2016, http://www.pbs.org/newshour/rundown/donald-trump-may-support-gay-rights-republican-party/.

10. Kate Shellnutt and Sarah Eekhoff Zylstra, "Who's Who of Trump's 'Tremendous' Faith Advisers," *Christianity Today*, June 22, 2016, http://www.christianitytoday.com/ct/2016/june-web-only/whos-who-of-trumps-tremendous-faith-advisors.html

11. Tom Gjelten, "Evangelical Leaders Under Attack for Criticizing Trump Supporters," National Public Radio, December 20, 2016, http://www.npr.org/2016/12/20/506248119/anti-trump-evangelical-faces-backlash.

12. Katherine Cramer, "How Rural Resentment Helps Explain the Surprising Victory of Donald Trump," *Washington Post*, November 13, 2016, https://www.washingtonpost.com/news/monkey-cage/wp/2016/11/13/how-rural-resentment-helps-explain-the-surprising-victory-of-donald-trump/?utm_term=.d6ba90d0cccf.

1. The 2016 Southern Electorate

1. Shirley, "How Gerald Ford Beat Ronald Reagan at the Last Contested GOP Convention," *Washington Post*, April 22, 2016, https://www.washingtonpost.com/opinions/how-gerald-ford-outmaneuvered-ronald-reagan-at-the-last-contested-gop-convention/2016/04/22/6bed14ec-07cf-11e6-b283-e79d81c63c1b_story.html?utm_term=.3e02c5f0ed8d.

2. Aaron Zitner, Dante Chinni, and Brian McGill, "How Clinton Won: How Clinton Overcame the Challenge of Bernie Sanders," *Wall Street Journal*, June 8, 2016, http://graphics.wsj.com/elections/2016/how-clinton-won/.

3. Bobby Ilich, "Clinton, Trump Electoral Map: With Tight Polls, Can Hillary Actually Win Red States Like Texas, South Carolina, and Mississippi?," *International Business Times*, September 30, 2016, http://www.ibtimes.com/clinton-trump-electoral-map-tight-polls-can-hillary-actually-win-red-states-texas-2424861.

4. "2016 Electoral College Voting Rankings," *Cook Political Report*, November 7, 2016, http://cookpolitical.com/presidential/charts/scorecard.

5. Robert S. Erikson, Michael B. MacKuen, and James A. Stimson, *The Macropolity* (Cambridge, MA: Cambridge University Press, 2002); Thomas M. Holbrook, *Do Campaigns Matter?* (Thousand Oaks: Sage Publications, 1996).

6. David Leip, "Dave Leip's Atlas of U.S. Presidential Elections," http://uselectionatlas.org.

7. Ibid.

8. Patrick R. Miller, "Demographic and Issue Cleavages in the Southern Electorate," in *Second Verse, Same as the First: The 2012 Presidential Election in the South*, ed. Scott E. Buchanan and Branwell DuBose Kapeluck (Fayetteville: The University of Arkansas Press, 2014), 3–20.

9. Leip, "Dave Leip's Atlas."

10. Angus Campbell, Phillip E. Converse, Warren E. Miller, and Donald E. Stokes, *The American Voter* (Chicago: University of Chicago Press, 1960).

11. Herbert F. Weisberg, *The Total Survey Error Approach: A Guide to the New Social Science of Survey Research* (Chicago: University of Chicago Press, 2005).

12. Jeffrey M. Jones, "Obama Job Approval Ratings Most Politically Polarized by Far," Gallup, January 25, 2017, http://www.gallup.com/poll/203006/obama-job-approval-ratings-politically-polarized-far.aspx.

13. Christopher Ellis and James A. Stimson, *Ideology in America* (New York: Cambridge University Press, 2012).

14. Erikson, MacKuen, and Stimson, *Macropolity*.

15. Nader Nekvasil, "Uninsured Down Since Obamacare; Cost, Quality Still

Concerns," Gallup, August 29, 2016, http://www.gallup.com/poll/195086/uninsured-down-obamacare-cost-quality-concerns.aspx.

16. Miller, "Demographics and Issue Cleavages."

17. Ibid.

18. Michael S. Lewis-Beck, Helmut Norporth, William G. Jacoby, and Herbert R. Weisberg, *The American Voter Revisited* (Ann Arbor: University of Michigan Press, 2008).

19. National Election Pool, "Presidential Exit Polls: Georgia," *CNN Politics*, 2008, http://www.cnn.com/ELECTION/2008/results/polls/#GAP00p1.

20. Ibid.

21. Lois Duke Whitaker, *Voting the Gender Gap* (Champaign: University of Illinois Press, 2008).

22. Steven K. Thompson, *Sampling* (Hoboken: John Wiley & Sons, 2012).

23. Lewis-Beck et al., *American Voter Revisited*.

24. Rob Suls, "Educational Divide in Vote Preferences on Track to Be Wider Than in Recent Elections," Pew Research Center, September 15, 2016, http://www.pewresearch.org/fact-tank/2016/09/15/educational-divide-in-vote-preferences-on-track-to-be-wider-than-in-recent-elections.

25. Whitaker, *Voting*.

26. Lewis-Beck et al., *American Voter Revisited*.

27. See, for example, Christopher Ingraham, "Why Rural Voters Don't Vote Democratic Anymore," November 23, 2016, *Washington Post*, https://www.washingtonpost.com/news/wonk/wp/2016/11/23/how-republican-gerrymanders-forced-democrats-to-abandon-rural-america/?utm_term=.db39a2f0a846; Danielle Kurtzleben, "Rural Voters Played a Big Part in Helping Trump Defeat Clinton," November 14, 2016, National Public Radio, http://www.npr.org/2016/11/14/501737150/rural-voters-played-a-big-part-in-helping-trump-defeat-clinton; Alex Roarty, "Rural Democrats: Party Ignored Us, Suffered the Consequences," November 29, 2016, *Roll Call*, http://www.rollcall.com/news/politics/rural-democrats-ignored-suffer-consequences.

28. Earl Black and Merle Black, *The Rise of Southern Republicans* (Cambridge, MA: The Belknap Press of Harvard University Press, 2002).

29. James N. Druckman, "Priming the Vote: Campaign Effects in a U.S. Senate Election," *Political Psychology* 25 (2004): 577–594.

30. Lydia Saad, "Trump and Clinton Finish with Historically Poor Images," Gallup, November 8, 2016, http://www.gallup.com/poll/197231/trump-clinton-finish-historically-poor-images.aspx.

31. Chris Cillizza, "Hillary Clinton's Email Problems Just Came Roaring Back," *Washington Post*, October 17, 2016, https://www.washingtonpost.com/news/the-fix/wp/2016/10/17/hillary-clintons-email-problems-just-came-roaring-back/?utm_term=.a5374439287e.

32. Ryan Teague Beckwith, "Trump: Debate Moderator Had 'Blood Coming Out of Her Wherever,'" *Time*, August 7, 2015, http://time.com/3989652/donald-trump-megyn-kelly-blood-wherever/; David A. Fahrenthold, "News Clips Show Trump Talking about Sex, Rating Women's Bodies, Reminiscing about Infidelity on Howard Stern's Show," *Washington Post*, October 14, 2016, https://www.washingtonpost.com/news/post-politics/wp/2016/10/14/

new-clips-show-trump-talking-about-sex-rating-womens-bodies-reminiscing-about-infidelity-on-howard-stern-show/?utm_term=.f46a080e0255; Clare Foran, "Donald Trump's Threats Risk Silencing Women," *Atlantic*, October 18, 2016, https://www.theatlantic.com/politics/archive/2016/10/trump-women-sexual-assault/504446/.

33. Anna Brown, "The Unique Challenges of Surveying U.S. Latinos," Pew Research Center, November 12, 2015, http://www.pewresearch.org/2015/11/12/the-unique-challenges-of-surveying-u-s-latinos/.

34. Gary Segura and Matt Barreto, "Lies, Damn Lies, and Exit Polls," Latino Decisions, November 10, 2016, http://www.latinodecisions.com/blog/2016/11/10/lies-damn-lies-and-exit-polls/.

35. F. Chris Garcia and Gabriel R. Sanchez, *Hispanics and the U.S. Political System: Moving into the Mainstream* (New York: Routledge, 2008).

36. Leip, "Dave Leip's Atlas."

37. Daron R. Shaw, *The Race to 270: The Electoral College and the Campaign Strategies of 2000 and 2004* (Chicago: University of Chicago Press, 2008).

38. Black and Black, *Rise of Southern Republicans.*

2. The 2016 Presidential Nomination Process

1. The seventeen Republican candidates in alphabetical order were: Jeb Bush, Ben Carson, Chris Christie, Ted Cruz, Carly Fiorina, Jim Gilmore, Lindsey Graham, Mike Huckabee, Bobby Jindal, John Kasich, George Pataki, Rand Paul, Rick Perry, Marco Rubio, Rick Santorum, Donald Trump, and Scott Walker.

2. Lincoln Chafee (RI), Martin O'Malley (MD), and Jim Webb (VA) also ran as Democrats and participated in the first debate, but they never gained traction.

3. These states were Michigan (last won by a Republican in 1988), Pennsylvania (last won by a Republican in 1988), and Wisconsin (last won by a Republican in 1984).

4. The term *post-reform* refers to the period starting in 1972 when primaries and caucuses became the means for determining the major party presidential nominees. This chapter conforms to the eleven-state definition of the South adopted in this edited volume and sometimes makes use of the important subregional distinction between Deep South (Alabama, Georgia, Louisiana, Mississippi, and South Carolina) and peripheral South (Arkansas, Florida, North Carolina, Tennessee, Texas, and Virginia) states.

5. James A. Stimson, *Tides of Consent: How Public Opinion Shapes American Politics* (Cambridge, MA: Cambridge University Press, 2004). If we consider independent voters to be a credible barometer of short-term political conditions, then it is worth pointing out that according to the national exit poll of presidential voters, independents went in favor of Trump over Clinton by a margin of 46 to 42 percent. Further, the national exit poll asked voters "which candidate quality mattered most" and provided the following four response options: "cares about me," "can bring change," "right experience," and "good

judgment." An impressive 39 percent plurality of voters chose the "can bring change" option, and 82 percent of them voted for Trump. Clinton won an overwhelming majority among voters who chose the other three response options as the candidate quality that mattered most to their vote decision. All exit poll data can be accessed at "Election 2016," *CNN Politics*, https://goo.gl/yybSzA.

6. In the National Election Pool Republican primary exit polls that were conducted in ten of the southern states (only Louisiana was excluded), for the question that asked voters what was the "top candidate quality" influencing their decision, they were given four response options: "electability," "shares my values," "tells it like it is," and "can bring change." Trump dominated the "can bring change" response option, only losing this category to Ted Cruz in Texas, the only southern state that Cruz won and that Trump lost. Across the ten southern state exit polls, the portion of respondents selecting "can bring change" ranged from a low of 28 percent in Florida and Tennessee to a high of 36 percent in Alabama and Georgia. The share of the vote Trump won in this response category ranged from a low of 43 percent in Texas and Virginia to a high of 57 percent in Mississippi. The exit poll data for primaries can be accessed at "Election 2016," *CNN Politics*, https://goo.gl/i4qhkY.

7. Scott H. Huffmon, H. Gibbs Knotts, and Seth C. McKee, "First in the South: The Importance of South Carolina in Presidential Politics," *Journal of Political Science* (forthcoming).

8. Charles D. Hadley and Harold W. Stanley, "Super Tuesday 1988: Regional Results, National Implications," *Publius: The Journal of Federalism* 19 (1989): 19–37.

9. Josh Putnam, "Presidential Primaries and Caucuses by Month (1988)," *FrontloadingHQ*, February 11, 2009, https://goo.gl/M3JuHr.

10. In 2016, the magic number of delegates needed to secure the Democratic nomination was 2,383, and it was 1,237 delegates to win the GOP nomination. Wilson Andrews, Kitty Bennett, and Alicia Parlapiano, "2016 Delegate Count and Primary Results," *New York Times*, July 5, 2016, https://goo.gl/P3e6AL. Some Republican contests provided for a winner-take-all pledged-delegate allocation (e.g., Arizona, Florida, and South Carolina).

11. Regressing Clinton's percentage of the popular vote onto a dummy for caucus contests (0 = primary); a dummy for whether the contest occurred before or on March 15 (0 = after March 15); and a South dummy (0 = nonsouthern) reveals that she did significantly worse in caucus contests (–17 percentage points; $p < .001$) and significantly better in southern states (+20 percentage points; $p < .001$). A model with the percentage of earned delegates as the dependent variable yields similar results. Speaking to the importance of black voters, regressing Clinton's percentage of the popular vote onto a Deep South dummy (0 = Peripheral South) and confining the model to the South (a simple bivariate regression) indicates that Clinton's vote share was 12 percentage points higher in the Deep South than in the peripheral South ($p = .002$). A model with the percentage of earned delegates as the dependent variable yields similar results.

12. An analysis of the Trump vote similar to the kind mentioned in the previous note for Clinton makes it obvious that the Republican nominee did no better or worse in southern primary contests (the South dummy is statistically

insignificant, as is a Deep South dummy in a model confined to the South). Trump's electoral success exhibited no regional bias. It is worth mentioning, however, that Trump did markedly worse in caucus contests where Cruz thrived. Cruz won 190 delegates in caucus contests, while Trump won 87. Andrews, Bennett, and Parlapiano, "2016 Delegate Count."

13. In the wake of the Indiana primary, Cruz and Kasich suspended their campaigns, leaving Trump the last man standing.

14. Seth C. McKee and Danny Hayes, "The Transformation of Southern Presidential Primaries," in *Presidential Elections in the South: Putting 2008 in Political Context*, ed. Branwell DuBose Kapeluck, Robert P. Steed, and Laurence W. Moreland (Boulder: Lynne Rienner Publishers, 2010), 39–69.

15. M. V. Hood III, Quentin Kidd, and Irwin L. Morris, *The Rational Southerner: Black Mobilization, Republican Growth, and the Partisan Transformation of the American South* (New York: Oxford University Press, 2012); Seth C. McKee and Melanie J. Springer, "A Tale of 'Two Souths': White Voting Behavior in Contemporary Southern Elections," *Social Science Quarterly* 96 (2015): 588–607.

16. Although Louisiana primary voters were not surveyed in the 2016 National Election Pool, the state holds closed party primaries (meaning that only voters registered with a major party can participate in that party's primary) and provides turnout data according to party registration and race (white, black, and other). In the March 5 Democratic presidential primary in Louisiana, 61 percent of those who participated were African American. "Find Results and Statistics," Louisiana Secretary of State, https://goo.gl/7mz3Rz.

17. Earl Black, "Presidential Address: The Newest Southern Politics," *Journal of Politics* 60 (1998): 591–612; Earl Black and Merle Black, *The Rise of Southern Republicans* (Cambridge, MA: Harvard University Press, 2002); Charles S. Bullock III and Ronald Keith Gaddie, *The Triumph of Voting Rights in the South* (Norman: University of Oklahoma Press, 2009).

18. Not all of the Democratic primary exit polls available on the CNN website provide a breakdown of gender by race (e.g., Arkansas), but most of them do, and the gender gap favoring women voters in southern Democratic primary elections is mainly driven by the significantly greater share of black female voters in comparison to black male voters. This disparity favoring black women is especially pronounced in the Deep South Democratic primary contests where African Americans are the majority of voters. For instance, in South Carolina, among the African American voters who comprised 61 percent of the Democratic primary electorate in 2016, 37 percent were women and 24 percent were men. In Mississippi, where over 70 percent of Democratic primary voters were African American, the gender split among black voters was 47 percent female and 23 percent male.

19. Danny Hayes and Seth C. McKee, "Toward A One-Party South?," *American Politics Research* 36 (2008): 3–32.

20. Earl Black and Merle Black, *Politics and Society in the South* (Cambridge, MA: Harvard University Press, 1987); Merle Black and Earl Black, "Deep South Politics: The Enduring Racial Division in National Elections," in *The Oxford Handbook of Southern Politics*, ed. Charles S. Bullock III and Mark J. Rozell (Oxford: Oxford University Press, 2012), 401–23.

21. The higher portion of independents participating in southern Republican primaries can be thought of as a Trump effect. In other words, there is no evidence of a dealignment trend in southern politics; rather, in 2016 the short-term political climate prompted more independents to participate in GOP primaries because of their attraction to Trump's candidacy.

22. V. O. Key, Jr., *Southern Politics in State and Nation* (New York: Alfred A. Knopf, 1949).

23. Alan I. Abramowitz, *The Disappearing Center: Engaged Citizens, Polarization, and American Democracy* (New Haven: Yale University Press, 2010).

24. Samuel L. Popkin, *The Reasoning Voter: Communication and Persuasion in Presidential Campaigns* (Chicago: University of Chicago Press, 1991).

25. In the South in 2016, the popular vote totals for the two Democratic contenders were as follows: Clinton: 5,091,683; Sanders: 2,473,427. Vote totals aggregated by the author from David Leip, "Dave Leip's Atlas of U.S. Presidential Elections," http://uselectionatlas.org.

26. Curiously, the National Election Pool only asked Democratic primary voters about their marital status and did not ask the question in every state where voters were polled. With the exception of South Carolina, Clinton tended to perform much better among married voters, which is likely correlated with an older population, a group in which she was particularly dominant.

27. Aaron Blake, "More Young People Voted for Bernie Sanders Than Trump and Clinton Combined—By a Lot," *Washington Post*, June 20, 2016, https://goo.gl/evH8KS.

28. Huffmon et al., "First in the South."

29. In the South in 2016, the popular vote totals for the six leading Republican contenders were as follows: Trump: 4,564,919; Cruz: 3,493,666; Rubio: 2,541,430; Kasich: 807,689; Carson: 531,433; Bush: 171,980. Vote totals aggregated by the author from Leip, "Dave Leip's Atlas."

30. The National Election Pool asked only Republican primary voters the "born-again or evangelical Christian" question. Given that Trump came across as anything but a pious crusader, among those voters who answered in the negative to this question, he won this group in every southern state except for Virginia, where Rubio was the plurality winner among these voters.

31. Josh Hafner, "Donald Trump Loves the 'Poorly Educated'—And They Love Him," *USA Today*, February 24, 2016, https://goo.gl/2AeRLC.

32. Black and Black, *Rise of Southern Republicans*.

33. Seth C. McKee and Danny Hayes, "Dixie's Kingmakers: Stability and Change in Southern Presidential Primary Electorates," *Presidential Studies Quarterly* 39 (2009): 400–417.

34. Huffmon et al., "First in the South."

3. Alabama

1. Mike Cason, "Bill Clinton Stops in Montgomery to Give Hillary a Super Tuesday Boost," *Birmingham News*, February 27, 2016, accessed December 13, 2016, https://goo.gl/lhxzW7.

2. Rick Harmon, "Hillary Clinton Scheduled to Speak in Hoover in October," *Montgomery Advertiser*, September 29, 2016, accessed December 13, 2016, https://goo.gl/lhxzW7.

3. Cameron Smith, "WikiLeaks Affirms Alabama Democrats have a Joe Reed Problem," *Birmingham News*, October 19 2016, accessed December 13, 2016, https://goo.gl/sFcV3Z.

4. The counties that yielded her lowest votes in the 2008 primary election produced her highest margins of victory in the 2016 race.

5. Sanders's highest support emerged from Blount County, with 38.6 percent of the votes. That county gave Clinton one of her highest margins (78 percent) in the state in 2008. The counties that produced her strongest numbers in 2008 were those that exhibited the strongest support for Sanders in 2016. Nevertheless, she carried each one of them in 2016.

6. CNN conducted exit polls of primary voters in each party, surveying 865 Democratic and 1,237 Republican voters. Results are available at "Election 2016," *CNN Politics*, https://goo.gl/5Rn4D2.

7. Clinton's highest polling numbers reached 78 percent in October 2015 in a WKRG News 5 poll. By February 17, Public Policy Polling had her down to 59 percent, but her numbers rebounded to 71 percent in a Monmouth Poll by Election Day. "Clinton Leads in 10 of 12 Early March Primaries; Benefits from Overwhelming Black Support," Public Policy Polling, February 17, 2016, accessed December 16, 2016, https://goo.gl/trdvWS.

8. Jordan LaPorta, "HUGE: Franklin Graham to Join Trump at Mobile Rally," *Yellowhammer News*, December 16, 2016, accessed December 16, 2016, https://goo.gl/hFlR8g.

9. Michael Barone, "Why Sen. Jeff Sessions Backed Trump," *Washington Examiner*, July 20, 2016, accessed December 11, 2016, https://goo.gl/jeNBF3.

10. Sessions was on the short list for Trump's vice presidential candidate and proved to be the first member of Congress to gamble on the Trump movement and never weaken his support. See Amber Phillips, "Ten Things to Know about Sen. Jeff Sessions, Donald Trump's Pick for Attorney General," *Washington Post*, November 18, 2016, accessed December 11, 2016, https://goo.gl/3kl6T6.

11. Paul Gattis, "Marco Rubio in Huntsville: Vows to Rebuild Military, Space Program," *Huntsville Times*, February 27, 2016, accessed November 30, 2016, https://goo.gl/smxOv0.

12. CNN's Republican exit polls for the Alabama primary surveyed 1,237 respondents. "Election 2016," *CNN Politics*, accessed September 15, 2016, https://goo.gl/AdlTpI.

13. Alabama GOP primary voters were over 96 percent white, and the sample size of minority respondents, at 4 percent (n = 45, approximately), was too small to reveal systemic differences.

14. In 2012, the plurality of men (34 percent) supported Newt Gingrich, while 38 percent of women supported Rick Santorum.

15. Of those with no college education, 55 percent indicated they voted for Trump. That support was 48 percent among those with some college, 39 percent among those who graduated college, and 28 percent among those with

postgraduate education. This last group is the only one in which he dropped to a tie with any candidate—Marco Rubio, who also carried 28 percent of respondents who had postgraduate education.

16. The remaining respondents who indicated that shared religious beliefs affected their vote split their support among Cruz, Rubio, and Carson. A majority (55 percent) of those who answered that shared beliefs did not affect their support voted for Trump.

17. John Sharp, "Why Bill and Hillary Clinton are Stumping in Deep Red Coastal Alabama," *Mobile Press-Register*, July 14, 2016, accessed December 1, 2016, https://goo.gl/HAPUWg.

18. Rick Journey, "Trump Jr. Campaigns for Dad in Birmingham," WBRC, October 14, 2016, accessed December 12, 2016, https://goo.gl/Ho6mkt.

19. Claire Aiello, "Several Alabama GOP Leaders Speak as Trump/Pence Bus Visits Huntsville," WHNT News, October 25, 2016, accessed December 4, 2016, https://goo.gl/kr8RFQ.

20. Brian Lyman, "At Trump Rally, Calls for Volunteers, GOP Support," *Montgomery Advertiser*, October 25, 2016, accessed December 8, 2016, https://goo.gl/gkGkk5.

21. Brian Lyman, "Terry Lathan, Jeff Sessions Stick by Donald Trump," *Montgomery Advertiser*, October 11, 2016, accessed December 8, 2016, https://goo.gl/qNV5tO.

22. Jordan LaPorta, "Here are the Alabama Republicans Who Have Withdrawn their Support from Trump," *Yellowhammer News*, October 10, 2016, accessed March 21, 2017 https://goo.gl/aLkH5y.

23. John Sharp, "Rep. Bradley Byrne Clarifies Position on Donald Trump: Supporting GOP Ticket," *Mobile Press-Register*, October 11, 2016, accessed December 8, 2016 https://goo.gl/QXP2Et.

24. Aderholt's primary challenger Phil Norris did not reside in the district, living and working over two hundred miles south of the district line. See J. Pepper Bryars, "Conservatives Could Knock Robert Aderholt Out in 2018 Primary," *Huntsville Times*, January 9, 2016, accessed December 7, 2016, https://goo.gl/TtGr1T.

25. In 2012, primary exit polls revealed that 66 percent of respondents supported Tea Party values. No such question was administered in 2016. However, 40 percent of 2016 respondents identified as "very conservative" and another 40 percent as "somewhat conservative." Only 20 percent identified as "moderate." This suggests voters may be ideologically receptive to Tea Party messages while reelecting establishment incumbents. See Jessica Taylor, "Will It Be Ruin or Resurgence for the Tea Party in Alabama Race?," MSNBC, October 24, 2013, accessed March 19, 2017, https://goo.gl/9mYZjV.

26. Brian Lyman, "Alabama Republicans—Including Bentley—Withdraw Trump Support," *Montgomery Advertiser*, October 8, 2016, accessed December 7, 2016, https://goo.gl/wlNVuE.

27. Roby was un-invited to the Pike County Republican Women's event in reaction to her intention to vote against Trump. She was replaced as the speaker by Alabama cochair of Trump's campaign, Perry Hooper. See Leada Gore, "Martha Roby's Donald Trump Fallout: GOP Group Pulls Speaking Invite,

Write-in Campaign Launched," *Birmingham News*, October 17, 2016, accessed December 7, 2016, https://goo.gl/qr184j.

28. "Martha Roby Faced Tough Re-election after Criticizing Trump, But Has No Regrets," Associated Press, November 9, 2016, accessed December 7, 2016, https://goo.gl/Ma7K31.

29. Other amendments expanded the Auburn University Board of Trustees by two seats and changed the amendment process that would be used in the future. Three amendments were specifically passed to clarify existing constitutional language, including an amendment to specify the vote threshold needed to convict someone on an impeachment charge. As of this writing, Gov. Robert Bentley was facing impeachment charges in the state legislature.

30. Alan Blinder, "Michael Hubbard, Alabama House Speaker, Is Convicted on 12 Felony Ethics Charges," *New York Times*, June 10, 2016, accessed December 7, 2016, https://goo.gl/MyQ4AK.

31. Mike Cason, "Former Alabama Speaker Mike Hubbard Seeks New Trial," *Birmingham News*, August 7, 2016, accessed December 10, 2016, https://goo.gl/kAtyaY.

32. Kyle Whitmire, "Robert Bentley's Scandal Isn't about Sex; It's about Mike Hubbard," *Birmingham News*, March 25, 2016, accessed November 30, 2016, https://goo.gl/tp6gCi.

33. Brian Lyman, "Bentley Impeachment Probe Suspended at AG's Request," *Montgomery Advertiser*, November 3, 2016, accessed November 30, 2016, https://goo.gl/Wc066M.

34. Luther Strange announced he would run for the seat in the 2018 elections, both signaling would-be primary challengers and indicating his interest in the seat for a gubernatorial appointment. Others who indicated interest included Rep. Robert Aderholt (AL-4), a close friend of Vice President Pence, Rep. Mo Brooks (AL-5), and state senator Arthur Orr (Decatur). See Mary Sell, "Aderholt a Contender to Replace Sessions," *Florence Times-Daily*, January 25, 2017, accessed March 10, 2017, goo.gl/IgMKzo.

35. Steve Marshall, "Attorney General Steven T. Marshall Statement Regarding Status of Attorney General Office Investigation of Governor Robert Bentley," Alabama Office of the Attorney General, February 15, 2017, accessed March 21, 2017, http://www.ago.state.al.us/News-995.

36. Amber Phillips, "Alabama Governor Resigns, Pleads Guilty to Charges Tied to Allegations He Tried to Cover Up Affair with a Top Aide," *Washington Post*, April 10, 2017, accessed April 17, 2017, https://goo.gl/E2F65q.

37. Roy Moore was removed by the Alabama Court of the Judiciary in 2003 after defying a federal court order to remove a Ten Commandments monument he had installed surreptitiously in 2001. When campaigning for the post in 2012, he promised not to revisit the issue and narrowly won the post. See Kent Faulk, "Roy Moore Timeline: Ten Commandments to Gay Marriage Stance," *Birmingham News*, May 6, 2016, accessed November 30, 2016, https://goo.gl/JANE7L.

38. No constitutional provision existed for the appeal after his colleagues on the supreme court recused themselves. The court set up a procedure for

the governor to identify fifty retired justices from which to draw. See "Retired Judges to Hear Moore Appeal," Associated Press, October 31, 2016, accessed December 3, 2016, https://goo.gl/0RnoNj.

39. Roy Moore's dramatic exit is characteristic of other public spectacles, such as riding a horse to vote in the 2012 Republican primary election. "Roy Moore Walks out of Court before Pool of Judges Chosen for His Appeal," Associated Press, October 27, 2016, accessed November 29, 2016, https://goo.gl/UO2Jfi.

40. "Moore Won't Remove Items from Courthouse Office," Associated Press, October 19, 2016, accessed December 4, 2016, https://goo.gl/7IFwti.

41. President Obama carried Conecuh (50.6 percent) and Bourbon (51.3 percent) Counties by slim margins. In 2008 these counties supported John McCain with 50.1 percent and 53.6 percent of the vote share, respectively.

42. Though the 2016 levels were not record breaking or in pace with 2008, they were still robust. See Jennifer Horton, "Alabama Turnout Was Third Highest in State History," WSFA, November 15, 2016, accessed December 13, 2016, https://goo.gl/0TB2C5. Actual votes cast dropped by roughly nine thousand from 2012; however, Alabama's official voter registration numbers have increased by almost five hundred thousand. This rise follows Alabama's implementation of online voter registration.

43. Regions of the state are composed of the following counties as determined by the author: Tennessee Valley: Colbert, Jackson, Lauderdale, Lawrence, Limestone, Marshall, Morgan; Hill Country: Autauga, Bibb, Blount, Calhoun, Chambers, Cherokee, Chilton, Clay, Cleburne, Coosa, Cullman, DeKalb, Elmore, Etowah, Fayette, Franklin, Lamar, Lee, Marion, Pickens, Randolph, Saint Clair, Shelby, Talladega, Tallapoosa, Walker, Winston; Black Belt: Barbour, Bullock, Butler, Choctaw, Dallas, Greene, Hale, Lowndes, Macon, Marengo, Perry, Pike, Russell, Sumter, Wilcox; Wiregrass: Coffee, Conecuh, Covington, Crenshaw, Dale, Escambia, Geneva, Henry, Houston; Coastal: Clarke, Baldwin, Monroe, Washington; Metropolitan: Jefferson, Madison, Mobile, Montgomery, Tuscaloosa.

44. Trump support was found among 76 percent of voters in Baldwin County and 72 percent in Shelby County, which reflected a drop from Romney's performance in 2012. Hillary Clinton's support was also lower than President Obama's in these counties, while support for independent candidates increased. Baldwin is adjacent to Mobile County and Shelby County neighbors Birmingham. Clinton support fell below 10 percent in Winston and Blount Counties (both 8 percent), and Trump surpassed 80 percent support in fifteen counties in the north-central portion of the state.

45. Rashad Snell, "Bipartisan Lawsuit Filed Against Gov. Bentley," AlabamaNews.net, March 6, 2017, accessed March 21, 2017, http://www.alabamanews.net/2017/03/06/bipartisan-lawsuit-filed-gov-bentley/.

46. Paul Gattis, "Gov. Kay Ivey 'Evaluating' Earlier Special Election for Senate Seat Held by Luther Strange," *Birmingham News*, April 12, 2017, accessed April 17, 2017, https://goo.gl/b3dm05.

4. Georgia

1. *Larios v. Cox*, 300 F. Supp. 2d 1320 (N. D. Ga. 2004).

2. Georgia voters indicate their race or ethnicity when registering. After each election, the secretary of state reports on turnout by race.

3. Ultimately, Mike Berlon received a five-year sentence. "Former Gwinnett Lawyer Sentenced to Prison for Stealing Funds from His Clients," press release issued by US Attorney's Office, Northern District of Georgia, May 15, 2015.

4. Greg Bluestein, "Candidates Aren't Visiting Georgia," *Atlanta Journal-Constitution*, August 29, 2016, A1, A6.

5. Aaron Gould Sheinin and Tamar Hallerman, "Sick of Campaign Ads? Try Living in Florida," *Atlanta Journal-Constitution*, November 2, 2016, A1, A6.

6. Tiffany's mother, Marla Maples, grew up in Georgia.

7. Ernie Scruggs, "With Clinton Leading Trump in Georgia, Reed Wants Campaign to Push," *Atlanta Journal-Constitution*, August 9, 2016, B1.

8. Telephone conversation with Clyde Tucker, December 28, 2016.

9. Other Republicans won by larger margins. In 2014 the average GOP advantage in ten statewide contests was 13 points, and only two candidates won by fewer than 10 points.

10. Greg Bluestein, "Nunn Memo Reveals Strategy, Weaknesses," *Atlanta Journal-Constitution*, July 29, 2014.

11. The exit poll estimated that blacks cast 30 percent of the vote. Exit polls are the best source in most states, but not in Georgia. The exit poll will still be used to describe voting patterns, but readers should keep in mind that race-based estimates are affected by slight distortions in the poll exit estimates.

12. Comparisons cannot be made with 2012 because, since Georgia was not seen as in play that year, no exit poll was conducted.

13. "Voter Registration Statistics," Georgia Secretary of State, http://sos.ga.gov/index.php/Elections/voter_registration_statistics.

14. Charlotte Alter, "Bottom Lines," *Time*, November 14, 2016, 34.

15. Greg Bluestein and Aaron Gould Sheinin, "No Easy Choice for Evangelicals," *Atlanta Journal-Constitution*, October 11, 2016, A7.

16. Ronald Brownstein, "How Obama Won: Marrying Old and New Democratic Coalitions," *Atlantic*, November 7, 2012.

17. Kristina Torres and Jennifer Peebles, "Georgia 2016 Voters Were Older, Whiter," *Atlanta Journal-Constitution*, January 1, 2017, B1.

18. Gwinnett has 209,186 whites among its 431,727 registrants. However, 53,376 registrants checked "Other" or did not indicate their race or ethnicity. If enough of these are white, then whites might still constitute a narrow majority.

19. Greg Bluestein, Tamar Hallerman and Aaron Gould Sheinin, "Campaigns Make Final Sprint in Georgia," *Atlanta Journal-Constitution*, November 6, 2016, A23.

20. Kristina Torres, "Campaigns War over Voting Rules," *Atlanta Journal-Constitution*, August 28, 2016, A15.

21. On the 1988 Super Tuesday, see Charles S. Bullock III, "The Nomination Process and Super Tuesday," in *The 1988 Presidential Election in the South*, ed.

Laurence W. Moreland, Robert P. Steed, and Tod A. Baker (New York: Praeger, 1991), 3–19.

22. Greg Bluestein and Jim Galloway, "Trump Takes a Beating in Ga. Districts," *Atlanta Journal-Constitution*, April 18, 2016, A1. A10.

23. Cohen, Richard E., and James A. Barnes, *The Almanac of American Politics, 2016* (New York: National Journal, 2015).

24. Greg Bluestein, "Challenger's Cash, Trump at Center of Ga. Senate Race," *Atlanta Journal-Constitution*, August 1, 2016, A1.

25. Final campaign expenditure figures were not available at the time of this writing.

26. "FollowTheMoney.org," accessed December 23, 2016, http://www.followthemoney.org.

27. Jim Galloway, "As Trump Flails, Georgia's Political Center Becomes More Attractive," *Atlanta Journal-Constitution*, August 18, 2016, B1.

28. Greg Bluestein, "Democrats Look for Path after Election," *Atlanta Journal-Constitution*, December 19, 2016, A1, A4.

5. Louisiana

1. Election results are from the Louisiana Secretary of State. "Find Results and Statistics," Louisiana Secretary of State, https://goo.gl/7mz3Rz.

2. Wayne Parent and Huey Perry, "Louisiana: African Americans, Republicans, and Party Competition," in *The New Politics of the Old South: An Introduction to Southern Politics*, 4th ed., ed. Charles S. Bullock III and Mark J. Rozell (Lanham: Rowman and Littlefield Publishers, 2010).

3. Campbell Robertson, "John Bel Edwards, Democrat, Defeats David Vitter in Louisiana Governor's Race," *New York Times*, November 21, 2015, accessed February 15, 2017, https://goo.gl/zXIR5M; Chris Cillizza, "Why Did David Vitter's Prostitute Problem Kill Him in 2015 and Not in 2010?," *Washington Post*, November 23, 2015, accessed February 15, 2017, https://goo.gl/K71xfi.

4. Deborah Barfield Berry, "Governor Bobby Jindal Announces He's Running for President," *USA Today*, June 24, 2015, accessed February 15, 2017, https://goo.gl/yCLZPC.

5. Jonathan Martin, "Bobby Jindal Quits Republican Presidential Race," *New York Times*, November 17, 2015, accessed February 17, 2017, https://goo.gl/387hte.

6. Josh Putnam, "Amended Bill Would Bump 2016 Louisiana Presidential Primary Up Two Weeks," *FrontloadingHQ*, May 31, 2014, https://goo.gl/XObzZu.

7. *The Green Papers*, https://goo.gl/EBUoUm.

8. Elizabeth Crisp, "Republican Frontrunner Donald Trump's Blunt Style Fires Up Massive, 'Amazing' Baton Rouge Crowd," *Baton Rouge Advocate*, March 2, 2016, accessed February 15, 2017, https://goo.gl/pIWmnv.

9. Jeff Adelson and Faimon A. Roberts III, "Donald Trump Yells 'Get Them' as Protesters Disrupt New Orleans Rally," *Baton Rouge Advocate*, March 4, 2016, accessed February 15, 2017, https://goo.gl/NsxOtq; Jeremy Diamond,

"More Than 2 Dozen Black Lives Matter Protesters Disrupt Trump Rally," *CNN Politics*, March 4, 2016, accessed February 15, 2017, https://goo.gl/CSA7TC; Danielle Dreilinger, "Ted Cruz Makes His Case to Louisiana on Presidential Primary Eve," *New Orleans Times-Picayune*, March 4, 2016, accessed February 15, 2017, https://goo.gl/0tBQj0.

10. Based on registration figures for March 1, 2016. "Find Results and Statistics," Louisiana Secretary of State, https://goo.gl/7mz3Rz.

11. All election registration statistics are from "Find Results and Statistics," Louisiana Secretary of State.

12. Ibid.

13. Elizabeth Crisp, "Louisiana Democrats Cast Presidential Nomination Votes During Democratic National Convention," *Baton Rouge Advocate*, July 26, 2016, accessed February 15, 2017, https://goo.gl/x4kKMl.

14. Rebecca Savransky, "Trump Campaign to Contest Louisiana Delegates Allocation," *The Hill*, March 28, 2016, accessed February 15, 2017, https://goo.gl/Fj4DhZ; Elizabeth Crisp, "Donald Trump Calls GOP Primary Politics 'Unfair,' Challenges Louisiana Delegate Distribution," *Baton Rouge Advocate*, March 29, 2016, accessed February 15, 2017, https://goo.gl/ZjlqaK.

15. Richard Rainey, "Louisiana GOP Leaders, Rubio Delegates Get Behind Trump," *New Orleans Times-Picayune*, May 5, 2016, accessed February 15, 2017, https://goo.gl/KT1b9W.

16. Holly Yan and Rosa Flores, "Louisiana Flood: Worst U.S. Disaster Since Hurricane Sandy, Red Cross Says," CNN, August 19, 2016, accessed February 15, 2017, https://goo.gl/JkLiV5.

17. Mark Berman and Jose A. DelReal, "Trump, Drawing Contrast to Obama, Visits Flood-Ravaged Baton Rouge," *Washington Post*, August 19, 2016, accessed February 15, 2017, https://goo.gl/0U2eWz.

18. Polling compiled by *FiveThirtyEight*, accessed February 15, 2017, https://goo.gl/XZWBYo.

19. Elizabeth Crisp, "Louisiana Democrats, Republicans Turn to Other States When They Want to Have an Impact on Presidential Race," *Baton Rouge Advocate*, November 4, 2016, accessed February 15, 2017, https://goo.gl/hWCeEP.

20. Data obtained from Federal Election Commission, accessed February 15, 2017, https://goo.gl/GkI8O.

21. Mark Ballard, "How Popular is Donald Trump in Louisiana? President-Elect Landed Highest Number of Votes Ever," *Baton Rouge Advocate*, November 9, 2016, accessed February 15, 2017, https://goo.gl/3qT20t.

22. For purposes of this analysis, the sixty-four parishes are divided into four regions. The Greater New Orleans region includes the following parishes: Jefferson, Orleans, Plaquemines, St. Bernard, and St. Tammany. The Acadiana region includes Acadia, Ascension, Assumption, Avoyelles, Calcasieu, Cameron, Evangeline, Iberia, Iberville, Jefferson Davis, Lafayette, Lafourche, Pointe Coupee, St. Charles, St. James, St. John the Baptist, St. Landry, St. Martin, St. Mary, Terrebonne, Vermilion, and West Baton Rouge. The Florida Parishes include East Baton Rouge, East Feliciana, Livingston, St. Helena, Tangipahoa, Washington, and West Feliciana. The north-central region includes the remaining thirty parishes not already listed.

23. The data are derived from cross tabulations compiled by Southern Opinion Media Research (released October 26, 2016). The telephone poll was conducted from October 19 to 21 and surveyed five hundred likely Louisiana voters. The results were weighted to normalize the sample to reflect the distribution of characteristics of state voters (race, age, and party affiliation).

24. Jon Huang, Samuel Jacoby, Michael Strickland, and K. K. Rebecca Lai, "Election 2016: Exit Polls," *New York Times*, November 8, 2016, accessed February 15, 2017, https://goo.gl/HMz1wh.

25. Robert E. Hogan and Joshua D. Hostetter, "Louisiana: For Republicans and Obama, Second Verse, Same as the First," in *Second Verse, Same as the First: The 2012 Presidential Election in the South*, ed. Scott E. Buchanan and Branwell DuBose Kapeluck (Fayetteville: The University of Arkansas Press, 2014).

26. Hogan and Hostetter, "Louisiana."

27. Ibid.

28. Huang et al., "Election 2016: Exit Polls."

29. Ibid.

30. Stephanie Coontz, "Why the White Working Class Ditched Clinton," CNN, November 11, 2016, accessed February 15, 2017, https://goo.gl/cBRCVD; Ronald Brownstein, "How the Rustbelt Paved Trump's Road to Victory," *Atlantic*, November 10, 2016, accessed February 15, 2017, https://goo.gl/GyOKKF.

31. Brian Schaffner, Matthew MacWilliams, and Tatishe Nteta, "Explaining White Polarization in the 2016 Vote for President: The Sobering Role of Racism and Sexism," paper presented at The U.S. Elections of 2016: Domestic and International Aspects, Interdisciplinary Center Herzliya, Israel, January 8–9, 2017.

32. Michael Henderson, "Election 2016: Everything Old is New Again," *Louisiana by the Numbers*, November 16, 2016, accessed February 15, 2017, https://goo.gl/wcQxAK.

33. The American Community Survey census data uses the five-year average for the period 2008–12. Additional analyses were conducted in which five-year American Community Survey data corresponding more closely to the election year pairs were examined, but the results were similar. This was due to the fact that the percentages of whites with no college do not change dramatically in most parishes over the time frames examined.

34. Federal Election Commission, accessed February 15, 2017, https://goo.gl/GkI8O.

35. Election results are from "Find Results and Statistics," Louisiana Secretary of State, https://goo.gl/7mz3Rz.

6. Mississippi

1. Emily Wagster Pettus, "McDaniel Says He Wants to Curb Federal Spending," *Northeast Mississippi Daily Journal*, May 29, 2014, 1A, 6A.

2. Jimmie E. Gates and Geoff Pender, "Protest, Message: Don't Discriminate," *Jackson Clarion-Ledger*, April 5, 2016, 1A, 4A.

3. Brian Perry, "Rand Paul's Republican Heterodoxy," *Starkville Daily News*, December 10, 2014, 4A.

4. Riley Manning, "Presidential Candidate Carson Speaks at Parkgate Fundraiser," *Northeast Mississippi Daily Journal*, February 18, 2015, 2A.

5. Emily Nitcher, "Rubio Praises American Dream," *Jackson Clarion-Ledger*, July 26, 2014, 1A, 9A.

6. Zack Orsborn, "Cruz Fires Up Supporters," *Northeast Mississippi Daily Journal*, August 12, 2015, 1A, 6A.

7. Brian Perry, "Presidential Primaries Take Shape in Miss.," *Starkville Daily News*, December 10, 2015, 4,5.

8. Mollie Bryant, "Trump Bashes and Blasts," *Jackson Clarion-Ledger*, January 3, 2016, p. 5A, 7A.

9. Bill Crawford, "Kasich Last Hope for Candidate with Character and Competency," *Northeast Mississippi Daily Journal*, February 22, 2016, 6A.

10. Editorial, "Kasich our Choice for GOP Nominee," *Jackson Clarion-Ledger*, March 6, 2016, 3C.

11. Emily Wagster Pettus, "Cruz Makes Campaign Appearance in Florence," *Jackson Clarion-Ledger*, March 8, 2016, 3A, 4A.

12. Mollie Bryant, "Trump: 'I Won't Be Forgetting Miss.,'" *Jackson Clarion-Ledger*, March 8, 2016, 1A, 7A.

13. Geoff Pender, "Miss. Businessman Yerger Throws Support to Trump," *Jackson Clarion-Ledger*, March 7, 2016, 4A.

14. Bracey Harris, "Civil Rights Activist Backs Trump," *Jackson Clarion-Ledger*, March 5, 2016, 1A.

15. Tim Wildmon, "Trump Seems on the Brink of Capturing Mississippi," *Northeast Mississippi Daily Journal*, March 6, 2016, 9A.

16. Jerry Mitchell, "Bill Clinton Urges Students to Vote," *Jackson Clarion-Ledger*, March 4, 2016, 1A, 4A.

17. "Mississippi Poll On-Line Results," Mississippi Poll, last updated December 16, 2014, https://goo.gl/GdEPrM.

18. "Summary of Mississippi Poll Methodology," Mississippi Poll, https://goo.gl/bzlQe8.

19. Susan Page, "Divisive Convention May Hurt GOP, Barbour Says," *USA Today*, April 22, 2016, 3A.

20. Therese Apel, "Giuliani Talks Trump, Terrorism," *Jackson Clarion-Ledger*, March 31, 2016, 3A.

21. Emily Wagster Pettus, "Lott: Trump 'Sucked All the Oxygen' out of GOP Opponents," *Northeast Mississippi Daily Journal*, May 5, 2016, 2A.

22. Emily Wagster Pettus, "Michelle Obama Urges Grads to Vote to Protect Civil Rights," *Northeast Mississippi Daily Journal*, April 24, 2016, 6A.

23. Deborah Barfield Berry, "Miss. Delegates, Party Leaders Believe Unity Will Prevail," *Jackson Clarion-Ledger*, July 17, 2016, 1A, 13A.

24. Deborah Barfield Berry, "Wicker: GOP-Run Senate a Must," *Jackson Clarion-Ledger*, July 19, 2016, 1A, 4A.

25. Deborah Barfield Berry, "Delegates, Drama," *Jackson Clarion-Ledger*, July 26, 2016, 1A, 4A.

26. Charlie Benton, "Trump Jr. Speaks at Neshoba County Fair," *Starkville Daily News*, July 27, 2016, 8A.

27. Geoff Pender, "Trump Jr. Talks," *Jackson Clarion-Ledger*, July 27, 2016, 7A.

28. Geoff Pender, "GOP Nominee Fires Up Faithful in Jackson, Calls Clinton 'a Bigot,'" *Jackson Clarion-Ledger*, August 25, 2016, 1A.

29. Jonathan Lemire, "Leader of British Movement to Leave EU Joins Trump at Rally," *Starkville Daily News*, August 26, 2016, 2A, 3A.

30. Associated Press, "Bryant, Other Top Mississippi Republicans Stick with Trump," *Jackson Clarion-Ledger*, October 16, 2016, 4A.

31. Geoff Pender, "Red and Blue Meet," *Jackson Clarion-Ledger*, October 27, 2016, 4A.

32. Bill Minor, "Clinton Holds a Previous Plus in Mississippi," *Northeast Mississippi Daily Journal*, September 29, 2016, 7A.

33. Robert S. McElvaine, "Don't Fall Prey to the Cult of Trump," *Jackson Clarion-Ledger*, November 4, 2016, 10A.

34. Caleb Bedillion, "Kelly Faces Clever in March Primary," *Northeast Mississippi Daily Journal*, February 28, 2016, 1A, 5A.

35. Jimmy D. Giles, "Jimmy Giles Declares Candidacy for Mississippi's Third Congressional District," News Mississippi, January 4, 2016, accessed November 25, 2016, https://goo.gl/SBdxuY.

36. Deborah Barfield Berry, "Confederate Emblem Removed at U.S. Capitol," *USA Today*, April 22, 2016, 2A.

37. Deborah Barfield Berry, "Palazzo Offers Bill to Aid Small Housing Agencies," *Jackson Clarion-Ledger*, April 14, 2016, 2C.

38. Emily Wagster Pettus, "Miss. Seeing Low-Key Campaigns," *Jackson Clarion-Ledger*, October 28, 2016, 3A, 5A.

39. Response rates had fallen to 26 percent and 31 percent in the 2012 and 2014 polls. See "Election 2016," *CNN Politics*, https://goo.gl/kHQbEj. Foreshadowing the likelihood that some prominent pollsters ended up under-sampling the Trump vote in 2016, the Mississippi Poll in 2014 greatly underestimated support for Tea Party "outsider" Chris McDaniel in the GOP primary. See "Election 2016," *CNN Politics*, https://goo.gl/4JtBMG.

40. This time period was selected because there was no significant change in the population's views on these issues over this time span. One county was omitted from the analysis due to its small size and absence of poll respondents. Though the pooled sample size is 3,625 people, with eighty-one counties, the median sample size for these attitudinal variables is about 30. Despite the sizable sample error for attitudinal indicators in some counties, the results suggested that we nevertheless obtained best estimates of the variables in each county.

41. Wyatt Emmerich. "Final Thoughts on the Nov. 8 Election," *Starkville Daily News*, November 2, 2016, 4A.

42. Daniel L. Gardner, "Sorry, Hillary; Nobody's Perfect," *Jackson Clarion-Ledger*, September 20, 2016, 8A.

43. In the seven presidential elections from 1988 through 2012 when the Mississippi Poll was conducted, the items for ideological self-identification and the perceived ideology of the major-party presidential candidates were measured on a 5-point scale ranging from 1 for very liberal to 5 for very conservative. The average scores for these seven elections was 2.25 for the Democratic nominee's

perceived position and 3.56 for the Republican's perceived position, and the average Mississippi respondent viewed himself or herself as a 3.44.

7. South Carolina

1. "Clinton/Trump Race Tight in South Carolina," Public Policy Polling, August 11, 2016, accessed December 10, 2016, https://goo.gl/Y2bUON.
2. Scott E. Buchanan, "The Dixiecrat Rebellion: Long-Term Partisan Implications in the Deep South," *Politics and Policy* 33 (2005): 754–69.
3. David McCullough, *Truman* (New York: Simon & Schuster, 1993).
4. William V. Moore, "Parties and Elections in South Carolina," in *South Carolina Government: An Introduction*, ed. Charlie B. Tyer (Columbia: University of South Carolina Press, 2002).
5. Earl Black and Merle Black, *The Vital South: How Presidents Are Elected* (Cambridge, MA: Harvard University Press, 1992).
6. Tom Benning, "South Carolina Shaping Up as a Focal Point for GOP Race," *Dallas Morning News*, January 5, 2012, accessed December 16, 2016, https://goo.gl/HvX88N.
7. All population figures based on 2015 census estimates found at "Census Quickfacts," US Bureau of the Census, accessed December 17, 2016, https://goo.gl/6Bj9x2.
8. The South Carolina State Survey included party identification questions from fall 1989 to fall 2006. It was conducted by the Institute of Public Affairs and Public Policy, University of South Carolina, Columbia.
9. "Winthrop Poll September 2016," Winthrop Poll, accessed November 29, 2016, https://goo.gl/VoI9ck.
10. Amanda Coyne, "Sanders Gets Third Black State Representative Endorsement in Two Weeks," *Greenville News*, February 2, 2016, accessed December 16, 2016, https://goo.gl/imyK9N.
11. "South Carolina Exit Polls," *New York Times*, February 27, 2016, accessed November 27, 2016, https://goo.gl/SOsqAa.
12. Jamie Self, "The Buzz: Who SC Elected Officials Support for President," *Columbia State*, January 9, 2016, accessed December 10, 2016, https://goo.gl/d0ahqW.
13. "South Carolina Exit Polls," *New York Times*, February 20, 2016, accessed November 27, 2016, https://goo.gl/cQF6hi.
14. "South Carolina: Trump vs. Clinton," *RealClearPolitics*, accessed December 17, 2016, https://goo.gl/fyu1Cm.

8. Arkansas

1. Like the remainder of the South, Arkansas did vote for Richard Nixon in 1972 but then reverted to form in supporting Democrat Jimmy Carter (with a larger percentage than in any state except his home state of Georgia) in 1976.
2. On the 2008 and 2012 presidential elections in Arkansas, see Jay Barth, Janine A. Parry, and Todd Shields, "Arkansas: He's Not One of (Most of)

Us," in *A Paler Shade of Red: The 2008 Presidential Election in the South*, ed. Branwell DuBose Kapeluck, Laurence W. Moreland, and Robert P. Steed (Fayetteville: The University of Arkansas Press, 2009) and Janine A. Parry and Jay Barth, "Arkansas: Another Anti-Obama Aftershock," in *Second Verse, Same as the First: The 2012 Presidential Election in the South*, ed. Scott E. Buchanan and Branwell DuBose Kapeluck (Fayetteville: The University of Arkansas Press, 2014).

3. Frank E. Lockwood, "Three Back Fiorina in a State Less Huckabee's," *Arkansas Democrat-Gazette*, November 17, 2015.

4. Ibid.

5. Erica Sweeney, "Recap: Trump Headlines Reagan Rockefeller Dinner," *Arkansas Money and Politics*, https://goo.gl/65fLkZ.

6. Andrew DeMillo, "Arkansas Up for Grabs after Huckabee Exit," Associated Press, February 7, 2016.

7. Benjamin Hardy, "Night at the Circus," *Arkansas Times*, February 11, 2016.

8. John Moritz, "Clinton Accuser Paula Jones Attends Little Rock Trump Rally," *Arkansas Democrat-Gazette*, February 5, 2016.

9. Jay Barth, "Arkansas's Moment," *Arkansas Times*, February 25, 2016.

10. "Arkansas Gov. Asa Hutchinson: Donald Trump's 'Words Are Frightening,'" *All Things Considered*, National Public Radio, Feb 24, 2016, https://goo.gl/Mzz9IB; John Brummett, "All Trumped Up," *Talk Business & Politics*, May/June 2016, 54–61. And the new participants were many. More than 630,000 voters participated in that party primary, nearly 100,000 more than any recent Arkansas primary. See table 8.1.

11. For a discussion of turnout patterns in Arkansas primary elections, see Diane D. Blair and Jay Barth, *Arkansas Politics and Government: Do the People Rule?*, 2nd ed. (Lincoln: University of Nebraska Press, 2005), 104–6.

12. Ara Janak, "Clinton Addresses Arkansas Democrats in NLR," *Arkansas Democrat-Gazette*, July 17, 2015.

13. Brian Fanney, "Clinton Touts State to LR Crowd," *Arkansas Democrat-Gazette*, September 22, 2015.

14. "O'Malley to Speak at Two LR Events," *Arkansas Democrat-Gazette*, Dec 4, 2015; Brian Fanney, "Candidate O'Malley's College Stop Draws Few," *Arkansas Democrat-Gazette*, Dec 5, 2015.

15. Arkansas has joined several states in a move away from headlining the party with the names of Thomas Jefferson and Andrew Jackson, party founders with pasts incommensurate with the party's current values. See Andrew DeMillo, "Arkansas Democrats Dropping Jefferson, Jackson from Dinner," Associated Press, May 26, 2016, https://goo.gl/nhX4B3.

16. Steve Brawner, "Clinton: Democrats Want More Perfect Union, While GOP Divisive," *Talk Business & Politics*, July 16, 2016, https://goo.gl/dpPofo.

17. Andrew DeMillo, "Bill Clinton Says Wife Can Bridge Partisan Divide," Associated Press, July 16, 2016; Jay Barth, "Bill Clinton Was Right," *Arkansas Times*, November 17, 2016.

18. Frank E. Lockwood, "In LR, Kaine Vows Fight for State in November," *Arkansas Democrat-Gazette*, August 24, 2016.

19. See "Full Text: Bill Clinton's DNC Speech," *Politico*, https://goo.gl/05W3tz.

20. Michelle Gorman, "Arkansas Delegates Cheer Two Old Friends, the Clintons, During DNC," *Newsweek*, July 28, 2016, https://goo.gl/mTMONx.

21. Jay Barth, "Hillary in Arkansas," *Arkansas Times*, Nov 3, 2016.

22. Glenn Kessler, "Fact Checker: The Facts about Hillary Clinton and the Kathy Shelton Rape Case," *Washington Post*, October 11 2016, https://goo.gl/orgRuk.

23. Bill Bowden, "Reed Says Laugh Didn't Target Girl," *Arkansas Democrat-Gazette*, October 12, 2016.

24. Frank E. Lockwood, "Hutchinson, Rutledge Rip Clinton in Speeches at GOP Convention," *Arkansas Democrat-Gazette*, July 20, 2016.

25. Frank E. Lockwood, "Two Arkansans Keep Clinton's A-List Supporters Visible, On Message," *Arkansas Democrat-Gazette*, Sept 28, 2016; Matt Flegenheimer, "Handling Cows by Day, Ever-Growing Clinton Rallies by Night," *New York Times*, Oct 12, 2016.

26. Jay Barth, "Hillary in Arkansas," *Arkansas Times*, Nov 3, 2016.

27. Frank E. Lockwood, "State Donations Favored Clinton," *Arkansas Democrat-Gazette*, Dec 11, 2016.

28. Max Brantley, "Arkansas Poultry Magnate Backs Trump PAC with $2 Million," *Arkansas Times*, https://goo.gl/9oIV0b.

29. David Leip, "Dave Leip's Atlas of U.S. Presidential Elections," https://goo.gl/kUci7Y.

30. Comparative congressional district data from David Nir, "Daily Kos Elections' Presidential Results by Congressional District for the 2016 and 2012 Elections," Daily Kos, November 19, 2016, https://goo.gl/RhHlT8.

31. Blair, Diane D., *Arkansas Politics and Government: Do the People Rule?* (Lincoln: University of Nebraska Press, 1988).

32. Barth, Parry, and Shields, "Arkansas: He's Not One"; Parry and Barth, "Arkansas: Another Anti-Obama Aftershock."

33. Steven Shepard, "Exit Polls Will Skip 22 States This Year," *Politico*, 7 Nov 2016, accessed 8 Jan 2016, https://goo.gl/FKg5ZQ.

34. See the Arkansas Poll, 2016, https://goo.gl/DzpIrN.

35. Ibid.

36. Allan Smith, "A Senate Candidate Provided a Blueprint for Democrats to Use Donald Trump in Their Attacks," *Business Insider*, May 11, 2016.

9. Florida

1. For detailed analyses of Florida's party development since the early 1990s, see William E. Hulbary, Anne E. Kelley, and Lewis Bowman, "Florida: A Muddled Election," in *The 1992 Presidential Election in the South: Current Patterns of Southern Party and Electoral Politics*, ed. Robert P. Steed, Lawrence W. Moreland and Tod A. Baker (Westport, CT: Praeger Publishers, 1994): 119–37; Kathryn Dunn Tenpas, William E. Hulbary, and Lewis Bowman, "Florida: An Election with Something for Everyone," in *The 1996 Presidential*

Election in the South: Party Politics in the 1990s, ed. Laurence W. Moreland and Robert P. Steed (Westport, CT: Praeger Publishers, 1997): 147–63; Steven Tauber and William E. Hulbary, "Florida: Too Close to Call," in *The 2000 Presidential Election in the South: Partisanship and Southern Party Systems in the 21st Century*, ed. Robert P. Steed and Laurence W. Moreland (Westport, CT: Praeger Publishers, 2002); Susan A. MacManus, "Florida: The South's Premier Battleground State," *American Review of Politics* 26 (Summer 2005): 155–84; Jonathan Knuckey, "Florida: Obama Gives GOP the 'Blues,'" in *The 2008 Presidential Election in the South: A Paler Shade of Red*, ed. Branwell DuBose Kapeluck, Laurence W. Moreland, and Robert P. Steed (Fayetteville: The University of Arkansas Press, 2009): 137–59; Jonathan Knuckey and Tyler Branz, "Florida: *Sí, Se Puede!*," in *Second Verse, Same as the First: The 2012 Presidential Election in the South*, ed. Scott E. Buchanan and Branwell DuBose Kapeluck (Fayetteville: The University of Arkansas Press, 2014): 137–59.

2. The full statement about Mexicans was: "When Mexico sends its people, they're not sending their best. . . . They're sending people that have lots of problems, and they're bringing those problems to us. They're bringing drugs. They're bringing crime. They're rapists. And some, I assume, are good people." Quoted in Michelle Ye Hee Lee, "Donald Trump's False Comments Connecting Mexican Immigrants and Crime," *Washington Post*, July 8, 2015, accessed December 21, 2016, https://goo.gl/syq7OH.

3. Steven Shepard, "Latino Voting Surge Rattles Trump Campaign," *Politico*, November 6, 2016, accessed December 21, 2016, https://goo.gl/QSBT6U.

4. Bill Nelson won 60 percent of the vote in the 2006 US Senate election and 55 percent in the 2012 US Senate election. Bob Graham won 62 percent of the vote in the 1998 US Senate election. Jeb Bush received 55 percent of the vote in the 1998 gubernatorial election and 56 percent in the 2002 gubernatorial election.

5. For a more detailed discussion of the 2014 midterm elections in Florida, see Susan A. MacManus, Aubrey Jewett, David J. Bonanza, and Thomas R. Dye, *Politics in Florida*, 4th ed., (Sarasota, FL: Peppertree Press, 2015): 91–146.

6. Quoted in Eli Stokols, "Florida Quietly Sets Up an Epic 2016 Primary Clash," *Politico.com*, May 19, 2015, accessed December 21, 2016, https://goo.gl/M50Prx.

7. Republican nomination polls compiled, and averages computed, by *RealClearPolitics*, accessed December 21, 2016, https://goo.gl/6zJdaF.

8. For comprehensive looks at why Jeb Bush did so poorly, see Sam Sanders, "Why Did Jeb Bush Fail? There Are Many Theories," National Public Radio, February 22, 2016, accessed December 21, 2016, https://goo.gl/IKpcUH; and Eli Stokols, "Inside Jeb Bush's $150 Million Failure," *Politico*, February 20, 2016, accessed December 21, 2016, https://goo.gl/PFwFf8.

9. Polls averaged by *RealClearPolitics*, accessed December 21, 2016, https://goo.gl/fvhfi6.

10. Matthew Dickinson, "What Did Rubio In?," *U.S. News & World Report*, March 18, 2016, accessed December 21, 2016, https://goo.gl/ZW30W9.

11. Florida presidential primary polls compiled by HuffPost Pollster, *Huffington Post*, accessed December 21, 2016, https://goo.gl/AkOoHg.

12. Josh Solomon, "With a Week to Go before Florida Primary, Bernie Sanders Shows Up to Campaign," *Tampa Bay Times*, March 8, 2016, accessed December 21, 2016, https://goo.gl/LRsFBs.

13. In 2008 the leading Democratic presidential candidates—Barack Obama, Hillary Clinton, and John Edwards—all had agreed not to campaign in Florida given that this was an event the Democratic National Committee had not sanctioned because the primary took place in a window reserved for Iowa, New Hampshire, South Carolina, and Nevada. Thus, the fact that the total number of votes cast in 2016 was similar to that of 2008 was perhaps a worrying sign for Democrats.

14. Democratic primary election data are from the Division of Elections, Florida Department of State, accessed December 21, 2016, https://goo.gl/sno3Eq.

15. Data for campaign visits are from National Popular Vote, accessed December 21, 2016, https://goo.gl/5lqaVb.

16. Ken Goldstein, John McCormick, and Andre Tartar, "Candidates Make Last Ditch Ad Spending Push Across 14-State Electoral Map," Bloomberg, November 2, 2016, accessed December 21, 2016, https://goo.gl/rxZZeQ.

17. Adam C. Smith, "In Florida, It's Donald Trump's Big Rallies vs. Hillary Clinton's Massive Organizing," *Tampa Bay Times*, August 12, 2016, accessed December 21, 2016, https://goo.gl/GOKlcG.

18. Michael Wines, "Florida Voter Registration Deadline Is Extended, a Win for Democrats," *New York Times*, October 12, 2016, accessed December 21, 2016, https://goo.gl/4svyTL.

19. "2016 Early Voting Period," Division of Elections, Florida Department of State, accessed December 21, 2016, https://goo.gl/q7pdCe.

20. Nico Pitney, "Florida's Early Vote Ends with Record Turnout in Democratic Strongholds," *Huffington Post*, November 7, 2016, accessed December 21, 2016, https://goo.gl/zRYajg.

21. Jeremy W. Peters, Richard Fausset, and Michael Wines, "Black Turnout Soft in Early Voting, Boding Ill for Hillary Clinton," *New York Times*, November 1, 2016, accessed December 21, 2016, https://goo.gl/dVwr1c.

22. Alex Wayne and Ben Brody, "FBI Absolves Clinton Again, Two Days Ahead of U.S. Election," Bloomberg, November 6, 2016, accessed December 21, 2016, https://goo.gl/VDi3yL.

23. Patricia Mazzei, Amy Sherman, and Steve Bousquet, "Democrats, Fueled by South Florida, Try to Build Clinton Firewall in Souls to the Polls," *Miami Herald*, November 6, 2016, accessed December 21, 2016, https://goo.gl/jEXZvH.

24. Turnout data are taken from Michael P. McDonald, "Voter Turnout," United States Elections Project, accessed December 21, 2016, https://goo.gl/VK8wXF.

25. Data are from "2016 National Popular Vote Tracker," *Cook Political Report*, accessed December 21, 2016, https://goo.gl/jxSx4p.

26. See Jonathan Knuckey, "The Structure of Party Competition in the South: The Case of Florida," *American Review of Politics* 25 (Spring 2004): 41–65.

27. A multiple regression analysis of the change in the county-by-county vote (not shown) revealed that the following three variables were the best predictors

in explaining why Trump did better (or worse) in a county than Romney had in 2012: Latino population share, percentage with a college degree, and median income. The smaller the Latino population share, the smaller the college-educated population share, and the lower the median income of a county, the better Trump performed relative to Romney.

28. Exit poll data for 2016 are taken from "Fox News Exit Polls," Fox News, accessed December 21, 2016, https://goo.gl/zDbbxa; and "Exit Polls," *CNN Politics*, accessed December 21, 2016, https://goo.gl/Nxvt2L. Data from 2012 are taken from "Exit Polls," *CNN Politics*, accessed December 21, 2016, https://goo.gl/TwNnFp.

29. See Florida data from the Univision-sponsored "Survey of Hispanic Voters in Battleground States Final Survey—November 2016," accessed December 21, 2016, https://goo.gl/iIYgW8. In late October, the survey found Clinton ahead of Trump by 60 to 30 percent among all Latinos in Florida but behind Trump among Cubans by a margin of 42 to 49 percent.

30. See Michael Tesler and David O. Sears, *Obama's Race: The 2008 Election and the Dream of a Post-Racial America* (Chicago: University of Chicago Press, 2010); Michael Tesler, *Post-Racial or Most Racial? Race and Politics in the Obama Era* (Chicago: University of Chicago Press, 2016).

31. In presidential elections in Florida since 1968, Trump's share of the white vote was exceeded in only three contests: by Richard Nixon in 1972 (with 78 percent), by Ronald Reagan in 1984 (with 71 percent), and by George H. W. Bush in 1988 (with 67 percent). On each of these occasions, the Republican candidate carried Florida by landslide margins (Nixon winning 72 percent of the vote, Reagan 65 percent, and Bush 61 percent). See Earl Black and Merle Black, *The Vital South: How Presidents are Elected* (Cambridge, MA: Harvard University Press 1992): 295.

32. Unfortunately, the percentage of the electorate for geography (urbanism) in 2016 cannot be reliably compared to 2012 because the dramatically different percentages reported for rural, urban, and suburban suggest that measurement or coding issues exist. As an example, it is highly unlikely that the percentage of urban voters jumped from 27 percent to 46 percent and suburban voters dropped from 60 percent to 45 percent when actual county-by-county numbers suggest changes much more modest than that.

33. For more details on the impact of the Fair District Amendments, see Aubrey Jewett, "New Rules for an Old Florida Game: Evaluating the 2012 Legislative and Congressional Redistricting Process," in *Jigsaw Puzzle Politics in the Sunshine State*, ed. Seth C. McKee, (Gainesville: University Press of Florida, 2015): 41–76; Aubrey Jewett, "'Fair' Districts in Florida: New Congressional Seats, New Constitutional Standards, Same Old Republican Advantage?" in *The Political Battle over Congressional Redistricting at the State Level*, ed. William Miller and Jeremy Walling (Lanham, MD: Lexington Books, 2013): 111–36.

34. Christine Sexton, "Gov. Scott: Running Against Sen. Nelson Is 'an Option' in 2018," *Politico*, November 15, 2016, accessed December 21, 2016, https://goo.gl/CW4sVn.

35. Knuckey and Branz, "Florida," 168.

36. See Jennifer Rubin, "GOP Autopsy Report Goes Bold," *Washington Post*, March 18, 2013, accessed December 21, 2016, https://goo.gl/nmtlB8.

10. North Carolina

1. Charles Prysby, "North Carolina: Color the Tar Heels Federal Red and State Blue," *American Review of Politics* 26 (2005): 185–202.

2. Charles Prysby, "North Carolina: Change and Continuity in 2008," in *A Paler Shade of Red: The 2008 Presidential Elections in the South*, ed. DuBose Kapeluck, Lawrence Moreland, and Robert Steed (Fayetteville: The University of Arkansas Press, 2009).

3. Charles Prysby, "North Carolina: No Longer Federal Red and State Blue?," in *Second Verse, Same as the First: The 2012 Presidential Election in the South*, ed. Scott E. Buchanan and Branwell DuBose Kapeluck (Fayetteville: The University of Arkansas Press, 2014).

4. Gerald M. Pomper, "The Nominating Contests and Conventions," in *The Election of 1976*, ed. Gerald M. Pomper (New York: David McKay, 1977).

5. Rhodes Cook, "The Nominating Process," in *The Elections of 1988*, ed. Michael Nelson (Washington, DC: CQ Press, 1989).

6. Charles Prysby, "North Carolina: Change and Continuity."

7. Colin Campbell and Taylor Knopf, "NC Leaders Want to Move All 2016 Primary Elections to March," *Raleigh News & Observer*, September 18, 2015.

8. M. V. Hood III and Seth C. McKee, "What Made Carolina Blue? In-migration and the 2008 North Carolina Presidential Vote," *American Politics Research* 38 (2010): 266–302.

9. For a definition of urban, suburban, and rural counties based on metropolitan statistical areas, see the Office of Management and Budget's Bulletin No. 13–01, February 28, 2013, accessed January 22, 2017, https://goo.gl/ZR5f1N.

10. Patrick Fisher, *Demographic Gaps in American Political Behavior* (Boulder: Westview Press, 2014), 141–66.

11. Voters born before 1945 are classified as the "silent" or "greatest" generation; voters born between 1946 and 1965 as "baby boomers"; voters born between 1966 and 1980 as "generation X"; and voters born 1981 and after as "millennials." Voter registration data compiled from the North Carolina State Board of Elections website, data file "ncvoter_Statewide.zip", accessed November 12, 2016, https://goo.gl/ZJfYyB.

12. National Election Pool, "2016 National Presidential Exit Poll," *CNN Politics*, accessed January 9, 2017, http://edition.cnn.com/election/results/exit-polls.

13. National Election Pool, "2012 National Presidential Exit Poll," *CNN Politics*, accessed January 9, 2017, https://goo.gl/YGeUZY.

14. Alan I. Abramowitz, *The Disappearing Center* (New Haven: Yale University Press, 2010).

15. The exit polls use a broad definition of independents that includes those who lean toward one party, so a sizable share of the independents are partisan

leaners who often are more similar to self-declared partisans than they are to pure independents.

16. Jonathan O. Knuckey, "Racial Resentment and the Changing Partisanship of Southern Whites," *Party Politics* 11 (2005): 5–28.

17. For a discussion of the role of candidate character traits in presidential elections, see David B. Holian and Charles L. Prysby, *Candidate Character Traits in Presidential Elections* (New York: Routledge, 2015).

18. Margaret Moffett, "HPU Poll: North Carolinians More Pessimistic About Government, Future," *Greensboro News and Record*, November 24, 2015.

19. Michael P. McDonald, "Voter Turnout," United States Elections Project, accessed January 4, 2017, https://goo.gl/VK8wXF.

20. Information on the racial composition of registered voters and of those who cast a ballot came from the North Carolina State Board of Elections website, accessed January 5, 2017, https://goo.gl/gvMIRa.

21. Registered voter turnout data compiled from the North Carolina State Board of Elections. We compared data file "historystats11xx08xx2016.zip" to "voterstats11xx08xx2016.zip", accessed January 16, 2017.

22. Information on the partisan composition of registered voters and of those who cast a ballot came from the North Carolina State Board of Elections website, accessed January 5, 2017, https://goo.gl/gvMIRa.

23. Ibid.

24. Kate Elizabeth Queram, "Tipping the Scales: Clinton, Trump Employ Different Tactics to Reach Voters," *Greensboro News and Record*, November 7, 2017.

25. "North Carolina Senate Race," Center for Responsive Politics, accessed January 9, 2016, https://goo.gl/9s971A.

26. Anne Blythe, Craig Jarvis, and Jim Morrill, "Federal Court Invalidates Maps of Two NC Congressional Districts," *Raleigh News & Observer*, February 5, 2016.

27. Election results data from the North Carolina State Board of Elections website, accessed January 16, 2017, https://goo.gl/8ivQts.

28. For an overview of the House Bill 2 controversy, see Trey Allen, "The General Assembly Preempts Local Antidiscrimination Measures," *Coates' Canons: NC Local Government Law*, March 24, 2016, accessed January 16, 2017, https://goo.gl/GgKoHw.

29. Steve Harrison, "McCrory: If Charlotte Approves LGBT Protections, 'Immediate' State Response Likely," *Charlotte Observer*, February 22, 2016, accessed January 16, 2017, https://goo.gl/ZFZJV8.

30. Steve Harrison, "N.C. Gov Pat McCrory Signs into Law Bill Restricting LGBT Protections," *Charlotte Observer*, March 23, 2016, accessed January 16, 2017, https://goo.gl/jb6EdQ.

31. Michael Gordon, Mark S. Price, and Katie Peralta, "Understanding HB2: North Carolina's Newest Law Solidifies State's Role in Defining Discrimination," *Charlotte Observer*, March 26, 2016, accessed January 16, 2017, https://goo.gl/7IOzOm.

32. Campbell Robertson, "North Carolina Voters Pass Same-Sex Marriage

Ban," *New York Times*, May 8, 2012, accessed January 16, 2017, https://goo.gl/2rEylg.

33. Matthew Burns and Laura Leslie, "Federal Appeals Court Overturns NC Voter ID Law," WRAL, July 29, 2016, accessed January 16, 2017, https://goo.gl/jXMb6p.

34. Election results data from the North Carolina State Board of Elections website, accessed January 16, 2017, https://goo.gl/8ivQts.

35. V. O. Key Jr., *Southern Politics in State and Nation* (New York: Alfred A. Knopf, 1949).

36. Paul Luebke, *Tar Heel Politics* (Chapel Hill: University of North Carolina Press, 1998).

37. Rob Christensen, *The Paradox of Tar Heel Politics* (Chapel Hill: University of North Carolina Press, 2008).

38. Tom Eamon, *The Making of a Southern Democracy: North Carolina Politics from Kerr Scott to Pat McCrory* (Chapel Hill: University of North Carolina Press, 2014).

11. Tennessee

1. John Shelton Reed, "Southern Culture on the Skids?," in *The American South in the Twentieth Century*, ed. Craig Pascoe, Karen Trahan Leathem, and Andy Ambrose (Athens: University of Georgia Press, 2005), 151.

2. Walt Hickey, "Which States are in the South?" *FiveThirtyEight*, April 30, 2014, http://fivethirtyeight.com/datalab/which-states-are-in-the-south/.

3. William Lyons, John Scheb, and Billy Stair, *Government and Politics in Tennessee* (Knoxville: University of Tennessee Press, 2001), 17.

4. Jeffrey Jones, "Red States Outnumber Blue for First Time in Gallup Tracking," Gallup, February 3, 2016, http://www.gallup.com/poll/8969/red-states-outnumber-blue-first-time-gallup-tracking.aspx.

5. Lyons, Scheb, and Stair, *Government and Politics in Tennessee*, 17.

6. David Woodard, *The New Southern Politics* (Boulder: Lynne Rienner Publishers, 2006), 17–18.

7. Amy Sayward, "Introduction," in *Tennessee's New Abolitionists*, ed. Amy Sayward and Margaret Vandiver (Knoxville: University of Tennessee Press, 2010), 7–8.

8. V. O. Key, *Southern Politics in State and Nation* (New York: Alfred. A. Knopf, 1949), 59.

9. David M. Brodsky, "Tennessee: Genuine Two-Party Politics," in *The New Politics of the Old South*, 1st ed., ed. Charles S. Bullock III and Mark Rozell (Lanham, MD: Rowman & Littlefield Publishers, 1998), 168.

10. Jack Bass and Walter Devries, *The Transformation of Southern Politics* (New York: Basic Books, 1977), 289.

11. Key, *Southern Politics*, 284.

12. Ibid., 277.

13. Bass and Devries, *The Transformation of Southern Politics*, 289.

14. Key, *Southern Politics*, 278.

15. Michael Nelson, "Tennessee: From Bluish to Reddish to Red" in *The New Politics of the Old South: An Introduction to Southern Politics*, 5th ed., ed. Charles Bullock, Mark Rozell, and Patrick Cotter (Lanham, MD: Rowman & Littlefield Publishers, 2014), 187.

16. John Lyman Mason, "Tennessee: Politics and Politicians that Matter Beyond State Borders," in *The New Politics of the Old South*, ed. Charles Bullock and Mark Rozell (Lanham, MD: Rowman & Littlefield Publishers, 2003), 184.

17. David Sutton, "No Tennessee Waltz in Appalachia: The Elections of 2000," *Appalachian Journal* 28, no. 3 (2001): 296.

18. Brodsky, "Tennessee," 170–73.

19. Lee Edwards, "The Conservative Consensus: Frank Meyer, Barry Goldwater, and the Politics of Fusionism," Heritage Foundation, January 22, 2007, http://www.heritage.org/home/research/reports/2007/01/the-conservative-consensus-frank-meyer-barry-goldwater-and-the-politics-of-fusionism.

20. M. V. Hood, Quentin Kidd, and Irwin Morris, "Tea Leaves and Southern Politics: Explaining Tea Party Support in the Region," *Social Science Quarterly* 96, no. 4 (2015): 16.

21. Phil Valentine, *Tax Revolt* (Nashville: Nelson Current, 2005), 2.

22. Ibid., 74.

23. Ibid., 224.

24. Lyons, Scheb, and Stair, *Government and Politics in Tennessee*, 372.

25. Roger Abramson, "Phil Bredesen Made a Successful Governor for One Mind-Blowing Reason: He Did Just What He Said," *Nashville Scene*, January 6, 2011, http://www.nashvillescene.com/nashville/phil-bredesen-made-a-successful-governor-for-one-mind-blowing-reason-he-did-just-what-he-said/Content?oid=2138062.

26. Carroll Van West, "Preface," in *The Tennessee Encyclopedia of History and Culture*, ed. Carroll Van West, Connie Lester, Margaret Duncan Binnicker, and Anne-Leslie Owens (Nashville: Rutledge Hill Press, 1998), xx.

27. Sekou M. Franklin, "The New South's Abolitionist Governor," in *Tennessee's New Abolitionists*, ed. Amy L. Sayward and Margaret Vandiver (Knoxville: University of Tennessee Press, 2010), 44–48.

28. Lee Seifert Greene, *Lead Me On: Frank Goad Clement and Tennessee Politics* (Knoxville: University of Tennessee Press, 1982), 375.

29. Richard Locker and Holly Meyer, "Haslam Signs Bill Giving Therapists Protections," *Tennessean* (Nashville), April 27, 2016, http://www.tennessean.com/story/news/politics/2016/04/27/haslam-signs-controversial-bill-giving-therapists-protections/83509448/.

30. Joey Garrison, "Ron Ramsey: Christians Should Consider Arming Themselves," *Tennessean* (Nashville), October 2, 2015, http://www.tennessean.com/story/news/2015/10/02/lt-gov-ramsey-christians-serious-faith-should-consider-handgun-permits/73203888/.

31. Nelson, "Tennessee: From Bluish," 203.

32. Anita Wadhwani, "Tennessee Amendment 1 Abortion Measure Passes," *Tennessean* (Nashville), November 6, 2014, http://www.tennessean.com/story/news/politics/2014/11/04/amendment-takes-early-lead/18493787/.

33. Eric Ostermeier, "Alexander Records Weakest Primary Win for US Senator in Tennessee History," *Smart Politics*, August 7, 2014, http://editions.lib.umn.edu/smartpolitics/2014 /08/07/alexander-records-weakest-ever/.

34. Jerry W. Taylor, "Insure Tennessee Merits Support and Approval," *Tennessean* (Nashville), December 29, 2014, http://www.tennessean.com/story/opinion/contributors/2014/12/29/insure-tennessee-merits-support-approval/20864011/.

35. Dave Boucher, "Politics Could Threaten Haslam's 'Insure Tennessee,'" *Tennessean* (Nashville), January 5, 2015, http://www.tennessean.com/story/news/politics/2015/01/05/politics-threaten-haslams-insure-tennessee/21266523/.

36. Kerry Roberts, "State Sen. Roberts Explains Insure Tennessee Vote", *Tennessean* (Nashville), February 10, 2015, http://www.tennessean.com/story/news/local/robertson/opinion/2015/02/08/state-sen-roberts-explains-insure-tennessee-vote/23097921/.

37. David Plazas, "Governor: Call New Special Session on Insure Tennessee," *Tennessean* (Nashville), April 19, 2015, http://www.tennessean.com/story/opinion/editorials/2015/04/18/call-special-session-insure-tennessee/25967287/

38. Ibid.

39. Katie Glueck, "Why Tennessee Will Matter in 2016," *Politico*, December 28, 2015, http://www.politico.com/story/2015/12/2016-presidential-election-tennessee-media-217134.

40. Ibid.

41. Joey Garrison, "Ted Cruz Rails Against 'Bipartisan Corruption' in NashvilleSpeech," *Tennessean* (Nashville), December 23, 2015, http://www.tennessean.com/story/news/politics/2015/12/22/ted-cruz-speaks-nashville-today/77693502/.

42. Dave Boucher, "MTSU Poll: Ben Carson Leads in Tennessee," *Tennessean* (Nashville), November 7, 2015, http://www.tennessean.com/story/news/politics/2015/11/07/mtsu-poll-ben-carson-leads-tennessee/75310988/.

43. Joey Garrison, "New Poll: Trump, Clinton Lead Big in Tennessee," *Tennessean* (Nashville), February 6, 2016, http://www.tennessean.com/story/news/politics /2016/01/28/mtsu-poll-trump-leads-cruz-tennessee-gop-race/79455886/.

44. Joey Garrison, "Poll: Trump, Clinton Dominating in Tennessee," *Tennessean* (Nashville), February 28, 2016, http://www.tennessean.com/story/news/politics/2016/02/28/new-poll-shows-trump-clinton-dominating-tennessee/81074450/.

45. Dave Boucher, "TN Sen. Beavers Agrees with Trump's Muslim Ban," *Tennessean* (Nashville), December 8, 2015, http://www.tennessean.com/story/news/politics/2015/12/08/mae-beavers-donald-trump-immigration/76974744/.

46. David Boucher, "Tennessee GOP Leader: Round Up Syrian Refugees, Remove from State," *Tennessean* (Nashville), November 19 2015, http://www.tennessean.com/story/news/politics/2015/11/17/tennessee-gop-leader-round-up-syrian-refugees-remove-state/75936660/.

47. Joey Garrison, "Tennessee Voters Could Help Catapult Trump, Clinton," *Tennessean* (Nashville), February 29, 2016, http:/www.tennessean.com/story/news/politics/2016/02/29/tennessee-voters-could-help-catapult-trump-clinton/81109512/.

48. Ibid.

49. Joel Ebert, "Hillary Clinton Makes Closing Arguments in Tennessee," *Tennessean* (Nashville), February 29, 2016, http://www.tennessean.com/story/news/politics/2016/02/28/hillary-clinton-speak-nashvilles-maherry-medical-college-today/80925186/.

50. Joey Garrison, "Tennessee Crushes Early Voting Record for Presidential Primary," *Tennessean* (Nashville), February 24, 2016, http://www.tennessean.com/story/news/politics/2016/02/24/tennessee-crushes-early-voting-record-08-primary/80853446/.

51. Joey Garrison, "Why Donald Trump Won Big in Clay County," *Tennessean* (Nashville), March 11, 2016, http://www.tennessean.com/story/news/politics/2016/03/11/why-donald-trump-won-big-clay-county-tennessee/81501114/.

52. "Tennessee Exit Polls," *CNN Politics*, March 1, 2016, www.cnn.com/election/primaries/polls/TN/Rep.

53. "Tennessee Exit Polls," *CNN Politics*, March 1, 2016, www.cnn.com/election/primaries/polls/tn/Dem.

54. Michael Collins, "Bob Corker Dismisses Donald Trump's Running Mate Theory," *Tennessean* (Nashville), May 10, 2016, http://www.tennessean.com/story/news/politics/2016/05/10/bob-corker-dismisses-donald-trump-running-mate-theory/84179096/.

55. Joel Ebert and Dave Boucher, "Anti-Islam Dutch Politician a Tennessee Guest at GOP Convention," *Tennessean* (Nashville), July 18, 2016, http://www.tennessean.com/story/news/politics/2016/07/18/anti-islam-dutch-politician-tennessee-guest-gop-convention/87250680/.

56. Stephen Shepard, "Exit Polls Will Skip 22 States Thus Year," *Politico*, November 7, 2016, http://www.politico.com/story/2016/11/2016-exit-polls-used-in-which-states-230892.

12. The Great Red Wall of Texas

1. Brian K. Arbour, "Texas: Big Red in the 2012 Elections," in *Second Verse, Same as the First: The 2012 Presidential Election in the South*, ed. Scott E. Buchanan and Branwell DuBose Kapeluck (Fayetteville: The University of Arkansas Press, 2014).

2. Katie Glueck, "Rick Perry Abandons Presidential Run," *Politico*, September 11, 2015, accessed January 5, 2017, https://goo.gl/Fgl9OX.

3. Cruz's speech was not a filibuster. Filibusters are used to prevent a law from passing or to take up time to run out the clock. When Cruz gave his marathon speech, the Senate had already invoked cloture and agreed to vote on a measure to fund the government the next afternoon.

4. Nick Corasaniti and Patrick Healy, "Ted Cruz Becomes First Major Presidential Candidate to Announce Presidential Bid for 2016," *New York Times*, March 23, 2015, accessed January 5, 2017, https://goo.gl/KpGM8m.

5. Republican primary poll results and aggregations are by HuffPost Pollster, *Huffington Post*, https://goo.gl/tEMGBk.

6. Republican nomination contest results are from Wilson Andrews, Kitty Bennett, and Alicia Parlapiano, "2016 Delegate Count and Primary Results," *New York Times*, https://goo.gl/NbCTZ8.

7. Katie Glueck and Shane Goldmacher, "Ted Cruz Drops Out of Presidential Race," *Politico*, May 3, 2016, accessed January 4, 2017, https://goo.gl/kf5qux.

8. Gabrielle Levy, "Take That, Trump: Perry Endorses Cruz," *U.S. News & World Report*, January 25, 2016, accessed January 4, 2017, https://goo.gl/oIPqkJ.

9. Patrick Svitek, "Greg Abbott Endorses Ted Cruz for President," *Texas Tribune*, February 24, 2016, accessed January 4, 2017, https://goo.gl/8zUrQL.

10. David Jackson, "Trump Taps Rick Perry for Energy Secretary," *USA Today*, December 14, 2016, accessed January 4, 2017, https://goo.gl/aFfRQG.

11. Max B. Baker, "Clinton Wins Big in Texas Democratic Primary," *Fort Worth Star-Telegram*, March 1, 2016, accessed January 4, 2017, https://goo.gl/OXcmAq.

12. "Texas Exit Polls," *New York Times*, March 1, 2016, accessed February 13, 2016, https://goo.gl/9XpraQ.

13. "Clinton Crushes Trump 3:1 in Air War," Wesleyan Media Project, November 3, 2016, accessed December 18, 2016, https://goo.gl/AqyzSx.

14. Data from "Travel Tracker," *National Journal*, http://traveltracker.nationaljournal.com/.

15. Matt Mackowiak, "Welcome to Texas, Donald Trump, But Why Are You Here," *The Hill*, August 23, 2016, accessed February 13, 2017, https://goo.gl/NjhX5w.

16. Abby Livingston, "Trump Family to Make Major Texas Fundraising Swings," *Texas Tribune*, September 7, 2016, accessed December 18, 2016, https://goo.gl/VHIY48; Brian Rogers and Jenny Deam, "One Arrested during Trump's Visit to Houston," *Houston Chronicle*, September 18, 2016, accessed December 18, 2016, https://goo.gl/VLljUL.

17. Justin Tilove, "Tim Kaine to Austin Democrats: 'We're Going to Go after Texas.'" *Austin American-Statesman*, August 9, 2016, accessed December 18, 2016, https://goo.gl/WJoEwg.

18. Patrick Svitek, "In Houston, Tim Kaine Seeks to Energize Texas Democrats," *Texas Tribune*, September 23, 2016, accessed December 18, 2016, https://goo.gl/oqfAHM.

19. Brooke A. Lewis, "Houston Headquarters for Clinton Opens," *Houston Chronicle*, September 15, 2016, accessed December 18, 2016, https://goo.gl/mg6cNp.

20. "Washington Post–Survey Money 50 State Poll: A New 50 State Poll Shows Exactly Why Clinton Holds the Advantage," *Washington Post*, n.d., https://goo.gl/ozkwc9.

21. Manny Fernandez, "Could Hillary Clinton Win Texas? Some Democrats Say Maybe," *New York Times*, October 24, 2016, accessed December 18, 2016, https://goo.gl/7rQLi3.

22. It should be noted that this is a great deal of controversy over this year's exit polls and their results for Latino voters. Gary Segura and Matt Barreto, who are political scientists and founders of a polling firm called Latino Decisions, argue that "The exit poll reports of Latino vote are profoundly and

demonstrably incorrect." Gary Segura and Matt Barreto, "Lies, Damn Lies, and Exit Polls," Latino Decisions, November 10, 2016, https://goo.gl/WsczNE. Harry Enten of *FiveThirtyEight* disagreed with Segura and Barreto, concluding that "Trump probably did no worse than Romney among Latinos, and probably did better." Harry Enten, "Trump Probably Did Better with Latino Voters Than Romney Did," *FiveThirtyEight*, November 18, 2016, https://goo.gl/YX0XLj. I use the exit poll results because they are the best available set of data for examining subgroup voting trends within the state. It is worth noting that these results, like all poll results, have a margin of error; the exact results are close to these numbers.

23. Ronald Brownstein, "The Parties Invert," *Atlantic*, May 23, 2016, accessed December 12, 2016, https://goo.gl/OHxbSO.

24. Poll results are available from the Texas Politics Project, University of Texas at Austin, June 2017, https://texaspolitics.utexas.edu/latest-poll.

25. Franklin Foer, "Donald Trump Hates Women: It's the One Position He's Never Changed," *Slate*, March 24, 2016, accessed December 18, 2016, https://goo.gl/N691VW; Ben Mathis-Lilley, "Trump Was Recorded in 2005 Bragging about Grabbing Women 'by the Pussy,'" *Slate*, October 7, 2016, accessed January 4, 2017, https://goo.gl/iurmn9.

26. "An Exhaustive List of the Allegations Women Have Made Against Donald Trump," The Cut, October 27, 2016, accessed January 4, 2017, https://goo.gl/sXMJPU.

27. Exit poll results for Texas in the 2016 general election from "Exit Polls," *CNN Politics*, https://goo.gl/6yibda.

28. The exit poll did not take a Texas only sample in 2012, which means I cannot make comparisons to that year.

29. For this analysis, the urban counties are Bexar (San Antonio), Dallas, Harris (Houston), Tarrant (Fort Worth), and Travis (Austin). Suburban counties are all those designated by the US Bureau of the Census as parts of the Austin, Dallas–Fort Worth, Houston, or San Antonio metropolitan areas except the urban counties listed above. All of the state's other counties are grouped together in the category of small towns and rural areas.

30. Alex Shephard, "Why Does Donald Trump Keep Going after Heidi Cruz?" *New Republic*, March 24, 2016, accessed January 4, 2016, https://goo.gl/QXcMTj.

31. Nolan D. McCaskill, "Trump Accuses Cruz's Father of Helping JFK's Assassin," *Politico*, May 3, 2016, accessed December 12, 2016, https://goo.gl/2RtILD.

32. Alex Altman, "Ted Cruz Makes a Big Gamble with Convention Speech," *Time*, July 20, 2016, accessed January 4, 2017, https://goo.gl/Np7T38.

33. Molly Ball, "Why D.C. Hates Ted Cruz," *Atlantic*, January 26, 2016, accessed January 4, 2017, https://goo.gl/CWlmQW.

34. Abby Livingston and Patrick Svitek, "GOP Sources: Rick Perry Encouraged Michael McCaul to Challenge Ted Cruz," *Texas Tribune*, October 31, 2016, accessed December 18, 2016, https://goo.gl/qiEH74.

35. Mimi Swartz, "Here Comes Trouble," *Texas Monthly*, Jan 2017, accessed February 13, 2017, https://goo.gl/ogZOnW.

36. Erica Grieder, "Master of the Senate," *Texas Monthly*, Dec 2014, accessed January 4, 2017, https://goo.gl/3tjZxA.

37. Joseph Bafumi, Robert S. Erikson, and Christopher Wlezien, "Balancing, Generic Polls, and Midterm Congressional Elections," *Journal of Politics* 72, no. 3 (2010): 705–19; Samuel Kernell, "Presidential Popularity and Negative Voting: An Alternative Explanation of the Midterm Congressional Decline of the President's Party," *American Political Science Review* 71, no. 1 (1977): 44–66; John R. Petrocik and Frederick T. Steeper, "The Midterm Referendum: The Importance of Attributions of Responsibility," *Political Behavior* 8, no. 3 (1986), 206–29.

38. James E. Campbell, *The Presidential Pulse of Midterm Elections*, 2nd ed. Lexington: University Press of Kentucky, 1997.

39. Albert D. Cover, "Surge and Decline in Congressional Elections," *Western Political Quarterly* 38, no. 4 (1985): 606–19.

13. Virginia

1. John J. McGlennon, "Virginia: Obama's Unexpected Firewall," in *Second Verse, Same as the First: The 2012 Presidential Election in the South*, ed. Scott E. Buchanan and Branwell DuBose Kapeluck (Fayetteville: The University of Arkansas Press, 2014) 213–31.

2. Ronald Brownstein, "The Most Valuable Voters of 2016," *Atlantic*, February 18, 2015, accessed January 1, 2017, https://goo.gl/W1dOvc.

3. Nate Cohn, "Clinton Has Solid Lead in Electoral College; Trump's Winning Map is Unclear," *New York Times*, November 5, 2016, accessed January 1, 2017, https://goo.gl/0aZBjW.

4. Abraham Moomaw and Andrew Cain, "Trump Pulling Some Campaign Staff out of Va.," *Richmond Times-Dispatch*, October 13, 2016, accessed January 1, 2017, https://goo.gl/hom4tA.

5. David Ress, "US Supreme Court Upholds New Lines for Virginia Congressional Districts," *Hampton Roads Daily Press*, May 23, 2016, accessed January 1, 2017, https://goo.gl/bEaFIM.

6. John J. McGlennon, "Virginia: The Triumph of Experience Over Hope," *American Review of Politics* 26, Summer (2005), 245–65.

7. Tal Kopan and Ariane de Vogue, "Supreme Court Vacates Former Virginia Gov. Bob McDonnell's Conviction," *CNN Politics*, June 27, 2016, accessed January 1, 2017, https://goo.gl/aqwuSc.

8. Jose A. DelReal and David Weigel, "Webb Exits the Democratic Presidential Primary," *Washington Post*, October 20, 2015, accessed January 1, 2017, https://goo.gl/wyD8yQ.

9. John Wagner, "O'Malley Suspends Presidential Bid after a Dismal Showing in Iowa," *Washington Post*, February 1, 2016, accessed January 1, 2017, https://goo.gl/ogrNfO.

10. "Trump Leads GOP Field, with Rubio and Cruz Next; Clinton Leads Sanders among Virginia Democrats," Judy Ford Wason Center for Public Policy, Christopher Newport University, February 16, 2016, accessed January 1, 2017, https://goo.gl/n3gVot.

11. Unless otherwise indicated, election data was accessed through the Virginia State Board of Elections website, http://www.elections.virginia.gov/resultsreports/election-results/.

12. Cooper Allen, "Jim Gilmore Drops out of GOP Presidential Race," *USA Today*, February 12, 2016, accessed January 1, 2017, https://goo.gl/DVTuZt.

13. Curt Mills, "Cruz Delegate Chief Seeks 2020 Rules Changes," *US News & World Report*, July 14, 2016, accessed January 1, 2017, https://goo.gl/kDsVsE.

14. Amy Chozick and Alan Rappeport, "Hillary Clinton and Tim Kaine Debut Ticket in Battleground of Florida," *New York Times*, July 23, 2016, accessed January 1, 2017, https://goo.gl/6POkZ7.

15. Richard A. Oppel Jr., "In Tribute to Son, Khizr Khan Offered Citizenship Lesson at Convention," *New York Times*, July 29, 2016, accessed January 1, 2017, https://goo.gl/ZZmRqI.

16. Emily Stewart, "Donald Trump Rode $5 Billion in Free Media to the White House," *The Street*, November 20, 2016, accessed January 1, 2017, https://goo.gl/Tkh4Qr.

17. Laura Vozzella, "Trump Confounds Many Republicans with Last-Minute Push in Virginia," *Washington Post*, October 24, 2016, accessed January 1, 2017, https://goo.gl/oLwgZ8.

18. Owen Minott, "Election Chartbook," *National Journal*, November 7, 2016.

19. Ann E. Marimow and Rachel Weiner, "Appeals Court Upholds Virginia Voter-ID Law," *Washington Post*, December 13, 2016, accessed January 1, 2017, https://goo.gl/X0fDkj.

20. Camila Domonoske, "Virginia Court Overturns Order That Restored Voting Rights to Felons," National Public Radio, July 22, 2016, accessed January 1, 2017, https://goo.gl/3aOSge.

21. Dan Roberts, "Virginia Makes Progress in Push to Restore Voting Rights to Ex-convicts," *Guardian*, October 14, 2016, accessed January 1, 2017, https://goo.gl/0gG3CH.

22. Jordain Carney, "VA Dems Jockey for Kaine's Seat," *The Hill*, October 21, 2016, accessed January 1, 2017, https://goo.gl/azvXme.

23. David Ress, "US Supreme Court Upholds New Lines for Virginia Congressional Districts," *Hampton Roads Daily Press*, May 23, 2016, accessed January 1, 2017, https://goo.gl/g1xe7h.

Conclusion

1. Theodore Schleifer, "30,000 Turn Out for Trump's Alabama Pep Rally," *CNN Politics*, August 25, 2015, accessed December 19, 2016, https://goo.gl/D2foOG.

2. Jordyn Phelps, "Trump Calls Electoral College 'Genius' as He Closes Out 'Thank You' Tour," *ABC News*, 17 Dec 2016, accessed December 19, 2016, https://goo.gl/8jxnhQ.

3. David Jackson, "Why the South Likes Donald Trump," *USA Today*, February 29, 2016, accessed December 19, 2016, https://goo.gl/2ukkWW.

4. Ibid.

5. See Kevin Phillips, *The Emerging Republican Majority* (New Rochelle, NY: Arlington House, 1969), and Robert P. Jones, "How Trump Remixed the Republican 'Southern Strategy,'" *Atlantic*, August 14, 2016, accessed December 19, 2016, https://goo.gl/ICW2h4.

6. Earl Black and Merle Black, *The Rise of Southern Republicans* (Cambridge, MA: Harvard University Press, 2002), 43.

7. Dan T. Carter, "What Donald Trump Owes George Wallace," *New York Times*, January 8, 2016, accessed December 19, 2016, https://goo.gl/tWRE34.

8. Ibid.

9. Megan Carpentier, "Why Do People Dislike Hillary Clinton? The Story Goes Far Back," *Guardian*, October 18, 2016, accessed March 8, 2017, https://goo.gl/NnCFyt.

10. Frank Newport, "Clinton's Image at Lowest Point in Two Decades," Gallup, July 25, 2016, accessed March 8, 2017, https://goo.gl/0yQtmS.

11. "State and Legislative Partisan Composition (2016 Election)," National Conference of State Legislatures, December 6, 2016, accessed December 20, 2016, https://goo.gl/mbSY2z.

12. Ibid.

13. David Leip, "Dave Leip's Atlas of U.S. Presidential Elections," accessed December 20, 2016, https://goo.gl/UIvuRV.

14. Ibid.

15. Ibid.

16. John C. Green, Lyman A. Kellstedt, Corwin E. Smidt, and James L. Guth, "The Soul of the South: Religion and Southern Politics in the New Millennium," in *The New Politics of the Old South: An Introduction to Southern Politics*, 5th ed., ed. Charles S. Bullock III, Mark J. Rozell, and Patrick Cotter (Lanham, MD: Rowman & Littlefield Publishers, 2014).

17. All 2016 exit poll data were obtained from "Exit Polls," *CNN Politics*, accessed December 19, 2016, https://goo.gl/79Fxl9.

18. Patrick Healy, "Donald Trump Fires Back at Sharp Rebuke by Pope Francis," *New York Times*, February 18, 2016, accessed December 19, 2016, https://goo.gl/FfIiNs.

19. All state-level election results were obtained from the *New York Times*, accessed December 21, 2016, https://goo.gl/Av2KBH.

20. Pearson correlation statistics represented by r values. Significance levels reported are $p \leq .01$ and $p \leq .05$ (two-tailed test). Nonsignificant findings are indicated with "NS."

21. M. V. Hood III, "Race, Class, Religion and the Southern Party System: A Field Report from Dixie," *Forum* 14 (2016): 95.

22. Matthew Fowler, "Race Still Matters: Political Ideology and the South," *PS: Political Science and Politics*, April 2016: 215–20.

23. J. Eric Oliver and Tali Mendelberg, "Reconsidering the Environmental Determinants of White Racial Attitudes," *American Journal of Political Science* 44 (2000): 574.

24. All state-level demographic information was obtained from the US Bureau of the Census, accessed December 21, 2016, https://goo.gl/pU3WyN.

25. Emily Badger, Quoctrung Bui, Adam Pearce, "The Election Highlighted a Growing Rural-Urban Split," *New York Times*, November 11, 2016, accessed December 20, 2016, https://goo.gl/fO69Wp.

26. Michael Henderson and Wayne Parent, "The Changing South," *PS: Political Science and Politics*, April 2016: 207–9.

27. Ibid.

28. Katherine J. Cramer, *The Politics of Resentment: Rural Consciousness in Wisconsin and the Rise of Scott Walker* (Chicago: University of Chicago Press, 2016).

29. Katherine Cramer, "How Rural Resentment Helps Explain the Surprising Victory of Donald Trump," *Washington Post*, November 13, 2016, accessed December 19, 2016, https://goo.gl/G4dvTn.

30. Ibid.

31. Data obtained from the US Bureau of the Census; calculations performed by the author.

32. Beau Dure, "Millennials Continue Urbanization of America, Leaving Small Towns," National Public Radio, October 21, 2016, accessed December 19, 2016, https://goo.gl/ZNUHy5.

33. Seth C. McKee and Jeremy M. Teigen, "The New Blue: Northern In-migration in Southern Presidential Elections," *PS: Political Science and Politics*, April 2016: 228–33.

34. Ibid.

35. Nate Cohn, "The New Blue and Red: An Educational Split Is Replacing the Culture War," *New York Times*, October 19, 2016, accessed December 19, 2016, https://goo.gl/e5eGT0.

36. "Growth and Opportunity Project," Republican National Committee, 2013, accessed December 19, 2016, https://goo.gl/Iqq34p.

37. Benjy Sarlin, "Sen. Graham: GOP in 'Demographic Death Spiral' Absent Immigration Reform," MSNBC, June 17, 2013, accessed December 19, 2016, https://goo.gl/kQciN9.

38. Emily Schultheis, "GOP Chairman Defends Trump on Claims of Rigged Election," CBS News, October 23, 2016, accessed December 19, 2016, https://goo.gl/5O3Q2t.

Contributors

Branwell DuBose Kapeluck is professor of political science at The Citadel. Since 2004, Professor Kapeluck has been codirector of The Citadel Symposium on Southern Politics. He is the author and editor of a number of publications, including *A Paler Shade of Red: The 2008 Presidential Election in the South*.

Scott E. Buchanan is professor of political science at The Citadel. Professor Buchanan has been the executive director of The Citadel Symposium on Southern Politics since 2009. His research focuses on southern politics and elections, and he is the author of the only published biography on former Georgia governor Marvin Griffin. Professor Buchanan's most recent book, with Charles S. Bullock III and Ronald Keith Gaddie, is *Georgia's Three Governors Controversy: Skullduggery, Machinations, and the Decline of Georgia's Progressive Politics*, the first scholarly examination of Georgia's 1947 three governors controversy.

Patrick R. Miller is assistant professor of political science at the University of Kansas. His primary research areas include public opinion, political psychology, elections, and survey and experimental methods. His has been published in *Social Science Quarterly*, *Public Opinion Quarterly*, *Political Psychology*, *Political Research Quarterly*, and *Politics, Groups, and Identities*, among other peer-reviewed journals.

Seth C. McKee is an associate professor of political science at Texas Tech University. He has published numerous journal articles and is the author of *Republican Ascendancy in Southern U.S. House Elections* (Westview Press, 2010), editor of *Jigsaw Puzzle Politics in the Sunshine State* (University Press of Florida, 2015), and author of the forthcoming textbook, *The Dynamics of Southern Politics: Causes and Consequences* (CQ Press).

Shannon L. Bridgmon is an associate professor of political science at Northeastern State University in Tahlequah, Oklahoma. Her primary research areas are southern politics and state political party issues. She is a graduate of the University of Alabama (PhD, MPA, BA) and contributes to various media outlets as an analyst on Alabama party politics. She has published in the *American Review of Politics* and the *Criminal Justice Policy Review*. Other research projects examine party responsibility in various policy areas, state party legislative performance, and the Alabama Constitution of 1901. She is cochair of Northwestern State University's American Democracy Project and also serves on the advisory council of the university's Center for Women's Studies.

Charles S. Bullock III is the Richard B. Russell Professor of Political Science and Josiah Meigs Distinguished Teaching Professor at the University of Georgia. He has authored, coauthored, edited, or coedited nearly thirty books and more than 150 articles. His most recent books are *Georgia's Three Governors Controversy: Skullduggery, Machinations, and the Decline of Georgia's Progressive Politics* (coauthored with Scott E. Buchanan and Ronald Keith Gaddie); the sixth edition of *The New Politics of the Old South* and *The Oxford Handbook of Southern Politics*, both coedited with Mark Rozell; *Georgia Politics in a State of Change*, second edition (coauthored with Keith Gaddie); *Redistricting: The Most Political Activity in America*; and *The Triumph of Voting Rights in the South* (coauthored with Keith Gaddie), winner of the V. O. Key Award as the best book published on southern politics in 2009.

Robert E. Hogan is the R. Downs Poindexter Professor of Political Science at Louisiana State University. He conducts research on various aspects of American electoral politics in the states. His most recent projects focus on candidate decision-making and the process of representation in state legislatures. His published work has appeared in a variety of academic journals including the *American Journal of Political Science*, *Political Research Quarterly*, and *Social Science Quarterly*.

David A. Breaux is dean of the College of Arts and Sciences at Delta State University. He has published articles in various academic journals including *Legislative Studies Quarterly*, *American Review of Politics*, *American Politics Quarterly*, and *Public Administration Review*. Dr. Breaux has also published numerous book chapters on state political party activists, state electoral politics, state policy making, and southern politics. In addition, he has been the recipient of various research grants, including three from the prestigious National Science Foundation.

Stephen D. Shaffer is a professor of political science at Mississippi State University. He has published extensively on Mississippi party organizations and political campaigns, as well as on national public opinion and federal elections. Professor Shaffer directs the Mississippi Poll and is coauthor of *Mississippi Government and Politics* and the 2006 V. O. Key Award–winning *Politics in the New South: Representation of African Americans in Southern State Legislatures*. He has published in such journals as *American Journal of Political Science*, *Western Political Quarterly*, and *Social Science Quarterly*.

Cole Blease Graham Jr. is executive professor and assistant dean at the George H. W. Bush School of Government and Public Service at Texas A&M University. He specializes in the study of American state and local government institutions and politics.

Janine A. Parry is professor of political science at the University of Arkansas and has directed the Diane D. Blair Center of Southern Politics and Society's Arkansas Poll since its inception in 1999. Her major fields of teaching and research include state politics and policy, public opinion and voter mobilization, and gender, politics, and policy. Her work has appeared in *Political Behavior*, *State Politics and Policy Quarterly*, *Social Science Quarterly*, the Presidential Elections in the South series, and other outlets.

Jay Barth is M. E. and Ima Graves Peace Distinguished Professor of Politics and Bill and Connie Bowen Odyssey Professor at Hendrix College in Conway, Arkansas. Barth's academic work includes research on the politics of the South, state government and politics, LGBT politics, and education policy. He is coauthor, with the late Diane Blair, of the second edition of *Arkansas Politics and Government: Do the People Rule?* Barth has authored or coauthored chapters in five previous collections in the Presidential Elections in the South series.

Jonathan Knuckey is an associate professor of political science at the University of Central Florida. His research focuses on southern politics, with an emphasis on the role of racial attitudes on voting behavior. His recent research has been published in *Party Politics*, *Presidential Studies Quarterly*, and *Social Science Quarterly*.

Aubrey Jewett is an associate professor of political science at the University of Central Florida. He is coauthor of *Politics in Florida*, fourth edition, and coeditor, with former Florida congressman Lou Frey, of *Political Rules of the Road*. Jewett has published numerous book chapters on Florida politics and scholarly articles in various journals including *Presidential Studies Quarterly*, *Legislative Studies Quarterly*, *Political Research Quarterly*, and *American Politics Review*. He served as an American Political Science Association (APSA) congressional fellow in 2003–2004 and received the Leon Weaver Award from the Representation and Electoral Systems section of the APSA for his study of ballot invalidation in Florida during the 2000 presidential election.

Charles Prysby is professor of political science at the University of North Carolina at Greensboro. His research interests are in elections, voting behavior, political parties, and southern politics. His research has appeared in the *Journal of Politics*, *Political Behavior*, *American Politics Quarterly*, *American Review of Politics*, and other journals. His most recent book is *Candidate Character Traits in Presidential Elections* (Routledge, 2015), coauthored with David Holian. He also is the coauthor, with Carmine Scavo, of the SETUPS Voting Behavior instructional modules.

J. Michael Bitzer is professor of politics and history at Catawba College, where he also serves as provost and dean of students. His academic research is on North Carolina politics and voting behavior, and he teaches in the fields of American politics, history, law, and public administration.

Vaughn May is professor and chair of political science at Belmont University. His research interests include southern politics, Tennessee politics, and the interplay of politics and popular culture. His work has appeared in a range of journals, including *Urban Education*, *Southeastern Political Review*, *College Teaching*, *Tennessee Historical Quarterly*, and *Studies in Popular Culture*.

Brian Arbour is an associate professor of political science at John Jay College, City University of New York. His research focuses on campaign message strategy and ethnicity in American elections. Professor Arbour also works on the decision desk for Fox News Channel, the election night group that analyzes exit poll results and calls races for the network.

John J. McGlennon is professor of government and public policy at the College of William & Mary. He has published widely on political party activists, Southern politics, and Virginia politics. His work has appeared in multiple book chapters and in the *Journal of Politics*, *International Review of Political Science*, and the *Australian Political Science Review*, among others. He is coauthor of *Party Activists in Virginia* and coeditor of *The Life of the Parties: Activists in Presidential Politics*. He was a participant in the National Science Foundation–funded Southern Grassroots Party Activists Project. He is a contributor to *Writing Southern Politics*, volumes resulting from the Southern Grassroots Party Activists Projects and The Citadel Symposium on Southern Politics, and previous volumes in this series.

Jakob Deel graduated in May 2016 from the College of William & Mary with dual majors in government and public policy. At William & Mary, he was the recipient of both the Gerald Tuttle Jr. Memorial Scholarship and the McGlennon Scholarship and was inducted as a member of the Phi Beta Kappa honor society. Mr. Deel has assisted Dr. John McGlennon with research in the areas of Virginia politics and southern political party activity. Additionally, he has researched and written about domestic welfare policy and drug testing welfare recipients in terms of both policy effectiveness and political attitudes.

H. Gibbs Knotts is professor and department chair in the Department of Political Science at the College of Charleston. His research focuses on southern politics, political participation, public administration, and the scholarship of teaching and learning. His book (coauthored with Christopher A. Cooper), *The Resilience of Southern Identity: Why the South Still Matters in the Minds of its People*, was published in 2017 by the University of North Carolina Press.

Index